SOCIETY FOR NEW TESTAMENT STUDIES

MONOGRAPH SERIES

General Editor: R. McL. Wilson, F.B.A.

Associate Editor: M.E. Thrall

47

HEBREWS AND PERFECTION

Hebrews and Perfection

An Examination of the Concept of Perfection in
the 'Epistle to the Hebrews'

DAVID PETERSON

CAMBRIDGE UNIVERSITY PRESS

CAMBRIDGE

LONDON   NEW YORK   NEW ROCHELLE

MELBOURNE   SYDNEY

Published by the Press Syndicate of the University of Cambridge
The Pitt Building, Trumpington Street, Cambridge CB2 1RP
32 East 57th Street, New York, NY 10022, USA
296 Beaconsfield Parade, Middle Park, Melbourne 3206, Australia

© Cambridge University Press 1982

First published 1982

Printed in Great Britain by Redwood Burn Ltd., Trowbridge

Library of Congress catalogue card number: 82-4188

British Library cataloguing in publication data
Peterson, David
    Hebrews and perfection – (Society for New Testament Studies monograph
    series; 47)
    1. Bible. N.T. Hebrews – Criticism, interpretation, etc. 2. Perfection
    I. Title   II. Series
    227'.8706   BS2860.H6
    ISBN 0 521 24408 0

CONTENTS

PREFACE

My interest in Hebrews was first aroused when I read the commentary by Professor F.F. Bruce in connection with undergraduate theological studies. It was therefore a great privilege for me to pursue my study of Hebrews at a postgraduate level under his supervision. His many writings and personal example have continued to challenge me, and I am especially grateful to him for the many hours spent in personal consultation over my work. This book is the modification of a doctoral dissertation accepted by the University of Manchester in 1978.

The research was made possible financially by the granting to me of the Joan Augusta Mackenzie Travelling Scholarship, by various provisions of the Principal and Executive Committee of Moore Theological College and by the awarding of a Research Studentship in Theology through the University of Manchester. To the relevant authorities in each case I offer again my sincere thanks.

I want to express my thanks to the editors of this Monograph Series for the many helpful suggestions made in connection with the revision of my thesis for publication. Dr Peter O'Brien was kind enough to read through the manuscript of this book, making helpful suggestions and pointing out errors. I would also like to record my appreciation of the typing assistance given by Mrs Margaret Kirton, Mrs Sue Westwood, Miss Lynda Graham and Miss Elizabeth Lockrey during various stages of the revision.

The work is dedicated to my wife and children, who have lived for so long in its shadow. During the period of research and writing and then during the revision, they have been a continual source of encouragement to me. Doubtless, they rejoice in the completion of the work and in my release from preoccupation with the project more than I do!

David Peterson
July, 1980

ABBREVIATIONS

AG	(Walter Bauer's) *Greek–English Lexicon of the New Testament and Other Early Christian Literature*, translated and adapted by W.F. Arndt and F.W. Gingrich (Chicago–Cambridge, 1957)
ATR	*Anglican Theological Review*
BDF	F. Blass and A. Debrunner, *A Greek Grammar of the New Testament and Other Early Christian Literature*, translated and edited by R.W. Funk (Chicago London, 1961)
BJRL	*Bulletin of the John Rylands Library*
BNTC	Black's New Testament Commentary
BZ	*Biblische Zeitschrift*
BZGBE	Beiträge zur Geschichte der biblischen Exegese
BZNW	Beiheft zur Zeitschrift für die neutestamentliche Wissenschaft
CBQ	*Catholic Biblical Quarterly*
EQ	*Evangelical Quarterly*
ET	English Translation
EVV	English Versions
ExpT	*Expository Times*
FS	*Festschrift*
HTR	*Harvard Theological Review*
HTS	Harvard Theological Studies
ICC	International Critical Commentary
JBL	*Journal of Biblical Literature*
JTS	*Journal of Theological Studies*
LSJ	*A Greek–English Lexicon*, by H.G. Liddell and R. Scott, revised by H.S. Jones (Oxford, 1940)
LXX	Septuagint version of the OT
MK	Meyer Kommentar (Kritisch–exegetischer Kommentar über das Neue Testament, begründet von H.A.W. Meyer)
MT	Massoretic Text of the Hebrew Bible
Migne *PG*	*Patrologia, Series Graeca*, edited by J.P. Migne (Paris, 1844–)
NEB	New English Bible

NKZ	*Neue kirchliche Zeitschrift*
NovT	*Novum Testamentum*
NRT	*Nouvelle Revue Théologique*
n.s.	new series
NTS	*New Testament Studies*
1QS	Rule of the Community (*serekh hayyahad*) from Qumran Cave 1
par	(and) parallel(s)
PTR	*Princeton Theological Review*
RSV	Revised Standard Version
RTR	*Reformed Theological Review*
S.B.L.	Society of Biblical Literature
SJT	*Scottish Journal of Theology*
TDNT	(G. Kittel's and G. Friedrich's) *Theological Dictionary of the New Testament*, translated by G. Bromiley (Index Volume compiled by R. Pitkin), 10 volumes (Grand Rapids, Michigan, 1964–76)
TKNT	(Herders) Theologischer Kommentar zum Neuen Testament
TLZ	*Theologische Literaturzeitung*
TZ	*Theologische Zeitschrift*
WUNT	Wissenschaftliche Untersuchungen zum Neuen Testament
ZK	Zahn Kommentar (Kommentar zum NT herausgegeben von Theodor Zahn)
ZNW	*Zeitschrift für die neutestamentliche Wissenschaft*

Abbreviations of the titles of the works of Philo and other ancient writers follow the pattern of *The New International Dictionary of New Testament Theology* (I, pp. 31–40), edited by Colin Brown (Exeter, 1975).

1

THE HERMENEUTICAL ISSUES

The justification for a full-scale study of the concept of perfection in the so-called 'Epistle to the Hebrews'[1] could simply be given in the words of Otto Michel: 'understanding Christian perfection is important, indeed central, for an interpretation of the Epistle to the Hebrews'.[2] The centrality of the concept to the writer's theology has been clearly recognised by those commentators who have provided extended notes on the subject and by the various authors of journal articles who have attempted to investigate the idea more closely. Three times in Hebrews the perfecting of Christ is mentioned (2: 10; 5: 9; 7: 28). On four occasions we are told that the Old Covenant ritual was unable to perfect the worshippers (7: 11, 19; 9: 9; 10: 1). On three specific occasions we are told that Christ alone is the source of perfection for believers (10: 14; 11: 40; 12: 23), though the use of related terminology elsewhere in the argument proclaims the same truth. Additionally, the writer urges his readers to 'maturity' (5: 11 – 6: 1) and points them to Christ as the 'perfecter' of faith (12: 2). An interpretation of these themes and their inter-relationship is clearly important for a proper understanding of Hebrews.

However, the multiplicity of opinions as to the background and purpose of this document is reflected in the variety of interpretations that have been offered to explain the concept of perfection it sets forward. The 'elastic adaptability'[3] of τέλειος and its derivatives in Biblical and extra-Biblical usage encourages interpreters of Hebrews to suggest the relevance of some associations and to reject others, according to their presuppositions about the religious context in which the document was written. This diversity of opinion suggests the need for a detailed exegesis of the relevant passages in Hebrews, in order to assess the validity of the various interpretations.

To set the discussion in its proper context, a selected history of interpretation will now be given. Having thus highlighted the various methodological and exegetical issues that others have raised, I will be in a position to specify certain questions, which subsequent chapters will seek to answer. The contributions summarised below are not necessarily given in chronological order and I have restricted myself to a representative group of twentieth-century scholars. Later chapters will show how others have followed and adapted the sort of arguments they present.

(a) J. Kögel[4]

It is often assumed by readers of the New Testament that any reference to perfection is to be understood in terms of a *moral* perfection. As a reaction to such interpretations of Hebrews in a number of nineteenth-century writings, Julius Kögel sought to establish what may be called the 'formal' interpretation. From his analysis of the use of τελειοῦν in classical Greek sources, Kögel came to the conclusion that this verb, which is used nine times in Hebrews, is 'a general term, without distinct content' (p. 39). It is a 'purely formal expression', and only the object of the verb and the context can indicate the particular sense in which it is being used on each occasion. Whereas τελεῖν puts the stress on 'the end as against the beginning or the middle', τελειοῦν, derived as it is from τέλειος, involves a more qualitative sense of 'wholeness', in contrast with what is fragmentary.

Turning to the LXX, Kögel observed that τέλειος is appropriately used there to render *šālēm, tāmîm and tām*, since these terms indicate 'wholeness' of personality, rather than 'sinlessness' (pp. 49f). Although he acknowledges an ethical colouring in the use of the verb at Sir. 31: 10, he does not consider that LXX usage of the verb goes beyond that of classical sources in any significant respect. In the NT, the verb is said to be used with much the same sense as τελεῖν, meaning 'to complete, finish', at Luke 2: 43; John 4: 34; 5: 36; 17: 4 and Acts 20: 24. However, in passages like 1 John 2: 5; 4: 12; 4: 17–18 and James 2: 22 it is to be understood more specifically in terms of bringing something to its pinnacle or to perfection. A final group of references in the NT shows the verb used *absolutely*, with respect to persons, and includes Luke 13: 32; Phil. 3: 12 and the usage of Hebrews. In none of these contexts is the concept of perfection a moral one.

Kögel takes Hebrews 9: 11, with its reference to 'the greater and more perfect tent', as the starting point for his exposition of the concept of perfection in Hebrews. As part of the writer's ongoing contrast between essence and sign, original and copy, heavenly and earthly, eternal and temporal, τέλειος belongs to the first category in each case and is equivalent to ἀληθινός (cf. 8: 2; 9: 24). The verb in 11: 40 and 12: 23 cannot mean moral perfection in the context but refers to the attaining of the goal of their earthly pilgrimage by believers, namely 'entrance into the heavenly inheritance' (pp. 55f). Through the work of Christ, believers are perfected 'as those who are taken into the eternal rest (4: 1ff) and have attained the δόξα determined for them from the beginning, that is, fellowship with the Father'. Working backwards through Hebrews, Kögel notes from 10: 14 that this perfecting is finally and objectively achieved by the sacrifice of Christ (τετελείωκεν), but that it must be subjectively appropriated by individuals in different generations (τοὺς ἁγιαζομένους). From 9: 9; 10: 1; 7: 11, 19 he argues that association with terminology such as ἁγιάζειν and λατρεύειν shows that 'in no way does an ethical idea combine with this word but only a religious one, whereby the action of man is not in view but exclusively the relationship with God' (p. 58).

Applying the principle that τελειοῦν is only given distinct content from its object in each particular context, Kögel argues from 2: 10 that Jesus' person as such is not perfected, but only his quality as 'pioneer of their salvation' (p. 61). Indeed, as a military leader is prepared for his task, Christ needed perfecting only in the external sense of being brought to 'glory and honour', not with respect to his 'inner being' (p. 62). The participle τελειωθείς in 5: 9 relates to Christ in his capacity as 'source of eternal salvation' and further describes his vocational perfecting. Although the contrast between 'men having weakness' and 'a Son perfected for ever' in 7: 28 could be taken to imply that τετελειωμένον was being used in a moral sense, he argues that the perfecting of Jesus as Son simply refers to the perfecting of his *Mittlerqualität* (pp. 63f).[5] This occurred through his humiliation and death, in connection with his installation to the high-priestly office.

If the perfecting of Christ was accomplished through his temptations, suffering and consequent learning of obedience, this was not in any sense to prove Christ but rather to enable him to *understand* the situation of the recipients of salvation and thus become 'a merciful and faithful high priest'.[6] The writer does not think in terms of the eternal Son of God proving his unfathomable love in temptation and suffering but rather of Jesus the man being thus prepared for his heavenly office, 'Son though he was' (p. 65). The 'learning' of 5: 8 means 'becoming acquainted with', though this is not simply 'an operation on the intellect but on the will'. It is clear from 2: 5–18 that Christ is perfected as 'pioneer' in order to bring about the perfecting of the 'many sons', whom he calls 'brothers'. In the final analysis, then, Kögel relates the perfecting of Christ to his exaltation or glorification, by which he opens the gate to God's glory for his people and thus perfects them.

(b) O. Michel[7]

Although Michel's great commentary on Hebrews contains significant
discussion of the concept of perfection at various points, his most
comprehensive exposition of the theme is found in a journal article,
published in 1935. Acknowledging much of value in Kögel's survey of the
evidence, Michel argues, nevertheless, that *the LXX is the proper basis on
which to interpret the NT evidence.* Kögel's dependence on classical Greek
parallels led him to one-sided and incorrect conclusions. Michel fundamentally wishes to argue that 'the Biblical concepts always carry with
them a concrete reference, and that they mostly stand in contrast to Greek
abstraction and Hellenistic formalism' (p. 335). Hebrews has taken over
the connection between δίκαιος and τέλειος that is frequently found in the
LXX and late Judaism, and does not use the terminology in a formal or
neutral sense (p. 336).

In the OT and Rabbinic interpretations of the OT,[8] perfection is the
situation of the person who 'acknowledges God's command and renders
obedience' (p. 337). It is not simply a moral quality alongside others, but
one that describes a person's whole position before God (Deut. 18: 13
LXX). For NT exegesis, the comparison between τέλειοι and μανθάνοντες
(1 Chr. 25: 8 LXX) is said to be particularly instructive (cf. Hebrews 5:
11ff; 1 Cor. 2: 6; Phil. 3: 15). Although there is a formal usage of
τελειοῦν in the LXX, there is also a 'religious' usage (eg., 2 Sam. 22: 26;
Sir. 31: 10; Wis. 4: 13), related to the use of the adjective and conveying
the sense of perfection in relation to God. The religious use of the
adjective and verb does not exclude cultic and moral content, but 'it is a
mistake to note exclusively the cultic and moral content of the concept'
(p. 340). The LXX 'goes beyond the classical Greek linguistic usage and
prepares both for the religious and the formal assertions of the NT'.

Having surveyed the use of the terminology elsewhere in the NT, Michel
turns specifically to Hebrews. He notes that 'Christ was Son and became
high priest; the way from sonship to his high priesthood was his perfection
(2: 10; 5: 9; 7: 28). Christ did not give up his sonship; on the contrary,
perfection consisted precisely in this, that sonship remained proven'
(p. 348). The real emphasis of Hebrews is on God's consecration of the
Son as high priest through suffering (2: 10) and confirmation of his cross
through ascension (5: 9). 'Sinlessness and obedience are the expressions of
inner perfection, the signs of proven sonship; cross and exaltation are the
events by which the outer, vocational perfection is reached' (p. 349). Yet,
*'it is impossible to distinguish the inner, personal perfection from the
outer, vocational. Hebrews has woven both lines into a unity.'* As learning

is the way to perfection in 1 Chr. 25: 8 (LXX), so for Christ 'sinlessness and obedience were not self-evident but had to be learned and struggled for'. The OT teaching on perfection is clearly in the background when Hebrews speaks of Jesus' offering himself freely, completely untarnished by sin (4: 15; 9: 14).

With regard to the perfecting of believers in Hebrews, Michel compares the perspective of Paul in Phil. 3: 12—15. Believers may be τέλειοι on earth, 'through the Spirit of God, through regeneration, through striving for the goal', but not 'perfected' (τετελειωμένοι). Christians only reach perfection with the Parousia of Christ (pp. 350f).[9] Michel notes the connection between purification, sanctification and perfection in Hebrews: the one action of God in Christ makes pure, sanctifies and perfects. Yet each of these terms has its own specific value in the argument. Furthermore, although each term is eschatologically considered by the writer, having its τέλος in eternity and beyond time, 'only perfection is *emphatically* eschatological' (p. 352). The purification of the conscience brings about the 'new heart' of Jer. 31: 31—4. The 'true heart' and the 'good conscience' are *'the fruit of forgiveness, the concrete content of Christian perfection and the first-fruit of the future world'* (p. 353). With Kögel, Michel concludes from the use of τέλειος in 9: 11 that the writer's linguistic usage identifies the heavenly and the perfect. In the final analysis, our writer's teaching about the perfection of believers supposes 'a becoming, a striving, a development, which draws nearer to the goal; and yet God reserves to himself the true perfection and gives it only to the citizens of the future city (12: 23)' (p. 355).

(c) E. Käsemann[10]

Observing the use of similar terminology in the Mandaean literature, quotations from Irenaeus about the teaching of the Valentinian Gnostics, the *Odes of Solomon* and the *Corpus Hermeticum*, Käsemann concludes that perfection in Hebrews is synonymous with 'glorification' or 'entrance into the heavenly sphere' (pp. 85f). He approves of Kögel's opposition to the moral interpretation but argues that, in the exegesis of the relevant texts in Hebrews, Kögel shows a subtle shift from the neutral or formal interpretation to an identification of perfection with glorification. Michel's contention is thus proved to be correct: there is no Hellenistic formalism in the usage of the terminology in Hebrews. However, Käsemann cannot follow Michel's suggestion that the LXX is the proper basis on which to interpret the NT evidence. In the light of his overall understanding of Hebrews, in terms of the Gnostic myth of the 'redeemed Redeemer', he reaches conclusions that are superficially similar to Kögel's. Perfection is equivalent to glorification, though in Käsemann's presentation there is a metaphysical emphasis not found in Kögel's approach.

Christ is said to have been perfected inasmuch as he has experienced 'a restored, qualitative transformation of his being, in which the sphere of humiliation is left behind. The one who is perfected is he who is transferred back into heaven, as he originates from heaven' (p. 86). The obedience of Jesus is 'an attribute of his earthly being, not moral proving but recognition of the plan of salvation and a sign of humiliation, which puts him on the same footing with the earthly church'. Käsemann's dependence on the Gnostic myth of the heavenly man thus brings him to conclude that obedience and perfecting are two *contrasting stages* in the journey of Christ, from heaven to earth and back to heaven again. The perfecting of believers is said to be clearly associated with transfer to the heavenly assembly in 11: 40 and 12: 23 and is easily understood in similar terms at 7: 11 and 7: 19. However, 9: 9; 10: 1 and 10: 14 connect the perfecting of believers with the concepts of purification and sanctification accomplished by Christ in his sacrifice (pp. 88f). Only Christ is 'perfecter' (12: 1), but believers are perfected by their attachment to him (10: 14) and as such may be called τέλειοι (5: 14).[11]

Believers are perfected already only inasmuch as they are 'those who are being sanctified' (10: 14): 'through consecration one becomes a member of the heavenly sphere, while still on earth' (p. 88). Such consecration to God is effected by the sacrifice of Christ, but 'a final and comprehensive perfecting is still outstanding, precisely with a view to which one is consecrated'.

The relationship between Christ's testing through suffering and his perfecting is taken up again at a later stage in Käsemann's work (pp. 142ff). He insists that it is misleading to portray Christ's perfecting as the result of a process of moral development on earth. Following K. Bornhäuser,[12] he argues that Jesus is portrayed in Hebrews as suffering not general human temptations but the 'proto-type' of specifically Christian temptations. These are not essentially moral dangers but 'the temptation to fall away from the eschatological hope'. In learning obedience through suffering, Christ 'realized the prerequisite' for perfection, 'not in the sense of a process of moral development' but in 'the absolute decision between hope and falling away' (p. 143).

(d) Th. Häring[13]

A totally different line of interpretation is initiated by Theodor Häring, which may conveniently be called the 'cultic' approach. The Christian hope is presented in Hebrews in cultic terms. Man is enabled to 'draw near to God' because of the high-priestly work of Christ. The parallelism between τελειοῦν, καθαρίζειν and ἁγιάζειν in the argument of Hebrews 9 and 10 shows that these are all the effects of the one sacrifice of Christ. More than both the other terms, τελειοῦν is said to be a formal concept, the particular meaning of which must be sought from the context. In this case, the context points to the meaning 'to consecrate' (*weihen*).

Häring acknowledges that classical Greek sources, Philo and the papyri offer no real support for such a cultic rendering of this verb.[14] Here the appropriate word for consecration is τελεῖν. However, he proposes that the former is used as an equivalent for the latter in the LXX rendering of the expression *millē' (yād)*, 'to fill (the hand)', i.e., 'to consecrate for the cult' (e.g., Exod. 29: 9, 29). 'The material significance of the Hebrew concept was still not extinguished from the translators' consciousness' when they chose πληροῦν to render the same Hebrew expression elsewhere (e.g., Exod. 32: 29; Jdg. 17: 5, 12). However, this is said to have entirely receded from view when they chose τελειοῦν. To suggest that these two Greek verbs were used synonymously, with the meaning 'to fill', shows little feeling for the Greek language, in Häring's view (p. 267).[15]

He then proceeds to argue that the cultic understanding of perfection best fits the context on each occasion.[16] Calvin is cited in support of this line of exegesis, though Calvin himself did not base his conclusions on a supposed cultic use of the verb in the LXX. Häring takes particular issue with those commentators who try to identify perfection with the concept of glorification (pp. 268ff). Although this is a possible interpretation of the verb in 2: 10 in view of the preceding verses (verses 5–9), the following section (verses 11–18) shows that the consecration of Christ to his priesthood was in the writer's mind. This is indicated even more clearly by the context when the perfecting of Christ is mentioned again (5: 9; 7: 28). Although glorification is possibly what is meant by the perfecting of believers at 11: 40 and 12: 23, the writer's preceding use of the verb in association with the concepts of cleansing, sanctification and drawing near to God suggests that the cultic sense is to be understood throughout.

The conclusion is thus reached that τελειοῦν in Hebrews may be consistently interpreted as a synonym for τελεῖν, particularly as the latter is used in the Mystery religions. However, our writer's usage is derived from a particular usage in the LXX and stresses that Christianity offers 'the true consecration', as opposed to all other means of consecration to God pursued by mankind (p. 275).

(e) E. Riggenbach[17]

Eduard Riggenbach's commentary on Hebrews, first published in 1913, contains a detailed analysis of the relevant texts, but no attempt to systematise the evidence relating to the concept of perfection. In a journal article responding to the arguments of Häring, he expresses himself more fully on the subject. A general review of the literature leads Riggenbach to the conclusion that 'an assured linguistic use of τελειοῦν and τελείωσις in the sense of consecration to the Mysteries does not exist' (p. 190).[18] The Hebrew expression *millē' (yād)*, 'to fill (the hand)', refers quite literally to the initial presentation of sacrificial offerings, by which action priests were installed to office. The LXX rendering πληροῦν τὰς χεῖρας expresses more conspicuously the concrete meaning of the Hebrew expression than τελειοῦν τὰς χεῖρας. However, even the latter keeps the literal sense in view, and τελειοῦν is used to indicate more specifically the 'spiritual significance' of the action: 'consecration with respect to the hands', that is, for the activity of a priest (p. 186).[19] The use of τελείωσις for *millû'-îm* (e.g., Exod. 29: 22, 26) is said to confirm this interpretation.

In the final analysis, Riggenbach is prepared to acknowledge 'an influence of the language of the Mysteries on the use of τελειοῦν in the manner of expression of the Pentateuch, but not in that of Hebrews' (p. 194). The perfect passive participle at Hebrews 7: 28 certainly recalls the use of Lev. 4: 5; 21: 10 (LXX). However, to interpret the verb in Hebrews in the sense of 'consecrated' would present a strange antithesis: Christ's consecration is for ever, whereas that of OT priests was somehow limited by sin (pp. 190f). In fact, 7: 11ff shows that the characteristic difference between the high priesthood of Christ and that of the OT is that 'it does not rest upon a legal arrangement, but on personal character' and has to do with *Christ's testing, death and heavenly exaltation.* We are not in the least prepared for a cultic application of the verb when it is first used (2: 10), and the following passage does not force a cultic interpretation upon us, as Häring proposes, since no hint has been given in the argument thus far that Christ needed to be consecrated himself to become 'the consecrator' (2: 11).

With reference to the perfecting of believers, Riggenbach notes that τελειοῦν in the LXX nowhere has the general sense of consecration that Häring wants to give it ('to place in a proper position in relation to God'). Our writer could certainly have effected such a new application of the verb, but this is unlikely because he denies absolutely that OT institutions could bring perfection (7: 11, 19; 10: 1). There was a measure of cleansing and sanctification possible under the Old Covenant (9: 10, 13f) and, if τελειοῦν was being used as a cultic term by our writer, a similar sort of *a fortiori* argument could be expected. Riggenbach concludes that there is no linguistic basis for interpreting the latter in terms of 'the true consecration'.

The terminology is said to be found frequently in Hebrews because of the situation of the original recipients. They were in danger of forfeiting their relationship with Christ because they were placing a higher value on the institutions of their Jewish background. The writer aims to show that everything that Judaism strove for, but did not attain, comes to fulfilment in Christ. Their perfection in Christ is only made possible because he himself was 'morally proved in suffering and brought to the goal of his vocation' (p. 195). Thus perfected, he is able to 'lead upward to perfection those who walk in fellowship with him'. The concept in Hebrews includes *a religious reference sometimes, an ethical one on occasions and sometimes a reference to the perfecting of man's state or condition.* The theme is central to the writer's purpose: 'readers only gain afresh the enthusiasm to declare themselves confidently for Christ when they become convinced that they achieved perfection in every respect in him and in him alone' (p. 195).[20]

(f) M. Dibelius[21]

In contrast to Riggenbach, Martin Dibelius contends that all attempts to read Hebrews as a message to a specific congregation in a specific situation impair the proper theological understanding of the document. Passages such as 10: 32–4 describe no single situation but 'typical experiences of a younger church' (p. 161), used by the writer to expound the theme of the Christian's 'better and more lasting possession' (10: 34). The exhortations are addressed to *the whole church*, 'whose final, eschatological distress is still pending' (p. 162). The writer treats his readers as immature (5: 11 – 6: 12) to 'admonish them to the utmost attentiveness'. He has no real knowledge of their situation and no real expectation of a renunciation of faith on their part.

The writer's purpose is a theological one: he sets out to portray Christian salvation in the form of 'a sublime *mystery-cult*, linking earth and heaven. Christ, the true high priest, opens the way through his death into the eternal sanctuary in heaven. He receives himself the initiation for this cult and makes Christians qualified to follow him, the Forerunner (6: 20), and become consecrated themselves in this cult' (p. 163). However, Jesus has accomplished his work in the framework of history – this cult is based on no myth – and all believers can 'draw near' to God in the heavenly sanctuary, as 12: 22 shows.

In two respects Hebrews is said to have withdrawn from what the early Christian kerygma held as historical tradition and has approximated its picture of Christ to that of the Gnostic Anthropos Myth (p. 164). The resurrection is played down in preference to the concept of Christ's entrance into the heavenly sanctuary, and there is a close parallelism between statements about Christ and statements about believers. An ethico-religious understanding of the concept of perfection is foreign to the NT, importing modern 'humanistic' ideas into the text. Only when it is observed that the goal of Christ and Christians is entrance into the heavenly sanctuary can it be seen that our writer means by $\tau\epsilon\lambda\epsilon\acute{\iota}\omega\sigma\iota\varsigma$ 'the consecration that will bring perfection (*die vollendende Weihe*)', and by $\tau\epsilon\lambda\epsilon\iota o\tilde{\upsilon}\nu$ 'the conferring of this consecration' (p. 166).[22]

Dibelius clearly builds on the arguments of Häring and opposes those of Riggenbach. It cannot be proved that the terminology was used with reference to consecration in the Mysteries. However, the use of the verb in the LXX for the expression 'to fill the hands' adds something to the plain meaning of the Hebrew original. It appears as a technical term, which is 'familiar to the LXX translator and his readers, according to which $\tau\epsilon\lambda\epsilon\iota o\tilde{\upsilon}\nu$ means "to consecrate", that is in the special sense "to perfect", so that the person concerned is qualified for priestly service' (p. 166). Since the consecration involves filling the hands with offerings, it is 'consecration with respect to the hands'. Dibelius goes on to argue the possibility of reading the verb in a cultic sense uniformly throughout Hebrews.[23]

The priesthood and ritual of the Old Covenant could not bestow 'the requisite cultic qualities' (pp. 167f). However, what the OT cult had previously denied is now affirmed for Christians (10: 14), namely 'the consecration that will bring perfection'. OT believers had to wait for Christians before experiencing this (11: 40). Those who have 'already received that consecration and have entered the heavenly sanctuary' are pictured in 12: 23.

The perfecting of Christ refers to 'the action which immediately precedes his entrance into the heavenly sanctuary', namely the consecration that is effected through his sacrifice (p. 170). This is shown by the sequence in 5: 7–10, where Christ's learning obedience through the things he suffered is a preliminary to his perfecting, not a part of it. God's intention to bestow this consecration on him through suffering is indicated in 2: 10, and 7: 28 asserts that his consecration is in no way transitory, since his sacrifice is effective 'for ever'. The 'last act' in our writer's presentation of the work of Christ is his entrance into the heavenly sanctuary for eternal ministry and the bold introduction of believers into that sanctuary.[24]

This activity of Christ is mentioned in 12: 2, where τελειωτής is said to mean 'consecrator' or 'mystagogue', rather than 'perfecter' (p. 171).

The exposition of a heavenly cult brings our writer to utter harsh words about the former cult (7: 18; 8: 13; 9: 8f; 10: 4–9). Such teaching not only passes judgement on Israelite–Jewish worship but 'on all cultic enterprises generally' (p. 173). Hebrews speaks unceremoniously, and without priestly allusion, of Christian assembly (10: 25; 13: 17, 24). This is not because the Church was still at a primitive stage of development but because of the writer's concern to express his central theological perception: 'sacrifice, consecration, the entrance of Jesus Christ into heaven and his priestly ministry are the only mystery-cult which still has value for Christians' (p. 175). Dibelius considers this highly significant in view of the 'early Catholicism' of 1 Clement. Our author's aim is to *put forward an exposition of Christian worship as participation in the cult of heaven, in which Christ himself is the only high priest.*

(g) C. Spicq[25]

In an excursus to his commentary on Hebrews, Ceslaus Spicq argues that the terminology of perfection is an important means by which the author contrasts the Old and New Covenants and their effects. Only the latter makes men 'morally and religiously perfect ... by leading them to their term, union with God'. When it is said that believers are τέλειοι (5: 14), the meaning is that 'they lack nothing, that they are justified, and that they entirely realise their vocation' (p. 214).[26]

The writer is concerned that each of his readers should aspire to become *un chrétien accompli* (5: 11 – 6: 1), arriving at the supreme state of development in his spiritual life. This perfection is characterised both by 'a more profound knowledge of the mystery of Christ and a moral conscience more refined and more rigorous; the latter, moreover, being dependent on the former' (p. 215). Like Michel, Spicq sees a particular parallel with Phil. 3: 12–15 and recalls Wis. 9: 6, where the idea is introduced that 'moral perfection is intrinsically a function of the religious knowledge of God. A man is not perfect, complete, unless he is united to the true God by faith and submissive to his will' (p. 216). The 'mature Hebrews' will no longer be tempted to return to Judaism when their faith is clarified and their conduct rectified.

The perfection of which 7: 11 speaks can only be properly understood against the background of LXX usage, notably with regard to the installation of the priests. It is said to be 'a technical term of sacerdotal ritual', and yet Spicq actually treats it as a formal concept when he argues that the 'perfection of priesthood' is 'to permit man to approach God' (p. 220). Thus, the New Covenant achieves what the Old Covenant could not: purification of the conscience, inner righteousness and the ultimate goal of entrance into heaven. Such perfection can only be obtained by believers thanks to the realisation of the ideal of priesthood by Christ.

The cultic use of the verb in the Pentateuch reminds us that 'the priest made perfect is the priest invested with the power of priesthood' (p. 221). The incarnate Son of God is 'the ideal priest, realizing all the requirements and possessing all the virtues of priesthood (cf. 1: 1–3)'. Both as Son (5: 8: 7: 28) and as leader of humanity (2: 10), Jesus is consecrated priest or 'consummated in his priesthood'. His perfection is 'religious' in the sense that he becomes a unique and eternal priest–king. It is 'moral' in the sense that, although morally perfect as Son of God, he must submit to God's will and carry out his commands, having his whole life oriented towards God.[27] It is thus that the great servants of God, such as Noah, Abraham or Job, are called τέλειος, and in this sense Christ is 'the consecrated *par excellence*' (p. 222). On the other hand, with respect to men, Christ becomes fully qualified to sympathise with the weakness of his brothers by virtue of his human life. 'His incarnation and his piety render him physically and religiously capable to offer the only sacrifice fully acceptable to God, being at the same time priest and victim' (pp. 222f).

The perfection of Christ in his priesthood 'after the order of Melchizedek' – his inner virtues, his sacrifice, his intercession in heaven, above all the efficacy of his mediation – earns him the title 'Perfecter' (12: 2), unique in Biblical and profane literature. The perfecting of believers means leading them 'to a state of completion' (p. 223). Everything necessary for the salvation of mankind has been acquired by the sacrifice of Christ (10: 14), including the heavenly inheritance. However, Christians are like exiles, aspiring to the heavenly city, who must pass from immaturity to maturity, 'to be in a position to reach the ultimate goal and be fully "accomplished", consummated in eternity' (p. 224).

Thus, in contrast to the attempt of certain writers to interpret the terminology uniformly throughout Hebrews, Spicq argues that particular contexts must show whether the accent is cultic, moral, intellectual or eschatological. Indeed, he seems to see evidence for almost every possible sense of the verb in his interpretation! However, the terminology always emphasises the idea of bringing something or someone to an appointed end, an end appointed and achieved by the grace and power of God.

(h) B. Rigaux[28]

The Dead Sea Scrolls reveal the existence of a first-century AD Jewish sect preoccupied with the procuring of perfection.[29] Rigaux attempts to expound the concept of perfection found in those documents and relate it to the teaching of the New Testament on that subject. He is in no doubt that the members of the Qumran Community borrowed their terminology from the OT. However, they use the terminology to mean 'obedience to the divine precepts, as they are practised at Qumran', which means 'acceptance of the whole monastic life, conceived as an expression of the divine will' (p. 238).[30]

Essential to the idea of perfection at Qumran is the concept of a *knowledge from God, reserved exclusively for the sectarians* (pp. 239f). The acquisition of perfection has something to do with knowledge of 'mysteries' or 'superior teaching'. This knowledge is imparted by the Holy Spirit (1QS 3: 13 – 4: 26) and is especially described as a divine gift reserved for the last times. Thus, we find a *moral* element in this concept of perfection – obedience and walking 'in the way' – a *mystical* element – surpassing human categories of knowledge, volition and action, the purification and gift of the Holy Spirit – and a *gnostic* element – knowledge of God's plan and God's law, 'bordering on a revelation of the activity of God and of the eternal destinies of man' (p. 241).

The members of the Community are not philosophers or mystagogues: 'they apply themselves above all to discover the divine plan and its realizations for their time' (p. 242). The illumination given to the Teacher of Righteousness and spiritual leaders at Qumran, conveyed in the form of *pesher* exegesis, 'contains a new revelation added to the text [of Scripture] itself' (p. 247). This revelation of the mysteries of God and of the prophetic words of Scripture constitutes the basis of the new life at Qumran.[31]

Turning to the Pauline epistles, Rigaux observes the relationship between perfection and knowledge, which is particularly stressed at Phil. 3: 15; Col. 1: 25–9 and 1 Cor. 2: 6. This knowledge is described by Paul in terms of the 'revelation of a mystery'. However, 'if the mystery appears to be revealed to all the saints in Colossians 1: 28 and Ephesians 4: 12–18, in 1 Corinthians this mystery is reserved for spiritual Christians' (p. 252).[32] Although there is a similarity of terminology at Qumran and in the NT here, 'the distance which separates the concepts is extremely great'. The Christian is classed among the perfect by Paul 'if he is capable of receiving spiritual teaching, by virtue of which his Christian experience will attain its fullness' (p. 257).

Although the terminology of perfection abounds in Hebrews, there is no explicit mention of a 'knowledge of the Mystery'. The warning of 5: 11 – 6: 3 shows that the readers have not passed the elementary stage of Christian understanding and moved towards perfection. In 5: 14 perfection is shown to involve both knowledge and discernment. Thus, without speaking of a mystery, 'the author will try to conduct the reader towards a perfect knowledge of the mystery of God' (p. 258). The following chapters show that *this is attained by understanding the perfection of Jesus Christ and the perfection that he has achieved for the Church.*

The author appears to deduce his teaching about the perfecting of Christ from Psalm 8: 4–6. 'Jesus accomplishes the mystery of the Scripture which has announced that he will be crowned with glory and honour (2: 9)' (p. 259). As the one who suffers and is glorified, Jesus is perfect, that is, 'completely man and completely Saviour'. Again in 5: 9 the perfecting of Christ is argued from a Scriptural citation (Psalm 110: 4), and this is taken up again in 7: 28. The teaching about the perfecting of Christians takes its departure from the prophecy of Jer. 31: 31–4. Such recourse to Scripture to illuminate the teaching on perfection is not presented in terms of a special 'charisma of revelation' on the author's part, but as an instrument of the Holy Spirit (p. 260).[33] Whereas all the members of the Qumran Sect are 'perfect', in Hebrews the τέλειος is the wise and virtuous Christian, who is 'apt to take hold of what is hidden to children' (p. 261). He is 'the adult who can comprehend the grandeur of the Christian realizations in the light of Scripture and theological speculation'. Knowledge of the perfection of Christ as high priest and of the perfection of the New Covenant 'confers on the Christian the knowledge of his own perfection' (p. 262).

(i) A. Wikgren[34]

The contributions to this debate by English-speaking writers have been few and far between. One of the most significant of these is by Allen Wikgren. The cultic—religious sense is basic, in his view, but 'concomitant aspects of intellectual, spiritual and moral or ethical growth and progess in the Christian life appear to be involved also in the author's thought and argument' (pp. 159f). There can be little doubt that Hebrews depicts the Christian life in terms of progress toward an end or goal, as in the figure of the wilderness journey of the people of God, which is 'a central feature of the author's typology'. This τέλος assumes 'different forms and emphases, ranging from a philosophical *summum bonum* to an eschatological identification with death as the ultimate "perfection"' (p. 160). Nevertheless, 'there appears throughout to be an underlying assumption of an ethical—

moral content and development in the use of τέλειος and its cognates, an element which significantly and explicitly appears as ethical exhortation and moral encouragement when the Epistle deviates from its main argument, and in its concluding three chapters'.

The greatest difficulty for the interpreter lies in relating the ethical—moral aspect, with its ideas of progression, to the person of Christ. In relating the 'perfectibility of Jesus' and the 'perfectibility of man', it is important to note carefully the parallels that the author draws between Jesus and man in the elaboration of his typology. The very possibility of man having a τέλος and attaining it 'depends upon a decisive act in which Christ as *redemptor* and *perfector* is the object of a response of faith by the believer. The latter is then in a sense proleptically *teleios* through initiation and participation in that community of faith which also constitutes this ideal goal (cf. 11: 40).'[35] This is described by Wikgren as a 'realized teleiology'. Although there are several points of contact with the idea of perfection in the Qumran literature,[36] the differences are also significant. The latter had an objective criterion by which to judge perfection or holiness, namely 'the law as objectified and interpreted in the rules and regulations of the community' (p. 162). In Hebrews, however, 'the Law perfected nothing' (7: 19), and the emphasis of the New Covenant is upon the Law being written by God on human hearts (8: 10; 10: 16).

In Hebrews, the ultimate goal is interpreted in terms of a 'rest' or 'Sabbath' (3: 11, 18; 4: 1, 3, 5, 10f), constituting the future state of perfect fellowship with God. Believers must 'strive' to enter that rest (4: 11). Thus, 'the end, though in a sense proleptically possessed, is neither fully nor automatically attained; its achievement involves struggle and suffering, a sharing, in fact, in the sufferings and in the death of Jesus himself (13: 13)' (p. 163). Such imitation and participation implies that 'the ideal has been objectified, made incarnate in Jesus Christ, and the believer should be prepared through faith to share objectively in his experiences'.

In 2: 10—18, where the parallels between Jesus and the believer are drawn most carefully, and in 5: 7—10, statements are made that seem to carry the assumption of an 'ethical—moral progression on the part of Jesus as well as man' (p. 164). Whilst certain titles express some differentiation of function and status on Christ's part, Wikgren argues against any attempt to limit Jesus' learning obedience to his function as perfect high priest. This 'contradicts the Epistle's concern with the atoning significance of the whole life of Jesus' (p. 165). Furthermore,

'attempts to resolve the difficulty by positing a difference between "perfect" (τέλειος) and "perfected" (τετελειωμένος) or by asserting that "perfection" is not to be identified with "sinlessness" are aspects of the view which would dissociate the quality of perfection from the person of the historical Jesus and ascribe it to him only in his function as exalted and heavenly high priest and mediator of salvation.'

Wikgren concludes that the writer aims to present, with his symbolic patterns of perfection, 'a kind of philosophy of history in which old and new, idealism and meliorism, being and becoming, are mutually related in what is for him a real continuity of meaning and emerge in a new structure of value, the new covenant' (p. 166). The Christian participates in this now in the community of faith, but its 'full and perfect realization still lies ahead, as the faithful press on toward the land of promise under the power of a τέλος defined as God revealed in Christ'. For in Christ 'the τέλος not only has been defined but also empirically demonstrated for the faithful in terms both of present potentiality and ultimate realization' (p. 167).

(j) L.K.K. Dey [37]

The teaching of Hebrews about perfection is one of a number of factors that suggest to L.K.K. Dey its closeness to the thought-world of Hellenistic Judaism, especially to the writings of Philo Judaeus. Dey argues that the sequence of comparisons between Jesus as 'Son' and the angels, the heavenly man, Moses, Aaron, Levi and Melchizedek, in Hebrews, points to 'a single religious thought world' from which it derives (p. 7). Here, such figures have 'to a large degree synonymous titles and interchangeable functions and they constitute the intermediary world between God and man'. This intermediary world mediates 'an inferior revelation and religious status of a secondary order', whereas 'the higher level of *perfection* is characterized by unmediated and direct access to God and participation in the primary gifts'. The readers addressed in Hebrews had an 'analogous frame of religious thought', which explains the writer's argument and the underlying issues.

In the first main section of his book, Dey expounds the idea of the intermediary world and patterns of perfection as found in the writings of Philo Judaeus. Occasional support is offered from other Jewish literature. Perfection is expressed in Philo in a variety of ways, but 'what is central is its unmediated relationship to God which transcends the leading of Sophia and mediation of the Logos' (p. 45 note 4). The patriarchs, Aaron, the levitical priesthood, Melchizedek and Moses all serve as 'exemplars' of the different levels of perfection, representing 'different dispositions of the soul, characters, types and virtues' (p. 46). The basis of the distinction amongst these exemplars of perfection is 'paideutic' — 'between those who are progressing to perfection through teaching and practice and those who are perfect by nature from the beginning and need neither teaching nor practice' (p. 68). Dey argues that other Philonic scholars have missed this central and important theme of religious perfection as 'unmediated access to God' (p. 79 note 14). 'It is the ideals of Greek paideia which give coherence to Philo's thought rather than, as Goodenough proposed, "mystery"' (pp. 80f).

In the Qumran literature, 'drawing near to God and the intercessory angel are seen in conjunction rather than in disjunction', whereas in Philo, 'the highest religious status or perfection requires that one pass beyond the intermediary world to God himself — an unmediated access' (p. 93).[38] In Hebrews, perfection and access to God are alternative forms of expression, indicating a closeness to the thought-world of Philo rather than to that of apocalyptic Judaism (p. 94). When Hebrews characterises perfection and access to God in terms of Christian faith and hope, it has reinterpreted with the aid of Christian beliefs 'a tradition which finds its closest analogy in Philo' (p. 95). Dey goes on to describe some of the features of apocalyptic literature that are missing in Philo and Hebrews but found at Qumran. The 'traditional eschatological pieces' found in Hebrews are 'rather simple in comparison to the much more elaborate apocalyptic themes in earlier Christian tradition ... and are used by the author mainly for the purpose of exhortation' (p. 96). As distinct from Philo and Hebrews, the teaching of Qumran on perfection is 'sectarian' in the sense that the 'perfect of the way' is the one who belongs to the Community and lives in total commitment to the ideology of the sect, specifically its eschatological self-understanding (pp. 96–8). Furthermore, the characteristic vocabulary associated with perfection in the OT, the Testaments of the Twelve Patriarchs and the Qumran literature, is not found in Philo and Hebrews (p. 110).

Turning specifically to the evidence of Hebrews, Dey argues from 7: 19 that perfection is 'proximity or access to God' (p. 122). Jesus is the one who effects this by his entry into the heavenly sanctuary (4: 14ff; 10: 19ff), and Christians procure such perfection for themselves by faith and hope. The series of comparisons between Christ and the various mediators of the 'intermediary world' suggests that the readers were in danger of identifying Jesus with this sphere and therefore of regarding the revelation and salvation that he mediates as inferior, 'a lower stage which could be surpassed on the path to perfection' (p. 123). The genius of the author lies in his 'use of the Christology of Jesus' suffering, death and exaltation as the "Son" to reinterpret this frame of religious thought' (p. 124). He concludes that the readers were not in danger of relapsing into a less taxing form of Judaism, which promised inferior salvific benefits to Christianity, nor were they in a 'state of post-apostolic fatigue', but rather their 'neglect' (2: 3) was occasioned by 'a particular tradition of Judaism which promised much more — perfection and immediacy to God without intervening mediators and the highest of (*sic*) religious status, like that of Aaron and Moses' (p. 126).

Most of the commentators on 2: 5–18 share the assumption that 'there is no real polemical situation in Hebrews and hence they seek for a singular theological point of view in the writing, whether apocalyptic or gnostic' (p. 215). Against these interpretations, Dey argues that the traditions of intermediaries and perfection can best explain the passage in its context. 'The Christian belief that the earthly Jesus, the man of flesh and blood, is the basis of salvation would have implied in this tradition imperfection rather than perfection/salvation. The perfect heavenly man is incorporeal, immortal and without any share (*ametochos*) in corruptible and earthly essence' (p. 217). Our writer 'shares with this tradition the understanding of sin and imperfection as the realm of flesh and blood, human weakness, ignorance, wandering, trial and temptation' (p. 219). However, his 'bold and revolutionary thesis' is that *Jesus has entered and participated in the realm of imperfection (flesh, blood and temptation) and has accomplished perfection within this realm and thereby has opened the way for others to participate in perfection within this realm of creation and not outside of it'* (p. 219). To achieve this end, the writer has used certain Christian apocalyptic traditions (e.g., 2: 5–9, 14*b*–15) to 'reinterpret the tradition of intermediaries and perfection, without such apocalypticism being the primary frame of his religious thought' (p. 221).

The writer presents that tradition of Jesus' suffering and temptation as the *paideia* or discipline that leads to progress or betterment and in the end to perfection (5: 7–10). Using the traditions of Hellenistic Judaism, in which martyrology has assimilated the ideals of Greek *paideia*, [39] and especially the tradition of Hellenistic Jewish prayer,[40] our writer represents Jesus in 5: 7ff as 'the one who achieved salvation for himself (= perfection) through ardent prayer and suffering, i.e., salvation from death and perfection through the education of suffering' (p. 224).[41] Jesus' participation in the realm of imperfection is given a 'further rationale along the lines that it was part of his education to perfection so that he could be a high priest who could be "merciful" and "sympathetic" to the human condition of imperfection' (p. 225).[42]

Hebrews insists that perfection is possible for the Christian here and now, even within this realm of imperfection. Christian faith and hope are the means of holding on to what is already possessed or can be possessed (p. 227). In this situation, Jesus is the Christian's exemplar (12: 1ff). Through the *paideia* of God (12: 8), 'which gives them the status of "sons", and through Christian instruction (5: 11 – 6: 20), believers progress from the status of children to that of the perfect' (p. 229). Contrary to the view of Käsemann, Michel and others, Dey insists that 'parenesis in Hebrews is a mode of Christian *paideia*, whose aim is to lead the Christians to the knowledge of God and the Christian "virtues" of faith and hope' (p. 229). Parenesis has as its main purpose 'to lead the learner to the knowledge of God and this knowledge informs and grounds their religious existence as faith and hope – and not the other way round'. The recipients of Hebrews have not reached the status of teachers (= perfection), but the author 'understands himself as a Christian teacher who has reached perfection – i.e., fully grounded in Christian faith and hope as a man of flesh and blood and beset with temptations' (p. 232). Hebrews 3: 14 is taken to mean that 'we become participants of Christ and remain so by holding on to the first principle of reality (hypostasis), namely, faith. It is in faith that we enter into God's own rest (= perfection).' Hence the insistence of the writer on holding fast to what is already possessed by faith.

(k) Conclusion

The preceding review of significant interpretations of the concept of perfection in Hebrews faces us with some important issues to resolve. In the first place, there are linguistic and methodological questions, which must be answered in the next chapter:

(i) To what extent does the 'formal' use of τέλειος and τελειοῦν in classical Greek literature carry over into the usage of NT writers in general and of Hebrews in particular?

(ii) To what extent does the use of the terminology in the LXX provide new content or material associations that may be assumed in NT usage?

(iii) What linguistic parallels can be adduced for the argument that τελειοῦν is used in Hebrews in the sense of 'glorification' or 'transfer to the heavenly sphere'?

(iv) To what extent can we argue a cultic meaning for the verb in Hebrews from the use of the expression τελειοῦν τὰς χεῖρας in the LXX?

In the second place, there are more general questions, which must be answered in the exegetical chapters that follow:

(i) Is the concept of perfection in Hebrews ethical, formal, cultic, metaphysical, eschatological, or a combination of these possibilities?

(ii) How rigorously is the parallelism between the perfecting of Christ and the perfecting of believers pursued (i.e., to what extent can the concept be interpreted uniformly, with respect to Christ and believers)?

(iii) What sort of polemic are we to understand behind our writer's use of the terminology of perfection?

(iv) How central is the exposition of this theme in Hebrews to the purpose of the writer?

2

THE LINGUISTIC BACKGROUND

The most thorough study of the terminology so far advanced is that of
P.J. Du Plessis, and it will be noted in the following pages to what extent
I am indebted to this work. However, his treatment of the *verb* in extra-
Biblical and Septuagintal usage is surprisingly inadequate. It is true that
Hebrews employs related terminology in important contexts,[1] but τελειοῦν
is more extensively used than any other member of this word group,
occurring nine times (2:10; 5:9; 7:19, 28; 9:9; 10:1, 14; 11:40; 12:23).
It must therefore be the focus of my study in this preliminary exercise.
Although the relevant article by G. Delling in the *Theological Dictionary
of the New Testament* (vol. VIII, pp. 49–87) makes up for this lack in
certain respects, its treatment of the Septuagintal evidence again leaves
much to be desired.

Classical Greek sources

Du Plessis begins by noting the significance of τέλος in this literature. The
'final notions of *telos* are never indicative of mere cessation, discontinu-
ation or suspended action. When finality is incurred, it is accompanied by
a hint of innate fulfilment' (p. 41). Thus, τέλος implies 'aim' or 'the
preconceived end'.[2] As a denomination of τέλος, the verb τελεῖν reflects
some of the characteristics of the noun. Its 'dynamic character is foremost:
to perform a task or execute what is expected' (p. 69). Its compass of
meanings includes 'to bring to an end', 'to finish' and the technical religious
sense 'to initiate',[3] or even 'to consecrate (to the priesthood)' (pp. 69–72).

It is argued that 'the distinct qualities of *telos* are to be kept in mind
when considering the circle of meanings characteristic of *teleios*' (p. 73).
Aristotle (*Metaphysics* IV.16.1021*b*) defines the latter as 'that which
constitutes an aggregate from which no component part is absent' and that
which has successfully reached its 'contemplated end'. Both a doctor and a
thief can be 'perfect' in their particular fields! Du Plessis argues that: 'the
dominant and fundamental quality of the adjective is *fullness*, derived

from the impletive disposition of *telos*, whose various intonations converge here on this one central idea. If *telos* expresses totality and maturity amongst other meanings, then *teleios* voices the same idea almost exclusively' (p. 77). After a comprehensive review of the adjective's use in Greek philosophy, Mysticism and Gnosticism, he argues that human perfection was essentially characterised throughout antiquity by 'the active desire of experiencing deity' (p. 93). Only the person who had reached this τέλος was truly τέλειος.

Du Plessis proposes that the verb τελειοῦν denotes the act of bringing something or someone to a state of entirety: 'to make complete and perfect', (in the passive) 'to attain maturity'. A certain parallelism between τελεῖν and τελειοῦν is evident because τέλος is fundamental to both, yet the former means essentially τέλος ποιεῖν and the latter τέλειον ποιεῖν.[4] 'The antonymity is in the former between "beginning" and "end", in the latter between "partiality" and "totality".'

Although this formal distinction may be proved in some cases, it is my contention that in general usage such a fine distinction of meaning cannot be pressed. This is especially so where *things, acts, works or time* are the subject or object of the verb. Thus, for instance, Thucydides (VI.32) uses τελεώσαντες to refer to the 'completion' of libations, in the sense of bringing them to an end. On the other hand, Pindar uses τελέσει with the sense of 'perfection', when he certifies that 'time, although his foot be slow, shall perfect' whatever share of excellence Fate has given him.[5] Here the implied contrast is between partiality and totality. Yet this could hardly be said of Sophocles' reference to the completion of a successful ambush (τὸν εὔαγρον τελειῶσαι λόχον),[6] or of Plato's reference to the fulfilment of the time of certain conditions (ἐπειδὴ γὰρ πάντων τούτων χρόνος ἐτελεώθη).[7] The latter means 'accomplished' in the sense of 'terminated'.

Something of the sense of bringing to completion in the sense of 'wholeness' is certainly implied in Aristotle's assertion that 'the pleasure completes the activity' (τελειοῖ τὴν ἐνέργειαν ἡ ἡδονή).[8] This nuance is also present in the extensive use of the verb with the sense of 'maturation', as applied to plants,[9] as well as to animals and man.[10] In the last case, growth in a moral sense is often implied, as well as physical maturation, but it is not the predominant meaning. The moral sense is not common, but is obvious in the statement attributed to Cleanthes: 'the evil are called imperfect and the serious-minded, perfected' (ἀτελεῖς μὲν ὄντας εἶναι φαύλους, τελειωθέντας δὲ σπουδαίους).[11] The use of this verb in essentially a non-moral sense, to refer to the perfecting of someone in a particular vocation, is of interest for our study. Herodotus reports how the simultaneous occurrence of certain events, 'as if by some predestination, made the election of Darius sure',[12] or '*sealed his success* in his claim to the monarchy' (ἐτελέωσε μιν ὥσπερ ἐκ συνθέτου τευ γενόμενα).[13] Sophocles' *Electra* (1508–10) concludes with the claim that the 'seed of Atreus', after many woes, has won his way into the path of freedom, 'being made perfect by the effort of today' (τῇ νῦν ὁρμῇ τελεωθέν). In avenging the wrong done to his father, Orestes is himself 'perfected'. Both of these references show how the completion of some task or the occurrence of some significant event can bring about the perfecting of someone in a particular role or calling.

Since, in the words of Du Plessis, 'the dominant and fundamental quality of the adjective is *fullness*' (p. 77), it is clear that the verb can mean 'to carry out fully' or 'to fulfil'.[14] Yet it cannot be denied that this is also the sense of τελεῖν in some contexts.[15] There is, however, one area where the distinction between the two verbs is most apparent. There is no evidence for the use of τελειοῦν in this period in a technical religious sense, paralleling the application of τελεῖν.[16] Of the whole word group, 'only τέλος and especially τελέω stand in any relation to the mysteries. Nor apart from allusions was the usage extensive in the pre-Christian and NT Age.'[17]

In conclusion, it must be said that Kögel's original contention about the formal nature of τελειοῦν in this literature is proved correct. Even in contexts where there are moral implications, the formal sense of the verb is obvious. The verb itself carries no material associations of a moral or technical kind, and distinct content can only be given by the context on each occasion.

The Septuagint

Du Plessis concludes that τέλος in the LXX 'did not belong to the religious vocabulary of the Alexandrinian (*sic*) translators' (p. 56). However, Eccles. 12: 13 describes the essential goal or fundamental principle of all existence: 'the knowledge of and communion with God' (pp. 64f). Aspiring to this end is '*going (hālak)* the way prescribed; its medium not intelligence but obedience (Deut. 18: 13)' (p. 66).

The purely formal use of τέλειος observed in classical Greek sources is also found in the LXX.[18] Du Plessis notes that the MT employs *tāmîm* predominantly in a *cultic and quantitative* sense, suggesting 'wholeness, entirety and intactness' (p. 94). However, apart from Exod. 12: 5, it is not τέλειος but ἄμωμος that is the usual LXX rendering in such contexts. The translators choose rather to employ the former when *tāmîm* is used in a *personal qualitative* sense (Gen. 6: 9; Deut. 18: 13; 2 Kgs 22: 26 LXX (2 Sam. 22: 26)). However, again it should be noted that other Greek words are more commonly used to render *tāmîm* and its derivatives in such contexts.[19]

It thus emerges that τέλειος is occasionally used in the LXX where the OT concept of perfection as 'entirety and wholeness in a divine relationship' is found.[20] Du Plessis insists that this concept is not formal or abstract: 'acquiring full proportion entails living in harmony with true standards'. Perfection in the OT is not essentially a moral concept, though it clearly involves loving obedience to God as the one who, in his mercy, has initiated the relationship with man. The expression *lēḇ(āḇ) šālēm*, conveying the idea of 'wholehearted allegiance to the Lord', is relevant here. It involves 'a stable integrity not contaminated by divergent motives or conflicts between thoughts and deeds' (p. 99). The LXX uses τέλειος to describe such an undivided heart at 1 Kgs 8: 61; 11: 4, 10 (B); 15: 3, 14 and 1 Chr. 28: 9, elsewhere employing πλήρης and ἀληθινός.

Although it appears that τέλειος acquires a certain 'religious' significance in some LXX contexts, my concern is to discover the extent to which τελειοῦν is similarly employed. More generally, I shall observe in what respects LXX usage of the verb goes beyond that of classical Greek sources and prepares for the usage of the NT.

(a) Formal Usage

The idea of bringing something to completion, where the implied contrast is between 'partiality' and 'totality', is apparent in Ezek. 27: 11, where mercenaries and their weapons, strung around the walls of Tyre, 'made perfect' her beauty.[21] Similarly, the son of Sirach advises: 'give a daughter in marriage; you will have perfected a great task'.[22] The same chapter urges: 'stretch forth your hand to the poor, so that your blessing may be complete' (ἵνα τελειωθῇ ἡ εὐλογία σου), the implication being that God will bless the person who does this 'in all the work of (his) hands'.[23]

On some occasions, the idea of completion seems to involve little more than the sense of bringing something to its proper conclusion, as in Sir. 50: 19, where the worship of the Lord is in view,[24] or 2 Esd. 16: 3 (Neh. 6: 3), where the work on the walls of Jerusalem is the object.[25] The use of ἐγενήθη τελειωθῆναι in 2 Esd. 16: 16 (Neh. 6: 16) to describe the accomplishment of the work on the wall 'with the help of our God', is an exaggerated rendering on the part of the Greek translators. It may be that their aim was to emphasise the idea that the great work was 'brought to fulfilment' with divine aid. This certainly seems to be the sense of the verb in Judith 10: 8, where the elders of the city pray that God might 'fulfil' Judith's plans.[26] On three occasions the Hebrew verb *tāmam* is translated with τελειοῦν. The sense in two cases is simply 'to finish',[27] and the third occasion, in 2 Sam. 22: 26 (LXX 2 Kgs 22: 26), comes in for special consideration below.

A final reference that must be considered at this point is 4 Macc. 7: 15. Here we read 'O blessed age, O reverend grey head, O life loyal to the law and perfected by the faithful seal of death' (ὃν πιστὴ θανάτου σφραγὶς ἐτελείωσεν).[28] The faithfulness of Eleazar to the Law found its ultimate expression in his torture and death. The verb τελειοῦν is being used as above in a purely formal sense to describe the consummation of the life of faith in martyrdom and has no special moral or mystical implications. Although there are similarities with the later Christian use of the verb to describe death, and more particularly the death of martyrs, there is nothing here to suggest anything beyond death as the goal of believers, or that death itself effects some change in their situation with respect to God.[29]

(b) Religious Usage

In his assessment of the Septuagintal evidence, Michel makes much of the fact that there is a 'religious' use of τελειοῦν, related to the use of the adjective and conveying the sense of perfection in relation to God.[30] In this respect the LXX is said to go beyond the classical Greek usage and prepare 'both for the religious and the formal assertions of the NT'. He points to 2 Sam. 22: 26 (LXX 2 Kgs 22: 26); Sir. 31: 10 and Wis. 4: 13. To these we might also add Daniel 3: 40 (LXX). In the first of these references, the Greek translators rather imperfectly convey the sense of the reflexive hithpa'el (*'im gibbôr tāmîm tittamām*) with the expression μετὰ ἀνδρὸς τελείου τελειωθήσῃ.[31] The fact that God shows himself to be perfect − or more particularly shows the perfection of his ways − only to those who are 'perfect' does not mean that God's nature is subject to change and depends on man's attitude. The promises of God are only fulfilled in the lives of those who are 'wholehearted' in their relationship with God.[32] Although the God of Israel is 'nowhere qualified as the *ens perfectissimum*, as being perfect in himself', nevertheless, his 'perfection' is described 'in terms of relationship with man, and with his covenant people in particular'.[33]

Although the use of τελειοῦν in 2 Kgs 22: 26 (LXX) conveys the sense of a wholehearted relationship, the reference is unusual in applying the concept to God. In Daniel 3: 40, which finds no parallel in the MT, the words καὶ τελειῶσαι ὄπισθέν σου ('and may we wholly follow thee' RSV

Song of the Three Young Men verse 17) apply the concept to believers walking in a wholehearted relationship with God.[34] Sir. 31: 10 refers to the rich man who has been 'tested' by riches and 'been found perfect'. The moral sense predominates here, as the parallel in verse 8 shows ('who is found blameless'), though the moralism of Sirach must be understood in terms of a wisdom that comes from the Lord and that is to be an expression of one's 'fear' of the Lord (cf. 1: 1ff; Wis. 9: 6).

In this same category I would place Wis. 4: 13 (τελειωθεὶς ἐν ὀλίγῳ ἐπλήρωσεν χρόνους μακρούς), where the context is dealing with the problem of the righteous dying young (verses 7ff). Some would argue that Enoch is alluded to as a typical instance of this problem in verse 10, where μετετέθη is used (cf. Gen. 5: 24; Sir. 44: 16) and that τελειωθεὶς is used with the sense of 'attaining martyrdom'[35] or heavenly 'translation'.[36] It must be admitted that there are several expressions in the context which would favour this interpretation, especially verses 7, 10f and 16. The last verse seems to parallel 'the righteous man who has died' with 'the youth that is quickly perfected', though τελεῖν is used in the last expression, rather than τελειοῦν. However, the actual wording of verses 13f rather favours the sense of moral or spiritual perfection, in terms of the maturity of a relationship with God.[37] The words ἐπλήρωσεν χρόνους μακρούς denote 'a long life' or 'a full life' (cf. Isa. 65: 20; Sir. 26: 2), yet Wis. 4: 8f insists that old age is not measured by 'number of years' but 'understanding is gray hair for men, and a blameless life is ripe old age'. Thus, 4: 13 is stressing that early moral and spiritual maturity, which gave the person in question 'a full life', brief though it was in terms of actual years. The righteous life of a young person may thus 'condemn the prolonged old age of the unrighteous man' (verse 16).[38]

In concluding this section, it should be noted that the use of τελειοῦν in the LXX with anything like the 'religious' sense of τέλειος *is very limited.* Only 2 Sam. 22: 26 (LXX 2 Kgs 22: 26) and Sir. 31: 10 are free from textual and exegetical uncertainties in this regard and, compared with the purely formal use of the verb in at least eleven references, the two or possibly even four 'religious' applications can hardly be described as setting a significant precedent for NT usage.

(c) Cultic Usage

It was noted above, in connection with extra-Biblical literature, that τελεῖν has a technical 'cultic' application, with respect to sacred rites such as sacrifices or the consecration of priests. The LXX uses that verb only rarely in such a sense, and only when the reference is to the practice of *foreign cults.* Thus, we find in Num. 25: 3 ἐτελέσθη Ισραηλ τῷ Βεελφεγωρ (Israel 'joined in the worship of the Baal of Peor' NEB).[39] The translators, however, never employ τελειοῦν in such contexts. Its use in the technical expression τελειοῦν τὰς χεῖρας with reference to the installation of the levitical priesthood, is quite often explained as giving birth to a cultic sense of this verb.[40]

In seven verses of the Pentateuch we find some variation of the expression first encountered at Exod. 29: 9 – καὶ τελειώσεις τὰς χεῖρας Ααρων καὶ τὰς χεῖρας τῶν υἱῶν (MT *ûmillē' tā yad 'harōn weyad bānāyw*).[41] In addition, there is one context where the translators have added the expression where the MT has only *hakōhēn hamāśîaḥ* (Lev. 4: 5, ὁ ἱερεὺς ὁ χριστὸς ὁ τετελειωμένος τὰς χεῖρας). The use of τετελειωμένου alone, without τὰς χεῖρας, at Lev. 21: 10 (MT *ûmillē' et yādô*) calls for special consideration.

When the translators render the same Hebrew expression with ἐμπιπλάναι τὰς χεῖρας (Exod. 28: 41) or πληροῦν τὰς χεῖρας, with a variety of meanings to be discussed below,[42] it is clear that they were seeking to be literal. A number of commentators agree with De Vaux in suggesting that the original meaning of the Hebrew expression may have been the filling of the hand with the first payment of a salary, by which a priest was engaged.[43] There may be some connection with the Akkadian equivalent, which means 'to put a man in charge of something' (i.e., 'to give him a task to perform'), or with the use of a similar expression in the Mari texts concerning the distribution of booty, part of which was assigned, as of right, to certain types of officers.[44] In the notoriously difficult Exod. 32: 29, a literal filling of the hand with swords is probably the primary meaning of the imperative in the MT, parallel in sense to the command of verse 27, with an oblique reference to the ceremony for the installation of priests: 'fill your hands today on behalf of Yahweh with your swords, and hereafter your hands shall be filled by another with (the blessing of) the priesthood'.[45] The LXX, Vulgate and Targum[0] read the indicative and apparently interpret the phrase to mean that the Levites had already effectively 'ordained' themselves by taking sword in hand to slay their idolatrous brethren.[46]

At 1 Chr. 29: 5 and 2 Chr. 29: 31 the RSV assumes that the expression has been used in a generalised sense to refer to the people of Israel 'consecrating' themselves to the Lord. However, it is better to see here a reference to their hands being filled with offerings and thus to render in terms of 'offering sacrifices'.[47] In Ezek. 43: 26 the Hebrew expression seems to have been adapted to mean 'consecrate', where the object in question is the altar, and the LXX has copied fairly closely.[48] Furthermore, in Num. 7:

88 the LXX has added πληρῶσαι τὰς χεῖρας αὐτοῦ,[49] as a virtual equivalent of ἁγιάσαι (cf. 7: 1 ἔχρισεν αὐτὴν καὶ ἡγίασεν αὐτήν). Nevertheless, even in these exceptional cases, it must be observed that it is the expression as a whole – both in Hebrew and Greek – that has come to mean 'consecrate', and it is not legitimate to assume that the verbs in either language attained a cultic significance *apart from this syntactical unit.*

It is clear from the narratives of Exod. 29 and Lev. 8 that a literal 'filling of the hands' was involved in the concept of 'installing' Aaron and his sons to the priesthood. Although some scholars argue that these traditions are post-Exilic attempts to 'give an explanation of a phrase whose original meaning had been forgotten',[50] it is reasonable to suppose that the LXX translators of these passages understood the expression in terms of the traditions they had before them. Exod. 29 is concerned with the rite to be observed in *consecrating* Aaron and his sons to be priests (verse 1). This includes washing, robing and anointing; but even the sacrifice of a bull as the sin-offering (verses 10–14) and a ram as the whole-offering (verses 15–18) only 'prepares for the act of ordination proper'.[51] This begins when the blood of the second ram, described as *êl millu'îm* (verse 22), is applied to parts of the body that are 'important in the performance of priestly actions',[52] as well as to the altar and the ceremonial dress. The climax of the whole action is described in verses 22–4, when parts of the 'ram of installation',[53] together with the offerings, are placed in the hands of Aaron and his sons and these things are 'waved' before the Lord for a 'wave-offering'. De Vaux appropriately describes the significance of this 'filling of the hands' as follows: 'by so performing for the first time the ritual gesture of a minister of the altar, the man was invested with priestly power'.[54]

It is my contention that the translators of the LXX had in view this literal 'filling of the hands' with sacrifices when they rendered the Hebrew expression τελειοῦν τὰς χεῖρας in the Pentateuch. By using τελειοῦν and τελείωσις in such contexts, instead of the more literal alternatives, they imparted a *particular nuance.* They wished to convey the sense that the high point of the consecration ceremony was the action to 'perfect' or 'qualify' the hands for priestly service and thus to 'perfect' or 'qualify' the man himself to act as a priest in offering sacrifices to God. Both τελειοῦν and τελείωσις are used here in a purely formal way.[55] In this respect I endorse the arguments of Riggenbach,[56] though τὰς χεῖρας will only be an 'accusative of relation' where the verb explicitly has a personal object as well.[57]

When Dibelius argues that the verb in this context is 'only explicable as a technical linguistic usage, which is familiar to the LXX translator and his readers, according to which τελειοῦν means "to consecrate" ',[58] he is making an unnecessary and unwarranted conclusion. There is no evidence for the employment of the verb in such a sense in extra-Biblical literature of the time, and the passages themselves point rather to the usual and formal sense of the verb. If there is a certain parallelism with ἁγιάζειν in these narratives (e.g., Exod. 29: 33 LXX), we are not at liberty to conclude from this that τελειοῦν *per se* acquires the meaning 'to consecrate' from the context. No one would suggest this about the verb ἐμπιπλάναι, which is used in a similar sentence construction in Exod. 28: 41 (LXX). Rather, the 'filling of the hands' is represented as the high point of the consecration ceremonies and, as such, it is most appropriately considered by the translators as the τελείωσις of the priests. If the 'perfecting of the hands' implies the qualification of the person concerned for priestly service, and thus the completion of his consecration, it is illegitimate to conclude that τελειοῦν is thus simply to be understood as an equivalent of ἁγιάζειν.

G. Delling pursues the cultic interpretation of τελειοῦν by suggesting that τελειοῦν τὰς χεῖρας means 'that someone's hands are made free from stain, or that he is made free from stain'.[59] There is no denying that the consecration of the priests involved a ritual cleansing from sin (Exod. 29: 19–21), but this is clearly a preparation for the 'filling of the hands' with sacrifices, which is the climax of the whole action and is described in the following verses (verses 22–5). In particular, I would take issue with Delling's conclusion that the abbreviated τετελειωμένου (without τὰς χεῖρας) of Lev. 21: 10 refers 'naturally to the cultic cleanness of the whole person'. This interpretation is used to support the later contention that τελειοῦν τινά in Hebrews means 'to put someone in the position in which he can come, or stand before God'.[60] The ceremony to which this verb in Lev. 21: 10 alludes is not that of ritual cleansing but the subsequent filling of the hands with offerings. The abbreviated rendering of the LXX is a short-hand way of referring to the latter, in much the same way as τελείωσις (for *millu 'îm*) is, in these chapters. M. Silva takes Lev. 21: 10 as proof that 'the technical sense of the idiom did transfer to the "head word" '.[61] However, even if this is so, such an obscure and singular example can scarcely indicate the development of a significant new linguistic usage. It is too far-fetched to suppose that Lev. 21:10 alone influenced the writer of Hebrews or that his readers would have made the necessary connection.

The assumption that τελειοῦν in the LXX has acquired such a cultic significance (apart from the words τὰς χεῖρας) that the writer to the Hebrews could expect his readers to understand immediately that he was using the word thus, seems to be quite invalid. Two comments from James

Barr are appropriate here. He argues that a great deal of difficulty arises in etymological research from a neglect of 'syntactical relations, and of groupings of words, factors just as important for the bearing of significance as the more purely lexicographical aspect of the single word'.[62] He also criticises those who allow 'etymological connections which appear to be theologically attractive ... to take charge of the whole interpretation and no real attention is given to the things being said and the *particular semantic contribution* of words used'.[63]

I have argued that τελειοῦν, used in the combination τελειοῦν τὰς χεῖρας in the Pentateuch, retains its formal sense 'to accomplish, make full, perfect' and, although not as literal a rendering of the Hebrew as ἐμπιπλάναι/πληροῦν τὰς χεῖρας, it is nevertheless to be understood in context as taking full account of the literal meaning of the Hebrew expression, as indicated by the narratives of Exod. 29 and Lev. 8. The formula as a whole has a technical, cultic meaning but not the verb *per se.* If the verb in Hebrews is to be given any cultic sense, it cannot be argued from this source.

The usage of Philo

The word group is clearly important and widespread in the writings of Philo. Apart from more than 400 uses of the adjective τέλειος, the verb τελειοῦν is found 53 times.[64] The formal sense of the latter is found in passages such as Philo's description of the creation being 'brought to completion',[65] or his statement that a thought is not perfected until it results in some action.[66] The verb is also used, as in classical Greek sources, with reference to the maturation of plants,[67] and to the physical maturation of human beings.[68] A further use, which is of general interest, concerns the fulfilment of Scripture: God will 'utter nothing at all which shall not certainly be performed (ὃ μὴ τελειωθήσεται βεβαίως), for his word is his deed'.[69] Similarly, we read of the Word of God as the source through whom 'both good and evil come to fulfilment' (συμβέβηκε τελειοῦσθαι).[70]

Philo's reference to Aaron's death as his perfection (*Leg. All.* III.45) is interesting in the light of our discussion of 4 Macc. 7: 15 and Wis. 4: 13 and provides us with an introduction to the complicated patterns of perfection in Philo's works. Commenting on Num. 20: 25, he asserts that 'when Aaron dies, that is, when he is made perfect (ὅταν τελειωθῇ), he goes up into Hor, which is "Light" '. In this context, perfection is not simply a synonym for death in the ordinary sense of the word. Aaron and Hor, who held up Moses' hands, are taken as being symbols respectively of the Logos and Light (= Truth). Philo allegorises the death of Aaron to assert that the τέλος of the Logos is Truth, and 'into it the Logos is eager to enter since it represents the *perfection of the Logos*'.[71]

Philo is concerned that the mind or the soul be perfected by escaping from the passions of the body and attaining the vision of God:

> 'When the soul in all utterances and all actions has attained to perfect sincerity and godlikeness, the voices of the senses cease and all those abominable sounds that used to vex it ... all these cease when the mind goes forth from the city of the soul and finds in God the spring and aim of its own doings and intents.'[72]

It is when the soul becomes 'no lover of the body, but a lover of God' that it can be described as 'perfected'.[73] However, L.K.K. Dey argues that there are *two* levels of religious status/perfection/existence in Philo's thought. Those who can be called 'sons of God' are those who 'live by the knowledge of the one God'. Those who are not worthy or adequate of such status can aim at being 'sons of the first-born Logos'. The Logos represents the whole intermediary world and has many names.[74] Perfection involves 'rising above the intermediary world of Logos, Sophia, Angel and Anthropos to the presence of God himself – unmediated access'.[75] In this pattern of thought, 'sight is primary, hearing is secondary; God gives the primary benefits, the intermediary world is the source of [the] secondary' and the τέλειοι belong to the class of the 'self-taught and self-instructed'. The patriarchs, Aaron, levitical priesthood and Melchizedek become 'exemplars of perfection' for Philo, representing different dispositions of the soul, characters, types and virtues.

Dey illustrates how the basis of the distinction among the exemplars of perfection is *paideutic* – 'between those who are progressing to perfection through teaching and practice and those who are perfect by nature from the beginning and need neither teaching nor practice'.[76] Thus, Abraham represents the type of character that progresses and is perfected by teaching and education. When he is brought to perfection, he is capable of begetting Isaac from Sarah, who is perfect virtue and wisdom (*Leg. All.* III.244–5). Isaac represents the highest form of 'paideutic perfection', namely self-learnt and self-taught virtue: he is perfect and good by nature from the beginning and able to dispense with the instruction of men (*Fug.* 168). Jacob is the type who is 'perfected as the result of discipline' (*Agric.* 42): when he exchanges hearing for sight and progress for perfection his name is changed to Israel, the one who sees God (*Ebr.* 82). Moses' perfection is self-learnt and self-taught like Isaac's, and his relationship to God is one of immediacy. Yet at times, Philo places the perfection of Moses above that of Isaac (*Sacr.* 5–8; *Praem.* 49–53). Philo's view of Moses is summarised by Goodenough in these terms:

> 'The career of Moses is not so much the career of one who, like
> Abraham and Jacob, had the experience of development which we
> may reproduce, but was the career of the saviour of men who, given
> to them as a special loan from God, can *lead them out of the world
> to the apprehension of God.* For the mystical experience of men
> consists in "going up to the aethereal heights with their reasonings,
> setting before them Moses, the type of existence beloved by God,
> to lead them on their way" (*Conf. Ling.* 95).'[77]

On Sinai, Moses went closer than any other man to 'a vision of God in his
essence',[78] and 'there he abides while he is made perfect in the most sacred
mysteries. And he not only becomes an initiate but also the hierophant of
the rites and teacher of divine things, which he will reveal to those whose
ears have been purified.'[79]

When Dey concludes that 'it is the ideals of Greek *paideia* which give
coherence to Philo's thought rather than, as Goodenough proposed,
"mystery"',[80] he perpetuates the dichotomy in thinking about the
evidence, which is common amongst scholars of Philo. Dey gives due
emphasis to the influence of Greek *paideia* but inadequate attention to that
of the Mystery religions. Allowing for the moral and paideutic elements in
Philo's concept of perfection, it is important to emphasise the mystical
elements, which are also there, particularly in the idea of the 'vision of
God' and of the spirit being released from the flesh in order to return to its
spiritual source in God.[81] At all events, we find in the writings of Philo an
extensive use of the terminology of perfection with a unique combination
of associations, as an essential part of his unique philosophy.

In assessing the evidence of Hebrews, I shall argue from several contexts
that the perfecting of believers is to be understood in terms of 'drawing
near to God'. There is also a sense in which Hebrews presents the tradition
of Jesus' suffering and temptation as the *paideia* that leads to progress or
betterment and in the end to perfection (5: 7–10), as Dey argues.[82] The
extent to which the writer may have been influenced by Philonic patterns
of thought in this regard will be discussed in more detail where appropriate.
However, here it must be acknowledged that the question of such influence
involves the assessment of issues far beyond the scope of the present study.
Dey's apparent neglect of the important work of R. Williamson is certainly
a serious demerit,[83] and his attempt to relate the *Sitz im Leben* of the
readers to a specifically Philonic frame of religious thought therefore remains superficial. Furthermore, whenever Dey acknowledges significant
differences between Hebrews and Philo, these are always signs for him of

the *reinterpretation* of Philonic views by the former, a position which is essentially unassailable by the critic!

The New Testament

(a) Luke—Acts

The verb $\tau\epsilon\lambda\epsilon\iota o\tilde{\upsilon}\nu$ is found in Lk. 2: 43; 13: 32 and Acts 20: 24 but it is also significant for our purpose to examine the use of $\tau\epsilon\lambda\epsilon\tilde{\iota}\nu$ (Lk. 2: 39; 12: 50; 18: 31; 22: 37; Acts 13: 29) and $\sigma\upsilon\nu\tau\epsilon\lambda\epsilon\tilde{\iota}\nu$ (Lk. 4: 2; 4: 13; Acts 21: 27).[84] The overlap in meaning between $\tau\epsilon\lambda\epsilon\iota o\tilde{\upsilon}\nu$ and $\tau\epsilon\lambda\epsilon\tilde{\iota}\nu$ is well illustrated by comparing Lk. 2: 39 and 2: 43. In the former we read that the parents of Jesus 'carried out' ($\dot{\epsilon}\tau\dot{\epsilon}\lambda\epsilon\sigma\alpha\nu$) conscientiously all the purification rites of the Law, and in the latter we read of their intention to leave Jerusalem 'when the feast was ended' ($\tau\epsilon\lambda\epsilon\iota\omega\sigma\dot{\alpha}\nu\tau\omega\nu$ $\tau\dot{\alpha}\varsigma$ $\dot{\eta}\mu\dot{\epsilon}\rho\alpha\varsigma$). Perhaps $\tau\epsilon\lambda\epsilon\iota o\tilde{\upsilon}\nu$ here stresses that the appointed worship was carried through to its proper conclusion (cf. Sir. 50: 19) but $\tau\epsilon\lambda\epsilon\tilde{\iota}\nu$ in 2: 39 also stresses the proper fulfilment of what the Law required, and 'a distinction is scarcely to be discerned'.[85] The three uses of $\sigma\upsilon\nu\tau\epsilon\lambda\epsilon\tilde{\iota}\nu$ also seem to stress the fulfilment of some important work or period of time: the period of Jesus' fasting (Lk. 4: 2), 'every temptation' that the Devil wishes to place before Jesus in the desert (Lk. 4: 13 — though Satan does not accomplish his goal of leading Jesus astray), and the seven days of Paul's purificatory rite in Jerusalem (Acts 21: 27).[86]

The verb $\tau\epsilon\lambda\epsilon\tilde{\iota}\nu$ is associated in four references with the idea of 'Jesus Christ as the Consummator in redemptive history'.[87] His mission is characterised by a *fulfilment of Scripture* in Lk. 18: 31 ('everything that is written of the Son of Man by the prophets will be accomplished'), Lk. 22: 37 ('this scripture must be fulfilled in me') and Acts 13: 29 ('when they had fulfilled all that was written of him'). Lk. 12: 50 describes the climactic event in Jesus' career, to which there is also reference in the above verses, as a 'baptism with which to be baptised', and Jesus is 'constrained' or 'distressed' until it is accomplished ($\dot{\epsilon}\omega\varsigma$ $\dot{\delta}\tau o\upsilon$ $\tau\epsilon\lambda\epsilon\sigma\theta\tilde{\eta}$). Jesus is presented as the one who willingly accepts this divinely decreed suffering and so brings history to its redemptive $\tau\dot{\epsilon}\lambda o\varsigma$.

The only place in the NT, apart from Hebrews, where the verb $\tau\epsilon\lambda\epsilon\iota o\tilde{\upsilon}\nu$ is specifically used in connection with the *person* of Christ is Lk. 13: 32. In view of the overlap with $\tau\epsilon\lambda\epsilon\tilde{\iota}\nu$ in Luke's usage and the important application of the latter in connection with Christ's redemptive work, it is not surprising that Lk. 13: 32 links the perfecting of Christ with the perfecting of his work. In response to the warning of certain Pharisees that

Herod is aiming to kill him, Jesus replies: Ἰδού ἐκβάλλω δαιμόνια καί ἰάσεις ἀποτελῶ σήμερον καί αὔριον, καί τῇ τρίτῃ τελειοῦμαι. If τελειοῦμαι is a middle, we may translate 'I finish my course' (RSV). This gives virtually the same sense as the saying attributed to Paul in Acts 20: 24, translated by the RSV 'if only I may accomplish my course' (ὡς τελειώσω τὸν δρόμον μοῦ). If τελειοῦμαι is taken as a passive, we may translate 'I am perfected' (RV) or 'I reach my goal' (NEB), and the emphasis will be on his messianic work being 'brought to a conclusion by God',[88] and thus on the perfecting of Jesus as Messiah. This suits the context best because there is an implied contrast between Herod's attempt to end Jesus' ministry and the *divinely appointed end* in Jerusalem (verse 33).

As indicated above, the author of Luke–Acts views the suffering and death of Jesus as the climax of God's will for his life and ministry: it is the fulfilment of Scripture and of God's redemptive plan.[89] It is not satisfactory to exclude Jesus' death from the concept of his perfecting and assume 'the casting out of demons and the healing as object understood' of τελειοῦμαι.[90] Although the πλήν at the beginning of verse 33 (which refers to Jesus' death) suggests a contrast between verses 32 and 33, there is a repetition in these verses that 'may well be deliberate and resumptive'.[91] The parallel phrases 'today and tomorrow and the third day' (verse 32) and 'today and tomorrow and the day following' (verse 33) probably mean 'a short, divinely appointed time, as in Hosea 6: 2',[92] and stress that God, not Herod, has determined how the short, remaining space of Christ's life shall be spent.[93] The verb τελειοῦμαι (verse 32) alludes to his death, as does ἀπολέσθαι (verse 33). The strong adversative πλήν is used to stress that, even though his time may be short and his end near, nevertheless he must continue on his way and perish, not in Herod's territory but in the place that is fitting for a prophet: in the Jerusalem whose rebellious history is then lamented.

Since Jesus' death is viewed as a pathway to resurrection and vindication (Lk. 9: 22; 18: 31–3), and Luke's total presentation of the suffering of Jesus gives to that event a redemptive and victorious significance,[94] we may conclude that 'death as crowned by victory' is implied in the perfecting of Jesus (13: 32).[95] However, E. Earle Ellis over-theologises when he asserts that 'the goal is his consecration and enthronement into the messianic office',[96] basing his interpretation on the supposed cultic meaning of τελειοῦν. The verb is used here, in fact, in a *formal sense*, identifying the perfecting of Jesus with the perfecting of his messianic work. It is not simply used, as in Patristic literature, to attest the perfection of a martyr's death but, within Luke's total presentation, Jesus' τέλος is a 'death as crowned by victory', which has a redemptive significance.[97]

(b) Johannine writings

The Fourth Gospel uses τελειοῦν in a number of important contexts (4: 34; 5: 36; 17: 4, 23; 19: 28) and, to a lesser extent, τελεῖν (19: 28, 30). In 4: 34 Jesus declares that his 'meat' is to do the will of the one who sent him and 'to accomplish' his work (τελειώσω αὐτοῦ τὸ ἔργον). The 'works' that Jesus does are the works that the Father has given him to accomplish (5: 36) and these show 'that he is manifestly sent from God, with a delegated divine authority'.[98] In his prayer to the Father in 17: 4, Jesus asserts that he has glorified God on earth in the accomplishment of the work given to him.

In each of these references, it is clear that 'the ministry of Jesus has no significance apart from the will of the Father; it is not the independent achievement of humanity but the fruit of submission'.[99] I would consequently endorse Bultmann's view that τελειοῦν is being used here with more than a sense of 'bringing something to a finish which has already been begun': it means 'the execution or completion of something *one has been commissioned to do*'.[100] However, the 'work' that the Father has given Jesus to complete is not entirely synonymous with the 'works' that Jesus has accomplished up to this point in the narrative: 'completion comes only in the whole complex of "the hour" stretching from 13 to 20',[101] and includes the crucifixion. It is not until we arrive at 19: 28–30 that we can see how 'that which in the prayer had been uttered *sub specie* of the completion of the work has now become historical reality'.[102]

The section in which this terminology is finally employed in relation to the completion of the Father's great work begins with the assertion that Jesus knew that 'all was now finished' (19: 28 ἤδη πάντα τετέλεσται). As he hangs on the cross, awaiting death, he cries out that he is thirsty 'so that the Scripture might be fulfilled' (ἵνα τελειωθῇ ἡ γραφή). This is the only place in the NT where τελειοῦν is used with reference to the fulfilment of Scripture, though we have observed the use of τελεῖν in such a fashion in Luke–Acts. Almost certainly, what we have here is simply a stylistic variation, virtually equivalent to πληροῦν,[103] and the verb is not to be given any special sense such as 'the conclusive fulfilment of the entire content of the Scriptures': 'the fulfilment of a particular passage of Scripture is meant'.[104]

The τετέλεσται of 19: 28, 30 recalls 4: 34; 5: 36; 17: 4 and the expression εἰς τέλος (13: 1), which means 'up to the end', as well as 'completely'. The verb in this context, therefore, 'does not simply mean "It is at an end", still less "It is endured", but rather "It is brought to an end", namely the work that has been commissioned'.[105] The overlap between τελεῖν and τελειοῦν in the Fourth Gospel is clear: 'the dominant τέλος conception behind these announcements agrees with the overall New Testament impress: Christ not only carries redemptive history to its τέλος, he is its τέλος'.[106] Bultmann introduces an inconsistency into the picture that is totally unnecessary when he agrees with Dodd's suggestion that τετέλεσται is probably derived from the Gnostic tradition in which the word 'could be thought of as a concluding formula of a mystery'.[107] Dodd suggests that 'as the liturgical term ἁγιάζειν is used of Christ's self-oblation in 17: 19, so here his death is declared to be the completion of the sacrifice, regarded as the means of man's regeneration, or initiation into eternal life'.[108] However, as Brown rightly suggests, 'the sacrificial connotation of τελεῖν is a fragile base to serve as a sole support for this interesting hypothesis'.[109]

The possibility of some influence from the Mystery religions on the clause in 17: 23 (ἵνα ὦσιν τετελειωμένοι εἰς ἕν) is also discussed by Bultmann. He argues that τελειοῦν is not used here in a purely formal sense, as it is found in 4: 34; 5: 36 and 17: 4, but has 'an eschatological sense like πληροῦν in verse 13'.[110] In the Mandaean writings, we are told, ' "perfection" frequently occurs as an eschatological predicate' and believers are called 'the perfected'. However, the particular semantic contribution of τετελειωμένοι in 17: 23 is the idea of 'completeness' and it is best to translate the clause: 'that they may attain perfect unity'.[111] Of course, 'final completeness and unity can ... be achieved only when the number of the elect is accomplished at the time of the end', but the following clause indicates that it has a present realisation (NEB 'then the world will learn that thou didst send me, that thou didst love them as thou didst me'). The previous clause indicates that it is a spiritual unity created by the presence of Christ in believers ('I in them and you in me'), a community of love that reflects the perfect unity of Father and Son.

A similar use of τελειοῦν is found in 1 John, where on four occasions the perfecting of love is in view. In 2: 5 we are told that 'whoever keeps his word, in him truly love for God is perfected' (ἡ ἀγάπη τοῦ θεοῦ τετελείωται). The RSV has assumed, with several commentators, that the genitive here is to be read as objective.[112] The NEB, however, reads a subjective genitive — 'in the man who is obedient to his word, the *divine love* has indeed come to its perfection'. Although the phrase remains somewhat ambiguous throughout 1 John, I would agree with Westcott that the fundamental idea is: ' "the love which God has made known, and which answers to his nature". This love communicated to man is effective in him towards the brethren and towards God himself. But however it may be manifested the essential conception that it is a *love divine in its origin and character is not lost.*'[113] Bultmann, who also argues for a subjective genitive here, nevertheless asserts that 'brotherly love is understood to be given as part of "God's love" and is included in "is perfected"'.[114] At all events, for our purposes the significance of τετελείωται is clear: it is used to convey the idea of completion or fulfilment of love in keeping his word.

In 4: 12 there seems little doubt from the context that ἡ ἀγάπη αὐτοῦ means 'God's love' since the demand for brotherly love 'is expressly grounded by the reference to the love with which God loved us (verses 9, 10a, 11, 19–21)'.[115] Thus, the expression ἡ ἀγάπη αὐτοῦ τετελειωμένη ἐν ἡμῖν ἐστιν means that 'the love of God conferred upon us reaches its goal' when we love one another. It is 'through man that "the love of God" finds its fulfilment on earth'.[116]

The final passage in 1 John in which this verb is used contains a number of exegetical difficulties, which cannot be adequately discussed here. It will be sufficient to note that in 4: 17 τετελείωται ἡ ἀγάπη μεθ' ἡμῶν means again that 'love has reached its goal, corresponding to the τετελειωμένη ... ἐστιν ("is perfected") of 4: 12'.[117] However, the real focus of this verse and the next is not on love but on παρρησία. God's love 'has fulfilled its aim in granting us "confidence"', writes Bultmann, but his attempted reconstruction of the verse removes the key phrase 'in the day of judgement'. The following verse makes it clear that 'confidence' involves 'freedom from fear', for 'fear has to do with punishment' (RSV), or 'fear brings with it the pains of judgement' (NEB). The 'perfect love' of verse 18 is equivalent to the love 'perfected with us' of verse 17. So, 'whoever still fears before God has still not *reached the goal opened up to him* by the gift of God's love: for him God's love has not yet become ἐν ἀληθείᾳ ("reality") (cf. 2 Jn. 3; 3 Jn. 1)'.[118] Thus, verse 18 concludes that 'he who fears is not perfected in love'.

I therefore conclude that the formal use of τελειοῦν is found with every application of the verb in the Johannine literature. With regard to the work of Christ, the context gives it the particular sense of 'the execution or completion of something one has been commissioned to do'. In 1 John it has the particular meaning 'to reach a goal' or 'to fulfil an aim'.

(c) Paul

It is remarkable that Paul employs τελειοῦν only once, although he quite often uses τελεῖν and its compounds.[119] Most commentators suggest that τελειοῦν is used in a special sense in Phil. 3: 12, in answer to the particular error he is attacking there and in all probability he is employing both τελειοῦν and τέλειος (verse 15) because the terminology was used by his opponents. The identification of those opponents and their point of view is clearly vital for a satisfactory interpretation of the passage. However, there is a great diversity of opinion on this issue and certainty is impossible.

Some have argued that the opponents were Jews who boasted of their perfection as those who were circumcised and keepers of the Law in its entirety.[120] However, such a position fails to deal adequately with the eschatological element in the debate and the argument of verses 17–21, which seems to have a form of antinomianism in view. There is more to be said for Lightfoot's view that Judaisers were under attack in verses 2–11 and 'the antinomian spirit, which in its rebound from Jewish formalism perverted liberty into licence' in verses 12ff.[121] This makes Paul's emphasis in the latter section 'the duty of moral and spiritual progress, as enforced by his own example'.[122] More recently, F.W. Beare has argued similarly that the opponents under attack in verses 2–11 were 'Christians of the Judaizing faction of the early Palestinian church',[123] and that Paul was turning against the dangers of antinomianism in the latter part of the chapter. However, Beare comes up with the remarkable conclusion, for which there is no linguistic support, that τετελείωμαι (verse 12) belongs to the terminology of the Mysteries: 'there is no thought of *moral* perfection here; it is more the notion of transition to a higher order of being effected through the operation of sacramental rites'.[124]

Strong criticism of Beare's approach is voiced by H. Koester, who argues that a single group of opponents is in view throughout the chapter. These are, like those of 2 Corinthians, 'Jewish-Christian apostles who boasted of their special spiritual qualities: however, in contrast to those of 2 Corinthians, their claim of the possession of the Spirit was essentially demonstrated by their complete fulfilment of the Law, including circumcision as the unique sign of such fulfilment.'[125] Koester criticises Beare's view of a non-moral perfection as being 'totally out of context', while similarly dismissing the view of W. Schmithals that the opponents were 'gnostische Pneumatiker' of Jewish descent, who showed an unbridled libertinism and had an immoral view of perfection.[126] The context of 3: 12 not only focusses on the problem of a Law-based righteousness but also on the eschatological implications of being in Christ (verses 10–11, 14, 20–1). This leads Koester to conclude that Paul is arguing here against a group 'which thinks of the resurrection as already achieved':[127] their perfectionism not only involves the assumption that they have achieved righteousness by complete fulfilment of the Law but also that they now possess 'the eschatological promises in full, that is, the Spirit and the spiritual experiences of such heavenly gifts as resurrection and freedom from suffering and death'.[128]

Koester's argument for a gnostic spiritualising of the resurrection hope certainly fits the context well but his exegesis of verses 18ff is unnatural. It is much more likely, as Schmithals suggests, that a denial of the theology of the cross on the supposed ground of being already raised to new life led to *libertinism*. Yet Schmithals deals inadequately with the exegesis of verses 2ff, in which Paul manifestly is concerned with opposing a concern for legal righteousness. In brief, it appears that the most satisfactory approach is to view Paul's opponents here as falling into two groups: the Judaisers who attacked the church from without and libertinist heretics who emerged from within. There is much to commend R. Jewett's suggestion that the common concern of these two groups was the promise of perfection, which each in its own way held out to the Philippians.[129]

Paul's answer is to stress what he 'has' and what he does not yet 'have' in his relationship with Christ. On the one hand, he possesses since his conversion a 'knowledge' of Christ (verse 8), a 'righteousness from God that depends on faith' (verse 9) and some realisation of 'the power of his resurrection' (verse 10). On the other hand, he emphasises that he must still await the consummation of all this at 'the resurrection from the dead' (verse 11). If $\tau o \hat{v} \tau o$ is read as the object understood of $\check{\epsilon}\lambda\alpha\beta o\nu$ (verse 12), the reference will be to the fulfilment of the relationship with Christ which the resurrection will bring (cf. verses 20–1).[130] The $\check{\eta}\delta\eta$ virtually transforms the aorist of $\check{\epsilon}\lambda\alpha\beta o\nu$ into a perfect tense, making the $\tau\epsilon\tau\epsilon\lambda\dot{\epsilon}\iota\omega\mu\alpha\iota$ a repetition of the same idea.[131] His opponents claim to have arrived at a state of perfection but Paul asserts that he has not yet reached that goal. Instead, 'he seeks to lay hold upon the hope set before him with ever firmer grip because ... Christ has laid his hand on him'.[132]

That $\tau\epsilon\lambda\epsilon\iota o\hat{v}\nu$ refers to eschatological consummation here is confirmed by the following verses. Paul does not rest secure in his present experience, considering that he has already laid hold of all that Christ offers, but constantly sets his sight on 'what lies ahead' (verse 13). Like an athlete in a race he presses on towards the goal, which in this case is the 'prize of the upward call of God in Christ Jesus' (verse 14). He has already indicated in verse 10 that this involves a willingness to share in Christ's sufferings, 'becoming like him in his death'. In view of the attack on self-indulgence and lawlessness in verses 17–19, it is certain that 'pressing on toward the goal' (verse 14) and 'holding true to what we have attained' (verse 16) involves a *moral* responsibility to Christ. Yet Pfitzner rightly stresses that perfection here is not essentially a moral concept or something that depends on human effort: 'perfection lies in the hands of God, who will bring to completion that which he has begun in calling me "in Christ Jesus" '.[133]

If Paul is keeping to the language of those who think that they have attained perfection already in verse 15 (ὅσοι οὖν τέλειοι), he will be using their term ironically: 'in Christian vocabulary, *perfect* can only mean "conscious that we are not perfect" and bent upon attaining a goal that has not yet been reached'.[134] It seems unlikely in such a context that τέλειοι simply means 'mature', as in 1 Cor. 2: 6; 14: 20 and Eph. 4: 13, though the paradox is still obvious with such a rendering. Paul holds himself up as an example to be followed (verse 17) in this matter of holding 'true to what we have attained' (verse 16), while at the same time 'straining forward to what lies ahead' (verse 13).

As a final illustration of the overlap in meaning of τελειοῦν and τελεῖν (and compounds) in the NT I will make some observations about Paul's use of the latter. The τὸν δρόμον τετέλεκα of 2 Tim. 4: 7 recalls a similar use of τελειοῦν in Acts 20: 24 and in its context means that 'he had already fully realized the expectancies of his apostolic office'.[135] Ἡ γὰρ δύναμις ἐν ἀσθενείᾳ τελεῖται in 2 Cor. 12: 9 is probably the original reading but τελειοῦται is an important variant.[136] Most commentators suggest that this means God's power becomes 'more conspicuous',[137] or 'more evident',[138] when the weakness of his servants is manifestly greater. I would therefore render the expression 'my power is fully expressed in weakness',[139] or 'where there is weakness, my power is shown the more completely' (J.B. Phillips). The ἐπιτελοῦντες ἁγιωσύνην ἐν φόβῳ θεοῦ of 2 Cor. 7: 1 suggests a similar use of the verb in its compound form, meaning to 'realise' or 'fully express' one's consecration to God. The preceding section (6: 14—18) asserts that sanctity is already the state of those who belong to Christ and 7: 1 is emphasising the need to '*put into operation* what they already have',[140] rather than the simple moralism of the RSV ('make holiness perfect in the fear of God').

With regard to the compounds of τελεῖν, J.H. Moulton concludes that, from post-Homeric times onwards, these have 'completely lost consciousness of the meaning originally borne by the prepositional element'.[141] The simplex outnumbers the compound use in the NT, but where the latter occurs, the prepositions have a 'perfective' effect on the verb's *Aktionsart*. However, from my survey of the Pauline usage, I would have to agree with the conclusion of Du Plessis that there is 'an ambivalent usage with little distinction' created by the use of the prepositions in compounds.[142] In Rom. 15: 28; 2 Cor. 8: 6; 8: 11 (twice); Gal. 3: 3; Phil. 1: 6, ἐπιτελεῖν is used with the sense of 'completing' a task already begun, though in some cases the meaning may be 'decisive' or 'effective completion'. In Rom. 9:

28, quoting Isa. 10: 23 LXX (λόγον γὰρ συντελῶν καὶ συντέμνων), decisive accomplishment or fulfilment of God's plan is stressed,[143] whereas 'fulfil' or 'carry out' is all that the simplex conveys in Rom. 2: 27 and Gal. 5: 16.

(d) James

The importance of τέλειος in this letter is shown by Du Plessis, who concludes that James' use of this word can be 'traced to the OT conception of *tamim* ... yet James applies it in his own distinct way, which is related to the basic theme of his letter, that of the profound unity of faith and works'.[144] The mutual relationship of faith and works is also expressed by the single use of the verb in 2: 22 (ἡ πίστις συνήργει τοῖς ἔργοις αὐτοῦ καὶ ἐκ τῶν ἔργων ἡ πίστις ἐτελειώθη). Abraham's faith was 'completed by works' (RSV) or 'fully proved' (NEB) in the sense that it was made fully effective according to the properties expected of true faith. This application of τελειοῦν is similar to that of 1 John inasmuch as both speak of an attitude or stance ('faith' or 'love') coming to full or ideal expression in some specified behaviour.

    In conclusion, I would note how frequently the NT uses τελειοῦν in a purely formal sense, with no particular moral or religious connotations. Lk. 13: 32 is an important exception, where the context relates the perfecting of Jesus to the perfecting of his messianic task and role. The verb is also used in a special sense in Phil. 3: 12 to refer to the consummation of the believer's relationship with Christ at the resurrection.

Early Christian literature

In this vast field, examples will only be given that offer significantly different applications from, or extensions of, usages noted above. The use of the verb noted previously with the sense of 'make perfect, complete or accomplish', and applied to things, acts, works or time, is widespread.[145] It is also used with the sense of 'fulfil, perform'.[146] However, the usage that is most significant in relation to our study of Hebrews is that related to the perfecting of Christ or the perfecting of Christians.

    The prayer that Christ might perfect his church in Didache X.5 (τελειῶσαι αὐτὴν ἐν τῇ ἀγάπῃ σοῦ) has both a moral and an eschatological sense implied by the context: 'save us from all evil' is the preceding petition, and 'make it holy and gather it together from the four winds into your kingdom' is what follows. The moral sense predominates in XVI.2, where continued faithfulness to Christ, expressed in obedience to his commands, is enjoined: 'for the whole time of your faith shall not profit you except ye be found perfect at the last time' (ἐὰν μὴ ἐν τῷ ἐσχάτῳ καιρῷ τελειωθῆτε).[147]

When 1 Clement declares 'in love were all the elect of God made perfect' (49: 5 ἐτελειώθησαν), it appears at first glance as though this perfection is viewed as a once-for-all achievement of Christ by his death. The following verse indeed speaks of the love of Christ in giving his blood for us, 'his flesh for our flesh, and his life for ours'. However, the immediate context shows that the writer's concern is to promote love and harmony amongst his readers. The sacrifice of Christ shows 'how great and amazing love is, and its perfection is beyond description' (50: 1). They are exhorted to pray for such 'love without human bias' and for God to make them irreproachable, since he alone is the source of such love (50: 2–3). Something of a parallel to 49: 5 is then provided in 50: 3, suggesting that 'all God's elect' in the former reference was a description of the godly in pre-Christian times: 'All the generations from Adam to our day have passed away, but those who, by the grace of God, have been made perfect in love have a place among the saints who will appear when Christ's Kingdom comes.'[148] It thus appears that, for this writer, perfection is a process of moral development, motivated by love: it involves keeping God's commandments 'in the harmony of love' (50: 12). Even though it is 'by the grace of God' that men are 'made perfect in love', this teaching differs from that of the NT by suggesting the need to win God's approval through love and so secure a place amongst the saints. The development of the idea of imitating Christ through rigorous asceticism and so fulfilling perfectly the 'law of Christ', is the next stage in the movement away from NT teaching. Such moral perfectionism is taught by the Encratics, the Montanists, the Novatians and Pelagius.[149]

The terminology of perfection is particularly important in the writings of the so-called Christian Platonists of Alexandria, Clement and Origen, and those influenced by them. LaRondelle observes that 'Clement and Origen construe basically the same synthesis of the Christian tradition and Hellenistic philosophy as Philo had done in Judaism.'[150] In this remarkable synthesis, we are told by Clement that philosophy was 'a preparation, paving the way for him who is perfected in Christ' (τὸν ὑπὸ Χριστοῦ τετελειούμενον).[151] In his *Paidagogos*, he declares that all reborn Christians have 'received the perfection for which we strive', and it is clear from the context that this means 'the knowledge of God and perfect forgiveness'.[152] However, in his *Stromateis* he envisages two types of believers: the class of 'medium believers' (τῶν μέσων) who 'only do medium or intermediate actions, procuring a lower grade of glory' and 'the perfect Gnostics who perform perfect actions (κατορθώματα), which raise them to the height of glory'.[153] The 'life-work of the perfected Gnostic' (ἡ ἐνέργεια τοῦ τελειωθέντος γνωστικοῦ) is: 'to hold communion with God through the great High Priest, being made like the Lord, as far as may be, by means of his service towards God, a service which extends to the salvation of men by his solicitous goodness towards us and also by public worship and by teaching and active kindness'.[154]

It is by γνῶσις that 'faith is made perfect, seeing that the man of faith only becomes perfect in this way'.[155] This γνῶσις involves intellectual insight but also love: 'perhaps he who has arrived at this stage has already attained equality with the angels'! The mystical aspect of this experience is described in the same passage: 'Herein lies the perfection (ἡ τελείωσις) of the gnostic soul, that having transcended all purifications and modes of ritual, it should be with the Lord, where he is, in immediate subordination to him.'

For both Clement and Origen, perfection apparently implied sinlessness: 'the disposition of complete disinterestedness in all the distractions of matter, i.e., a continuous passionless state, undisturbed by pleasure or profit, in the contemplation of heaven'.[156] Just as Origen develops a threefold system of Biblical exegesis – the typical (literal), the spiritual (moral) and the mystical (pneumatic) – so he speaks of three types of believers: 'the common people, the spiritually growing, and those who are truly perfect'.[157] In his development of the idea that perfection can be attained by ascetic mortification of the body and by 'the contemplative life of intensified, ecstatic prayer', Origen becomes 'the precursor of Monasticism'.[158]

Within the confines of this study it is not possible to deal adequately with the employment of the terminology of perfection in all of the various systems that may be labelled 'Gnostic'. However, certain basic elements common to them all may be enumerated as a basis for commenting on Gnostic views of perfection. The belief that 'man in his true nature is essentially akin to the divine, a spark of the heavenly light imprisoned in a material body and subjected in this world to the dominance of the Demiurge and his powers' means that man is yearning for some sort of deliverance from this situation.[159] Saving γνῶσις is the means by which 'that deliverance is effected and man awakened to the consciousness of his own true nature and heavenly origin'. Through γνῶσις 'the eventual return of the imprisoned sparks of light to their heavenly abode' is made possible. Thus it comes about that the only souls to be saved, according to the Apocryphon of John, are: 'those on whom the spirit of life comes down and who have united with the power ... become perfect and become worthy to go up to the great lights'.[160] Thus also the Valentinians are reputed to have taught: 'the end will come when all that is spiritual is shaped and perfected through knowledge, and that means spiritual men who possess the perfect knowledge of God and are initiated into the mysteries of Achamoth'.[161]

This emphasis on γνῶσις as the means to perfection means that believers are classified into different groups, as we have seen in the case of Clement and Origen. The Valentinians are said to have described ordinary Church members as those who are 'strengthened by works and mere faith and do not have perfect knowledge'.[162] Continence and good works are said to be necessary for such 'psychic men' that 'by means of them, we may come to the place of the "Middle"'. However, for those who are called 'spiritual and perfect' these are not necessary: 'for it is not conduct that leads to the Pleroma, but the seed, sent forth from there in an immature state, but brought to perfection here'.[163]

Consequently, although working in many respects from similar presuppositions about the nature of man and the dilemma of his existence, it is possible for some writers like Clement and Origen to propose asceticism as part of the programme for attaining perfection and others to propose licence. The disciples of Basilides, for instance, are said to have propounded this libertine doctrine, either 'on the grounds that they have the right even to sin because of their perfection, or that they will in any case be saved by nature even if they sin now, because of their inborn state of election'.[164]

In conclusion it may be said that perfection in these writings generally means the escape of the human spirit from the imprisonment of the material body and the dominion of hostile powers, to return to its heavenly abode. Whether this is regarded as an experience that is immediately accessible to the 'spiritual men' or something that ultimately awaits the ἀποκατάστασις πάντων, the means of attaining this goal differs significantly from system to system. Certainly, the possession of the appropriate γνῶσις is always a prerequisite in each case, though the content of this will vary from system to system and the consequences of that possession will lead to different modes of behaviour.

Two special uses of τελειοῦν in early Christian literature remain to be discussed: what may be termed a 'cultic' application and the use of the verb as a synonym for death. The idea of perfecting people through sacramental agency or initiation into sacred Mysteries has already been alluded to above, in connection with the Valentinians. So too, the Gnostic Justinus is said to have conducted men 'to the Good One, consummating the initiated (by admitting them into) the unspeakable mysteries' (ἐπὶ τὸν ἀγαθὸν ἄγει τελειῶν τοὺς μύστας τὰ ἄλαλα μυστήρια).[165] When Clement of Alexandria is describing Christian baptism, he uses the terminology as follows:

> 'Straightway, on our regeneration, we attained that perfection after which we aspired. For we were illuminated, which is to know God. He is not then imperfect who knows what is perfect ... Being baptized we are illuminated, illuminated we become sons, being made sons we are made perfect, being made perfect we are made immortal ... This work is variously called grace (χάρισμα), and illumination, and perfection, and washing; washing by which we cleanse away our sins, grace by which the penalties accruing to transgressions are remitted, and illumination by which that holy light of salvation is beheld, that is, by which we see God clearly.'[166]

Eusebius also speaks about Constantine at his baptism being 'regenerated and perfected'.[167]

I would argue that in none of these references is τελειοῦν being used as τελεῖν is used, with the sense, 'to initiate', but rather that it retains its formal sense 'to complete' or 'to consummate'. So although the verb is used here in a cultic context, it is not being used as a strictly cultic term. It must certainly be understood as an expression of the broader philosophy of salvation being expounded by the particular writer and in that regard be given specific content. However, it is not legitimate to argue that it thereby becomes synonymous with ἁγιάζειν or καθαρίζειν. On the other hand, it is plain to see how the verb could become an equivalent for such concepts in later writings. Thus, Gregory Nazianzen uses it to describe the installation of OT priests,[168] and Pseudo-Dionysius ('the Areopagite') uses it extensively to refer to the ordination of Christian priests,[169] and for the consecration of baptismal water.[170] G.W.H. Lampe notes some references in Athanasius where the verb is said to be used for 'consecration' of a Church building.[171] However, I would judge that the verb is used in its normal sense to describe the 'completion' of the building and that ἐποίησας τὰ ἐγκαίνια is Athanasius' expression for 'celebrating the dedication' here (cf. 2 Macc. 2: 9). It must be concluded that an explicitly technical application of τελειοῦν in a cultic sense is a late development and that its use in this way is not common, even in the fourth century AD.

The extensive use of τελειοῦν in early Christian writings with reference to death, especially the death of martyrs, is significant. The idea of martyrdom consummating the life of faith is present in 4 Macc. 7: 15 and the concept of Jesus' being perfected by his death and subsequent exaltation is emphasised in Lk. 13: 32 and the usage of Hebrews, as I shall show. The Christian hope of resurrection seems to lie behind the development of this usage in Patristic writings. When martyrdom is specifically under discussion, it is clear that the end of life is viewed as a particular goal or duty to be performed to the glory of God. In such contexts, the verb not only means 'to reach the end of one's course' but also suggests 'the perfection of dying blessedly'.[172] In some contexts, τελειοῦν is simply used as a synonym for death *per se*, as when Eusebius writes of the death of the Emperor's mother (τοῦ μὲν οὖν βασιλέως ἐτελειοῦτο ἡ μήτηρ),[173] or when Athanasius writes of the brethren urging St Antony to stay with them and 'there to die' (κακεῖ τελειωθῆναι).[174] It does not appear that τελειοῦν is used specifically as an equivalent for μαρτυρεῖν. It must be used in association with that verb to convey such a sense — as when Athanasius writes of St Antony having 'received and brought on their way those who were being martyred until they were perfected'[175] — or in an expression such as μαρτυρίῳ τελειωθῆναι.[176]

Athanasius uses τελειοῦν in connexion with the crucifixion of Jesus, when he writes that 'only he that is perfected on the cross dies in the air' (μόνος γὰρ ἐν τῷ ἀέρι τις ἀποθνήσκει ὁ σταυρῷ τελειούμενος).[177] Here the verb seems to be used as above, as an equivalent for the verb 'to die', and carries no special theological significance. It is therefore unwarranted to render a similar expression (σταυρῷ τετελείωται ὑπὲρ τῆς πάντων σωτηρίας) as 'he was *sacrificed* on a cross for the salvation of all'.[178]

General conclusions

The preceding analysis illustrates the extent to which the formal sense of 'make perfect, complete, accomplish, fulfil' is found throughout the literature as the meaning of τελειοῦν. The overlap with τελεῖν is most obvious where *things, acts, works or time* are subject or object of the verb. In contexts where τελειοῦν is related to a *person*, Delling's description of the verb as 'factitive', with the meanings 'to make τέλειος' or 'to become τέλειος', is most apposite. In such contexts it is important to determine the particular writer's measure of τέλειος, whether it is a physical, moral, philosophical or religious concept. Thus, although Philo and early Christian writers use the verb in conjunction with their respective soteriologies, it cannot be assumed that the word carries similar material associations in other contexts. The usage of Hebrews must be examined by detailed exegesis of relevant passages and against the background of the writer's overall theological emphases.

Although there is evidence of a 'religious' use of the verb in the LXX, related to the special application of τέλειος and conveying the sense of completeness in a relationship with God, this usage is rare and can hardly be described as setting a significant precedent for NT writers. Indeed, I find that the NT, apart from Hebrews, most frequently uses the verb in a purely formal sense, with no particular moral or religious connotations. Phil. 3: 12 is an important exception where Paul, apparently taking up the language of his opponents, refers to the consummation of the Christian's relationship with Christ at the resurrection. Here the verb could be understood as in some sense a synonym for δοξάζειν. Lk. 13: 32 is also an important exception, where the consummation of Christ's messianic work by death is in view, and thus the perfecting of Christ himself as Messiah. The use of the verb by early Christian writers in connection with death and martyrdom is clearly related to the latter, though Lk. 13: 32 has important redemptive overtones, in Luke's presentation.

The technical 'cultic' application of τελεῖν for 'initiation' or 'consecration' does not appear to be shared by τελειοῦν until well into the Christian era. The latter retains its formal sense in the LXX expression τελειοῦν τὰς χεῖρας. Although not as literal a rendering of the Hebrew as ἐμπιπλάναι or πληροῦν τὰς χεῖρας, τελειοῦν is to be understood in context as taking full account of the literal meaning of the Hebrew expression, as indicated by the narratives of Exod. 29 and Lev. 8. The formula as a whole has a technical, cultic meaning but τελειοῦν itself does not thereby become an equivalent for 'consecrate' or 'cleanse'. This usage has more in common with the 'vocational' application of Herodotus III.86, Sophocles' *Electra* 1508–10 and Lk. 13: 32, whereby the perfecting of some task or the fulfilment of some great event can bring about the perfecting of someone in a particular role. Clearly, the perfecting of a priest may be considered in terms of his consecration, but it cannot be argued that τελειοῦν in Hebrews carries the sense of 'priestly consecration' on the basis of LXX usage.

Kögel's contention that the verb is 'a general term, without distinct content' may be simplistic. The formal use of the verb throughout the literature predominates, but there is an amazing range of specific applications. This suggests the correctness of Kögel's methodology with regard to the interpretation of this verb in a given passage. Only the context in general and the object of the verb in particular can indicate the particular sense on each occasion. This will be my starting point and method of approach with regard to the usage of Hebrews, though I will have occasion to differ significantly with Kögel's conclusions.

Du Plessis takes issue with this sort of approach, describing it as 'unfortunate' because: 'the term and its derivatives have acquired by elastic adaptibility (*sic*) various stable associations from religious, profane and colloquial usage. To wield it as a materially neutral concept is an unjustifiable abstraction. By recognizing the inherence of material associations we approximate the plenitude of characteristics which may have suggestive value for exegetical labours.'[179] This argument begs the question as to which of the 'various stable associations' are to be applied in the interpretation of Hebrews' use of the terminology. This question is often answered implicitly by interpreters who argue for a specific religious context for our writer, such as Philonism or Gnostic thinking. In the continuing debate about the *Sitz im Leben* of Hebrews, the writer's use of the terminology of perfection is often put forward by supporters of different positions to uphold their arguments. However, to proceed on the assumption that distinct content can only be given to $\tau\epsilon\lambda\epsilon\iota o\tilde{\upsilon}\nu$ by a given context seems the most valid approach to this problem. Such an approach does not permit the interpreter to ignore the various applications of the terminology by other writers, though the extent to which parallels may be evinced will depend on a careful exegesis of the relevant contexts in Hebrews.

3

THE PERFECTING OF CHRIST: THE BROAD PERSPECTIVE

The first reference to the perfecting of Christ in Hebrews comes in a passage filled with themes of supreme importance for the consequent argument of the writer. Eschatology, Christology and Soteriology are interwoven in a remarkably concise and profound manner. Detailed exegesis of 2: 5–18 is necessary, therefore, not only for the proper interpretation of 2: 10 but also for an understanding of our writer's theology in general.

The centrality of 2: 10 to the argument of the passage as a whole can easily be seen. The perfecting of Christ appears to be related to the theme of his humiliation, suffering and exaltation, introduced in verses 6–9 and enlarged upon in verses 14–18. The 'many sons' who benefit from the perfecting of Christ are further defined in verses 11–13 and the way in which Christ brings them to 'glory' is somewhat elaborated in verses 14–18.

Although subsequent passages associate the perfecting of Christ particularly with the concept of his earthly struggle (5: 9 in context) or the concept of his heavenly exaltation (7: 28 in context), I will argue that 2: 10 in its context embraces both emphases. Here, where such a broad perspective on the achievement of Christ is given, I will argue that the perfecting of Christ is a *process*,[1] the particular aspects of which are to be expounded in subsequent chapters.

The significance and structure of 2: 5–18

According to Vanhoye's detailed analysis of the structure of Hebrews, 1: 1–4 serves as an introduction to the whole work and concludes with an announcement of what will be the subject of the first main division: 'the name which is more excellent than that of the angels'.[2] Vanhoye argues that the word 'angels' is 'le *terme caractéristique*' of the whole section from 1: 5 to 2: 18 – it reappears regularly (1: 5, 6, 7, 13; 2: 2, 5, 7, 9, 16) but is not used again until 12: 22 and 13: 2 – and forms a large 'inclusion' (although 2: 17–18 constitutes the 'announcement of the following part').[3]

The writer of Hebrews is certainly concerned in this whole section (1: 5 − 2: 18) with the exposition of the 'name' of Christ, not simply presenting us with various titles for Christ but showing us different aspects of his character and work. J. Bligh has argued, however, that the section 'cannot be satisfactorily united under the title "Christ is superior to the angels" since this is only one of the three or four themes elaborated in it'.[4] He suggests that Vanhoye's analysis does not reveal the true relationship between the introduction and 1: 5 − 2: 18 because:

> 'in 2: 5–9*a* the subject is Christ's session at the right hand of the Father and in 2: 9*b* − 2: 18 the subject is his redemptive death, and ... these two subjects are announced in 1: 3 (not 1: 4). Furthermore, the hortatory passage 2: 1–4 draws the conclusion from 1: 1–2. Thus the whole introduction (1: 1–4) is the signpost. It contains in the order A, B, C, the ideas developed in the three parts of the section 1: 5 − 2: 18 in the order C (1: 5–14), A (2: 1–4), B (2: 5–18).'

Bligh certainly offers a helpful analysis of the relationship between 1: 1–4 and the three sections of the argument from 1: 5 to 2: 18, and it is true that Christ's relationship to the angels is only one of several themes in these chapters. The importance of verse 3 as an anticipation of the argument in 2: 5ff is also suggested by the presentation of O. Hofius, who argues that the theme of pre-existence (incarnation), death and exaltation is first stated in 1: 3 and then elaborated in 2: 5ff.[5] Nevertheless, there is still validity in Vanhoye's assessment. The very fact that references to angels persist in the argument, at least as far as 2: 9 with some frequency, and that these references appear in each of the three sections outlined by Bligh, suggests that this provides a link for all the other themes and is a major concern for the author.[6]

Examining more specifically the internal structure of the section 1: 5 to 2: 18, Vanhoye notes that the first paragraph (1: 5–14) is *doctrinal* in content and consists of an accumulation of scriptural testimonies provided by the author to demonstrate the superiority of the Son to the angels. The second paragraph (2: 1–4) is *parenetic*, drawing out for the readers a practical conclusion to the argument so far: if angels were mediators of the covenant at Sinai and the penalty for disregarding that revelation was so severe, how much more severe the penalty for those who drift from the word of salvation proclaimed by the Son of God himself. The third paragraph (2: 5–18) is *doctrinal* in content and resumes the theme of Christ's eschatological rule, in which angels are merely 'ministering spirits' (cf. 1: 13f).[7] However, the emphasis in this new section is on the fact that Christ assumes his dominion by fulfilment of Psalm 8: 4–6. This changes the focus to explore the implications of Christ's incarnation both for himself, *vis-à-vis* the angels, and for those he came to save (not the angels but the 'sons of Abraham', verse 16). The purpose of this paragraph, therefore, is *to consider the necessity for Christ's temporary humiliation 'lower than the angels', particularly with respect to his suffering, and to show how he came to be 'crowned with glory and honour', as 'the heir of all things' and Saviour of his people.*

Exegesis of 2: 5–18

(a) Jesus as the Man crowned with glory and honour (2: 5–9)[8]

There are two issues in particular with which the writer is concerned in these verses, perhaps in response to specific challenges or questions from his readers or perhaps to anticipate such objections. The first problem may be stated in this fashion: if Jesus Christ is 'the Son', as expounded in the opening chapter, why is his rule not complete and apparent to all? The second problem is this: why did the Son have to suffer and die, as the apostolic tradition maintains that he did? In seeking to deal with these issues, the writer introduces the idea of Christ as the Man who fulfils Psalm 8. In 2: 10–16 this concept is developed to show how his achievement as 'pioneer' brings salvation to the many sons with whom he identifies himself. Finally, in 2: 17–18 we see how the concept of Christ as representative Man becomes the basis for the writer's exposition of Christ's work as high priest. Thus, far from being a digression, the section 2: 5–18 establishes a vital foundation on which the christological discussion of later sections will be dependent.

A preliminary question which, at first glance, may seem to be of little importance, leads us to the heart of the issue: is Psalm 8 used in a directly 'messianic' sense, applied to Christ immediately from verse 5? Several commentators expound the view that the psalm here is used primarily to express 'the true identity of man' (up to, and including, verse 8), and that it is only when the author has shown that the psalm is not, in fact, fulfilled at present by men that he turns to apply it to Christ (verse 9). Thus, Moffatt comments: 'human nature is not "crowned with glory and honour" at present. How can it be, when the terror of death and the devil enslaves it (verse 15)?'[9] Commenting on verse 8 (with reference to verse 5), Westcott says: 'God did not subject the future world to angels *for* he promised man an absolute sovereignty which still has to be assured in that coming order.'[10] There is strength in this argument since it presupposes in the first place an interpretation of the psalm that is more obviously related to the original intention of the psalmist. Furthermore, the name of Jesus is not associated with the interpretation of the psalm until verse 9 and the concept of 'bringing many sons to glory' (verse 10) shows how much the writer's concern is with the destiny of men.

Despite the obvious strength of this position, I would argue that the writer is not introducing a new contrast between *man* and the angels in 2: 5 but resuming the contrast between *Christ* and the angels, begun in chapter 1 and interrupted by the exhortation in 2: 1–4. The assertion that 'it was not to angels that (God) subjected the world to come' (2: 5) recalls the promise of absolute dominion to Christ in Psalm 110: 1 (cf. 1: 13). It then provides the link to a second scriptural testimony to Christ, which explains how that promised dominion is obtained by him. However, such an interpretation by no means supposes that the anthropological significance of Psalm 8 was ignored by the writer in his application of the words to Christ. On the contrary, mankind benefits from the achievement of Christ as representative Man.

Michel notes that 'a messianic application of Psalm 8 is not found in Rabbinic writings, but possibly in Apocalyptic'.[11] However, it is significant that Paul applies Psalm 8: 6 (8: 7 LXX) to Christ in 1 Cor. 15: 27, in the development of an Adam–Christ typology (verses 20–3, 45–9). The text is used in parallel with an allusion to Psalm 110: 1 (verse 25), to describe the ultimate triumph of Christ as the one who 'must reign until he has put all his enemies under his feet'.[12] In Eph. 1: 22 the same verse from Psalm 8 is used, following a similar allusion to Psalm 110: 1 (verse 20). However, the reference here is to the present exercise of authority by the risen and ascended Christ. In Phil. 3: 21 there is a further allusion to Psalm 8: 6, to assure the readers that Christ 'will change our lowly body to be like his glorious body, by the power which enables him even to subject all things to himself'. The language of both psalm texts may also be reflected in 1 Pet. 3: 22, with reference to the ascension of Christ.[13]

The linking of the two psalms in 1 Cor. 15: 25–7; Eph. 1: 20–2; Hebrews 1: 13 – 2: 8; and possibly 1 Pet. 3: 22 points to *an established christological association of these texts in Christian tradition.*[14] Psalm 8: 6 seems to have been applied to Christ because the words 'putting all things in subjection under his feet' are reminiscent of the theme of Christ's absolute dominion in Psalm 110: 1. However, our writer goes further than others when he relates the preceding verse of Psalm 8 to the incarnation and heavenly exaltation of Jesus. It is not an understanding of Jesus as Son of Man that underlies the use of Psalm 8 in Hebrews,[15] but the idea of him as head of a redeemed humanity in a 'new creation'.

The 'world to come', asserts the writer in 2: 5, has been placed by God under the authority of Christ, and not of angels. Christ is the one appointed 'heir of all things' (1: 3), whom God has invited to sit at his right hand (1: 13). The expression τὴν οἰκουμένην τὴν μέλλουσαν originates from late Jewish and primitive Christian eschatology. The new age brings 'the transformation of heaven and earth with it: the future "world" and the coming "city" (13: 14) are expressions of this kind which, on the one hand stand close to the old apocalyptic motif (Apoc. 21: 1–2), and on the other hand have lost their typically Palestinian colouring'.[16] We are not simply dealing with a spiritualised eschatology here: this 'spatial' concept and the related 'temporal' concept of 6: 5 (μέλλων αἰών) correspond to 'the common primitive Christian notion of the Kingdom of God'.[17] However, Vanhoye rightly argues that τὴν μέλλουσαν is *not to be understood in a strictly chronological sense*, as if the new 'world-order' were totally future. It designates 'the definitive reality which certainly has not yet unfolded all its virtualities, but which is none the less already present and active'.[18] The miracles and charismatic gifts (2: 4) are a manifestation of the latter truth (cf. 6: 4f). Moffatt also captures the balance between future and present in the writer's eschatology when he describes the 'world to come' as 'the new order of things in which the σωτηρία of 1: 14, 2: 2–3 is to be realized (see 9: 28 ἀπεκδεχομένοις εἰς σωτηρίαν) and from which already influences are pouring down into the life of Christians'.[19]

With 2: 5ff the writer thus reiterates the theme of Christ's enthronement as the Son, destined to rule over all and receive the glory and honour due to God himself. However, the important dimension introduced by the supporting citation in 2: 6ff is the implication that Christ achieves this dominion as a man, made 'for a little while lower than the angels'.[20] The necessity for this is explained in the rest of the chapter and is a theme of continuing importance in our writer's presentation. However, Psalm 8 also seems to be used here to assure the readers that, despite all appearances to the contrary, and perhaps their own expressed doubts, all things *will* ultimately be brought into submission to Christ, since he is the one to whom the promise primarily applies ('putting all things in subjection under his feet').[21] As if to reinforce the point, the writer claims in verse 8 that the words just quoted can only mean that God left 'nothing that is not subject' (cf. 1 Cor. 15: 27). However, the problem is that 'we do *not yet* see all things subject to him'. Spicq rightly suggests that, if these words are to be understood with reference to Christ (αὐτῷ), the writer is reflecting 'the anguish, if not the discouragement, of the despised and persecuted Christians, vainly awaiting the advent of God's kingdom on earth'.[22] Michel also assumes that the psalm is being interpreted of Christ in verse 8:

'now the revelation of Christ's world-dominion has still not happened. The eschatological οὔπω has its parallel in Mark 13: 7, 1 John 3: 2, Apocalypse 17: 10, 12. The primitive Christian tension between now and then is concealed in this "not yet". The contrast lies between the still not fulfilled world-dominion and the already occurring humiliation and exaltation.'[23]

This assumes that the crowning with glory and honour of which the psalm speaks has been fulfilled in the ascension—enthronement of Christ.[24]

This brings us to a consideration of the second main issue with which the paragraph is concerned: why did Jesus as 'the Son' of chapter 1, destined to have dominion over all things, have to suffer as the apostolic tradition maintains that he did? For the writer of Hebrews the answer is to be found again in the wording of Psalm 8. We do not yet see all things subject to Christ but we *do* see the fulfilment of the prior statement in the psalm, namely Jesus 'for a little while made lower than the angels, crowned with glory and honour' (verse 9). In its original application, the psalm expresses 'the nobility of man's nature which falls but little short of the divine'.[25] However, applied to Christ, these words become a prophecy of his humiliation in the incarnation and of the subsequent glorification in his resurrection—ascension. In repeating the words from the psalm that acknowledge the temporary humiliation of the Son, our writer inserts the important words διὰ τὸ πάθημα τοῦ θανάτου before completing the citation. This interpretative addition reveals that, for the writer, it was essentially because of 'the suffering of death' that Christ received the promised crowning with glory and honour.[26] As in Phil. 2: 6–9, death appears as the ultimate expression of Christ's humiliation and the ground of his exaltation.[27]

Throughout the section 2: 5–18 Westcott observes a 'tacit reference to the objections which were raised against the Lord's claims to Messiahship on the ground of the actual facts of his life and suffering'.[28] It is certainly true that, unless explained, the cross formed very strong evidence against Jesus' messiahship, and the hint of some apologetic on this subject may be indicated by the unusual expression 'it was fitting' (verse 10). However, as I shall argue in my concluding chapter, our writer's treatment of the sufferings of Christ may be directly related to the apparent questioning of the readers about their own sufferings (cf. 12: 1–13).

There is some uncertainty amongst commentators about the relationship of the final clause in verse 9 to the preceding clauses. Some argue, as Michel does, that the 'concluding ὅπως does not connect logically; it points back to the humiliation of the Son of Man, apparently jumping

back over the "crowned with glory and honour" '.[29] Whereas the words
'because of the suffering of death' point to Christ's death as the ground of
his exaltation, the words 'so that by the grace of God he might taste death
for every one' point to that death as 'the divine remedy for the human
predicament'.[30] However, Spicq and Vanhoye insist that the final clause
connects logically with the preceding words ('crowned with glory and
honour'), suggesting that 'the crowning has a repercussion on his death. It
confers an influence (*rayonnement*) on it, a universal efficacy. Because it
resulted in glorification, the death of Christ is a death useful for all mankind.'[31] Although Westcott says 'the particle is not strictly connected with
ἐστεφανωμένον alone, but refers to all that precedes — to the Passion
crowned by the Ascension', he comes to the same conclusion that 'the
glory which followed the death marked its universal efficacy'.[32] The last
two explanations are preferable to the first because they propose a more
natural syntax and are in keeping with the later stress on the importance
of Christ's ascension as the means by which he becomes the perpetual
source of mercy and grace (4: 14–16; 7: 23–5; 9: 11f, 24).

(b) Jesus as the saviour of his brethren (2: 10–16)

The suggestion of a divine plan to be fulfilled to meet the needs of people
everywhere and at all times (verse 9) is taken up and expounded in verse
10. Although this is said to have taken place 'by the grace of God',[33] our
writer also asserts that it was 'fitting' for God (ἔπρεπεν γὰρ αὐτῷ) to
achieve the salvation of his people in the humiliation, death and exaltation
of the Son.

The argument about what 'befits' God finds no parallel elsewhere in
the Bible in precisely the same language,[34] but William Manson reminds us
that the OT prophets constantly appeal to God by reference to his own
revealed character: 'they judge God by God, so to speak, and insist on the
divine consistency'.[35] As suggested above, the use of such an unusual
expression implies an apologetic aim in the passage. Westcott argues that:
'this argument from "fitness" is distinct from that of logical necessity
(δεῖ verse 1) and of obligation from a position which has been assumed
(ὤφειλεν verse 17) ... the standard lies in what man (made in the image of
God) can recognise as conformable to the divine attributes'.[36] However,
the 'fitness' in this case also has reference to the condition of man,[37]
hinted at in verse 9 and now to be expounded in some detail. Indeed, it
could be said that 'verses 11–18 explain this fittingness; 11–15 in respect
to those he is to save, and 16–18 in respect of the Saviour', but behind
this is an argument 'from God's character to what he will do'.[38]

It is assumed that the αὐτῷ in verse 10 refers to God, since he is pictured as the one who initiates the salvation of mankind in verse 9 ('by the grace of God') and in the preceding chapter. The epithet 'for whom and through whom all things exist' points to the freedom of God in his sovereignty to do what is fitting, both with respect to his own character and plans for creation and with respect to the needs of mankind. God will also be the subject (understood) of τελειῶσαι, and the accusative participle ἀγαγόντα is best explained as agreeing with the unexpressed subject of the infinitive. Käsemann argues that the participle is an 'ingressive aorist' and refers to Christ as τὸν ἀρχηγόν: 'as Leader, the Heavenly Man began to lead many sons to heavenly glory in his earthly humiliation'.[39] However, since an 'ingressive aorist' is normally only understood with verbs 'whose Present denotes a state or condition',[40] Käsemann's rendering is inappropriate. It is much more likely that we have here a 'simultaneous aorist',[41] or a 'proleptic aorist which envisages the work of Christ and its consequences for mankind as a unity'.[42]

God's purpose for his people is to lead them 'to glory' (εἰς δόξαν) by perfecting Christ. Mention of 'glory' recalls the previous section: the glory of the Son (2: 7, 9) is to become the glory of men.[43] Reference to the perfecting of Christ 'through sufferings' (διὰ παθημάτων) suggests that men only attain this glory 'through a Jesus who had won it for them by suffering'.[44] The description of those who benefit from the perfecting of Christ as 'many sons' introduces what might be called the 'particularist emphasis' of our passage,[45] and I shall examine the writer's exposition of this theme more closely in verses 11–13. Although it is said in verse 9 that he tasted death 'for every one', it is clear from what follows that the benefits of that death are only enjoyed by a particular group within humanity.[46]

In his comments on the words 'crowned with glory and honour' in Psalm 8, Artur Weiser says:

> 'the king of the universe has even gone so far as to install man as the king of the earth and to "crown" him with the regalia of "majesty and glory" which really are the attributes of God's own presence. It is in this sense that we can speak of man here being created "in the image of God and after his likeness" (Gen. 1: 26–28, 2: 19f).'[47]

In its reflections on the status of man in creation, Psalm 8 does not appear to take into account the Fall narrative of Gen. 3, but speaks of man in ideal terms.[48] For Paul and the writer of Hebrews, however, this glory is the eschatological goal of man in Christ: it is the promise of becoming like Christ in his glorified state. G. Kittel observes:

'when the NT refers to the eschatological participation of believers in δόξα this is simply part of the general statement of salvation history concerning the connexion and parallelism between the resurrection of Christ and the resurrection and the new aeon of believers. Participation in δόξα, whether here in hope or one day in consummation, is participation in Christ.'[49]

The reference in 2: 10 to glory as the *destination* of the many sons means that the term is being used here as something of a synonym for 'the world to come' (verse 5), though the latter more particularly designates the *sphere* in which the glory will be realised.

There is general agreement among scholars as to the importance of the title ἀρχηγός in the Christology of Hebrews, but some dissension as to its background and meaning here. The significance of this title for an understanding of the writer's concept of perfection is clear, since it occurs as the object of τελειῶσαι in verse 10. The noun is also applied to Christ in 12: 2 and Acts 3: 15; 5: 31. E.K. Simpson notes that the word hovers between the two senses of 'Chieftain' and 'Founder' in Greek literature generally and in the papyri.[50] He contends that the meaning 'author' or 'initiator' unquestionably suits Hebrews 2: 10; 12: 2 and Acts 3: 15 best because the word is followed in each of these texts by a possessive case. In the examples he gives, this construction conveys the notion of 'prime agent' or 'factor'. Only in Acts 5: 31 does he read 'leader' or 'prince'.

Most modern commentators, however, argue that the context demands the sense of 'leader' or 'pioneer' in Hebrews 2: 10. Moffatt acknowledges that 'the general idea in ἀρχηγός is that of originator or personal source', but says 'it is doubtful how far the writer was determined, in choosing the term, by its varied associations'.[51] Westcott maintains that 'the preceding ἀγαγόντα seems to fix the rendering "leader" here (as in 12: 2). Christ is the "Leader of our salvation" inasmuch as he travelled by the way which we must follow to come to God.'[52] Michel insists on being guided exclusively by LXX usage, where ἀρχηγός translates nāśîʾ,[53] śar,[54] and above all rō̄ ʾš,[55] as well as other Hebrew words denoting leadership. The three Hebrew words particularly noted here are also translated in the LXX by ἄρχων on a great number of occasions.

The most thorough investigation of the history of interpretation and etymology of ἀρχηγός has been carried out by P.G. Müller. Having analysed the use of the term in various sources, he seeks to relate it to the fundamental theme of OT theology that Israel is a people uniquely *led by God*.[56] The idea of Christ as the new leader of God's people has been derived from this tradition, rather than from Gnostic traditions, which speak of souls being led back to their source in God.[57] In Hebrews 2: 10, Christ is led by God through suffering to glory, thus becoming the leader of his people on the journey to salvation: the title indicates 'the soteriological role the exalted Christ has for the faith experience of the earthly church'.[58] The closest parallel is the title 'forerunner' ($\pi\rho\delta\rho\rho\mu\sigma$) in 6: 20, rather than 'source of eternal salvation' ($\alpha\iota\tau\iota\sigma\varsigma$ $\sigma\omega\tau\eta\rho\iota\alpha\varsigma$ $\alpha\iota\omega\nu\iota\sigma\nu$) in 5: 9.[59]

Despite the obvious strength of these arguments, and particularly the fact that 2: 10 points to Christ's role as $\dot{\alpha}\rho\chi\eta\gamma\dot{\sigma}\varsigma$ in relation to God's plan to 'lead many sons to glory', there are also suggestions in the context that the word conveys something of the sense of 'originator' or 'initiator'.[60] In the first place, the concluding clause of verse 9 indicates that Christ accomplished something unique by his death and exaltation *on behalf of others*: by the grace of God he tasted death 'for every one' ($\dot{\upsilon}\pi\dot{\epsilon}\rho$ $\pi\alpha\nu\tau\dot{\sigma}\varsigma$).[61] Although it is true that the expression 'he tasted death' is essentially a graphic description of 'the hard and painful reality of dying which is experienced by man and which was suffered also by Jesus',[62] the immediate context makes it clear that Jesus' death was more than simply an identification with mankind or an example to men as to how they should die. In 2: 14f we are told that his death was in order to 'break the power of him who had death at his command, that is, the devil' (NEB) and to liberate men from the fear of death. Elsewhere, Christ's death is associated with the death of every man, but its unique purpose 'to bear the sins of many' is stressed (9: 27f).

A second factor that suggests that the sense of 'author', 'originator' or 'initiator' cannot be excluded from the context here is the qualification $\tau\dot{\eta}\varsigma$ $\sigma\omega\tau\eta\rho\iota\alpha\varsigma$ $\alpha\dot{\upsilon}\tau\dot{\omega}\nu$. The pronoun $\alpha\dot{\upsilon}\tau\dot{\omega}\nu$ emphasises again that Christ accomplished a deliverance for his 'brothers' or the 'many sons' that they could not accomplish for themselves. He did not need to be saved himself in the same way that his people needed saving.[63] He leads them along the path to glory and is able to save them completely (cf. 7: 25; 9: 28) because he has already secured for them an 'eternal redemption' in his death and exaltation (9: 11f). This is made more explicit when the writer says 'he became the source ($\alpha\dot{\iota}\tau\iota\sigma\varsigma$) of eternal salvation to all who obey him' (5: 9). I contend that the difference between this description of Christ and that of 2: 10 is not as great as some have argued.[64] The NEB appears to combine the ideas of Christ as trail-blazer and unique redeemer with the rendering 'the leader who delivers them'.

A detailed examination of the words $\delta\iota\dot{\alpha}$ $\pi\alpha\theta\eta\mu\dot{\alpha}\tau\omega\nu$ $\tau\epsilon\lambda\epsilon\iota\tilde{\omega}\sigma\alpha\iota$ will be given at the conclusion of this chapter when an exegesis of the passage as a whole has been presented.

Underlying the argument of 2: 5–10 has been the assumption of a certain solidarity between Christ as the Man who fulfils Psalm 8 and mankind in general, or between Christ as the Son and the many sons he leads to glory. This assumption is made explicit in 2: 11 and illustrated by citations from the OT in 2: 12f. In effect, these verses explain who benefits from the perfecting of Christ.

According to Vanhoye, the designation ὁ ἁγιάζων (verse 11) is never applied to man in the OT but is always reserved for God.[65] Certain men, however, receive the order of 'sanctifier' with respect to others: the commission 'to set them apart for cultic functions by consecrating them with a rite'.[66] Moffatt echoes a similar point of view when he maintains that in 2: 11 and 13: 12 'Jesus is assigned the *divine prerogative* of ἁγιάζειν ... i.e., of making God's people his very own, by bringing them into vital relationship with himself.'[67] This verb in Hebrews is essentially associated with the establishment of New Covenant relations between God and man.[68] It is a sacerdotal metaphor inasmuch as the consecrating work of Christ is presented as a high-priestly action, fulfilling the ritual of the Day of Atonement. However, the broader covenantal reference must not be obscured in the interpretation of this term. The NEB translation of 2: 11*a* ('for a consecrating priest and those whom he consecrates are all one stock') must be criticised for narrowing the meaning of this verb too much in a sacerdotal direction and for making explicit Christ's priestly function before the writer does (2: 17f). Michel lifts the concept of sanctification entirely from the realm of the cult when he interprets 2: 11*a* in terms of 'a removal from earthly realities and an establishment in God's new world, which comes in with Jesus Christ'.[69]

Some commentators interpret the phrase ἐξ ἑνὸς πάντες to mean that the Son as consecrator and the sons as those who are consecrated are members of *the one spiritual family*, the 'one' referring to God. Thus, Moffatt proposes: 'it is implied, though the writer does not explain the matter further, that Christ's common tie with mankind goes back to the pre-incarnate period; there was a close bond between them, even before he was born into the world; indeed the incarnation was the consequence of this solidarity or tie'.[70] The quotation from Isa. 8: 18 in verse 13 would seem to confirm this conclusion: those whom Christ is not ashamed to call his 'brothers' (verses 11*b*–12) are in fact 'the children' God has given him (verse 13*b*). They are given to Christ by God so that he might 'proclaim God's name' to them (verse 12) and lead them to glory (verse 10). The incarnation is then shown to be a necessary condition for the fulfilment of the divine plan by the argument of verse 14: since 'the children' share in flesh and blood he also had to partake of the same nature.

Other commentators, however, prefer to see ἐξ ἑνός as a reference to Adam: 'it is just one more instance of our writer's insistence that it is as true Man that our Lord wins our salvation ... And it is *because* he is as Man descended from Adam as we too are, that he calls us his brethren; in spite of our fallen state, he is not ashamed to call us so.'[71] The strength of this interpretation is its obvious continuation of the theme of verse 10: it was fitting for God to perfect Christ 'through suffering' because this pattern of redemption perfectly meets the needs of fallen humanity. The consecrator and the consecrated are bound together by 'the community of human nature'.[72] Its weakness lies in the implication that Jesus is not ashamed to call men his brothers simply because they are *men* (verse 11*b* δι' ἣν αἰτίαν points back emphatically to ἐξ ἑνός πάντες), whereas the quotation in verse 12 identifies them as God's ἐκκλησία and the quotation in verse 13*b* continues the suggestion that they are a special group within humanity, given to Christ by God.[73] Christ is not ashamed to call them brothers because of the spiritual bond linking the Son and the sons, a bond that originates in the will and purpose of God. 'What the sanctifier is and what the sanctified become, they are such and become such through God: sonship and brotherhood already become combined here.'[74] However, for that purpose of God to be fulfilled in the actual creation of a new humanity, it was necessary for the Son not only to become incarnate but also to experience suffering and ultimately death 'for every one'.

Vanhoye seeks to interpret the three OT citations in verses 12–13 as descriptive of the ministry of *the glorified Christ*. If our writer was observing the sequence of Psalm 22, it is likely that the citation of verse 22 (LXX 21: 23) means that 'it is the resurrected Christ who will announce God's name to his brothers and will praise God in the midst of the congregation'.[75] On the other hand, the flow of the argument in Hebrews 2: 10–12 may suggest that the whole Christ event is to be placed under the category of proclaiming the name of God to his people.[76] There seems little point in denying that our writer applies the citations of 2: 13 to the earthly ministry of Christ. Vanhoye's argument at this point is strained and unnecessary.[77] Perhaps the most satisfactory summary of the author's train of thought here is provided by Kistemaker:

'It is the motif of glory and honour which has been the bridge between the last half of Psalm 8 and the second part of Psalm 22. Yet the first part of Psalm 22 is not entirely lost out of sight. Once again the author seems to reach back to the agony of Christ on the cross, when he heard his scoffers say "he trusteth on God" (πέποιθεν ἐπί); for the author quotes a verse found in Isaiah 8: 17 and 2 Samuel 22: 3 "I will put my trust in him" (πεποιθὼς ἐπί). The addition of this citation serves the purpose of affirming the intermediate work of the high priest in the person of Christ'.[78]

The three citations establish and reinforce the theological assertions of verses 10–11. The 'brothers' with whom Christ is not ashamed to be identified are from one point of view the eschatological congregation (ἐκκλησία) of God, already assembled around the exalted Christ (12: 22–4). They are constituted as such because Christ faithfully fulfilled the ministry given to him by God. From another point of view, they are the 'children' of Christ,[79] who are still very much in the world (2: 14–18), on their way to glory. As such, they need to appreciate how much Christ has identified with them in their human situation, by virtue of his incarnation and sufferings, and how he is able to help them reach their heavenly destination.

To express historically his fellowship with the 'children' and bring about God's ultimate purpose for them, it was necessary for the Son to enter upon a physical unity with them by incarnation. The expression κεκοινώνηκεν αἵματος καὶ σαρκός (verse 14) emphasises a 'community of nature', but a nature that involves frailty and weakness.[80] Westcott notes that, whereas 'κεκοινώνηκεν marks the common nature ever shared among men as long as the race lasts', 'μετέσχεν expresses the unique fact of the incarnation as a voluntary acceptance of humanity'.[81] The distinction in the use of the tenses in his argument is quite valid but the suggestion that there is a significant difference in the meaning of the verbs themselves cannot be maintained: in the examples he gives they appear to be used synonymously. The adverb παραπλησίως does not indicate clearly how far the similarity goes, but it is used in situations 'where no differentiation is intended, in the sense *in just the same way*'.[82] Both verse 14 and verse 17 (κατὰ πάντα) only become meaningful when *equality* rather than *resemblance* is understood.[83]

The purpose of the incarnation, as described in 2: 14b–15, is victory over the Devil as the one who 'has the power of death' and the liberation of his prisoners. The instrument in both cases is Christ's death (διὰ τοῦ θανάτου).[84] Michel shows how the proposition that the Devil has the power of death belongs to a Palestinian tradition, in which there was a tendency to identify Satan and the angel of death in the OT.[85] In particular we may note the perspective of Wis. 2: 23f: 'for God created man for incorruption, and made him in the image of his own eternity, but through the devil's envy death entered the world, and those who belong to his party experience it' (RSV). If we ask how the death of Jesus is envisaged as the means of robbing the Devil of his power (καταργήσῃ),[86] and how it can deliver men from the fear of death, we may observe that the writer is more interested in 'the result of Christ's sacrifice than its mode and progress'.[87] The method of the sacrifice recedes into the background and he says little about 'the theory or doctrine behind these symbolic representations'. Nevertheless, some suggestion that his death has a substitutionary value is given in 2: 9, and in 2: 17 it is represented as an atoning sacrifice for the sins of his people. In 9: 15 his death explicitly achieves 'redemption' from transgressions (cf. 9: 12), and in 9: 28 he offers himself 'to bear the sins of many'.

In the background of 2: 5–10 and 2: 14–15 we may see the picture of Gen. 1–3 and the teaching of Prophetic and Apocalyptic writers about the restoration of paradise in the End-time, the victory over death and sin and Satan. Implicit in this context is the assumption that death is the divine punishment for sin, which Satan wields as a power over man's life within the divine economy. The Devil is deprived of his power over death when Christ provides forgiveness for sin through his atoning sacrifice (cf. 10: 15–18) and thereby the possibility of passing through death into 'the promised eternal inheritance' (9: 15). Men can be released from the 'fear of death' (2: 15) and therefore, in a sense, from bondage to the Devil's power, by coming to believe in the effectiveness of the redemption achieved by Christ. The imagery at 2: 14f reinforces the conclusion that our writer is developing an Adam Christology with the use of Psalm 8 in 2: 5–9.

The concluding verse of this section (2: 16) is one of the author's 'terse parentheses',[88] in which he apparently alludes to Isa. 41: 8f (with ἐπιλαμβάνεται instead of ἀντελαβόμην) and restates the theme of the Son becoming temporarily 'lower than the angels' to meet the needs of mankind. E.K. Simpson rightly argues that ἐπιλαμβάνεται should be rendered 'to take hold of', and not weakened to 'to help'.[89] The same verb at 8: 9, in a quotation from Jer. 31: 32 (LXX), refers to God's 'taking hold' of the hand of Israel to lead them out of the bondage of Egypt. Following the theme of deliverance from bondage to the Devil and fear of death, 2: 16 suggests that Christ 'takes hold' of the 'seed of Abraham' to rescue them in this way. The verse describes the *purpose* of the incarnation, rather than the fact of it.[90] The phrase 'seed of Abraham' is probably chosen with Isa. 41: 8f in mind but also with regard to the promises of Gen. 13: 16; 15: 5; 22: 18 (cf. Hebrews 11: 12, 18). The reference is neither to mankind in general nor to Israel in particular: 'seed of Abraham' ranks with 'brothers' and 'children' as 'words of honour which God's Word grants to the faithful'.[91] Reappearance of the word 'angels', as the characteristic term of this whole section, indicates that the section is drawing to a close and that the next verses form a transition to an entirely new stage of the argument.

(c) Jesus as the merciful and faithful high priest (2: 17–18)

Although notice of the high-priestly work of Christ is given in 1: 3, and possibly in 2: 11, it is not until 2: 17 that we are introduced to the title 'high priest' which, together with 'Son', supports the Christology of Hebrews. The terminology and perspective up to this point has been similar to that of the rest of the NT: salvation from the coming wrath (2: 2f), a share in the coming kingdom and glory of Christ through his death (2: 5–10), Christians as sons of God and brothers of Christ sharing together in his victory (2: 11–16). Although the traditional eschatology continues to reappear in the argument that follows (e.g., 3: 1 – 4: 13; 6: 1–18; 9: 27f; 10: 23–9), it is the cultic presentation of the work of Christ that begins to predominate from 2: 17.

Scholars continue to debate the question of precedents for our writer's high-priestly Christology and suggest different sources of influence on his thinking in this regard.[92] It may be that the title 'high priest' belonged to some fixed form of confession already known to the readers (cf. 3: 1; 4: 14), though I will argue in connection with 4: 14 that this is unlikely. If our writer was the first Christian explicitly to describe Christ in these terms, it must be remembered that there are several elements in other Christologies known to us from the NT that could have given rise to this particular presentation of the person and work of Christ. The idea of Christ as the heavenly intercessor (Rom. 8: 34; 1 John 2: 1f) may have been current already and inspired our writer to interpret Psalm 110: 1 in the light of the fourth verse of the psalm.[93] The idea of Jesus as Servant of the Lord may provide one of 'several converging elements that bring the author to see Jesus' death as a priestly act'.[94] The concept of Jesus as Son of Man has also been proposed as a source of this Christology, but the context (2: 5–18) does not lend the support to this theory that is claimed by its advocates.[95] It is specifically an Adam Christology that merges into the picture of Christ as the perfect representative of his people in a priestly ministry, making atonement for their sins before God. The theology of high priesthood and sacrifice becomes the means of explaining how Christ, as 'the leader who delivers them', can actually bring his people into the promised inheritance.

Moffatt observes that the key clause in 2: 10 receives further explanation in 2: 17f: 'The idea of τελειῶσαι in verse 10 is being explicitly stated; the sufferings of Christ on earth had a reflex influence upon himself as Saviour, fitting him for the proper discharge of his vocation. But the vocation is described from a new angle of vision; instead of ἀρχηγός or ὁ ἁγιάζων Jesus is suddenly called ἀρχιερεύς.'[96] In these verses there is a particular concern to draw out the implications of the expression διὰ παθημάτων (verse 10), not simply with reference to his redemptive death but also to 'the much wider range of human experience which constitutes an important preparation for the discharge of the instrumental aspect of his priesthood'.[97]

The parallel between verse 17 and verse 14 has already been noted, however, the κατὰ πάντα of 2: 17 seems to refer to Christ's becoming like men *in all the experiences of life*, whereas 2: 14 refers more specifically to *the adoption of human nature*.[98] The experiences of his incarnate life were designed to make him a 'merciful and faithful high priest'. Use of the adjective 'merciful' with respect to the high priesthood of Christ perhaps implies a strong contrast with contemporary counterparts in Judaism.[99] The stress here is on his experience of suffering and temptation, which makes him perfectly sympathetic to the needs of his people (verse 18 cf. 4: 15f). That same experience was the means by which he expressed his faithfulness to God (cf. 5: 7—9; 10: 5—10; 12: 2).[100] Vanhoye argues that the faithfulness of Christ in this context must mean he is worthy of absolute confidence on the part of his people.[101] This is certainly the stress in 4: 14—16; 7: 19, 25 and 10: 19—22, and it may be that we should allow the adjective πιστός to have a double meaning here.[102] Christ is the object of hope and confidence for believers because he faithfully fulfilled his God-given charge, even through suffering, and now continues faithfully to exercise a ministry of 'help' for them (verse 18).

Although verse 18 goes on to explore the theme of Christ's qualification in a personal sense to exercise a ministry of help towards those who are tested, verse 17 concludes with a description of his ministry in more conventional and technical priestly terms. The words εἰς τὸ ἱλάσκεσθαι τὰς ἁμαρτίας τοῦ λαοῦ mean 'to expiate the sins of the people, to rob them of their validity and significance before God'.[103] If (ἐξ)ιλάσκεσθαι in the LXX is 'directly concerned with removing sin, not with placating God',[104] it must be remembered that the sacrifices of expiation are 'directed towards placating the anger of God in this sense that, by removing sin, expiation removes what provokes God's anger'.[105] The expression in 2: 17 is a general description of Jesus' priestly function. In later texts the writer makes it clear that the means by which Christ atones for or expiates sin is his own self-giving in death (e.g., 7: 27). The victim is the priest himself, and this unity of the priest and sacrifice 'brings the old offering to an end, cf. 9: 12, 25'.[106]

In expounding the sacrificial work of Christ, our author insists on its unique and unrepeatable character (7: 27; 9: 24–8; 10: 10, 12, 14), in contrast to the numerous and repeated offerings prescribed by the Law. It is reading too much into the present tense of ἰλάσκεσθαι in 2: 17 to say that 'the one (eternal) act of Christ (10: 12–14) is here regarded in its continuous present application to men (comp. 5: 1–2)'.[107] Vanhoye has argued that it refers to 'an activity of the glorified Christ', and draws attention to the present infinitive ἐντυγχάνειν in 7: 25 as a parallel expression.[108] However, the present infinitive in 2: 17 most naturally refers to the sacrifice and offering of Christ, which is 'generally viewed in retrospect, with the employment of the aorist tense', but in 2: 17 is viewed 'in prospect'.[109] The writer speaks of the necessity for Christ's incarnation so that his self-offering for sins could take place. In 2: 18 he moves on immediately to discuss the practical help that Christ is able to give to 'those who are tempted'. This help clearly includes the expiation of sins or 'mercy' (4: 16) for those who have fallen, but the emphasis on Christ's own practical experience of temptation suggests that the help includes strength to stand firm in the face of temptation.

The words ἐν ᾧ γὰρ πέπονθεν αὐτός, which connect verse 18 with verse 17, give support to the interpretation offered above. The idea of making expiation for the sins of the people by his death recalls the suffering associated with that death (verses 9, 10). However, the stress is now on the fact that the suffering of Jesus – whether in prospect or actual experience – was the source of temptation for him (πειρασθείς).[110] Our writer does not mean that Christ 'suffered by his temptations' but rather that his sufferings were the particular source of temptation for him:

'The aorist participle πειρασθείς has a causal force and assigns the temptation-aspect of his sufferings as the ground for his ability to succor. It is not the memory of suffering in general that evokes his sympathy: the thought is much more concrete and specific: the sufferings which he had behind him and carries with him as a past experience (notice the perfect tense πέπονθεν) enable him to know what force of temptation suffering exerts to make the sinner fall. His mercy thus grasps the sufferer in his moral capacity, in the very crisis where suffering threatens to issue into sin or actually issues into the same.'[111]

Further discussion of the way in which Christ helps his people when tempted will be presented in connection with 4: 14–16 and 7: 25. The situation of the readers will be examined more closely in my concluding chapter. Here it may be noted that they appear to have been tempted to withdraw from explicit identification with Christ for fear of the hardships involved, in particular the prospect of further suffering (10: 32–9; 12: 1–13). Riggenbach appropriately draws attention to the parallel between the situation of the readers and that of Christ in his earthly ministry, a parallel implied by 2: 18: 'as the readers are tempted through suffering to disassociate themselves in despair and unbelief from Christ, so also Jesus has been tempted through suffering to give up his calling as Redeemer and abandon obedient submission to the will of God (5: 8)'.[112] If there is truly an apologetic thrust in what the writer has to say about the death of Jesus in verses 9–10, a similar tendency may be observed here too. As Riggenbach puts it: 'just the very thing which was objectionable to the readers in the person of Jesus, namely his suffering of death, has qualified the Lord to be the proper helper for them in their situation of suffering'.

The concept of perfection

I am now in a position to provide a detailed examination of the words διὰ παθημάτων τελειῶσαι in their context. In the preceding chapter, Kögel's contention that τελειοῦν is 'a general term, without distinct content' was shown to be an exaggeration. In the usage of certain writers, it has acquired moral, cultic or eschatological associations, making it almost a technical term. Nevertheless, the formal use of this verb predominates throughout the literature and has clearly given rise to specific applications in particular contexts. The very diversity of possible applications suggests the correctness of Kögel's methodology for the interpretation of this verb in a given passage: only the context in general and the object of the verb in particular can indicate the meaning on each occasion.

Observing that Jesus is the object of this verb in his role as τὸν ἀρχηγὸν τῆς σωτηρίας αὐτῶν, Kögel asserted that Jesus' person as such was not perfected but rather his 'quality as mediator of salvation' (*Heilsmittlerqualität*).[113] The use of τελειοῦν in what may be called a 'vocational' sense has been illustrated in the preceding chapter[114] and is adopted by a number of modern commentators in connection with the usage of Hebrews. Christ is 'qualified',[115] or 'made completely adequate',[116] as 'the leader who delivers them' (2: 10), as 'the author of eternal salvation' (5: 9), and as 'Son', appointed 'priest for ever after the order of Melchizedek' (7: 28). However, critics of Kögel have rightly drawn attention to his rather arbitrary exclusion of any idea of moral or inner development on the part of Christ. The extent to which the writer envisages some personal development in Christ is a vexed issue and will be discussed in connection with 5: 7–9, where it seems most appropriate. However, even in the present context, the hint of such a process is given with the words διὰ παθημάτων and in 2: 18. Kögel was only willing to speak of the suffering and temptation of Christ as being necessary for *the beneficiaries of salvation*, so that Christ might gain 'a full understanding' of their situation.[117] I will argue that these experiences were thought by the writer of Hebrews to be more significant *personally* for Christ.

Du Plessis speaks of 2: 10 as radiating a 'personal qualitative sense, firstly as far as vocational aptitude is concerned and secondly in relation to moral and spiritual capacity'.[118] To make such a statement about this particular verse is probably to anticipate too much the perspective of later verses, though in the final analysis it seems a well-balanced assessment of the writer's total perspective on the perfecting of Christ. The qualifications for priesthood discussed particularly from 4: 14 to 5: 10 include the necessity for the *person of Christ* to be prepared for his salvific ministry. Only with this in view can the conclusion of G. Vos be endorsed, that τελειοῦν 'always designates that (Christ's) qualifications for the high-priestly office were perfected, that he received the full-orbed equipment which his priestly ministry requires'.[119]

If we assume that τελειοῦν is being used in 2: 10 in a vocational sense, the context gives a very broad perspective on what that perfecting involved. In the first place, it must have something to do with his ascension and enthronement as the one 'crowned with glory and honour', destined to rule over all in 'the world to come' (verses 5–9). In the second place, it must include 'the suffering of death', which is the ground of his exaltation (verse 9), the means by which he robs the Devil of his power and delivers his people from 'lifelong bondage' (verses 14–15), and the means by which he expiates the sins of the people (verse 17). Finally, it may be seen to involve his whole incarnate experience, by means of which he became 'a merciful and faithful high priest' (verse 17), but particularly his suffering, which equipped him to help those who are similarly tested. Commentators who emphasise one of these elements at the expense of the rest are not doing justice to our writer's concept of the perfecting of Christ.

Kögel, for instance, went on to identify the concept of perfection with that of glorification, and this position is reflected in a number of more recent approaches to Hebrews. Riggenbach argued for the essential identity of τελειῶσαι and ἄγειν εἰς δόξαν from the connection of verse 10a with verse 9, where Christ is said to have been 'crowned with glory and honour because of the suffering of death'. He also observed that perfection in 5: 9 and 7: 28 is contrasted with 'the weakness of the flesh' and 'the necessity for development and suffering that goes with it'.[120] In dealing with 2: 18 and 5: 9 he gives due attention to the role of suffering in the preparation of Jesus for his heavenly high-priesthood — 'without this Jesus would not have been qualified for the special office of the high-priesthood' — but still concludes (in the light of 2: 10) that the writer's emphasis is on 'the resurrection from death, ascension and resultant exaltation of the Lord in the situation of perfect life and final achievement of his destination'.[121]

Pursuing his interpretation of Hebrews in terms of the Gnostic Redeemer myth, Käsemann also stresses that Christ is made perfect by attaining heaven: his perfection is 'a restored, qualitative transformation of his being, in which the sphere of humiliation is left behind. The one who is perfected is he who is transferred back into heaven as he originates from heaven.'[122] A. Cody, without any thesis of Gnostic influence on the thought of Hebrews, makes much of the writer's dualism between the heavenly and the earthly, the perfect and the imperfect, and defines the perfection of Christ as the 'raising of the humanity of Christ to the celestial plane of existence where it can completely enter into the glory and privileges which the divine nature enjoys in strict eternity ... Christ as man is made completely perfect ($\tau\acute{\epsilon}\lambda\epsilon\iota\sigma\varsigma$) when he reaches his celestial term ($\tau\acute{\epsilon}\lambda\sigma\varsigma$) and is glorified in heaven.'[123]

The importance of Christ's ascension for the establishment of his heavenly high-priesthood is certainly stressed by our writer in his chapters 7 to 9, and a detailed treatment of this subject will be presented when dealing with that section. In the present context, Jesus' exaltation is important on several counts. It places him in that position of authority and power by virtue of which everything is put 'in subjection under his feet' (2: 8; cf. 10: 12f). The crowning with glory and honour also marks the universal efficacy of Christ's death, as I have argued in connection with the final clause of 2: 9. Much of the argument of Hebrews 7–9 is a development of this theme in the unusual imagery of the cult, in which Christ is high priest 'for ever'. Finally, as the ascended 'leader who delivers them', Christ is able to lead believers to glory (2: 10) and give them a share in 'the world to come' (2: 5), over which he rules.

For all that, it is misleading to place the emphasis on Christ's exaltation to the heavenly sphere *per se* as the means by which he is essentially qualified or perfected. The statement that he was perfected $\delta\iota\grave{\alpha}$ $\pi\alpha\theta\eta\mu\acute{\alpha}\tau\omega\nu$ suggests that suffering was *part of the process by which he was perfected*, not merely a preliminary to it or the ground of it. The $\delta\iota\grave{\alpha}$ $\pi\alpha\theta\eta\mu\acute{\alpha}\tau\omega\nu$ of 2: 10 is not simply synonymous with the expression $\delta\iota\grave{\alpha}$ $\tau\grave{o}$ $\pi\acute{\alpha}\theta\eta\mu\alpha$ $\tau\sigma\tilde{v}$ $\theta\alpha\nu\acute{\alpha}\tau\sigma\tilde{v}$ of 2: 9. The use of $\delta\iota\acute{\alpha}$ with the accusative in verse 9 stresses that the suffering of death was the *ground* of Christ's exaltation, whereas the genitive with the preposition in verse 10 stresses that suffering was something *through* which Christ had to pass. The singular $\pi\acute{\alpha}\theta\eta\mu\alpha$, with the qualifying τοῦ θανάτου, probably refers 'not to sufferings as a special form or accompaniment of the death of Jesus but to the suffering which consists in death',[124] but the plural παθημάτων seems to reflect a broader perspective.

In 5: 7f, Jesus' suffering includes at least the events in Gethsemane. The hostility that Jesus is said to have endured against himself (12: 3) was certainly a form of suffering and cannot be restricted to the actual process of crucifixion. It is clear that in 9: 26 and 13: 12 the focus is on the redemptive achievement of Christ's suffering, and yet there is a parenetic thrust in the writer's choice of language in 13: 12, made explicit by the following verse.[125] His emphasis is not simply on the fact that Jesus died a shameful death 'outside the city' but that he 'suffered' there: the writer 'naturally dwells on the painful condition by which the triumph was prepared because he wishes to encourage his readers to endurance in suffering'.[126] The attempt of Michaelis to limit 5: 8 and 2: 18 'exclusively to the death of Jesus'[127] is unnatural and disregards the parenetic aspect of our writer's presentation of the suffering of Christ (cf. 12: 1ff). I thus conclude that the expression 'through sufferings' (2: 10) has in view the whole experience of suffering associated with and leading up to the death of Jesus.[128]

That Christ's perfecting involved at least his death, in addition to his heavenly exaltation, may be argued from another point of view. Christ's sacrifice and entrance into the 'heavenly sanctuary' are considered as different facets of the one redemptive action, in the later presentation of his work as high priest (9: 11f, 24–8; 10: 12–14, 19f). Although the title 'the leader who delivers them' is not sacerdotal and τελειῶσαι cannot be interpreted simply in terms of his 'consecration' to heavenly high priesthood, later exposition of the work of Christ in cultic terms illustrates the sense in which he fulfils his vocation. As heavenly high priest he is able to save absolutely 'those who draw near to God through him', since he always lives to apply the benefits of his once-for-all sacrifice to the needs of his people.[129] The title ἀρχηγός belongs to the imagery of redemption from bondage, exodus and journey to the promised 'rest'. In terms of this imagery, we are told that Christ has secured a redemption from transgressions, which enables 'those who are called' to receive 'the promised eternal inheritance' (9: 15). Only by virtue of his atoning death is he the leader of his people to heavenly glory. The perfecting of Christ as 'the leader who delivers them' involves the completion of his redemptive sacrifice as well as his transfer to God's right hand.

Such a perspective is lost if our writer's use of τελειοῦν is interpreted in terms of 'a restored, qualitative transformation' of Christ's being or of 'the raising of the humanity of Christ to the celestial plane of existence'.

Although such metaphysical and theological inferences are not inconsistent with our writer's presentation of the person and work of Christ, it cannot be argued that this is the essential framework of his thinking. The glorification of Christ in 2: 5–10 is presented primarily in terms of his achieving the *dominion* over all things promised in Psalm 8 and thereby enabling many sons to share in that eschatological rule. Our writer does not focus on the changes involved in the 'being' of Christ so much as on the consequences of his redemptive achievement and exalted status for his pilgrim people.

M. Silva relates the perfecting of Christ to the concept of 'the Son' – 'what Jesus is and always has been *by divine nature*' (1: 2) – inheriting the messianic title 'Son' (1: 4ff) and all that goes with it.[130] This theme seems to be present in 7: 28 ('a Son perfected for ever') and I shall have occasion to deal with it more thoroughly in exegeting that verse. However, Silva restricts the perfecting of Christ to 'some type of change *in his human nature*': 'at the resurrection Christ *became* life-giving Spirit (1 Cor. 15: 45) and received the exalted sonship which is the crown of his messianic work'.[131] Apart from the fact that Christ's resurrection *per se* does not figure so centrally in our writer's thinking, Christ's inheritance of 'the name' depends as much on his making purification for sins as on his ascension—enthronement (1: 3). The Son's eschatological inheritance could not be secured nor his Sonship decisively manifested for the salvation of his people until he had carried out the earthly ministry destined for him as Messiah.[132] The perfecting of the Son involved both suffering and exaltation and is not simply to be identified with the latter.

Our contention is that the vocational understanding of the perfecting of Christ is the only interpretation that allows for all the dimensions in our writer's presentation. In 5: 7–9 the personal qualification of Christ as his people's Saviour and high priest is connected with his learning obedience through suffering and a similar focus on the importance of his suffering and temptation is reflected in 2: 18 and 4: 15f. In other passages the focus is on his death alone, viewed as the redemptive event that destroys the Devil's power over death (2: 14f) and provides the perfect sacrifice for the 'sanctification' of his people (7: 27; 10: 5–10; 13: 12). In some passages the entrance of Christ into the heavenly sphere is given as the basis for confidence in him, because this makes him both a perpetual mediator in the presence of God himself (4: 14ff; 7: 16–26) and the forerunner of his people (6: 19f). A final group of passages emphasise both death and exaltation as the means by which Christ meets the needs of his people (9: 11–14, 15–26; 10: 12–13, 19–21). If the perfecting of Christ is his qualification to act as Saviour and high priest of his people, it is clear that our writer envisages *a whole sequence of events* as equipping him to act in this way. Michel has achieved the proper balance when he concludes that the perfecting of Christ describes 'his proving in temptation, his fulfilment of the priestly requirements and his exaltation as Redeemer of the heavenly world'.[133]

The cultic understanding of perfection is clearly related to what I have more broadly designated the vocational. John Calvin seems to have been particularly influenced by the proximity of ἀγιάζειν (2: 11) to render τελειῶσαι in 2: 10 by *consecrare*. He comments:

'as the word τελειῶσαι which (the writer) uses is of doubtful meaning, I think it clear that the word I have adopted is more suitable to the context. For what is meant is the settled and regular way or method by which the sons of God are initiated, so that they may obtain their own honour and be thus separated from the rest of the world; and then immediately sanctification is mentioned.'[134]

A number of commentators in this century have developed similar arguments, adding the apparently significant use of τελειοῦν in the LXX and early Christian literature as support for a cultic interpretation.[135] In the preceding chapter it was argued that the use of this verb in the expression τελειοῦν τὰς χεῖρας cannot be taken as an indication that the verb in Hebrews means 'to consecrate'. Parallels with early Christian literature were also discounted: cultic use of this verb is late and rare. It is especially surprising to note how Du Plessis attributes a sacral—cultic character to this verb, 'despite the crucial doubt that τελειοῦν was technically applied, or that it functioned as (*sic*) stereotyped expression for initiation and sacred consecration'.[136] Since he rejects all Gnostic and mystical associations for this verb in Hebrews, the only basis for his assertion is 'a passage like Lev. 21: 10, where the verb alone, without the addition of τὰς χεῖρας expresses the inauguration (of the priests)'. This single example is a very weak base on which to build such an argument, as I have shown.[137] Du Plessis then goes on to assert that 'the motif of consummation in respect of vocational qualities does not merely supersede but subsumes the character of consecration'.[138]

Even allowing for the possibility that the verb could have a technical, cultic meaning, there are few indications in the context that this was our writer's meaning. Although the concept of Christ as 'the leader who delivers them' may be related to the writer's concept of Christ as high priest, and the exposition soon moves into a cultic presentation of the person and work of Christ (2: 17f), the focus in 2: 5—16 is on Christ as the Man of Psalm 8 who restores to man his dominion over all things and as the

Saviour who opens the way into 'the world to come' or 'glory'. It seems that the writer was concerned to set his christological and soteriological discussion within the framework of traditional apocalyptic images and expectations and to make his cultic interpretation of the person and work of Christ arise from this. Hints of that cultic perspective are given in 1: 3; 2: 11 and in the picture of Christ leading the worship of God in the congregation of his brothers (2: 12). Nevertheless, it is my contention that these are not sufficient to demand a cultic understanding of perfection in 2: 10.

Commentators who point to the proximity of ἁγιάζειν in 2: 11, also point to the apparent equation of perfection and sanctification or consecration in 10: 14 ('he has perfected for all time those who are sanctified'). However, I will argue in connection with the latter verse that the terms are not simply synonymous in our writer's usage.[139] The perfecting of believers certainly involves a definitive consecration to God by means of the sacrifice of Christ but seems to go *beyond the idea of consecration to embrace the concept of glorification.* The verb ἁγιάζειν is never used in Hebrews with the sense of consecration to priesthood but more generally with reference to the establishment of New Covenant relations between God and man.[140] This is something Christ achieves *for others* by his sacrifice (10: 10, 14, 29; 13: 12), not something he is ever said to need for himself. The parallelism between the perfecting of Christ and the perfecting of believers cannot simply be drawn in terms of their need for consecration.

The attempt to establish that perfection means consecration to priesthood, by comparing 2: 10f with the language of the Fourth Gospel,[141] must also be rejected. John never speaks of the perfecting of Christ but only of the perfecting of the work given to him by the Father (4: 34; 5: 36; 17: 4, and cf. 19: 28, 30). Hebrews goes further in speaking of the personal perfecting of Christ 'through sufferings'. There is no cultic application of τελειοῦν in John, though the self-consecration of Christ in 17: 19 ('for their sake I consecrate myself, that they also may be consecrated in truth') is sometimes given sacerdotal significance.[142] Hebrews never explicitly describes Jesus' self-offering as a consecration of himself to God. This may be implied in 9: 14 and 10: 5–10 and may therefore be related to his perfecting. Nevertheless, it is the Father who perfects Christ in 2: 10 and the passives in 5: 9 and 7: 28 suggest a similar perspective: the perfecting of Christ involves more than his obedient self-consecration to the Father's will. A closer parallel to 2: 10 might be John 10: 36, where the Father is said to have 'consecrated' the Son and sent him into the world. Here 'the whole mission of Jesus, not his death only, is in mind',[143] and the LXX usage of ἁγιάζειν with regard to the setting apart of prophets for their mission (e.g., Jer. 1: 5; Sir. 45: 4) provides us with a more appropriate background than the sacerdotal application. However, John 10: 36 refers to an action of the Father prior to the incarnation, whereas Hebrews 2: 10; 5: 9 and 7: 28 refer to a process that included the earthly sufferings and death of Jesus as well as his exaltation to the heavenly sphere.

Conclusion

The vocational understanding of the perfecting of Christ is the only interpretation that allows for all the dimensions in our writer's presentation. Adopting the rendering 'to qualify' or 'to make completely adequate' for τελειῶσαι in 2: 10, I have shown how much of this passage is concerned to explicate the meaning of this concept, with respect to Christ as 'the leader who delivers them'. It was necessary first that he identify with those he came to save in a real incarnation ('for a little while made lower than the angels'). This enables him to 'taste death for everyone' and through death, not only rob the Devil of his power over death and liberate men from the fear of death, but also open the way into the world to come. Through his death and exaltation the 'many sons' can now share in the glory that is his.

The transition to the presentation of the work of Christ in high-priestly terms at 2: 17 is highly significant. The incarnation is necessary that he might become 'a merciful and faithful high priest', expiating the sins of the people by his death. At the same time, through his experience of being tempted by suffering to abandon the will of God, he is qualified to help his people in similar situations. These verses and subsequent development of the themes they announce provide a further explanation of the perfecting of Christ. That perfecting involved a whole sequence of events: his proving in suffering, his redemptive death to fulfil the divine requirements for the perfect expiation of sins and his exaltation to glory and honour. Thus perfected or qualified, he not only provides his brothers with the promise of sharing in his glory, but also continues to provide them with the necessary help to persevere in their calling and reach their heavenly destination.

4

THE PERFECTING OF CHRIST: HIS EARTHLY STRUGGLE

Further study of our writer's teaching on the perfecting of Christ requires me to examine in some detail the whole section from 4: 14 to 5: 10. It is true that the subject with which I am concerned is only explicitly dealt with in 5: 7–10, but the relationship between these verses and the preceding section (4: 14 – 5: 6) is such as to demand careful exegesis of the whole.

The significance and structure of 4: 14 – 5: 10

Vanhoye's criteria for establishing the structure of Hebrews lead him to propose that the second main section of the argument ('Grand-prêtre fidèle et miséricordieux') begins at 3: 1 and proceeds to 5: 10 as follows: the theme of Jesus as 'faithful' is developed in 3: 1 – 4: 14 and that of Jesus as 'merciful high priest' in 4: 15 – 5: 10.[1] The former section involves an exposition of the fidelity of Moses and the fidelity of Jesus (3: 1–6) and parenesis based on Psalm 95 (3: 7 – 4: 14) to encourage the readers to imitate the faithfulness of Jesus and thus reach their heavenly destination. Here, as elsewhere, it may be argued that Vanhoye's distinction between 'exposé' and 'parénèse' is too precise and artificial since the whole of chapters 3–4 involves an intricate combination of both.[2] The presentation of the theme of Christ the merciful high priest is said to begin with parenesis (4: 15–16) and proceed to exposition (5: 1–10).

Although there is some agreement amongst the commentators as to the division of these chapters on such lines, there is disagreement as to the exact point at which the section begins. Vanhoye proposes that 3: 1 – 4: 14 forms an 'inclusion', with 4: 14 recalling the language of 3: 1 and providing a perfect 'conclusion–transition'. Most commentators and the EVV, however, indicate that the literary unit ends at 4: 13, with the next section beginning at 4: 14.[3] It must be acknowledged that 4: 14 forms such a perfect bridge between the two main themes of our section that we cannot confidently assert whether the writer intended this verse to be the conclusion of one theme or the beginning of the next. For our purposes, this verse will be considered as the beginning of the section I am to examine in detail.

The function of 4: 14–16 as a recapitulation is particularly noted by Spicq: 'it is an explicit conclusion (οὖν) of the doctrinal theme on the priesthood of Christ set forth in 2: 17 – 3: 1 and of the exhortation to faithfulness pursued to 4: 11 – κρατῶμεν τῆς ὁμολογίας (cf. 3: 1)'.[4] However, the importance of these verses as an introduction to the new paragraph (5: 1–10) must not be overlooked: Christ's ability to sympathise, his experience of human weakness and his testing through suffering are highlighted there.

Exegesis of 4: 14 – 5: 10

(a) Challenge to respond appropriately to the high priesthood of Christ (4: 14–16)

Although much remains to be explained about the nature of Jesus' priesthood and his qualification to act in this capacity, enough has been said already to warrant the challenge of 4: 14–16. The previous exhortation to 'consider Jesus' as 'the apostle and high priest of our confession' (3: 1) is taken up and developed, with particular focus on the latter element. The exhortation of 10: 19–25, which concludes the detailed exposition of Christ's priesthood and sacrifice in 7: 1 – 10: 18, is remarkably parallel to 4: 14–16 and may be considered as a further development of the preliminary challenge. Indeed, these two exhortations (4: 14–16; 10: 19–25) form a sort of inclusion to the central theological argument of Hebrews, and it is important for the exegesis of the intervening material to give detailed attention to the former at this stage.

In 3: 1 and 4: 14 Jesus is described as the object of Christian ὁμολογία (cf. 10: 23). It has become popular to view the usage of this word in Hebrews as quite technical. Thus, Michel proposes:

'the ὁμολογία of Hebrews is a firmly outlined, liturgically set tradition by which the community must abide. We are to think of an ecclesiastical confession of faith or baptismal confession to which the hearers are already committed – the formula of divine sonship (4: 14, 6: 6, 10: 29) is frequently enough attested as the content of the baptismal confession – or possibly of a liturgy of praise which is connected with the various predicates of Christ (3: 1, 4: 14f).'[5]

G. Bornkamm goes so far as to identify the confession of faith mentioned in 3: 1; 4: 14 and 10: 23 with an alleged hymn in 1: 3.[6] V.H. Neufeld argues that the Christian's confession is a brief statement of what he confesses publicly — essentially that Jesus is Lord — and in form is a continuation of the Jewish *shema*.[7] Neufeld argues from 4: 14 that the confession known to readers was 'Jesus is the Son of God' and that the words 'apostle' and 'high priest' are 'not part of the content of the *homologia* but refer to offices mentioned in the author's comparison between Jesus and Moses'.[8] As to the *Sitz im Leben* of the confession, Neufeld argues that the concern of the writer is not with the original situation in which it was expressed — for example, at baptism or in worship — but with the necessity for the readers to 'cling to their faith as expressed in the *homologia*, which they once accepted and have openly declared'.[9]

The more cautious approach of Neufeld as to the content and *Sitz im Leben* of the confession in Hebrews is commendable in view of the sparsity of evidence. However, it may still be asked whether the evidence warrants even the assumption of a fixed formula or confession of faith.[10] At all events, I would endorse the conclusion of Westcott that the crisis faced by the readers 'claimed not simply private conviction but a clear declaration of belief openly in the face of men'.[11]

The great incentive for maintaining this confession of Christ is the fact that he is both 'Jesus the Son of God' and 'a great high priest who has passed through the heavens'. The call for an appropriate response to Jesus as 'the Son' has been stressed in 1: 5 — 2: 4 and the call for confidence in Christ as 'a great high priest' is anticipated in 2: 17 — 3: 1. However, the new element in 4: 14 — not elaborated until 6: 19–20 and 9: 11–14, 23–4 — is the assertion that the greatness of Jesus as high priest consists in his 'access to God, not through any material veil, but through the upper heavens; he has penetrated to the very throne of God in virtue of his perfect sacrifice'.[12] Michel rightly suggests that διεληλυθότα τοὺς οὐρανούς is a 'summary-term for ascension which comes from Apocalyptic and Gnosis' and οἱ οὐρανοί is not here simply 'heaven as the place of God, also not only a rendering of the Hebrew expression *šāmayîm* but the different layers of supernatural spheres which are situated between God and man, the holy place and earth'.[13]

Such emphasis on the transcendence of Christ suggests his remoteness from the problems of his people on earth and so the following verse anticipates such an objection by asserting that 'the perfectness of his sympathy is the ground for clinging to the faith which answers to our needs'.[14] Christ carries with him into that exalted sphere a genuine sympathy with the situation of his people, derived from his own earthly experience. It was argued above, in connection with 2: 10 and 2: 17f, that this is a major theme in the writer's presentation of the person and work of Christ and is central to his understanding of the perfecting of Christ. It is clear from what follows in 4: 15–16 and 5: 7–8 that the sympathy of Christ the exalted high priest is 'not simply the compassion of one who regards suffering from without, but the feeling of one who enters into the suffering and makes it his own'.[15]

Most commentators endorse the view that ταῖς ἀσθενείαις ἡμῶν in 4: 15 refers to the 'weakness with which sin is not necessarily connected though it may render human nature susceptible to temptation and sin'.[16] Although G. Stählin proposes that ἀσθένεια has almost the sense of sin in 4: 15, by analogy with 7: 28,[17] Westcott's analysis of the relevant texts is more careful. He acknowledges that in 7: 28 the expression ἀρχιερεῖς ἔχοντας ἀσθένειαν (*singular*) 'includes both the actual limitations of humanity as it is, and the personal imperfections and sins of the particular priest'.[18] Just as physical weakness and moral deficiencies in general are implied in 11: 34, so in 4: 15 the reference is to the general weakness of humanity. Jesus gave warning of this to the disciples during the testing experience in Gethsemane (Mk. 14: 38 = Matt. 26: 41 'The spirit indeed is willing, but the flesh is weak') and it is likely that our writer has a similar emphasis, particularly if Gethsemane is in view, when he illustrates Christ's experience of human weakness in 5: 7. Vos rightly suggests that Christ, like the readers, 'had been called upon "to hold fast the confession" when *the human ἀσθένεια consisting in the fear of suffering* tempted him to swerve from his appointed path'.[19]

That Christ experienced human weakness and the temptations arising from this source is confirmed by the following clause: πεπειρασμένον δὲ κατὰ πάντα καθ' ὁμοιότητα χωρὶς ἁμαρτίας.[20] However, much debate arises with regard to the exact meaning of these words. R. A. Stewart reminds us that 'the New Testament consistently attributes sinlessness to Christ, quite independently of the sacerdotal office' (2 Cor. 5: 21; 1 Pet. 2: 22; John 7: 18; 8: 46; 1 John 3: 5; cf. Matt. 3: 14; 19: 17) and that it is in Hebrews that 'the doctrine and the office are brought into juxtaposition'.[21] In searching for parallels, Stewart finds that 'Jewish literature did not and could not postulate any sinlessness in the mortal representative of the high priesthood.'[22] The hypothesis of direct borrowing from Philo is unlikely: 'the sinless high priest of Philo is really the divine Logos and something of an intellectual abstraction'.[23] On this same question, Michel notes how the righteous Messiah in the Targums sometimes bears priestly characteristics, but that he should be sinless 'is actually not expected. In general, there is no thought of a Messiah who surpasses human proportion.'[24] However, Michel demonstrates that the sinlessness of the Messiah and of his eschatological community is 'an established feature of the apocalyptic picture'.[25] Despite this last point, Michel's basic thesis is that the testimony of Hebrews about the sinlessness of Jesus is 'a distinct interpretation of the historicity of Jesus, which is indeed connected with the Synoptics but at the same time also interprets them'.[26]

The claim that Christ was tempted $\kappa\alpha\theta$' $\dot{o}\mu o\iota\dot{o}\tau\eta\tau\alpha$ may mean 'according to the likeness of our temptations',[27] but the NEB rendering 'in virtue of his likeness to us' seems preferable because it recalls the language of 2: 17f ($\kappa\alpha\tau\dot{\alpha}$ $\pi\dot{\alpha}\nu\tau\alpha$ $\tauo\hat{\iota}\varsigma$ $\dot{\alpha}\delta\epsilon\lambda\phio\hat{\iota}\varsigma$ $\dot{o}\mu o\iota\omega\theta\hat{\eta}\nu\alpha\iota$).[28] The words $\kappa\alpha\tau\dot{\alpha}$ $\pi\dot{\alpha}\nu\tau\alpha$ would seem to imply 'exempted of no human temptation',[29] and yet the testing of Jesus outlined in the Synoptic tradition is quite specifically related to his mission and, 'in the strict sense, "tempted as we are" (Heb. 4: 15) may not be substantiated' from that source.[30] In this connection, I have already argued in favour of the suggestion that Christ's temptations in Hebrews are viewed as specifically arising from his call to suffer in obedience to the will of his Father.[31] However, it is not necessary to limit the scope of $\kappa\alpha\tau\dot{\alpha}$ $\pi\dot{\alpha}\nu\tau\alpha$ on this basis: in both cases (4: 15; 2: 17f) the stress is on the reality of his humanity and the extent of his human experience. If the writer narrows his attention to the particular temptations experienced by Christ in the face of suffering, it is because the victory of Christ in this area was so vital for the achievement of salvation and because the writer is concerned to warn and encourage his readers about the danger of apostasy. The ability of Christ to sympathise and help *in their particular situation* is thus emphasised by concentration on a particular aspect of his earthly experience.

The problem that remains when we note how emphatically Jesus' humanity is asserted in Hebrews 4: 15 is expressed by one writer in this fashion: 'what seems implied by the phrase $\chi\omega\rho\grave{\iota}\varsigma$ $\dot{\alpha}\mu\alpha\rho\tau\acute{\iota}\alpha\varsigma$ contradicts this emphasis on the unimpaired genuineness of the humanity'.[32] A discussion of the meaning and implications of $\chi\omega\rho\grave{\iota}\varsigma$ $\dot{\alpha}\mu\alpha\rho\tau\acute{\iota}\alpha\varsigma$ for the doctrine of Christ's perfection is provided in Appendix A. Consideration is also given there to the related suggestion of some commentators that Christ had to offer for his own sins first and then for those of the people (7: 27; cf. 5: 3).

The challenge to 'draw near to the throne of grace' (verse 16) is based particularly on the presentation of Jesus' earthly experience in verse 15 and his consequent ability to 'sympathize with our weaknesses'. The verb $\pi\rho o\sigma\acute{\epsilon}\rho\chi\epsilon\sigma\theta\alpha\iota$ appears at a number of significant points in our writer's argument (4: 16; 7: 25; 10: 1, 22; 11: 6; 12: 18, 22; cf. $\dot{\epsilon}\gamma\gamma\acute{\iota}\zeta\epsilon\iota\nu$ 7: 19) and I will show how closely the concept is related to that of the perfecting of believers. Description of the Israelites in 10: 1 as $\tauo\grave{\upsilon}\varsigma$ $\pi\rho o\sigma\epsilon\rho\chi o\mu\acute{\epsilon}\nu o\upsilon\varsigma$

— those who approach God in cultic worship — recalls a common application of this verb in the LXX.[33] On the other hand, the use of the same verb in 11: 6, to describe a relationship with God in a more general and non-cultic sense, should warn us against the interpretation of this concept in Hebrews in purely cultic terms.[34] In 7: 25, the context indicates that the sense of a new relationship with God through the mediation of Christ is primarily in focus (cf. 7: 19). Nevertheless, such a definitive 'drawing near' to God is portrayed in terms of transformed cultic terminology: it is through the high-priestly mediation of Christ in his death and exaltation that one is enabled to enter the heavenly sanctuary of God's own presence. In 12: 18ff there is an extended contrast between the approach of the Israelites to God at Mt Sinai and the approach of Christians to God in the heavenly Jerusalem. The perfect tense in 12: 22 ($\pi\rho o\sigma\epsilon\lambda\eta\lambda\upsilon\theta\alpha\tau\epsilon$) would seem to locate this new approach to God at some decisive moment in the past, namely at their baptism or conversion.[35]

Viewed against this background, the present imperatives of 4: 16 and 10: 22 ($\pi\rho o\sigma\epsilon\rho\chi\omega\mu\epsilon\theta\alpha$) call for special comment. In both contexts the challenge is based on a statement of Jesus' high-priestly work, which leads to an opening of the heavenly sanctuary for men in a new way. Whether the 'throne of grace' (4: 16) is taken as 'the antitype, in our author's mind, to the "mercy seat" in the earthly sanctuary',[36] or simply as 'a Hebraic periphrasis for God himself',[37] the sense of the verb is much the same. The direct approach to God with 'confidence', which is the essence of the Christian position (12: 22ff), needs to be expressed continually as an ongoing relationship of trust and dependence (10: 22, 'with a true heart in full assurance of faith'). The particular need expressed in 4: 16 — to 'receive mercy' and find 'timely help' for running the Christian race — indicates the activity of prayer. In this case, $\pi\rho o\sigma\epsilon\rho\chi\epsilon\sigma\theta\alpha\iota$ has a special reference.[38] However, such prayer is to be understood as the means of expressing the reality of a relationship already existing through the mediatorial work of Christ. In 10: 22 the drawing near is not particularly related to prayer, though the context may indicate something like 'the reception of the gifts of salvation in the act of divine worship',[39] which may involve prayer.

The exhortation to draw near $\mu\epsilon\tau\alpha$ $\pi\alpha\rho\rho\eta\sigma\iota\alpha\varsigma$ confronts us with another key concept in our writer's presentation. Schlier has shown that in the Greek political sphere the word $\pi\alpha\rho\rho\eta\sigma\iota\alpha$ was used with three shades of meaning: the right of the full citizen to say anything in the city assembly, 'openness to truth' and 'the courage of openness, i.e., candour'.[40] In the private sphere it denoted candour and was especially used to describe the freedom of friends to speak the truth and not flatter one another. The LXX goes beyond the use of Hellenism in passages where it is stated that 'God gives the people παρρησία and that divine σοφία has παρρησία' or where there is reference to παρρησία towards God or to the παρρησία of God himself.[41] However, W. C. van Unnik has rightly cautioned that it is not a central idea in the religious terminology of the OT and 'there is no indication whatsoever that it directly influenced the NT usage, not even texts like Wisdom 5: 1 and 4 Macc. 4: 10'.[42] The NT uses the terminology more frequently than the OT and it is clearly a more important term in the usage of some writers.

In assessing the use of this word in Hebrews (3: 6; 4: 16; 10: 19, 35), we may observe again the parallel between the central exhortations of 4: 16 and 10: 22. Here, the way in which the readers are to draw near to God is 'with confidence' (4: 16) or 'with a true heart in full assurance of faith' (10: 22). The latter phrase indicates that what is required is both that 'openness which need not be ashamed when it stands before the Judge',[43] and that confidence in the promises of God and the achievement of Christ (10: 19–21), which alone can take away the fear of death and judgement (cf. 2: 14–15; 9: 27–8). We see specifically from 10: 19 that the confidence to enter the 'holy place' is 'by the blood of Jesus'. In both of these contexts, the idea of free access to God is associated with that of maintaining their Christian profession (4: 14; 10: 23), and in 3: 6 it is specifically said that the mark of a true Christian is to hold fast this confidence and maintain exultant hope. The challenge of 10: 35 not to 'throw away' this confidence assumes that the readers have this as a present possession and that it was manifested on a previous occasion, but that it is in danger of being discarded. Van Unnik's summary of the evidence in Hebrews is apposite:

> 'the "freedom of speech" has two sides: the free right to approach God, given in the sacrifice of Christ, which is the essence of the Christian faith, and the open confession of this faith, which is an unshakeable hope. These two sides are an inseparable unity. In the situation in which the Christians live they need it as a gift and a task.'[44]

Since λάβωμεν ἔλεος and χάριν εὕρωμεν are chiastically related to one another, the question may be raised as to whether 'mercy' and 'grace' should be distinguished from one another. While there is obviously an overlap in meaning between ἔλεος and χάρις as 'qualities and gifts of God',[45] the suggestion of Westcott and others that the former refers to 'mercy for past failures' and the latter to 'grace for present and future work' seems valid enough.[46] The phrase εἰς εὔκαιρον βοήθειαν ('for timely help')[47] suggests that 'the help comes when it is needed and not till then'. The help involved means more than mercy for past failures if the obvious connection with 2: 18 is made (τοῖς πειραζομένοις βοηθῆσαι). Michel observes: 'the help consists of this, that I accept the promise of the high priest who intercedes for me, who suffered for me — knowing that this word spoken for me, this sacrifice offered for me, is precisely what helps me in temptation.'[48] Accepting the validity of this explanation, I would add that our writer seems to imply more: although he has nothing comparable to Paul's teaching on the role of the Spirit as inner strengthener of believers (Gal. 5: 16–25; 2 Cor. 4: 13–18; Rom. 8: 26–7; Eph. 1: 19ff; 3: 14ff), the promise of strength from Christ to endure testing seems to be involved at 2: 18 and 4: 16.

(b) The qualifications for earthly high priesthood (5: 1–4)

Three times in the argument so far (2: 17f; 3: 1; 4: 14) Jesus has been described as high priest, but here in chapter 5 we have the first formal attempt to establish the validity of that assertion and describe the nature of his priesthood. The argument that begins here is taken up and developed in chapter 7, after the important challenge of 5: 11 – 6: 20. Most commentators note the chiastic arrangement in 5: 1–10, where the author compares the qualifications for earthly high priesthood (verses 1–4) with those of Christ for his high priesthood (verses 5–10).[49] However, the author does not simply present us with 'all the necessary conditions for being a high priest' in the first paragraph,[50] but rather focusses on certain features of human priesthood that are relevant to his exposition of the priesthood of Christ. The attempt of some writers to draw an exaggerated parallelism between the two paragraphs in 5: 1–10[51] will be criticised in the course of the exegesis.

The general description of high priesthood given in verse 1 places the emphasis on men being appointed to act on behalf of other men in 'matters pertaining to God' (τὰ πρὸς τὸν θεόν). The principal clause is καθίσταται τὰ πρὸς τὸν θεόν and this is further explicated by the ἵνα clause that follows. In contrast to the assertion of Moffatt that δῶρά τε καὶ θυσίας ὑπὲρ ἁμαρτιῶν is a 'generic term for sacrifices or offerings without any distinction',[52] it is probably more accurate to see δῶρα as a comprehensive term, including thank-offerings and food-offerings, and to see θυσίαι as sin-offerings in particular.[53] Nevertheless, it seems best to attach ὑπὲρ ἁμαρτιῶν to the verb or to view it as qualifying δῶρά τε καὶ θυσίας as a whole.[54] In other words, the clause as a whole places the emphasis on the expiatory role of the high priest.[55]

Thus, 5: 1 is reminiscent of 2: 17, with its assertion that high priesthood 'in matters pertaining to God' involves making expiation for the sins of the people. However, this does not justify the conclusion that the expression 'chosen from among men' (5: 1) means that the prime requisite for the priestly office is 'that of belonging to the human race',[56] by analogy with the opening words of 2: 17. The latter certainly indicates that the incarnation was essential for Christ to be qualified as a merciful and faithful high priest, but the clause in 5: 1 has a different function in the argument.

It is a common assumption, particularly among Roman Catholic commentators, that the perfection of Christ's priesthood lies in the union of the divine and human natures in his person. Consequently, he is said to have been consecrated priest at the moment of his incarnation. However, in Appendix B it is argued that such a line of reasoning goes beyond the evidence and the argument of the writer. In 5: 1 the expression ἐξ ἀνθρώπων λαμβανόμενος ὑπὲρ ἀνθρώπων is clearly subordinate, both grammatically and theologically, to καθίσταται τὰ πρὸς τὸν θεόν. This latter clause is then explicated in the following clause ('to offer gifts and sacrifices for sins'): the essence of the priest's mediatorial role is his atoning work. The writer's use of the expression 'chosen from among men' in 5: 1 is simply to be understood as a way of differentiating earthly priesthood – priesthood that has its locus on earth – from the heavenly high priesthood of the Son of God, already alluded to in 4: 14 and soon to be expounded in 5: 5–10. To put the emphasis on the union of the divine and human in the person of the mediator diverts attention from the centrality of *atonement* as the means of mediation between God and man. The centrality of Christ's death to the concept of his work as mediator is stressed in 9: 15. It is his perfect sacrifice that makes Christ the perfect high priest or mediator between God and man.

The emphasis of our writer on the experiences of Christ 'in the days of his flesh' (verse 7) is rather to be explained from a consideration of verse 2. Here, it is the ability of high priests to exercise their mediatorial role with a particular quality of restraint or moderation that is in focus. High priests should have this quality by virtue of their humanity, since they themselves are 'beset with weakness'. The Son of God had to be 'made like his brethren in every respect' (2: 17) in order to achieve a perfect sympathy with men in their weakness (4: 15) and then to offer himself as the perfect sacrifice for their sins.

The OT made no moral specifications for the role of the high priest, but it may be that our writer considered that the provision discussed in verse 3 – the necessity for the high priests to offer for their own sins – was designed in part to achieve that end. Insistence on the importance of this quality may arise also from our writer's observation of the *need* for such a quality in the Jewish system of priesthood. At all events, his main concern is to emphasise the sympathy that Christ now exercises towards his people (4: 15f; 2: 17f), a sympathy 'learned' through his earthly experience (5: 7f). In a sense, the writer's understanding of the ideal priesthood of Jesus has thrown new light for him on the pattern of ministry that ought to have been reflected in the priesthood of Jerusalem.

Most commentators draw attention to the sense of moderation implied by the word μετριοπαθεῖν, which occurs only here in the Greek Bible but is well-attested elsewhere. E.K. Simpson argues for 'to treat considerately' as the best, though inadequate rendering.[57] More recently E.J. Yarnold has reviewed the same evidence and come to the conclusion that it is best rendered 'to restrain or moderate one's anger'.[58] In this article, he specifically criticises those who treat this verb and συμπαθῆσαι (4: 15) as virtual equivalents.[59] A similar conclusion is reached by W. Michaelis, who describes μετριοπαθεῖν as 'closely related to the συμπαθῆσαι of 4: 15' but 'not identical': the picture in 5: 2 is that of the high priest aware of his own weakness and sin and therefore 'moderate in his (justifiable) displeasure and anger at the sins of the people'.[60] Moffatt also notices the rather limited quality of 5: 2 in comparison with 'the deeper idea that Jesus qualified himself by a moral discipline to be ἀρχιερεύς in a pre-eminent sense'.[61] Since Christ was 'without sin' he had no need to offer for his own sins first,[62] nevertheless his involvement in human affairs ('in the days of his "flesh"') was an involvement with human weakness, providing him with the necessary qualification for effective priesthood. Indeed, not only is he able to moderate his anger against sin, because of his truly human experience, but also more positively, able to express a true fellow-feeling (4: 15) with his people, providing them with timely help for perseverance in the Christian way (4: 16).

The suggestion that τοῖς ἀγνοοῦσιν καὶ πλανωμένοις is practically a hendiadys, giving the sense 'the people who go astray through ignorance',[63] is attractive because it recalls the OT distinction between 'unintentional sins' and sins committed 'with a high hand' (Lev. 4: 2; 5: 15; Num. 15: 22–31). The former were offences for which the priests could make atonement, but the latter put a person outside these provisions. That our writer has taken over and adapted this OT teaching is made clear when we consider the way he views the sin of apostasy (10: 26, ἑκουσίως. Cf. 6: 6; 3: 12).

The provision for the high priest's own sin-offering (verse 3) recalls the directions for the Day of Atonement ritual (Lev. 16: 6–17).[64] It highlights the difference between Christ and the priests of Judaism, so well described by Westcott: 'It is necessary that the true high priest should be able to sympathise with the *manifold forms of weakness from which sins spring*, as himself conscious of the nature of sin, but it is not necessary that he should actually share the feelings of sinners as himself having sinned.'[65] Any suggestion that Christ 'offers' for himself in the prayers and supplications of verse 7 and then for the people through his suffering (verses 8–9),[66] presses the parallel between Christ and the priests of Judaism too closely and reads too much into the προσενέγκας of verse 7. This is 'at most a subconscious echo of προσφέρειν in verses 1–3':[67] there is no equivalent in Jesus to the sacrifice offered by the OT high priest for his own sins.

The second qualification for authentic high priesthood is not a moral quality (as in verses 2–3) but involves the necessity for a divine calling (verse 4). Westcott points to the way this requirement is related to the preceding: 'of himself a man could not presume to take upon himself such an office. He could not draw near to God being himself sinful: still less could he draw near to intercede for others.'[68] The divine call in the case of the high priesthood of Christ, however, has to be established, not because there is a question of his fitness to draw near to God, but because a new order of priesthood seems to be implied.

(c) The qualifications for heavenly high priesthood (5: 5–10)

As suggested above, the words 'chosen from among men' (5: 1) have the particular function of focussing our attention for a moment on the role of earthly high priests. This is in preparation for the exposition of the high priesthood of 'Jesus the Son of God', who has 'passed through the heavens' (4: 14). The vexed question as to *when* Jesus became high priest is dealt with in Appendix B. Here it will be noted that the two psalm citations in verses 5–6 alert us to the fact that, despite the parallels soon to be drawn, Jesus' high priesthood is fundamentally of a different order from that of the levitical priests, discussed in verses 1–4.

There is clearly a vital connection in our writer's thinking between the titles 'high priest' and 'Son', and it may be that the linking of Psalm 2: 7 and Psalm 110: 4 here is meant to indicate that 'the position of divine Son carried with it, in some sense, the role of ἀρχιερεύς'.[69] Vanhoye rather plays down the significance of the first citation when he says it 'forms part of the periphrasis and designates God; the second citation, which alone speaks of priesthood, also alone constitutes the scriptural argument in favour of the thesis'.[70] The link between the two citations is Psalm 110: 1, which sets the priesthood 'after the order of Melchizedek' within the context of *enthronement*. The reappearance of Psalm 2: 7 at this point has the function of recalling the argument of 1: 1–13, with its emphasis on the absolute supremacy of the Son and the salvation he came to provide. In 1: 5, where the previous verses (verses 3–4) draw particular attention to the significance of Christ's enthronement, Psalm 2: 7 with its σήμερον γεγέννηκα is best taken as a reference to the manifestation of Christ's sonship at the *inauguration of his heavenly rule as Son*, through resurrection–ascension.[71] This interpretation is consistent with the enthronement setting of Psalm 2 itself and finds a parallel in Acts 13: 33, where Paul is said to have used it with reference to the resurrection.[72]

Spicq, on the other hand, argues for the moment of incarnation as the occasion when the Father makes this 'double declaration' of 5: 5f to his priest-Son.[73] In taking this line, Spicq is controlled by a theory of Christ's priesthood that I have already had occasion to criticise, namely the idea that Christ became a perfect mediator by union of his divine nature with that human nature which he acquired at the incarnation.[74] It is true that the Synoptic tradition applies Psalm 2: 7 to Jesus at his baptism (Mk 1: 11 par. and especially Lk. 3: 22 in Western texts) and at his transfiguration (Mk 9: 7 par.). Yet even Michel's suggestion that σήμερον refers to the 'totality of the messianic time of salvation' in Hebrews (3: 7 – 4: 7) and that the writer means that 'the Son's installation is expressed in different events' fails to give adequate stress to the enthronement setting of the citation in 1: 5.[75]

It is certainly important to notice that our writer assumes Christ to have been Son already during the period of his earthly ministry (1: 2; 5: 8): he does not imply that Christ was first raised to this status by his ascension–enthronement.[76] If Psalm 2: 7 is used in 1: 5 and 5: 5 with the latter event particularly in view, it will mean that our writer envisaged that event as inaugurating a new 'situation' for Christ, by virtue of his incarnation and sacrifice: it is now as the triumphant Man of Psalm 8 and messianic priest-king of Psalm 110 that he sits at the Father's right hand. The messianic connotations of Psalm 2 will therefore be in view. It was when he was enthroned as the Christ that his unique and essential relationship to God as Son was decisively manifested. God's plan was for the Son to enter into his inheritance through suffering and exaltation. In Appendix B it is argued that 'the crucifixion belongs to the high-priestly office of Christ as well as his present rule in the sanctuary. His office comprises both the penetrating movement of his saving action and the lofty calm of his constant giving.'[77] Just as the enthronement marks the consummation of his work as Messiah and the manifestation of his sonship, so it marks the consummation of his work viewed from a sacerdotal point of view and the manifestation of his heavenly high priesthood to all.

As Hebrews 7 shows, our writer is not content to establish the validity of Christ's high priesthood merely by citation of Psalm 110: 4. However, for the moment that suffices to indicate that 'Christ did not confer upon himself the glory of becoming high priest' (NEB). The one who addressed him as Son in Psalm 2: 7, designated him as high priest of an entirely new 'order' in Psalm 110: 4.[78] Since Psalm 110: 1 has already been used as a direct testimony to Christ, as the one enthroned at God's right hand (1: 13 cf. 1: 3), our writer could have used that text in connection with the fourth verse of the psalm to demonstrate the promise of heavenly kingship and priesthood for the Messiah. However, his preference for Psalm 2: 7 in connection with Psalm 110: 4 here seems to be governed by his preference for Son rather than Lord as the designation for Christ.

If 5: 5–6 takes up the issue of Christ's divine calling to be high priest corresponding to verse 4, 5: 7–8 appears to take up the question of that other quality for high priesthood discussed in verses 2–3. Just as 5: 5–6 implies a significant difference between Christ and the priests of Judaism, so also 5: 7–8 implies a sympathy with human weakness that surpasses the μετριοπαθεῖν of verse 2 and a perfect obedience to the will of God that requires him to make no sin-offering for himself. The writer is concerned both to compare and contrast the priesthood of Christ with the levitical system. Thus, the chiastic structure of 5: 1–10 is completed with a general description of Christ's function as high priest of a new order (verses 9–10), corresponding to the general description of the high-priestly role in verse 1.[79] However, as with the previous points of comparison, the superiority of Christ's achievement is stressed: once 'qualified' (τελειωθείς verse 9) he is able to provide *eternal salvation* to those who obey him.

A preliminary question with regard to the interpretation of verse 7, which actually has important bearing on particular details of exegesis in this section, is whether the Gethsemane scene alone is in focus or whether the wider experience of Christ is meant. The wider view may seem to be implied by the words 'in the days of his flesh', which may generally refer to 'the days in which he was subject to the weakness of the natural earthly life, and therefore had to conquer the dread of pain and death which is inseparable from this state'.[80] Furthermore, the words 'with loud cries and tears', which find no parallel in the Gospel records of Gethsemane, together with the general scope of the passage, may suggest 'the application of the words to other prayers and times of peculiar trial in the Lord's life'.[81] The third evangelist in particular pictures Jesus at prayer at critical moments in his ministry and gives us the impression that Gethsemane was the climax of a lifetime of commitment and rededication to the will of God through prayer.[82]

However, as far as we can tell, the pre-Gethsemane prayers of Jesus contained nothing like the prayer for the cup of suffering to be taken away which we find in Mk 14: 36, Matt. 26: 39 and Lk. 22: 42. The words πρὸς τὸν δυνάμενον σῴζειν ἐκ θανάτου are more than a periphrasis for God: they indicate the way in which Jesus approached God in prayer and the particular help sought.[83] The loud cries of Jesus on the cross (Mk 15: 34, 37 = Matt. 27: 46, 50) may also be in view, but it is doubtful that these involved prayer to be saved ἐκ θανάτου.[84] Only the Gethsemane traditions offer us a clear picture of Jesus under the dread of death and seeking escape from it.

It may be that the words 'with loud cries and tears' were added by our writer to bring out the full significance of this event for Jesus.[85] In this regard, he could have been inspired by the wording of Mk 14: 33, or the additions to the Lucan account found in some MSS (Lk 22: 43f), which emphasise the intensity of Jesus' agony in Gethsemane. On the other hand, it may be that our writer was informed of the incident in the garden by a source − oral or written − independent from our Gospel accounts.[86] Various attempts to uncover the alleged tradition or hymn underlying this section have been made, some of which are contradictory. In reviewing some of these theories, Michel concludes: 'more and more there emerges an ancient tradition about Christ, which Hebrews has taken over. It corresponds only partially with the report of the Gospels but has at the same time conspicuous peculiarities.'[87] The influence of various psalms, either directly on the presentation of our writer or on the tradition which came to him, has been proposed.[88] Thus, Strobel argues for the influence of Psalm 116 (LXX 114), which serves to 'illuminate and deepen the passion of Christ, because it is impressed with the martyrological content of the psalm'.[89] E. Brandenburger goes a step further in proposing that we have here the fragment of an early Christian hymn, based on the language of that psalm, in which the Hellenistic-Jewish Christian congregations 'recognized the history of their Lord'.[90] He argues that the use of Mk 14 as a basis for interpreting our verse has led to unwarranted historicising and psychologising.

While it may be legitimate to suggest some general influence of the language of the psalms on this verse, it is neither legitimate nor necessary to loose it from the Gethsemane situation, as Brandenburger has done. The words πρὸς τὸν δυνάμενον σῴζειν αὐτὸν ἐκ θανάτου and the words εἰσακουσθεὶς ἀπὸ τῆς εὐλαβείας, as I shall demonstrate, most particularly point to Gethsemane. Even though the writer speaks of Christ being tempted κατὰ πάντα καθ' ὁμοιότητα (4: 15), the particular way in which he illustrates this in 5: 7f focusses our attention only on one sort of temptation for Christ, namely the temptation to swerve from the will of God because of the suffering and anguish involved. Gethsemane is presented in the Synoptic Gospels and Hebrews as the supreme moment of testing for Christ in this regard. The extent to which our writer may have been influenced by John 12: 27f is dealt with below.

Although I have argued that the words πρὸς τὸν δυνάμενον σώζειν αὐτὸν ἐκ θανάτου point to Jesus' prayers in Gethsemane to be kept from the approaching suffering and death, there are some commentators who argue differently on the basis of the preposition ἐκ in that clause. Thus, G. Vos argues that Christ's prayers were:

> 'not that he might be saved from death but that he might be saved out of it; they were expressions of that obedience he was learning, not expressions of a mood of weakness he had to unlearn. For the writer adds that he was heard, he obtained what he prayed for, and this was not escape from death, but salvation through and out of death.'[91]

This comment is strange in the light of his previous assertion that Christ had to 'conquer the dread of pain and death'. He really plays down the humanity of Jesus that our writer aims to stress and fails to take account of the very real fear of death expressed by Jesus in the Gethsemane accounts. Furthermore, we must ask what evidence there is in the Gospel traditions for Christ praying to be saved 'out of death'.

Those writers who propose that Hebrews uses traditions independent from the Synoptic Gospels would not be troubled by such a question. Some argue for a closer link between Hebrews 5: 7 and John 12: 27f. Here the words πάτερ σῶσόν με ἐκ τῆς ὥρας ταύτης have a likeness to the words I am examining. Westcott suggests that the ἐκ indicates a petition 'for deliverance *out of* ... and not for deliverance *from* (ἀπό) the crisis of trial. So that the sense appears to be "bring me safely out of the conflict" (Heb. 5: 7), and not simply "keep me from entering it".'[92] Apart from the fact that ἐκ can be used where one might expect ἀπό and that there is overlap in the usage of these prepositions,[93] the context in John 12: 27f scarcely favours Westcott's reading: there is little point to the corrective clause following ('but for this purpose I have come to this hour') if the previous clause does not express a desire to escape from 'this hour'. Even if the words are taken as a prayer for preservation *from* the approaching crisis, J. Jeremias argues that they are replaced by another prayer for exaltation ('Father, glorify your name' verse 28 cf. 17: 5) and that this interpretation of the Gethsemane prayer lies before us in Hebrews 5: 7.[94]

If it is true, as Jeremias and others suggest, that the Johannine pericope sounds a more triumphant note than the Gethsemane narratives in the Synoptics, we may endorse the comment of E. Brandenburger that such a triumphant note is far from the 'loud cries and tears' of Hebrews 5: 7.[95] Yet, the Johannine pericope is not so different from the Synoptic tradition as may first appear.[96] In particular, the prayer for glorification of the Father's name is to be understood in the light of 7: 18 and 8: 50, rather than 17: 5: it is not a prayer for Jesus' exaltation to the Father's presence but a parallel to the Synoptic 'yet not what I will, but what you will.'[97] Thus, I would argue for the same two-stage presentation in John 12: 27f as in the Synoptics: Jesus prays for deliverance from the approaching crisis (even if John 12: 27 makes this a deliberative question and therefore only a contemplated wish), but then submits willingly to the Father's will. Hebrews 5: 7 shows awareness of these two stages or aspects to the prayer of Jesus. The offering of 'prayers and petitions, with loud cries and tears, to the one who was able to deliver him from death' corresponds to the first stage and the statement that 'because of his humble submission his prayer was heard' (NEB) corresponds to the second.[98]

The assumption that $\dot{\alpha}\pi\dot{o}$ $\tau\hat{\eta}\varsigma$ $\epsilon\dot{v}\lambda\alpha\beta\epsilon\dot{\iota}\alpha\varsigma$ means 'because of his humble submission' (NEB) or 'for his godly fear' (RSV) is not shared by a number of commentators, ancient and modern.[99] They take $\epsilon\dot{v}\lambda\dot{\alpha}\beta\epsilon\iota\alpha$ with the sense of 'fear, anxiety' and understand that Jesus was 'heard' in the sense that he was delivered from fear of death, rather than from death itself. O. Cullmann puts it this way:

> 'the whole context forces upon one the sense of ordinary human fear as the meaning of $\epsilon\dot{v}\lambda\dot{\alpha}\beta\epsilon\iota\alpha$. This is just what the *temptation* is. The $\dot{\alpha}\sigma\theta\dot{\epsilon}\nu\epsilon\iota\alpha$ of Jesus shows itself precisely in the fact that he was afraid, that he had the ordinary human fear of death! And he was heard because he conquered his fear when he prayed "not my will ...".'[100]

This interpretation certainly takes account of the attitude of Jesus recorded in the Synoptic Gethsemane accounts and John 12: 27 ('now is my soul troubled') and of our writer's emphasis on the full participation of Jesus in the weakness of humanity. However, if one takes this line of interpretation, it is well to note with Brandenburger that more than a creaturely fear of death will be implied: Jesus' fear was a fear of death as the 'place of expulsion and of God-forsakenness'.[101]

Nevertheless, there are difficulties with this position. H.W. Montefiore, who is one of its advocates, takes the whole phrase as a pregnant construction — 'and being heard (was set free) from fear' — but acknowledges that the phrase is cryptic and that 'Jesus' liberation from fear is only indirectly relevant to the main point of the sentence, which is that Jesus learnt obedience from his sufferings.'[102] We may indeed ask whether, in the light of his later use of Psalm 22: 1 (Mk 15: 34 = Matt. 27: 46), Jesus was in fact delivered from fear of death. P. Andriessen, another advocate of this sort of interpretation, acknowledges the difficulty with the brachylogy and proposes instead 'he was heard *after* having endured the anguish of death'.[103] He argues that there is a parallel use of ἀπό in 11: 34 (ἐδυναμώθησαν ἀπὸ ἀσθενείας) and says the provenance of the formula εἰσακουσθεὶς ἀπὸ τῆς εὐλαβείας is not the Gethsemane traditions but Psalm 22: 'the Psalmist and Christ have supplicated God, with great clamour, to save them from death, they have become resigned to their lot; "no response". Both have submitted to the anguish of death to the end. Afterwards, God heard them.'[104] Apart from the fact that Andriessen proposes a most awkward reading of ἀπό in this context, he has actually extended the meaning of εὐλάβεια from 'fear (of death)' to 'endurance of the anguish of death'. No parallels are offered to justify this extraordinary interpretation of εὐλάβεια.

Writers like Andriessen and Bultmann argue that 'anxiety' is the best rendering of εὐλάβεια in 5:7 and 12: 28, the only places in the NT where this substantive occurs.[105] The former even renders εὐλαβηθείς in 11: 7 'filled with fear before the imminent catastrophe' though Bultmann allows that it may mean 'reverent awe'. If, however, 'caution' or 'circumspection' is the basic meaning of this word-group, as Bultmann maintains, it is most natural to read the verb that way in 11: 7 (NEB 'took good heed').[106] Andriessen stresses that the words μετὰ εὐλαβείας καὶ δέους in 12: 28 must be interpreted in the light of the following verse ('for our God is a consuming fire'), which recalls the perspective of 10: 27—31 and 12: 18—21. However, this is to ignore the balancing effect of the opening words of 12: 28, which recall verses 22—4 and the *contrast* between the Israelites, full of fear at Sinai, and Christians who have drawn near with confidence to the heavenly Zion. Despite the certainty of their standing before God, emphasised in verses 22—4, 28a, Christians must go on heeding the voice that calls them from heaven (verses 25—7). Even though the writer warns of the judgement awaiting apostates, it is not anguish or anxiety he wishes to promote (such as Moses experienced verse 21) but circumspection or reverent awe, in response to God's grace and holiness, considered together.

Although the description of Jesus' prayers in 5: 7a recalls the anxiety and anguish of the Gethsemane scene and suggests that εὐλάβεια has that sense, I would argue that the writer is consistent in his use of this terminology and that 'reverent awe' or 'godly fear' is meant. In our view, this is

confirmed when one examines the relationship between the words
εἰσακουσθεὶς ἀπὸ τῆς εὐλαβείας and the following verse. J. Jeremias argues
that verse 8 is an inserted parenthesis that serves to explain the sense of
ἀπὸ τῆς εὐλαβείας. The sequence should then be translated: 'and was
heard because of his piety (although Son, he learned obedience in
suffering) and was brought to perfection'.[107] The relationship between
these verses has been a matter of some scholarly debate.[108] Bultmann
follows Harnack in suggesting that an original οὐκ has been dropped from
before εἰσακουσθεὶς.[109] Brandenburger, with a similar desire to give full
weight to καίπερ ὢν υἱός, proposes that the writer has imperfectly joined
one fragment of an early Christian hymn (verse 7) to the fragment of
another (verses 8–10).[110] However, the latter is not as distinct in 'language,
presentation-setting and theme' from verse 7 as Brandenburger argues. The
words ἀφ' ὧν ἔπαθεν take up the theme of Christ agonising in prayer, as he
anticipates the suffering of death, and the words ἔμαθεν ... τὴν ὑπακοήν
suggest the bringing of his will into submission to the will of the Father,
which is the measure of true piety (εὐλάβεια).[111] In repeating the twofold
emphasis of verse 7 — suffering and godly fear — verse 8 adds the startling
words καίπερ ὢν υἱός to remind the readers that the one in question is
none other than the one addressed by God as Υἱός μου (verse 5). The
apparent incongruity of these words is discussed below.

One of the arguments against the reading 'heard for his godly fear' is
the supposition that 'the hearing could then only consist in his deliverance
from death'.[112] Amongst those who adopt the sense of 'godly fear' for
εὐλάβεια, however, there is diversity of opinion as to the meaning of
εἰσακουσθεὶς. Some would say the answer to Christ's prayer was strength
to endure the bitter ordeal facing him.[113] Others would see this solution as
inadequate: 'the prayer was to be saved from death, and the hearing must
correspond to this; mere strengthening to bear death (Luke 22: 43) seems
to fall far below its meaning'.[114] Thus it is proposed that Christ was 'heard'
in the sense of being delivered from the final triumph of death by resurrection, though it has to be acknowledged that the answer to the prayer was
not quite as offered. R.E. Omark, on the other hand, argues that Jesus
needed saving from 'potential forfeiture of sonship, high priesthood,
saviourhood, messiahship: indeed eternal fellowship with the heavenly
Father!'[115] The answer to Jesus' prayer was salvation, 'not *from* temporal
torment and death, but *in* and *through* such a death *from* the infinite
failure and loss of saving Sonship and Messiahship. To go to death in saving
ministry for others meant security for himself. To avoid death was to miss
the achievement of his mission, and the forfeiture of his divine relationship.'[116]

Omark rightly stresses the two stages in the prayers of Jesus, reflected in Hebrews 5: 7f and in the Gethsemane traditions. Jesus pleads for escape from the sufferings and death awaiting him but then submits to the Father's will and interest: because of his godly fear, his 'prayer for salvation from death issued in the glory and victory of the Cross'.[117] Spicq has a similar suggestion, but without Omark's proposal that 'the ascent to the Cross became the Son's salvation': Christ was heard,

> 'not with respect to his immediate object, exemption from death, but with regard to his final and ultimate object ... agreement with the will of the Father, ἀλλ' οὐ τί ἐγὼ θέλω ἀλλὰ τί σύ (Mark 14: 36); Πάτερ, δόξασόν σου τὸ ὄνομα (John 12: 28). Thereby, moreover, Christ obtains deliverance from death in quite a superior form, resurrection (Acts 2: 27, 32), triumph over death.'[118]

Omark's discussion of the potential loss for Jesus takes us into the realm of speculation, but this does not destroy the value of his proposal that the glory and victory of the cross were the answer to Jesus' prayer for the Father's will to be done. E. Riggenbach similarly argues that the recipients of Hebrews would have known from their oral tradition what readers of the Gospels know today, that 'the greatest concern of the prayers of Jesus in Gethsemane was not for protection from the fate of death but perfect agreement with the divine will'.[119] It was Jesus' prayer *for the Father's will to be done* that was answered in the events that followed.

J. Jeremias has a similar argument, backed up by the suggestion that τελειωθείς in verse 9 explains εἰσακουσθείς in verse 7. However, he interprets the former as 'exaltation in perfection, crowning with δόξα and τιμή (Hebrews 2: 7)'.[120] It was argued in connection with 2: 10 that the limitation of Christ's perfecting to his crowning with glory and honour gives an inadequate perspective to our writer's use of this concept. Here too, although I have expressed agreement with the view that verse 8 is parenthetical, I would question the attempt to exclude from the concept of Christ's perfecting the process referred to in verses 7–8. In verse 7, our writer recalls the struggle of Jesus to do the will of God when the ordinary human fear of death and suffering, and the particular fear of death as the place of expulsion and God-forsakenness, tempted him to turn aside. When, in reverent awe, he submitted himself to the Father's will, his prayer was heard and answered in the death, resurrection and ascension—enthronement that followed. In verse 8, our writer draws out the significance of the previous verse: the process of learning to obey God in the face of suffering was necessary even for the Son. The τελειωθείς at the beginning of verse 9 explains that necessity in terms of his qualification to be 'the source of eternal salvation'. As in 2: 10, a process is in view, and it is not just the final events of death, resurrection and ascension that are comprehended by the concept. Precisely how that process of learning obedience through what he suffered was essential for his perfecting will be dealt with below.

The stark incongruity of the words καίπερ ὢν υἱός (verse 8) is only appreciated when one understands that 'Son' with a capital letter is the writer's intention: 'as applied to Jesus, υἱός means something special. As divine υἱός in the sense of 1: 1f it might have been expected that he would be exempt from such a discipline.'[121] It is true that, in one sense, 'the idea of sonship suggests that of obedience',[122] but the sonship of Jesus has been expounded in such a fashion in Hebrews 1 as to highlight the apparent incongruity of such words as 'he learned obedience through what he suffered' being applied to him. Deliberate emphasis on the unique and exalted nature of Christ's sonship, together with a stress on the reality of his humanity and earthly experience, is characteristic of our writer (1: 1–13; cf. 2: 5–18) and in 5: 8 he presents both themes in careful juxtaposition.[123] As indicated above, the reason for the Son's having to learn obedience through what he suffered is given in verse 9.

The formula ἔμαθεν ἀφ' ὧν ἔπαθεν already had a long history when it came to be used by the writer of Hebrews. In a full-scale analysis of this usage, J. Coste observes how the theme of ἔμαθον–ἔπαθον in Greek literature 'has been rather more developed in its negative and pessimistic aspect than in its positive aspect'.[124] When we turn to the OT, although we find the educative effect of suffering voiced in passages like Proverbs 3: 11f; 15: 5, 'chastisement is here a sign of love and it is as such that it appears as a good thing'.[125] In general, Coste concludes that the religious thought of Israel 'appears to have spontaneously preferred, instead of the profane idea of "educative" suffering, helping man to form himself a treasure of wisdom and experience, the religious notion of a suffering leading to the acknowledgement of God and invocation'.[126] In a detailed examination of Philo's use of the ἔμαθον–ἔπαθον theme, Coste shows how the Biblical and Greek perspectives are both in evidence.

Turning to Hebrews 5: 8, Coste concludes that the Christology of Hebrews as a whole will not allow us to interpret this expression in terms of the profane notion of 'educative correction'. There is no suggestion of an original imperfection in Christ that must be gradually overcome. Neither the OT nor Philo are said to provide sufficient help to explain the sense of the verse.[127] In the end, one must be struck by 'the irreducible originality' of Christ's experience: no previous human experience can suffice to explain it.

Although I would endorse in general terms Coste's conclusions about the originality of the verse, I would point to an important OT precedent. Particularly in the case of Moses, Elijah and Jeremiah, there emerges the concept of suffering in consequence of being a mediator. This teaching finds special expression in Isa. 50: 4–9, where the Lord's servant is represented as both learner and teacher and as one who willingly submits to suffering in the cause of his ministry. There are points of affinity with the laments of Jeremiah here but also significant differences:

> 'the cry of the mediator so passionately and wildly voiced by Jeremiah is silenced. Some radical change has come about, and a new factor entered into God's dealings with his chosen people – the lament of the mediator who is attacked and defamed because of his task here develops, for the first time, into assent to and acceptance of his suffering.'[128]

The theme of the Servant as willing victim in the face of unjust suffering is given its ultimate expression in Isa. 53 where there are clear pointers to 'an expiatory sacrifice as the explanation of the meaning of the Servant's suffering and death'.[129]

In Hebrews 12: 2f the theme of Jesus' enduring hostility against himself and then the cross, 'despising the shame', is presented. Again in 10: 5–10 the theme of Jesus' offering himself completely to do the will of God and thereby becoming 'a single sacrifice for sins' (verse 12) is found. If our exegesis of 5: 7 is correct, the same sequence of thought is present in 5: 7–9. Although fearful of death and its consequences, he willingly submits to the Father's plan and all that it involves, in order to become the unique source of eternal salvation (verse 9).[130] The language of 9: 28 appears to echo the actual wording of Isa. 53: 12, just as 7: 27 recalls the concept of the Servant making 'himself an offering for sin' (Isa. 53: 10).[131] If the cross is the focus of our writer's thinking with respect to the self-offering of Christ, it would seem from 5: 7f that experiences prior to the cross (notably Gethsemane) were designed to elicit and test the reality of that obedience which found its ultimate expression at Calvary.

Jesus' suffering in consequence of being a mediator has a unique, redemptive outcome. His learning obedience through the things he suffered must be related first and foremost to this: his sufferings were the means by which he could assent to and express obedience to the will of God for his life. At Gethsemane, 'he wrestles with and accepts the impending and climactic suffering of Calvary, and in doing so he completes the perfection of his obedience to the will of the Father'.[132] Commentators who seek to avoid any sense of 'an increasing capacity for obedience or of a developing maturity of Jesus for the fulfilment of his task',[133] are really applying limitations to the character and experience of Jesus which the NT itself does not require. On the other hand, apart from Lk. 2: 39f, 52, where his human development is described in similar terms to that of John the Baptist (1: 80), the NT shows little interest in this subject. There is no justification for saying, on the basis of the Gospel evidence, that Jesus needed divine chastisement for disobedience or that his character needed correcting through suffering. If Hebrews is considering the 'moral development' of Jesus, it is the development of one who could be uniquely judged without sin (4: 15) at every stage of his human life. Nevertheless, it is entirely consistent with the picture of Jesus' humanity in the NT to suggest that he was prepared for the ultimate act of obedience by the various experiences of suffering and temptation that came his way.

Coste suggests that the emphasis in 5: 8 is on the ἔπαθεν, rather than on the words ἔμαθεν ... τὴν ὑπακοήν, in accordance with the 'glissement sémantique' of ἔμαθεν–ἔπαθεν, which he claims is particularly evident in Philo's use of the word-play.[134] This tends to 'accentuate the idea of experience' and give ἔμαθεν the special sense of positive spiritual learning through experience. Coste is right to stress that our writer puts the emphasis on the positive learning experienced by Christ, rather than on the need for correction. However, in view of the close connection between verse 7 and verse 8, it is clear that ἔπαθεν involves specifically the physical and mental anguish leading up to, and associated with, Jesus' death.

I have already suggested that there was a need for Christ to *express* obedience to God in the context of the human situation: 'to bring into the conscious experience of action, that which is present as an avowed principle antecedent to the action. There is a difference between the desire and the resolve to obey and the carrying through of this attitude of mind in the concrete circumstances of life, whilst natural inclinations assert themselves in the opposite direction.'[135] As well as the redemptive aspect of his learning obedience, we may note the need for Christ to *experience* 'just what obedience to God involved in practice, in the conditions of human life on earth'.[136] Thus, Spicq writes of the necessity for Christ to 'display' the virtue of obedience 'in all circumstances, even to the point of heroism': Jesus thereby acquires 'an enriching psychological experience, a practical comprehension and an appreciation of suffering which was indispensable for him to sympathize as priest with those who are his brothers'.[137] Jesus needs to learn obedience through the things he suffers not only to effect the sacrificial aspect of his priestly ministry but also to enable him to administer its benefits sympathetically. The writer has prepared us for this perspective in 4: 14–16 and the chiastic structure of 5: 1–10 is designed to show how Christ is better qualified in this respect (verses 7–8) than the priests of Judaism (verses 2–3). It is not simply that Christ knows what it is like to be human and experience the difficulties of obeying God in the face of suffering and the temptation to forsake God's will. He can provide practical help for those who are similarly tempted and sympathetically administer the benefits of his once-for-all sacrifice to those who seek mercy (4: 16; 7: 25).

John Calvin writes of the need for Christ to habituate himself to obedience, as an *example* to his people:

> 'not that he was driven to this by force, or that he had need of being thus exercised, as the case is with oxen or horses when their ferocity is to be tamed, for he was abundantly willing to render to his Father the obedience which he owed. But this was done from a regard to our benefit, that he might exhibit to us an instance and an example of subjection even to death itself.'[138]

He gives some attention to the subjective effect on Christ himself, when he writes that 'Christ was by his sufferings taught how far God ought to be submitted to and obeyed', but he does not relate this to the συμπαθῆσαι of 4: 15.[139] The point he makes is that Christians should 'by his example be taught and prepared by various sorrows and at length by death itself, to render obedience to God'.[140] This perspective finds expression in 12: 1–11 and 13; 13, where the suffering of believers is specifically related to the experience of Christ.[141] That it was present in our writer's mind in 5: 9 may be suggested by the words 'to all who obey him' in association with the obedience of Jesus mentioned in verse 8. Here Calvin comments: 'if we then desire that Christ's obedience should be profitable to us, we must imitate him; for the Apostle means that its benefit shall come to none but to those who obey'.[142] That true faith is expressed in obedience, has already been implied by our writer in 3: 18f and 4: 6, 11.

The concept of perfection

A number of comments about the concept of perfection in this passage have already been made. However, it is now possible to examine more closely the meaning of τελειωθείς within its immediate context, drawing on the exegetical conclusions above.

The theme of Christ the merciful high priest dominates the section 4: 14 – 5: 10. The challenge of 4: 14–16 arises from preceding sections of the argument but also serves to introduce the new paragraph (5: 1–10) where the focus is on his qualifications for priesthood. The section as a whole begins with the announcement that Jesus is 'a great high priest who has passed through the heavens' (4: 14) and ends with the assertion that he was 'designated by God a high priest after the order of Melchizedek' (5: 10). It is not surprising, therefore, to find that commentators have given a cultic interpretation of τελεωθείς in this context.

Thus, Calvin renders the verb *sanctificatus* and argues that the ultimate end of Christ's suffering was that 'he might thus become initiated into his priesthood, as though the Apostle had said that the enduring of the cross and death were to Christ a solemn kind of consecration, by which he intimates that all his sufferings had a regard for our salvation ... he by his obedience blotted out our transgressions'.[143] It is certainly true that 5: 7f gives a picture of Christ consecrating himself to the will of God through suffering (cf. John 17: 19), though I have argued that this can hardly be restricted to 'the enduring of the cross and death'. It was noted in connection with 2: 10 that it is *the Father who perfects Christ*, and the passives of 5: 9 and 7: 28 suggest a similar perspective: the perfecting of Christ involves more than his own self-consecration to the Father's will. Furthermore, the linguistic basis for a cultic rendering of τελεωθείς is thin. It is more accurate to take this verb in the broader sense of vocational qualification and personal consummation, which 'does not merely supersede but subsumes the character of consecration'.[144]

In 5: 9, as in 2: 10, Christ is 'qualified' in his capacity as Saviour of his people. The description of his function in this case is 'source of eternal salvation',[145] which is not a sacerdotal expression but which picks up the imagery of 2: 5–16, with its emphasis on Christ as the leader of his people on the pathway to glory and unique deliverer by means of his death and heavenly exaltation. The statement that he was 'designated by God' in Psalm 110: 4 'a high priest after the order of Melchizedek' (5: 10) immediately indicates that Christ's achievement of eternal salvation is to be considered by the writer in sacerdotal terms (Hebrews 7–10). However, we are not compelled by this to give τελεωθείς a specifically cultic rendering.

Apart from the linguistic issue, our writer does not clearly pinpoint the *moment* when Christ 'became' high priest (see Appendix B), but commentators who press for the cultic interpretation of the verb tend to focus on a particular event by which he is said to have been consecrated. Thus, Dibelius lists seven characteristics of Jewish high priesthood from 5: 1–4 and seeks to show how parallels are drawn in each case with respect to Christ in 5: 5–10. This leads him to the erroneous conclusion that Christ's offering of prayers for himself (verse 7) corresponds to the sacrifice of the high priest for himself (verse 3) and that Christ's offering for the people is the subject of verse 8. Instead of taking verse 8 as a further explanation of the significance of verse 7, he limits the expression 'through what he suffered) to the death of Jesus and ignores the significance of 'he learned obedience'. In this context, τελειωθείς is said to refer only to 'the action which immediately precedes his entrance into the heavenly sanctuary, to the consecration of Christ'.[146]

There is a similar tendency to play down the sense of Christ's personal consummation on the part of those commentators who press for the understanding of his perfecting essentially in terms of his transfer to the heavenly sphere. Thus, Käsemann argues against the view that Christ is perfected as 'source of eternal salvation' – 'his τελείωσις is rather the prerequisite for that becoming "source of eternal salvation"'.[147] He then proposes that it is misleading to describe Christ's perfecting 'as the result of a process of moral development on earth'.[148] He follows K. Bornhäuser in arguing that Jesus is portrayed in Hebrews as suffering not general human temptations but the 'proto-type' of specifically Christian temptations: not moral dangers but 'the temptation to fall away from the eschatological hope'.[149] Käsemann stresses that 'the interest in the human nature of Jesus tends to be just in the Redeemer's becoming like his "brothers"'. In learning obedience through suffering, Christ 'realized the prerequisite for τελείωσις', but 'not in the sense of a process of moral development, but the absolute decision between hope and falling away'.[150] In Kögel's view, the temptations of Jesus are 'not indispensable for his person, as though necessary for proving him and for overcoming in the struggle'.[151]

Without doubt, the ascension or heavenly exaltation of Jesus is stressed in our passage. Jesus is the great high priest who has 'passed through the heavens' (4: 14), and the linking of the two psalm citations in 5: 5–6 suggests the importance of his ascension–enthronement for the exercise of the eternal priesthood after the order of Melchizedek. However, in this regard it becomes important to establish the relationship of τελειωθείς to the preceding verses. If 5: 8 is merely a parenthesis explaining εὐλάβεια, as Jeremias suggests, the perfecting of Christ may simply be identified with his resurrection–ascension (τελειωθείς = εἰσακουσθείς). However, I have argued that 5: 8 is stating in more general terms the significance for Jesus of the sort of experience outlined in 5: 7. The τελειωθείς at the beginning of 5: 9 then explains the necessity for the Son's learning obedience through what he suffered in terms of his qualification to become 'source of eternal salvation'.[152]

If one views the exaltation of Christ as an essential part of his becoming source of eternal salvation, it is neither valid nor necessary to exclude the concept of some prior 'development' from the concept of his perfecting. E. Riggenbach, who views the perfecting of Christ fundamentally in terms of his exaltation, observes that the connection between τελειωθείς and verses 7f is 'scarcely questionable'.[153] The writer wishes to indicate, at least in part, something of the 'inner perfecting of the person of the Lord'. Without this, 'Jesus would not have been qualified for the special office of high priest'. While it may be true, as Käsemann suggests, that Christ was confronted with 'the absolute decision between hope and falling away', it is reasonable to suppose with Cullmann that Jesus had to ' "learn" to carry out the task of the *ebed Yahweh* to its end'.[154] This implies that Jesus' experience was not simply designed to acquaint him with the human situation, but to prepare him for the climactic act of self-sacrifice, by which he became source of eternal salvation. His exaltation proclaims the eternity of his high priesthood (7: 23ff) and the eternal or heavenly significance of his sacrifice and the salvation that it brings (9: 11–14, 23–6; 10: 12–14, 19ff).

We may further note with Cullmann that the κατὰ πάντα of 2: 17 and 4: 15 appears to go

> 'far beyond both the temptations in the wilderness and the temptations presented by Jesus' opponents in doctrinal debates (Mark 8: 33, 12: 15, John 8: 1ff) ... The author of Hebrews really thinks of the common temptations connected with our human weakness, the temptations to which we are exposed simply because we are men. "In every respect as we are" refers not only to form but also to content.'[155]

He strongly asserts that 'Hebrews' claim that Jesus was sinless becomes really meaningful only in connection with the strong emphasis on his susceptibility to temptation. Unless he was really tempted, the claim that Jesus was without sin is fundamentally meaningless.'[156] It is true that our writer focusses on the temptations that Jesus experienced with regard to the fulfilment of his redemptive mission, but we cannot limit the scope κατὰ πάντα on this basis, as Bornhäuser and Käsemann do.

With regard to the perfecting of Christ, Cullmann proposes that 'in order to lead humanity to its completion, the High Priest himself must go through the various stages of human life'.[157] Although the writer focusses primarily on the final phase of Christ's life and passion, 'the High Priest must realize the τελείωσις through his whole life until the final sacrifice of his voluntary death'. If Cullmann means that the τελείωσις of Christ is a static moral quality that has to be expressed 'through the various stages of human life', he is using the terminology in a way that differs significantly from our writer's usage. However, this is unlikely to be his meaning, since he later asserts that 'the life of Jesus would not be really human if its course did not manifest a *development*'.[158] P.E. Hughes interprets the perfecting of Christ fundamentally in moral terms, but seeks to relate this to the assertion of Christ's sinlessness:

> 'This perfection was progressively achieved as he moved towards the cross which marked the consummation of his suffering and obedience. His perfection consisted in the retention of his integrity, in the face of every kind of assault on his integrity, and thereby the establishment of his integrity. Had he failed at any point, his integrity would have been impaired and his perfection lost, with the consequence that he would have been disqualified to act as mediator and redeemer. What was essential was that, starting, like Adam, with a pure human nature, he should succeed where Adam had failed. His sufferings both tested and, victoriously endured, attested his perfection, free from failure and defeat.'[159]

It is wrong to minimise the development of Jesus with respect to his humanity and the sense in which he was prepared by his experiences for his high-priestly activity. However, I would question whether Hebrews pictures the perfecting of Christ essentially as these writers suggest, in terms of his moral development or his leading 'humanity to its perfection'. Cullmann notes how 'we approach at times very close to the Son of Man concept. Since the task of the High Priest is to be the Mediator between God and man, the crowning of his work is the realization of the perfect man.'[160] He does not develop this particular line of thought, but we find it expressed by Westcott: 'In studying this τελείωσις of Christ, account must be taken both (1) of his life as man ... so far as he fulfilled in a true human life the destiny of man personally; and (2) of his life as the Son of Man, so far as he fulfilled in his life, as Head of the race, the destiny of humanity by redemption and consummation.'[161]

In the previous chapter, I argued for an Adam Christology underlying our writer's use of Psalm 8 and the exposition that follows (2: 5–15). Here we are told of man's dominion over death being restored by Christ and many sons being enabled to share in the glory that Christ has achieved and now enjoys in his exalted state. The writer's *pesher* on Psalm 8 in 2: 9 reveals that it is specifically 'because of the suffering of death' that Jesus is 'crowned with glory and honour' and it is by 'tasting death for every one' that he enables others to share in his glory. This passage certainly suggests that Christ fulfilled 'the destiny of humanity by redemption and consummation', though our writer emphasises the significance of his suffering death, rather than his life, as the means by which this was achieved. To what extent does our writer develop the theme of Christ fulfilling in a true human life the destiny of man personally?

There is a clearer indication of the concept of the personal consummation of Christ in his humanity in 5: 7–9. Here we catch a glimpse of how Christ 'realised to the uttermost the absolute dependence of humanity upon God in the fulness of personal communion with him, even through the last issues of sin and death'.[162] Again, in 10: 5–10 we read of Christ presenting his body as a living sacrifice to God, realising perfectly in his own life the obedience that fulfils the ideal of sacrifice and achieves a definitive sanctification of believers. Nevertheless, in both of these passages the focus is on the *death* of Christ as the means by which the salvation of men is achieved. His incarnate experience and development as a man is presented in 2: 5–18 and 4: 14 – 5: 10 particularly as a vital preparation and qualification for his redemptive role. In this way he learns perfect sympathy with his people, shows them how far God ought to be obeyed, and learns that obedience by which the final and decisive act of self-sacrifice is achieved. Westcott seems to obscure the fact that the need for an atonement and a reconciling priestly ministry is made the foundation of everything in Hebrews, and 'the incarnation is defined solely by relation to it'.[163]

In the final analysis, therefore, I would question the accuracy of Westcott's assessment, especially in the following statement: 'The conception of τελείωσις is that of bringing Christ to the full moral perfection of his humanity (cf. Luke 13: 32) which carries with it the completeness of power and dignity ... This "perfection" was not reached till after death: 5: 9, 7: 28. It lay, indeed in part in the triumph over death by resurrection.'[164] Here we have a development of the writer's theology, which takes its rise from key concepts in our writer's presentation, but actually says more than our writer says on the subject. Particularly questionable is the assumption that τελειοῦν in Hebrews and Lk. 13: 32 primarily refers to the bringing of Christ 'to the full perfection of his humanity'. There is no hint of such a meaning in Lk. 13: 32, where Jesus' approaching passion and exaltation are viewed as the climax of God's will for his life and ministry, and therefore as his personal consummation.[165] Hebrews similarly points to these climactic events as the fulfilment of his messianic–priestly destiny and therefore his own personal consummation as Messiah and high priest. Here, the functional or vocational understanding of Christ's perfecting should not be allowed to exclude the concept of his personal development as man and preparation for his salvific roles. On the other hand, to give primary emphasis to the perfecting of Christ as *man*, rather than as Saviour, is to obscure the real focus of our writer in favour of a subsidiary theme.

A similar criticism must be levelled at the conclusions of Vanhoye. He begins with the assumption that if one applies the concept of perfection to an ordinary man 'one understands it quite naturally in a moral sense'.[166] In fact, our analysis of the use of τελειοῦν in a wide range of literature showed that this sense was by no means common. Furthermore, I shall show that the perfecting of believers in Hebrews has to do with their *relationship* with God through Jesus Christ: the perfecting of humanity in our writer's presentation is not essentially a moral concept.

In Vanhoye's view, the perfecting of Christ means this: 'by enduring suffering (2: 10, 5: 8), by confronting testings or temptations (2: 18, 4: 15), by practising obedience (5: 8), Jesus has acquired moral perfection'. He suggests that writers who shy away from the moral interpretation are approaching Hebrews with preconceived ideas about the mystery of the incarnation. We must certainly not imagine in Jesus 'the slightest moral blemish', he continues, and 5: 8 cannot be interpreted to mean that Jesus was once rebellious but was brought to submission. However, in rejecting the idea of moral progress altogether, we must ignore Lk. 2: 52, where a real physical development is associated with the development of his human spirit, 'by reacting to exterior influences in full conformity to the will of God'.[167] One can say, in a sense, that Jesus was perfect from his birth and that he was so afterward, at each stage of his existence. Yet, 'Jesus as a child did not have the moral perfection of an adult. Before suffering, he did not have the moral perfection that gives acceptance of suffering. Otherwise, he would not have been truly man and the incarnation would not have been genuine.'[168]

Exception cannot be taken to the last statement, which is true both to the evidence of Hebrews and to the evidence of the Gospels. However, Vanhoye himself has qualified considerably the sense in which moral progress can be attributed to Jesus and I would go further and insist that our writer's presentation of this theme is specifically related to the preparation of Christ for his high-priestly ministry. To insist that the primary sense of Christ's perfecting is his vocational qualification, rather than his moral perfection, is not to approach Hebrews with 'preconceived ideas about the mystery of the incarnation', but rather an attempt to reflect the balance in our writer's presentation. In the final analysis, it is his redemptive death that qualifies Christ to act as heavenly high priest, since the primary function of priesthood is 'to expiate the sins of the people' (2: 17; cf. 5: 1; 7: 27; 8: 3; 9: 28). In this respect, I would endorse the remarks of Spicq:

'his incarnation and his piety render him physically and religiously capable to offer the only sacrifice fully acceptable to God, being at the same time priest and victim. When it is said that God makes this

priest "perfect through suffering" (2: 9–10) and that effectively the
Saviour offers himself to his Father (10: 1–18), it is necessary to
understand that it is solely to realize the object of his priesthood: to
obtain pardon for sins, to unite men to God (5: 9).'[169]

Conclusion

The vocational reading of $\tau \epsilon \lambda \epsilon \iota o \tilde{u} \nu$, in terms of Christ's being qualified to
be high priest of a new order and 'source of eternal salvation', has been
pursued. Assessment of various comments in the light of the text has enabled us to conclude that those who interpret this qualification in strictly
official terms, either as a consecration through death or transfer to the
heavenly sphere, fail to give adequate expression to our writer's total
perspective. The personal preparation of Christ to offer his once-for-all
sacrifice and to be a merciful and faithful heavenly high priest is particularly emphasised in 4: 14 – 5: 10. His experience of suffering and temptation was not only for the purpose of acquainting him with the situation
of his 'brothers', so that he could achieve perfect sympathy with them and
show 'mercy' and 'grace to help in time of need'. It was also to show men
'how far God ought to be submitted to and obeyed' and so that he himself
might ' "learn" to carry out the task of the *ebed Yahweh* to its end'.

Any view that recoils from the concept of development and proving,
with respect to the incarnate Christ, is saying less than our writer says. On
the other hand, to interpret the perfecting of Christ essentially in terms of
his moral development or his 'realization of the perfect man' is to put the
emphasis where our writer does not put it. Christ is perfected as man, but
his qualification to be 'source of eternal salvation' and 'high priest after
the order of Melchizedek' does not simply occur because he fulfilled 'in a
true human life the destiny of man personally'. The focus is on his
redemptive death and the heavenly exaltation that marks the eternity of
his priesthood and of his sacrifice. His human experience is presented as a
preparation for his once-for-all act of atonement and the extension of this
work into eternity (7: 25). The adequacy of Michel's summary can therefore be asserted again:[170] the perfecting of Christ involves 'his proving in
temptation, his fulfilment of the priestly requirements and his exaltation
as Redeemer of the heavenly world'.

5

THE PERFECTING OF CHRIST: HIS EXALTATION

The theme of exaltation 'because of the suffering of death' was announced and applied to Christ in the first context in Hebrews in which he is said to have been perfected (2: 5–10). There, because of the proximity of these themes, several commentators have argued for an interpretation of the perfecting of Christ simply or essentially in terms of his exaltation to heavenly glory and honour. However, the summary nature of 2: 10 was stressed in the exegesis of that passage and the words 'through sufferings' were related to the interpretation of 5: 7–9. In the latter context, it was argued that the perfecting of Christ involved the whole process of temptation and testing that culminated in his crucifixion. On this basis it was concluded that the perfecting of Christ in 2: 10 could not be limited to the concept of exaltation.

The final reference to the perfecting of Christ (7: 28) comes in a context where the focus is particularly on his exaltation, and only brief mention is made of the preceding sacrifice (7: 27) and the personal qualities that make him superior to any earthly mediators (7: 26). Here, as I shall demonstrate, the concluding verse can only be properly understood in the light of an exegesis of the whole chapter, since it recalls, in a series of intricate contrasts, the preceding arguments. However, the τετελειωμένον of that verse cannot be understood in terms of the preceding context alone. It must be insisted, in particular, that the emphasis of 5: 7–9 on Christ's perfecting through earthly struggle and self-sacrifice is included in the writer's application of the term.

The significance and structure of chapter 7

The centrality of this chapter to the argument of Hebrews has often been observed. Spicq refers to the preceding six chapters as only a preparation and the following six as 'an explication and consequence'.[1] Here, at last, is the 'solid food' that suits the mature (5: 12–14), which the writer has promised his readers (6: 1–3). Michel describes chapter 7 as the 'essential heart' of Hebrews and the 'disclosure of secrets' intimated in the preceding word of exhortation (5: 11 − 6: 20).[2] Such an emphasis, however, is exaggerated unless one goes on to assert, as Michel does, that chapter 7 is but the *beginning* of the central section. The opening verse of chapter 8 tells us the writer's 'main point' ($\kappa\epsilon\phi\acute{a}\lambda\alpha\iota o\nu$). The words 'we have such a high priest' take up the main thrust of chapter 7, relate it to the fundamental affirmation of 1: 3 ('one who sat down at the right hand of the throne of the Majesty in heaven'), and lead into the concept of his heavenly liturgy ('a minister of the sanctuary and the true tent'). The latter theme is suggested in 7: 25 but dominates the argument of 8: 1 − 9: 28. It is clearly the central and most distinctive aspect of our writer's presentation of the saving work of Christ.[3]

Chapter 7 itself may be split into seven divisions, as a number of commentators have shown,[4] but there is a compelling logic to the presentation of Vanhoye, both in terms of the criteria used to determine the structure and in terms of the balance achieved.[5] The first major inclusion is formed between 7: 1 and 7: 10 by the words $\sigma\upsilon\nu\alpha\nu\tau\acute{\eta}\sigma\alpha\varsigma$ and $\sigma\upsilon\nu\acute{\eta}\nu\tau\eta\sigma\epsilon\nu$ respectively, and deals with 'Melchizedek and his priesthood, according to Gen. 14'. The second major inclusion is formed between 7: 11 and 7: 28 by the words $\tau\epsilon\lambda\epsilon\acute{\iota}\omega\sigma\iota\varsigma$ and $\tau\epsilon\tau\epsilon\lambda\epsilon\iota\omega\mu\acute{\epsilon}\nu o\nu$ and is called 'The Aaronic order and the order of Melchizedek, according to Psalm 110'. The first division really only prepares for the exposition of Psalm 110: 4, which follows in verses 11−28. The second division is composed of two subdivisions: the words $\tau\epsilon\lambda\epsilon\acute{\iota}\omega\sigma\iota\varsigma$ and $\dot{\epsilon}\tau\epsilon\lambda\epsilon\acute{\iota}\omega\sigma\epsilon\nu$ in 7: 11 and 7: 19 respectively form an inclusion (reinforced by the mention of $\nu\acute{o}\mu o\varsigma$ in each case) and the word $\dot{o}\rho\kappa\omega\mu o\sigma\acute{\iota}\alpha\varsigma$ in 7: 20 and 7: 28 forms a further inclusion. The difference of perspective in the two subdivisions is particularly due to the difference in the way Psalm 110: 4 is employed. In 7: 11−19, the name of Melchizedek is constantly opposed to that of Aaron and the dominant theme is that of the *change* of order, provoked by the insufficiency of the levitical priesthood. In 7: 20−8, Melchizedek is mentioned only once but the ideas of an 'oath' and 'eternity' are taken from the psalm citation and the dominant theme is the *superiority* of the new priesthood. The concluding verses (7: 26−8) form an important conclusion to the chapter as a whole, recalling and restating the major themes, and also preparing for the following section (8: 1 − 9: 28) with the introduction of new ideas.

Exegesis of chapter 7

(a) Melchizedek and his priesthood, according to Gen. 14 (7: 1–10)

Considering the sparsity of information about Melchizedek in the OT it-self or, as David M. Hay has suggested, 'perhaps partly *because* of that exiguity',[6] there is a remarkable amount of speculation about this figure in Jewish, Samaritan, Christian and Gnostic literature. However, although the teaching within Hebrews 7: 1–3 indicates to some scholars 'a special tradition of teaching about Melchizedek, teaching very possibly of a Gnostic or proto-Gnostic character',[7] Hay concludes from his survey: 'In various ways Hebrews seems to reflect and stand critically over against a variety of traditions concerning Melchizedek. To specify precisely which traditions ... the epistle's author knew, and which he did not, is im-possible.'[8] The remarkable restraint with which the writer interprets the narrative of Gen. 14: 18–20 is due to the fact that the real basis of his argument in this chapter is Psalm 110: 4. The Melchizedek story is only of interest to him insofar as it explains the assertions of that key verse of prophecy and intimates the superiority of the priesthood 'after the order of Melchizedek'.[9]

The key to understanding the writer's argument in this section is the clause ἀφωμοιωμένος δὲ τῷ υἱῷ τοῦ θεοῦ (verse 3). The verb ἀφομοιοῦν, which only occurs here in the NT and rarely in the LXX, may simply give the clause the meaning 'he is like the Son of God' (so NEB). However, taking the passive in a strict sense, we may render the clause 'he is made to resemble the Son of God' (i.e., in Scripture).[10] This would be consistent with the writer's apparent assumption that the Son of God is proto-type (*Urbild*) for the Biblical presentation of Melchizedek: 'God is the sculptor who lets a sign of primitive times correspond to the event of the End-time.'[11] The resemblance lies 'in the biblical representation and not primarily in Melchizedek himself. The comparison is not between Christ and Melchizedek, but between Christ and the isolated portraiture of Melchizedek.'[12]

In what way is Melchizedek thought to point to the Son of God? First, with respect to his name and title, 'king of righteousness' and 'king of peace' (verse 2), his character is shown to be that of a king 'in whom and through whom righteousness and peace are realised'.[13] Secondly, with respect to his office (verse 3), he combines the prerogatives of royalty and priesthood. This appears to have been the primary reason for the allusion to Melchizedek by the writer of Psalm 110: 4, who envisaged the ap-pearance of another figure, combining these two offices in his own person: a Davidic king, with a priesthood like Melchizedek's, not apparently based on physical descent from any known priesthood but nevertheless divinely appointed. Our writer expresses this perspective with the words 'without father, or mother or genealogy'. Rather than interpret the words 'without father or mother' as a reference to his heavenly origin, it seems best to understand them in the light of the following 'without genealogy'. 'Melchizedek does not have at his disposal a legitimate family tree.'[14] Since genealogy and knowledge of a person's parents were important to the Semitic mind, particularly for the establishment of the legitimacy of priesthood, the *absence* of these details with respect to Melchizedek is taken as a matter of great significance. Our writer assumes an intentional omission in the Genesis narrative. Arguing from the silence of Scripture, he asserts the uniqueness of Melchizedek's priesthood: he belongs to no dynasty, with no predecessors and no successors.[15]

The third assertion concerning Melchizedek sees him as 'an earthly figure of the eternal Son of God, who in reality possesses neither beginning of days nor end of personal existence'.[16] For the Melchizedek of Scripture, there is no record of his birth or death. B. A. Demarest argues that 'it is precisely the notion of eternity, foreshadowed in Melchizedek and realized in Christ, which repeatedly emerges as the leading refrain and unifying feature of the text and of Hebrews as a whole'.[17] The incarnate Son of God 'had no need of human priestly ancestry to legitimize his unique and never-ending priesthood'. Thus it can be said that Melchizedek 'continues a priest for ever' (verse 3), because he is invested in the Genesis record 'with a symbolic resemblance to the anti-typical priest of the New Covenant'. In this respect pre-eminently, Melchizedek is made to resemble the Son of God.

The writer then proceeds to show from the narrative of Gen. 14 how Melchizedek was superior to Abraham and to the priesthood that traces its descent from Abraham. The aim of this section (verses 4–10) is to prepare for the argument that the priesthood of Jesus is superior to and supersedes the priesthood of the tribe of Levi (verses 11–19). In what respect is Melchizedek greater than Abraham? First, in the reception of tithes from Abraham. It is assumed that 'the receiver of tithe is greater than the giver of tithe: in the case of the less familiar blessing this superiority is affirmed (verse 7)'.[18] The levitical tithe rested on a specific ordinance (κατὰ τὸν νόμον) but the offering in Gen. 14 appears to be a spontaneous recognition of the dignity of Melchizedek. Secondly, in exercising the priestly function of blessing Abraham, Melchizedek certainly showed his superiority. As the one bearing the promise of God's special blessing and the promise of being a source of blessing to others (Gen. 12: 3), Abraham 'might have seemed to be raised above the acceptance of any human blessing'.[19]

As a final point of comparison, our writer returns to the theme of Melchizedek's perpetual priesthood. In contrast to mortal men like the Levites, to whom tithes were normally paid, tithes were paid in this case to one 'whom Scripture affirms to be alive' (verse 8 NEB).[20] Almost as an afterthought, the writer suggests that Levi may be thought of as paying tithes through Abraham (verses 9–10). Although it is true that 'an ancestor is regarded in Biblical thought as containing within himself all his descendants',[21] the argument is strange enough for the writer to preface it with the unusual ὡς ἔπος εἰπεῖν (NEB: 'it might even be said')![22]

(b) The Aaronic order and the order of Melchizedek, according to Psalm 110: 4 (7: 11–28)

The central point of our chapter, that of demonstrating the superiority of Jesus' priesthood 'after the order of Melchizedek' to the one 'named after the order of Aaron', now becomes abundantly clear. Furthermore, although Psalm 110: 4 'glitters behind the fabric of 7: 1–10',[23] its importance to the writer's argument becomes explicit in the second half of the chapter, where it is expounded in detail.

(i) The insufficiency of the old priesthood (verses 11–19)
A searching question is first posed: why did Psalm 110: 4 prophesy the coming of another priest 'after the order of Melchizedek' if 'perfection' had been attainable under the existing priesthood? With this question we are confronted for the first time by the concept of perfection as applied to believers, rather than Christ. It is typical of our writer to insert such a reference, tantalising in its brevity, in anticipation of a later development of the theme. A second reference in this vein in 7: 19 gives more indication of the sense in which the terminology is being used, but a complete picture cannot be presented until I have examined related references in their context (9: 9; 10: 1; 10: 14; 11: 40; 12: 23). This will be the task of my next chapters and I shall therefore postpone consideration of the concept of perfection in 7: 11–19 until then.

Here, however, we may note the close connection between Law and priesthood in our writer's argument. In 7: 11 it is the levitical priesthood that, by implication, is unable to secure perfection but in 7: 19 it is the Law that 'perfected nothing'. In the former verse the writer explicitly states that 'the law rested on the priesthood' (ὁ λαὸς γὰρ ἐπ᾽ αὐτῆς νενομοθέτηται),[24] so that 'a change of priesthood must mean a change of law' (verse 12 NEB). Truly, for Hebrews 'the fate of the law hangs upon the fate of the priesthood'.[25] The weakness of the Mosaic Law, as a system by which men were related to God, is connected by our writer with the weakness of the priesthood that supported it.

Many commentators draw attention to the similar conclusions about the temporary and ineffective nature of the law reached by Paul (e.g., Gal. 3–4). However, Paul and Hebrews view the Law from different standpoints. Although Paul does not make any fundamental distinction between cultic and ethical commandments, or between the Decalogue and the rest of the Law, 'he works out his position primarily with reference to the ethical commandments, especially those of the Decalogue which apply to all men'.[26] Hebrews is not concerned with the Law as 'a prescription for the behaviour of the individual, but as the sum of sacrificial regulations for the ancient cultic community'.[27] Michel rightly suggest that Hebrews is nearer to John than Paul in stressing the OT as a 'hidden witness to Christ'.[28] There is, on the one hand, a certain *correspondence* noted between the Old Covenant and the New: some OT categories and concepts are taken over (sacrifice, priesthood, covenant, sanctuary). On the other hand, 'better' is a characteristic word for our writer and *supersession* is argued: the New Covenant has better and more effective gifts and institutions than the corresponding gifts and institutions of the Old. Finally, the New Covenant has, in contrast to the Old 'the true sacrifice, the heavenly sanctuary, the eternal priesthood. $\dot{\alpha}\lambda\eta\theta\iota\nu\dot{o}\varsigma$, $\dot{\epsilon}\pi o\nu\rho\dot{\alpha}\nu\iota o\varsigma$ $\alpha\dot{\iota}\dot{\omega}\nu\iota o\varsigma$ are the indications of "perfection".'[29]

That 7: 12 forms a parenthesis to the main argument becomes apparent when, in 7: 13–14, we are told in what sense a priest has arisen who can be described as $\dot{\epsilon}\tau\epsilon\rho o\varsigma$ and $o\dot{\upsilon}$ $\kappa\alpha\tau\dot{\alpha}$ $\tau\dot{\eta}\nu$ $\tau\dot{\alpha}\xi\iota\nu$ $A\alpha\rho\dot{\omega}\nu$ (verse 11). At the simplest level, this means a priest who does not come from the priestly tribe of Levi, and Christian tradition clearly asserts that Jesus was from the tribe of Judah.[30] We may perhaps discern a polemic here against persons who disputed any claim of priesthood for Jesus in the 'confession' of the readers,[31] or simply suppose that the author is covering himself against such objections as he unfolds for the first time the concept of Jesus as high priest. However, the difference between Jesus' priesthood and that of the Levites is not simply to be found in this question of physical descent. As the following verses show (verses 15–17), 'this promised priesthood was after a wholly different type, not legal but spiritual, not sacerdotal only but royal, not transitory but eternal'.[32] These conclusions are based on the fact that Psalm 110: 4 points to another priest who is 'in the likeness of Melchizedek'.

The substitution of $\kappa\alpha\tau\dot{\alpha}$ $\tau\dot{\eta}\nu$ $\dot{o}\mu o\iota\dot{o}\tau\eta\tau\alpha$ for the $\kappa\alpha\tau\dot{\alpha}$ $\tau\dot{\eta}\nu$ $\tau\dot{\alpha}\xi\iota\nu$ of the psalm in verse 15 significantly points us back to the $\dot{\alpha}\phi\omega\mu o\iota\omega\mu\dot{\epsilon}\nu o\varsigma$ of verse 3 and to the argument of verses 1–10. The Melchizedek of Gen. 14:

18–20, in his person and office, is a type of the Son of God in his priest-hood. This 'likeness' is now described by way of a contrast between the priesthood of Jesus and the levitical priesthood. The latter is characterised as κατὰ νόμον ἐντολῆς σαρκίνης and the former as κατὰ δύναμιν ζωῆς ἀκαταλύτου. The contrast is firstly between νόμος and δύναμις as respect-ively characterising the old priesthood and the new: 'the "law" is an out-ward restraint; the "power" is an inward force'.[33] It seems best to interpret ἐντολῆς σαρκίνης and ζωῆς ἀκαταλύτου as genitives of content, giving us, in the first instance, 'the law consisting in the carnal commandment'.[34] Michel aptly describes the ἐντολὴ σαρκίνη as 'not that which proceeds from the flesh, also not the commandment provoking sin but only the commandment which is *inhibited in its operation, aimed at the "flesh"*'.[35] In the present context, this will refer particularly to the fact that the Old Covenant demanded a certain physical descent and certain standards of outward purity for the priesthood, not moral or personal qualities. Since this Law 'belongs to the earthly sphere' in its operation, it 'does not have the power of indestructible life, as heavenly things have'.[36]

In contrast, then, to the 'law consisting in the carnal commandment', by which the levitical priests were instituted and conducted their ministry, Christ has become high priest 'by the power of an indestructible life'. The commentators are divided as to whether this phrase describes a *quality* possessed by the historic Jesus or an *objective event* in which he partici-pated.[37] On the one hand, there are those like Montefiore who argue that Christ's divine nature, united to his humanity, conferred upon the latter the power 'of a life that nothing can destroy ... This union of natures took place when the Son came into the world, and it was then that he was given his priestly office (10: 5).'[38] I have already had occasion to argue that the union of two natures in Christ is not the basis on which our author establishes his high priesthood.[39] On the contrary, Christ's priesthood in Hebrews seems to be bound up with the heavenly world and the age to come (6: 19–20; 7: 26; 8: 1–4; 9: 11ff). B.A. Demarest concludes a history of the exegesis of this verse with the following helpful assessment:

'Bearing in mind the two-age doctrine in Hebrews and the teaching of the NT as a whole that the cross and resurrection of Jesus signalled a partial manifestation of the new age, δύναμις ζωῆς ἀκαταλύτου (7: 16) must be regarded as the new quality of life with which Christ was endowed upon his exaltation to the heavenly world. Christ's earthly life *did* experience κατάλυσις. However, not only did Christ expire but he came back to life via resurrection and, having been "exalted above the heavens" (7: 26), he is now "seated at the right hand of the throne of Majesty in heaven" (8: 1). Thus, ζωὴ ἀκατάλυτος is principally descriptive of Christ as Son and High Priest in his ascended and eternal state.[40]

In identifying this phrase with the resurrection—ascension experience of Christ, Demarest finds a number of supporters.[41] There are those, however, who seek to combine both perspectives and suggest, like Büchsel, that: 'unceasing life belongs particularly to Jesus after his resurrection, though it does not begin then, for in Hebrews the historical as well as the risen Jesus is high priest. If it is by his resurrection, on the basis of his death, that he is fully what he is, he begins to be it already in his historical life.'[42] However, such an interpretation still has to deal with the problem raised by Demarest: 'Christ's earthly life *did* experience κατάλυσις.' Büchsel is forced to say that Christ's death is 'not the decease of a man like other men. It is upheld by the power of an indestructible life', and yet our writer stresses the complete identity of Jesus in life and death with other men (2: 9; 2: 14ff; 4: 15; 5: 7—8). The introduction of 9: 14 into this argument is inappropriate, since it stresses the motive and power by which he offers himself in death, not that he somehow 'offered himself as living in death by the eternal spirit',[43] which is an incomprehensible notion.

Thus, it seems best to interpret 7: 16*b* as a reference to the heavenly exaltation of Christ, whereby he is enabled to exercise that perpetual priesthood of which the psalm citation speaks (verse 17). This exaltation and its consequences is the major theme of verses 23—8. In reaching this conclusion about 7: 16*b* I am bound to discuss the connection between Christ's self-sacrifice and his heavenly priesthood, since the former seems to be viewed as a high-priestly action by our writer. This discussion is undertaken below in connection with 7: 25 and in Appendix B.

The idea introduced in verse 12, that a change in the priesthood necessitates a change in the system based upon that priesthood, is now developed further. The μετάθεσις of verse 12 is explained negatively in verse 18 (ἀθέτησις μέν ...) and positively in verse 19 (ἐπεισαγωγὴ δέ ...). The 'former commandment' (προαγούσης ἐντολῆς) means 'an earlier commandment' as well as 'a foregoing commandment'.[44] In other words, the primary reference is to the ordinance of priesthood mentioned in verse 16. However, since the whole Mosaic system was based on the priesthood (verse 11), the system as a whole is declared invalid, nullified, set aside,[45] when the ordinance of priesthood is set aside. This is made clear by the parenthesis of verse 19 ('for the law made nothing perfect'). This dramatic change in God's manner of dealing with his people takes place because of the 'weakness and uselessness' of the ordinance of priesthood in particular and of the legal system in general (verse 19*a*).

The annulling (ἀθέτησις) of the commandment was accompanied by the introduction of a 'better hope'. Westcott maintains that 'the comparison is between the commandment characteristic of the law and the hope characteristic of the Gospel; and not between the temporal hope of the law and the spiritual hope of the Gospel'.[46] However, the use of κρείττων in other such comparisons (7: 22; 8: 6; 9: 23; 11: 40) would speak to the contrary: 'the new ἐλπίς is κρείττων by its effectiveness (6: 18); it accomplishes what the νόμος and its ἱερωσύνη had failed to realise for men, viz. a direct and lasting access to God'.[47] Westcott's distinction between the two covenants is too absolute and is partly due to an exaggerated emphasis on the significance of the clause 'through which we draw near to God'. Noting the rare usage of ἐγγίζειν τῷ θεῷ in the LXX in relation to the priestly ministry, he concludes: 'that which was before (in a figure) the privilege of a class has become (in reality) the privilege of all and thus man is enabled to gain through fellowship with God the attainment of his destiny (τελείωσις)'.[48] However, the more general use of ἐγγίζειν (with or without τῷ θεῷ or πρὸς τὸν θεόν) in LXX and Philo, as an expression for *encounter with God*, should warn us against reading a particularly sacerdotal meaning into its usage here (cf. James 4: 8).[49] As I have argued in connection with the use of προσέρχεσθαι, our writer does not deny the people of the Old Covenant the possibility of drawing near to God absolutely (10: 1; 11: 6; 12: 18ff). The significant difference for the Christian is the *better hope* by which he draws near to God: 'the certainty of the actualisation of the drawing near is now stronger and surer and more complete than in the O.T. and later Judaism'.[50] It is too simplistic to say that the contrast is between the limited priesthood of the Old Covenant and the 'priesthood of all believers'. In actual fact the contrast in the present passage is between the *limited effectiveness of the former priesthood and the absolute effectiveness of the priesthood of Christ.*

(ii) The permanence and effectiveness of the new priesthood (verses 20–8)
The weakness and ineffectiveness of the levitical priesthood and the system based upon it are mentioned briefly in verses 16 and 19. The development of that theme is continued now as the superiority of the new priesthood is expounded. That superiority is illustrated in terms of the oath (verses 20–2) and the eternity (verses 23–5) of Christ's priesthood and in terms of the character, achievement and status of the Christian's high priest (verses 26–8).

Our writer sees great significance in the fact that the Scripture 'appointing' Christ to his priesthood was prefaced by a divine oath (verse 21). No such oath was associated with the appointment of the levitical priests. The argument of 6: 13ff has already shown, in connection with the divine promise to Abraham (Gen. 22: 16), that God, 'desiring to show even more clearly ... how unchanging was his purpose, guaranteed it by oath' (6: 17 NEB). Thus, for our writer, 'in the concept of the oath lies absoluteness and eternal validity'.[51] The promise to Abraham with an oath and the promise of the Melchizedek priesthood with an oath apparently hang together in our writer's thinking, and 'as Paul worked out the one in Galatians so our author will work out the other'.[52] Above all, our writer wishes to assert that the divine oath makes Jesus 'the surety of a better covenant' (verse 22).

The 'better covenant' picks up the thought of the 'better hope' of verse 19, using the word 'covenant' for the first time.[53] The relationship between Christ's priesthood and his covenantal role is also found in 8: 6 and 9: 15, where he is declared mediator of a new and better covenant (cf. 12: 24). The concepts of 'mediator' ($\mu\epsilon\sigma\iota\tau\eta\varsigma$) and 'surety' or 'guarantor' ($\check{\epsilon}\gamma\gamma\upsilon o\varsigma$) are related but not identical. In Michel's words, the mediator 'steps into the gap between God and man (Psalm 106: 23, Ezekiel 22: 30): the surety, however, *stakes his person and his life for his word*'.[54] In Jesus' case, 'the word proclaimed is conveyed and supported through the priestly ministry which stands behind him'. Jesus is the surety of a new and better covenant because of the divine oath associated with his priesthood (verse 22) and because he 'always lives to make intercession' for the recipients of the covenant (verse 25).[55]

The levitical priesthood had been appointed an 'everlasting priesthood throughout their generations' (Exod. 40: 15): it was only perpetual because a succession of priests was provided to fulfil the ministry. For our writer, plurality is apparently a sign of incompleteness and imperfection (1: 1ff; 10: 1ff) and thus the superiority of Christ's priesthood is illustrated in the fact that he uniquely, as an individual, 'continues for ever' (7: 24).[56] The many priests of the levitical order were prevented from 'continuing in office' by the simple fact of death.[57] Christ, however, 'holds his priesthood permanently' (verse 24).[58]

An important logical inference from the previous assertion is then indicated by the $\check{o}\theta\epsilon\nu$ at the beginning of verse 25.[59] Westcott insists that the message of this verse is for believers and not for the world, since the writer speaks of the 'working out of salvation to the uttermost in those who have received the Gospel'.[60] The present tense ($\sigma\dot\omega\check{\zeta}\epsilon\iota\nu$) has its full force: 'the support comes at each moment of trial' (cf. 1 Cor. 15: 2; Jude 23 and Hebrews 5: 7). This is an attractive interpretation in the light of 4: 14−16 and the whole emphasis of Hebrews on looking to Jesus for help to run the race and reach the heavenly goal (3: 1ff; 6: 18ff; 12: 1ff).

Westcott takes εἰς τὸ παντελές to mean 'completely, wholly, to the uttermost' (NEB: 'absolutely'). Even if this phrase is taken to mean 'forever,
for all time', as it may be,[61] the overall sense is much the same: for
Hebrews, the perfection and the eternity of salvation 'are always bound up
with one another'.[62] If, however, εἰς τὸ παντελές is taken as simply 'a
literary variant for πάντοτε',[63] and attached to the δύναται, we arrive at
the translation 'hence for all time he is able to save' (so RSV). This implies
that Christ is ever able to offer men salvation *simpliciter*, but provides us
with a less natural reading of the syntax of this verse.

Christ's ability to save his people absolutely or forever has to do with
his ministry of heavenly intercession ('since he always lives to make intercession for them'). The history of exegesis shows considerable disagreement
as to what that intercession involves.[64] The NT uses ἐντυγχάνειν twice
with the meaning 'to approach someone with a complaint' (Rom. 11: 2;
Acts 25: 24) and four times with the sense 'to intercede as a
representative' (Rom. 8: 26f (the Spirit); 8: 34 (Christ) and Heb.
7: 25). The idea of Jesus as heavenly intercessor, witness or judge to
men is 'firmly embedded in the synoptic tradition',[65] and is most likely
implied in the vision of Acts 7: 55–6.[66] However, only Rom. 8: 34;
Hebrews 7: 25; Acts 7: 55–6 and possibly 1 Pet. 3: 21–2 seems to
connect the idea of heavenly intercession with Christ's position at the
right hand of God.[67]

D.M. Hay argues that the suggestion of an ongoing priestly ministry in
heaven here seems to conflict with the author's dominant view of the
atonement as something accomplished once-for-all in Jesus' death: 'Why
should he need to intercede after offering an utterly adequate sacrifice?
Moreover, if the intercession is central to the author's soteriology, why
does he mention it directly only once and never discuss it systematically as
he does Jesus' death?'[68] These are important questions, but Hay's suggestion
that 7: 25 is 'best viewed as a foreign element or "seam", indicative of the
uniting of two fundamentally different ideas of Jesus' work' is a poor
solution. I have already argued that the perspective of 4: 14–16, with
Christ the ascended high priest who is able to sympathise with our weaknesses and provide mercy and grace to help in time of need, is *central* to
our writer's aim in his 'word of exhortation' (13: 22).[69] Here in 7: 25 we
have again the fundamental idea of drawing near to God through Christ
(προσέρχεσθαι as in 4: 16 and 10: 22). In 10: 19–25, the death of Christ
is made the basis for confidence to approach God. Thus, 7: 25 is not a
'foreign element' to the writer's presentation but reflects the perspective
of the two pivotal exhortations in 4: 14–16 and 10: 19–25. The three
references are concerned in their context with Christians persevering to the

end. The 'mercy' promised to those in need and the 'help' that is available from the ascended Christ (4: 14–16; 13: 20) suggest the picture of a heavenly intercessor (7: 25; cf. 1 John 2: 1f). However, the emphasis on the finished nature of his atoning work, particularly in 10: 11ff, means that believers are being challenged to enjoy the ongoing benefits of that work (10: 19ff) and the image of the intercessor is used to emphasise Christ's willingness and ability to go on applying those benefits (cf. 12: 24).

There is no justification for the view that, by some continuous liturgical action in heaven, Christ 'pleads the sacrifice' made on Calvary.[70] Although Christ appears to fulfil a double function as high priest – the once-for-all act of atonement and the extension of this work into eternity – Cullmann rightly points out that this is actually no double function 'but only one, for everything rests on the one act of sacrifice'.[71] Indeed, Hebrews considers 'the present lordship of Christ as a high priestly office'. If we ask how his presence at the Father's right hand can be of itself the extension of this work into eternity, the traditional interpretation in terms of the ritual of the Day of Atonement seems most applicable: the very presence of the high priest in the Holy of Holies witnessed 'to the continued preservation of the established relation of man to God'.[72] Thus, the climax of the work of Christ can be described in terms of his entry into heaven 'now to appear before the presence of God on our behalf' (9: 24). As Cody puts it, 'the historical acts of salvation are done, and yet something of them is gone over into glory, into the celestial, eternal sphere, and is prolonged in eternity, outside the limits of space and time'.[73] The very presence of the crucified and yet glorified Christ with God is the reality behind the concept of his intercession and this is 'really and simply equivalent to his expiatory activity, carried out once in earthly history and brought up against eternity in the celestial order'.

Montefiore reflects a Patristic mode of exegesis when he proposes that 'it is in virtue of his glorified and perfected humanity that Jesus intercedes'.[74] Cody more accurately relates this intercession to his sacrificial work but includes the concept of Christ's glorified humanity in the perspective: 'the reality behind the concept is that of the presence of the glorified humanity of Christ with God, and of the value of his act of salvation in confrontation and interaction with the divine power, for the perfection of many sons in glory (2: 10)'.[75] The glorification of Christ 'above the heavens' (verse 26) is certainly related to the concept of his ministry of intercession (verse 25) but the extent to which our writer emphasises the glorification of Christ's humanity will be discussed in connection with verse 28. The τοιοῦτος of verse 26 clearly relates back to the description of Christ as high priest in the previous verse but also provides a bridge to the description that follows.[76] The complete correspondence between Christ as he is and the needs of believers (ἡμῖν),[77] may be recognised by faith to be entirely appropriate (ἔπρεπεν) to our situation.[78]

The three adjectives used to describe the personal qualities of the Christian's high priest in verse 26 (ὅσιος, ἄκακος, ἀμίαντος) explain why his sacrifice was so perfect, needing no repetition (verse 27). His exaltation above the heavens (verse 26) explains how he nevertheless 'always lives' to apply the benefits of that sacrifice (verse 25). If ὅσιος is taken in the sense in which it is used in the LXX, its basic meaning is 'faithfulness to Yahweh'[79] or 'devout' (NEB). Spicq rightly associates this word with Christ's accomplishment of the Father's will (10: 5–10) and his 'godly fear' (5: 7f), proved through the experiences of his earthly life: Christ is presented by our writer as 'wholly consecrated to the service of the glory of God'.[80] He is also 'without guile' (ἄκακος) in relation to men (cf. Isa. 53: 9; 1 Pet. 2: 22) and 'undefiled' (ἀμίαντος) in spite of his complete involvement in the life of sinful humanity.[81] With this terminology, our writer contrasts the spiritual and moral perfection of the Christian's high priest with the outward characteristics demanded of the levitical high priests.[82] There is good reason to understand the words 'separated from sinners' in relation to the preceding adjectives and to translate 'different from sinful men'.[83] However, most commentators seem to relate it to what follows and understand Christ to be 'separated from sinful men' by being exalted to the heavenly world. The clause is certainly a link between the two concepts and we may fairly conclude: 'This separation is, on the one hand inward and moral, and on the other hand the consequence of his being now exalted to the right hand of God, withdrawn from the midst of a sinful world.'[84]

It is important to see the perspective of earlier passages reflected in the words 'devout, guileless, undefiled'. These describe one who remained obedient to God through great testing; the outcome of such a life and not simply static moral qualities. What, then, is the connection between the moral perfection of Jesus and his exaltation above the heavens? The answer is provided in verse 27 where, for the first time, mention is made of *the offering of himself*, by which the whole system of levitical sacrifices is replaced: 'to the grandeur of Christ belongs also his separation from sacrificial ministry'.[85] Having offered the perfect sacrifice, he has no need to perform a daily sacrificial service, as earthly priests do.[86] The perfection of this sacrifice is clearly associated with the perfection of the victim, in this case, the priest himself: he offered himself 'without blemish' to God

(9: 14). Its efficacy is proclaimed by the fact that Christ as high priest thereby secures entrance into heaven itself, a theme that the writer will develop in detail later.

A certain technical inexactitude is apparent in the use of the words τοῦτο γὰρ ἐποίησεν. G.W. Buchanan has recently revived the interpretation that the expression speaks of Jesus' sacrificing for his own sins as well as for the sins of the people. This is only possible because he takes χωρὶς ἁμαρτίας in 4: 15 as a reference to 'the crucifixion alone, and not to Jesus' entire life'.[87] I have argued against such an interpretation in Appendix A and would therefore conclude that the writer is making a general comparison in 7: 27 with the OT priesthood and ritual: 'whatever the Aaronic high priest did in symbol, as a sinful man, that Christ did perfectly as sinless in his humanity for men'.[88] Having already asserted the sinlessness of Jesus (4: 15; 7: 26), our writer clearly did not envisage any need for Jesus to be personally cleansed from sin.

The truths expounded in the preceding verses are now recalled and restated in 7: 28, in a series of important contrasts. The first contrast is between 'the law' and 'the word of the oath which came later than the law'. The weakness and ineffectiveness of the OT system in general, and the law appointing the levitical priests in particular, is the subject of 7: 11–19. The superiority of 'the word of the oath' (Psalm 110: 4) and the priesthood that it proclaims is the subject of 7: 20–2. There it is asserted that the establishment of Jesus' priesthood by divine oath makes him 'the surety of a better covenant'. That same sense of supersession is implied in 7: 28 by the words τῆς μετὰ τὸν νόμον (cf. 8: 13). The supersession proclaimed in Psalm 110: 4 'came into effect when the Messiah appeared and vindicated his high-priestly title on the basis of a perfect sacrifice'.[89] The particular aspect of Jesus' priesthood that the oath guarantees and our writer emphasises is its permanency (εἰς τὸν αἰῶνα). Here is the essential likeness to the priesthood of Melchizedek proclaimed in verses 1–10 and the essential contrast with the priesthood of the Levites asserted in verses 23–5.

The second major contrast in verse 28 is between 'men in their weakness' and 'a Son who has been made perfect for ever'. Within this broad statement, two particular contrasts are implied. In the first place, the plural 'men' contrasted with the singular 'Son' reminds us of the argument in verses 23ff, where the need for many priests, 'prevented by death from continuing in office', is contrasted with the one priest of the New Covenant who continues 'for ever'. In the second place, the many priests of Judaism are characterised as 'having weakness' whereas the high priest of the Christian's confession is 'a Son who has been made perfect for ever' (υἱὸν εἰς τὸν αἰῶνα τετελειωμένον).

The concept of perfection

It is important to observe that 7: 28 not only recalls some of the themes but also the argument of previous passages. The description of the high priests of Judaism as ἀνθρώπους ... ἔχοντας ἀσθένειαν recalls the assertion of 5: 2 that they were 'beset with weakness' (περίκειται ἀσθένειαν). There it was argued that this characteristic had the positive consequence of enabling the high priest to 'moderate his anger' with regard to the 'ignorant and wayward', but the negative consequence of necessitating a 'sacrifice for his own sins as well as for those of the people' (5: 3).

A contrast is clearly implied in the case of the high priest of the New Covenant (7: 28), though his involvement with human 'weakness' was such that he continues to 'sympathize with our weaknesses' (4: 15).[90] I have already had occasion to endorse the conclusion of Westcott that 'this "weakness" includes both the actual limitations of humanity as it is, and the personal imperfections and sins of the particular priest'.[91] Our writer's presentation of the human experience of Christ ('in the days of his flesh') would lead us to suggest that he knew from first-hand experience 'the actual limitations of humanity as it is', in terms of temptation (2: 18; 4: 15), fear of death (5: 7) and learning obedience through what he suffered (5: 8). However, in the final analysis, he does not 'lose heart and grow faint' (12: 3) and is never depicted as 'weak' in the sense of 'abandoned to temptation'.[92]

When Jesus is described as 'perfected for ever', then, the picture is not that of a heavenly being completely unacquainted with human weakness but of one who proved himself in the events of his human experience 'devout, guileless, undefiled', and who is now 'raised high above the heavens' and, in that sense, 'separated from sinners'. Once again, the immediate context (7: 26f) suggests that our writer meant by the perfecting of Christ *his proving in temptation, his death as a sacrifice for sins and his heavenly exaltation.* The perfect participle in this case (τετελειωμένον) suggests that Christ has all these experiences through which he passed 'always behind him',[93] and thus 'qualified' he is able to 'save absolutely those who approach God through him' (7: 25 NEB).

The description of Jesus as 'son' recalls the argument of 1: 2ff and 5: 5–10. Even though the Son is the one whom God has made 'heir to the whole universe and through whom he created all orders of existence' (1: 2 NEB), his entrance into that inheritance has to do with 'the purgation of sins' and the taking of his seat 'at the right hand of Majesty on high' (1: 3 NEB). Psalm 2: 7 ('You are my Son, today I have begotten you') is best understood at 1: 5 and 5: 5 as applying to *the inauguration of Christ's heavenly rule as Son*, and hence to *the manifestation of his Sonship*, which takes place through his ascension–enthronement. The idea of Christ entering into his inheritance through suffering and exaltation is also expounded in 2: 5–9, in relation to Psalm 8: 4–6, though the title 'Son' is not used in that context.

When our writer mentions that Jesus was Son during his public ministry as he spoke to men (1: 2), and as he 'learned obedience through the things he suffered' (5: 8), it seems clear that the title could be perfectly applied to Christ before his resurrection–ascension. The reference to the Son as the one through whom God 'created all orders of existence' (1: 2) indicates that our writer had no hesitation in conceiving of the Son as pre-existent.[94] Against the theory of two Christologies in Hebrews, Hofius rightly asserts that 'the Son *becomes* as the Exalted One, what he already *is* as the Pre-Existent One'.[95] The kingly glory of Christ, previously hidden, becomes *manifest* to all with his enthronement and reception of 'the name' (1: 4). The Son's eschatological inheritance could not be secured nor his Sonship decisively manifested for the salvation of his people until he had carried out the earthly ministry destined for him as Messiah. I therefore endorse the view of Kögel that the perfecting of Christ as Son in 7: 28 'points to the vocation which Jesus has'.[96] The perfecting of Christ as Son involves the perfecting of his *Mittlerqualität*: the fulfilment of the Messianic role in humiliation, death and exaltation. In previous discussions of Kögel's point of view, I took issue with his absolute exclusion of any idea of moral or inner development on the part of Christ. Nevertheless, with the qualifications I have made previously, the 'vocational' understanding of Christ's perfecting is appropriate here, as well as in 2: 10 and 5: 9.[97]

The perfecting of the Son in 7: 28, as in 5: 5–10, is associated with his becoming 'a priest for ever after the order of Melchizedek'. In the argument of chapter 7, it is clearly *the eternity of Christ's priesthood* that is mainly in focus (verses 3, 8, 16–17, 23–5), and this is recalled in the last verse with the words εἰς τὸν αἰῶνα. However, it is unwarranted literalism to restrict the exercise of Christ's priesthood 'after the order of Melchizedek' to his heavenly session and intercession (see Appendix B). His sacrifice, which is mentioned in 7: 27 is the basis of his high-priestly work. His ascension–enthronement makes it possible for him to apply continually the benefits of his once-for-all sacrifice to the needs of his people (7: 25): it makes his sacrifice eternal in its effects (9: 12, 23–6; 10: 12–14, 19ff).

Käsemann's view of Christ's perfecting in terms of 'a new qualitative transformation of his being whereby the sphere of humiliation is left behind'[98] may be thought particularly relevant to the interpretation of 7: 28. His assertion that 'between the earthly priests encircled with weakness, and the perfected and eternal Son, exist no ethical gradations of development',[99] seems to capture well the stark contrast of that verse. However, the preceding verses stress the obedience that led to the offering of the perfect sacrifice and consequent exaltation of Christ (verses 26–7) and preceding passages stress an intimate connection between his testing and learning of obedience and perfecting as high priest (2: 17f; 5: 7–10). Käsemann views the obedience of Jesus as an 'attribute of his earthly being, not moral proving, but recognition of the plan of salvation and sign of humiliation, which puts him on the same level with the earthly church'.[100] Through his obedience, Christ 'realized the prerequisite for $\tau\epsilon\lambda\epsilon\acute{\iota}\omega\sigma\iota\varsigma$',[101] the sacrificial death which, as a penetration through the hindering curtain of his flesh, becomes the means of entry into heaven (10: 20). Käsemann's dependence on the Gnostic myth of the heavenly man thus brings him to conclude that obedience and perfection are two contrasting stages in the journey of the heavenly man, from heaven to earth and back to heaven again. However, such an absolute distinction between Christ's period of obedience–humiliation and the concept of his perfection is not faithful to the presentation of our writer. The wording of 2: 10 suggests that suffering is more than simply the prerequisite for his perfecting: it is at least part of the process by which Christ is perfected. Furthermore, the sufferings envisaged cannot be limited to the actual experience of death itself but include a period of testing and preparation for that final act of obedience (2: 18; 4: 15; 5: 7f). So 7: 28 does not simply provide us with a 'metaphysical contrast', as Käsemann suggests, but recalls the triumph of Christ in life and death, which culminated in his exaltation to the right hand of God.

The extent to which our writer envisaged a transformation of Christ's being through heavenly exaltation, is best discussed in consideration of the views of A. Cody. His particular emphasis is on the perfecting of the Son's human nature through resurrection–ascension:

'Christ is "perfectly" Son, with both human nature and divine nature at last actually on the same celestial plane of existence, only when the power of God has raised him from the dead and set him in the power and glory of heaven, so that the human nature of Christ is on the celestial level of power and glory with his divine nature and can, in virtue of his being so perfected, use the perfected power of his human nature to bring to glory his brethren, who are also "sons".'[102]

Such an interpretation has its own appeal, especially when Cody describes the resurrection–ascension of Christ in terms of 'the glorification of the humanity of the Son of God after he willingly reached the nadir of fleshly existence in death ... By the triumph and exaltation of his resurrection and ascension our Lord effected his *transitus* from the realm of sin and death to the divine realm of consummate perfection in the glory of God.'[103] Our writer nowhere expresses an explicit theology of 'the glorification of the humanity of the Son of God' though it may be supposed that this under-lies passages like 4: 14f and 9: 23 (and therefore, to some extent, 7: 25). However, I would question the argument that this is our writer's essential meaning when he speaks of the perfecting of the Son or the perfecting of his priesthood.

It was argued in connection with 2: 5−10 that Christ's glorification is presented there primarily in terms of his achieving the *dominion* over all things, as promised in Psalm 8, and thereby enabling many sons to share in that dominion. Our writer does not focus on the changes involved in the 'being' of Christ so much as on the consequences of his achievements and new status for us. The entrance of the Son into his messianic inheritance through death and exaltation also seems to be the concept behind our writer's use of Psalm 2: 7 and therefore, as I have argued, behind the reference to the perfecting of the Son in 7: 28. To view the perfecting of the Son primarily in a vocational, rather than a metaphysical sense is more consistent with the argument of preceding chapters in Hebrews. Cody also acknowledges that the ascension of Christ is fundamentally of importance for our writer 'because of its term, the Session which has taken place once and for all and continues into eternity, the Session in glory and power.'[104] However, he immediately goes on to define the session as that which 'perfects the saving humanity of Christ and correspondingly, envisaged in the cult reference of the heavenly sanctuary, perfects the priesthood of Christ'. In this latter statement Cody seems to confuse the significance of what he calls the *transitus* (i.e. the Ascension) with the concept of Christ's session, because he argues on the very next page that 'the *transitus* of Jesus, his Ascension, perfects him as a priest'. It is certainly true that the concept of Christ's *transitus* is important to our writer's typological exposition of Christ's work (4: 14; 9: 11f; 9: 23),[105] but it is doubtful that these verses carry as much theological and metaphysical significance as Cody suggests.

If we are thinking in terms of the perfecting of Christ's priesthood, it seems clear that the appearance before God on our behalf constitutes the climax of the type-complex of the Day of Atonement's sin-expiating ritual (9: 23). However, if the *transitus* is included in the concept of his perfecting as priest, why not also his self-offering in death and the preceding life of obedience which culminated in that death? To focus on the perfecting of the humanity of Christ through ascension is to obscure the wider perspec-tive of our writer concerning the consummation of Christ as high priest.

Perhaps the heart of our disagreement with Cody concerns his theory that Hebrews' use of τελειοῦν combines Alexandrian and Johannine perspectives:

> 'From the Alexandrian point of view, the heavenliness and perfection of our Lord's priesthood seems to be heavenliness and perfection in the order of being, and to be related to the hypostatic union, in which Christ's human nature was clasped to the absolute heavenliness and sanctity of the Word. But from the other point of view, they seem to be related more to the order of operation, in which Christ carried out on earth the will of his Father (10: 5–10), was perfected by his suffering (5: 9), and achieved the coronation of the fruits of his sanctity by becoming "higher than the heavens" (7: 26), so that being at the term and pinnacle of perfection in glory he might exercise his priestly office by bringing his brethren to glory with him (2: 10).'[106]

The so-called Alexandrian point of view leads to an interpretation of the perfecting of Christ that is not consistent with our writer's use of the terminology. This is obvious when Cody speaks of Jesus the Son of God 'perfected by entrance into glory',[107] when our writer clearly asserts that he was perfected 'through sufferings' (2: 10). What Cody describes as the Johannine view is also the view in 7: 26–8, as I have shown. The relationship between the typological presentation of the work of Christ in 8: 1 – 9: 26 and the presentation that predominates in the preceding seven chapters remains to be assessed. However, the relating of Christ's priesthood to the concept of the hypostatic union is a theological importation into the perspective of Hebrews. It is a theory based on the assumption that Christ became a priest from the instant of his incarnation and it is supported by a simplistic exegesis of 5: 1.[108] Our writer in fact provides no evidence for the view that 'Christ is consecrated priest at the very moment of his incarnation, when his human nature is created and at the same time united with the divine in the person of the eternal Son of God.'[109] The most that can be said is that 'the Son exhibited and authenticated himself as a priest in the performance of his priestly functions'.[110]

The relationship between the participle τετελειωμένον (7: 28) and the following section (8: 1 – 9: 28) is much emphasised by A. Vanhoye. Following the lead of L. Vaganay, he proposes that the three clauses of 5: 9–10 designate in advance the subject matter of what he calls the third main part of Hebrews (7: 1 – 10: 35). The high priesthood of Christ 'after the order of Melchizedek' is the subject of 7: 1–28, his being brought to perfection is said to be the subject of 8: 1 – 9: 28 and his becoming 'source of eternal salvation for all who obey him' the subject of 10: 1–18 (with a concluding exhortation in 10: 19–35).[111] The τετελειωμένον of 7: 28 serves to remind the reader that the perfecting of Christ will be the author's main concern in the following section. Vanhoye argues that any consideration of the concept of perfection in Hebrews will be incomplete and inexact that does not take account of these observations.[112] In an earlier article, Vanhoye shows in some detail how the contrast begun in 7: 26–8 between the levitical high priesthood and the high priesthood of Jesus is continued in the following chapters where we find the inadequacies of the levitical system outlined in 8: 3 – 9: 10 and the achievements of Christ in his priesthood in 9: 11–28.[113] In a concluding assessment, Vanhoye proposes that the perfecting of Christ means:

'to pass beyond the stage of carnal rites, powerless to purify the conscience (9: 1–10) and to offer himself, in fulness of spirit, by the shedding of his own blood (9: 11–14); to pass beyond the stage of the first covenant, impersonal and provisional in effect, precisely the stage of the impotence of rites (8: 6–13), and to become mediator of the New Covenant thanks to the ability of his blood to purify (9: 15–23); in a word, to pass beyond the stage of the earthly, figurative cult (8: 3–5) and really end up, once for all, in heaven, "to appear before the face of God on our behalf" (9: 24–8).'[114]

As a summary of the argument in 8: 1 – 9: 28, this last paragraph is brief but adequate. It also agrees with much that I have said previously about the perfecting of Christ: the consummation of his Messianic vocation in death, resurrection–ascension and heavenly session is here viewed in terms of his fulfilment of the high-priestly office and his mediation of a new covenant. Although the τετελειωμένον of 7: 28 appears to be separated from 9: 11–28 by the nature and extent of the intervening verses, Vanhoye has demonstrated the intricate connections between the sections (7: 26–8; 8: 1 – 9: 10; 9: 11–28). The suggested link between 5: 9–10 and chapters 7 to 10 is not as far-fetched as may at first appear, when the details of Vanhoye's analysis are considered.

However, the correct method of approach must be the testing of Vanhoye's conclusions from his theory of literary structure in the light of previous exegesis. The immediate contexts of 2: 10; 5: 9 and 7: 28 supply us with a progressive understanding of the concept of Christ's perfecting. It is only against this background that we can see validity in the argument that 8: 1 – 9: 28 deals in certain respects with this theme. The idea that Christ is perfected as heavenly high priest becomes progressively more apparent in 2: 10–18; 4: 14 – 5: 10 and 7: 1–28. In 8: 1 – 9: 28 we are told what this involves in terms of his fulfilment of the high-priestly office: a 'heavenly liturgy' with respect to the heavenly sanctuary. Again we may say that the vocational understanding of Christ's perfecting is confirmed by exegesis to be central to our writer's use of $\tau\epsilon\lambda\epsilon\iota o\tilde{\upsilon}\nu$, though I cannot agree that this word was understood with the particular sense of sacerdotal investiture.[115]

One important dimension that is emphasised particularly in 2: 10–18 and 4: 14 – 5: 10 but not so much in 7: 28 and not at all in Vanhoye's assessment of 8: 1 – 9: 28, is the *personal* preparation and qualification of Christ for his work in terms of temptation, suffering and learning obedience. In my previous chapter, I showed how Vanhoye, in his *Situation du Christ*, stresses the 'moral' perfecting of Christ. In that later publication, he seeks to relate the latter to the 'plan religieux' that dominates the context of 2: 10; 5: 9 and 7: 28. He introduces 1 Cor. 15: 50 ('flesh and blood cannot inherit the kingdom of God') to support his assertion that: 'the humanity of Christ, bound up with our own, has need, therefore, to be "made perfect" by a profound transformation. It must pass from a carnal mode of existence to a perfectly spiritual mode of existence.'[116] Christ's obedience through suffering, leading to his self-offering, is what is said to render his human nature perfect, by establishing it in a new relationship with God and man. However, I have argued in connection with Cody's position that our writer's focus is not on the perfection of Christ's humanity in such a metaphysical sense. The transfer to heavenly glory, which leads to his 'appearance' in the heavenly tabernacle and his heavenly session, may well imply such a concept, but this is not the essential meaning of the perfecting of Christ. Nowhere, in all his writings, does Vanhoye appear to provide a satisfactory integration of all the evidence of Hebrews on this subject.[117]

Conclusion

The leading refrain of Hebrews 7 is the notion of an eternal priesthood, foreshadowed in Melchizedek and realised in Christ. Our writer focusses on the resurrection–ascension experience of Christ, which put him in a position where he can exercise that perpetual priesthood of which Psalm 110: 4 speaks (verses 16–17, 23ff). The divine oath associated with his appointment makes him the surety of a new and better covenant because the eternity of his priesthood is guaranteed by God (verses 20–2). In contrast with the levitical priests, 'he always lives to make intercession' for those who draw near to God through him (verse 25). The reality behind this concept of intercession is the presence of the crucified and yet glorified Christ with God.

Although the emphasis of this chapter is on the significance of Christ's heavenly exaltation for himself and his people, mention is also made of the personal qualities that make him the perfect high priest (verse 26) and the perfect sacrifice (verse 27). The terminology of verse 26 recalls the perspective of 2: 18; 4: 15 and 5: 7f, where his proving through earthly circumstances is suggested. It is not simply the fact that he is 'exalted above the heavens' that makes him a perfect high priest. It is because he lived and died as he did, offering the perfect sacrifice (verse 27), that he was exalted to God's right hand and always lives to make intercession for his people. The sequence of thought in verses 26—8 suggests the importance of Jesus' proving in temptation, his self-sacrifice in obedience to the Father and his heavenly exaltation, for his perfecting as high priest after the order of Melchizedek.

Despite the fact that the chapter as a whole is concerned to explicate the significance of Psalm 110: 4 for Christ as high priest of the New Covenant, it is ultimately as 'Son' that he is said to have been perfected (verse 28). It would seem that our writer's presentation is best understood here again in vocational terms. The Son's eschatological inheritance could not be secured nor his Sonship decisively manifested for the salvation of his people until he had carried out the earthly ministry designed for him as Messiah. However, the messianic task is interpreted by our writer in sacerdotal terms because he wants to indicate the supersession of the priesthood and cult of the Old Testament and focus the attention of his readers on the practical consequences of the eternal priesthood of Christ.

6

THE PERFECTING OF BELIEVERS

Leaving aside the particular application of the terminology in 5: 14; 6: 1 and 12: 2 for consideration in the next chapter, our concern here is to interpret those contexts in which the perfecting of believers is specifically in view. It may reasonably be supposed that there are similarities in the use of the terminology with respect to Christ and to believers, though the precise nature of the relationship will not be analysed until the next chapter, when the present exegetical survey is completed.

The assumption that was fundamental to the interpretation of τελειοῦν in previous chapters is also maintained here: distinct content can only be given to this verb from its context in each case and its object in particular. However, a problem arises when it is observed that this verb in some contexts appears to be associated with ἁγιάζειν and καθαρίζειν and in other contexts with the τέλος of man's earthly pilgrimage, the attainment of 'the δόξα determined from the beginning, that is, fellowship with the Father'.[1] The relating of these two different perspectives remains a central problem for the interpreter. Although some have argued that our writer is using τελειοῦν at 11: 40 and 12: 23 in a different sense from the application in previous passages,[2] I will maintain that he consistently has in view the totality of Christ's work for believers on every occasion. The evidence will be considered in the order in which it is unfolded, illustrating that a proper assessment of this terminology depends on an understanding of the argument generally, as it develops in these central chapters of Hebrews.

The weakness of the levitical system

(a) An inadequate priesthood (7: 11–19)

In the exposition of Hebrews 7 presented above, it was argued that the main purpose of 7: 11–19 was to illustrate the insufficiency of the levitical priesthood. The very fact that Psalm 110: 4 prophesied the coming of a priest of a new order implied a weakness in the existing order. When Christ is enabled to exercise that eternal priesthood of which the psalm citation speaks (verse 17), by virtue of his heavenly exaltation (verse 16), it is clear that the better priesthood, with its better hope (verse 19), has arrived.

Seeking to indicate more specifically the ways in which the levitical priesthood was inadequate, the writer speaks of its failure to secure τελείωσις (verse 11). This first and only use of the noun in Hebrews must be related to the use of the verb in 7: 19. Delling shows how the LXX employs this word with the range of meanings found in extra-Biblical Greek. It is used for the 'execution' of a plan (Judith 10: 9),[3] the 'completion' of wisdom in truthful lips (Sir. 34: 8), the 'conclusion' or 'completion' of the temple (2 Macc. 2: 9),[4] and the 'maturity' of Israel in love for God (Jer. 2: 2).[5] We also find in the LXX the peculiar use of this noun in connection with the installation of the priests.[6] Here, the Greek translators have rendered fairly literally what is already a technical use of *millu'îm* in the MT. In chapter 2, it was argued that this usage has to be understood as a shorthand reference to the more complete verbal expression τελειοῦν τὰς χεῖρας. The primary reference is to the filling of the hands of the prospective priest with a wave-offering, thereby enabling him to perform the priestly function for the first time. The preference for τελειοῦν and τελείωσις in these narratives, rather than πληροῦν and πλήρωσις, may be due to the desire of the translators to convey the sense of 'consummation', 'completion' or 'qualification' with respect to the vocation of priesthood.

However, the attempt of Delling and others to interpret Hebrews 7: 11 in the light of this cultic use of τελείωσις is not legitimate. It may be true to say from the context that 'through the levitical priesthood the state is not reached in which "one can come before God"',[7] but this is not indicated by the supposed cultic implications of τελείωσις. Neither is it true that 'in the context the reference is to the priest who is not qualified by the Aaronic order to intercede for the people before God'. The relevant expression in 7: 11 is not speaking of the failure of the levitical system to qualify its own officials to 'come before God'.[8] The writer speaks of the hypothetical possibility of perfection being obtained *through* the levitical priesthood (διά with the genitive). In the Pentateuch, the ordination offering was for the 'perfecting' of *the priests*, not something applied to the people by the priests. Yet in 7: 19 the perfecting that the Law could not achieve is clearly related to that better hope 'by which we draw near to God' (cf. 7: 25). In other words, our writer is contrasting the failure of the levitical priesthood to bring perfection to the people of God, and the success of Jesus in this regard. Furthermore, if the terminology of perfection was being used in a modified cultic sense, I would expect the same kind of comparison as is found in the application of ἀγιάξειν and καθαρίξειν. With regard to these terms, we are told that the Law provided some measure of cleansing and sanctification (9: 13, 19ff), but our writer denies *absolutely* that perfection was available under the former system ('for the law made nothing perfect', 7: 19).

With these considerations in mind I would argue that the more usual sense of 'consummation' or 'completion' is meant. Lk. 1: 45 is the only other place in the NT where τελείωσις is used, and here we are told of Mary's belief that there would be 'a *fulfilment* of what was spoken to her from the Lord'.[9] Michel argues that in Hebrews 'the issue is not the fulfilment of the promise but the qualification for heavenly sacrifice and priestly service, the definitive consecration',[10] supposing an allusion to the τελείωσις of the priests in the Pentateuch. However, the sense of 'fulfilment' is much more appropriate to the context and to our writer's overall argument, where the emphasis is not on the fulfilment of Scripture, as in Lk. 1: 45, but on the fulfilment or consummation of mankind in an eternal relationship with God.

As suggested above, the first clue to the specific meaning of this perfection can be taken from 7: 19. Although it is *the Law* that is said to have failed in bringing perfection, the writer has already shown how the Law rested on the priesthood (verse 11),[11] and 7: 18f actually speaks of the setting aside of the particular ordinance of priesthood ('a former commandment') because of its weakness and uselessness. In other words, the failure of the Law in general to perfect is specifically related to the failure of the levitical priesthood in this regard. The οὐδέν of 7: 19 as the object of ἐτελείωσεν gives the same general sense as 7: 11 – 'nothing was brought to its appointed end'[12] – but the particular concern in this context is the failure to bring people into a right relationship with God. In Riggenbach's words, 'although given by God, the law was still not able to perfect. All its institutions such as priesthood, sacrifice, atonement, and the like, fall short of what they should have been to bring about a definitive arrangement of the relationship with God.'[13]

Several commentators follow this line, interpreting the perfecting of 7: 19, which the Law did not achieve, in terms of the 'better hope by which we draw near to God'. Thus, Moffatt speaks of the uselessness of the law to secure 'a real access or fellowship' with God,[14] and W. Manson describes perfection in this context as 'the complete facilitation of our approach to God'.[15] Du Plessis also notes the connection between ἐτελείωσεν and ἐγγίζομεν τῷ θεῷ and concludes that man's perfection is to be found in drawing near to God through Christ: 'they who do so become beneficiaries of salvation and are called the people of God'.[16] Of course, perfection cannot simply be identified with drawing near to God. As argued in the previous chapter, drawing near to God was not a complete impossibility for people under the Old Covenant, neither was it the privilege of the priests alone. Our writer's stress is on *the better hope* with which the Christian encounters God (7: 19).[17] This better hope is due to the 'better covenant' of which Jesus is surety (7: 22) and mediator (8: 6; 12: 24): it is enacted on 'better promises' (8: 6) and is eternal in its consequences (13: 20).

Mention of the 'better hope' suggests a future dimension to the perfecting of believers. The better hope is clearly related to the *eternity* of Christ's priesthood, which is so stressed in the context. Jesus is the 'surety of a better covenant' (verse 22) by virtue of the divine oath appointing him 'a priest for ever'. Whereas the levitical priests were prevented by death from continuing in office, Christ is able to save 'for all time' those who draw near to God through him, 'since he always lives to make intercession for them' (verse 25). His exaltation on the basis of a perfect obedience, culminating in a perfect sacrifice (verse 26f), qualifies him to bring people into an intimate relationship with God and keep them in that relationship through his continual 'intercession' on their behalf. The final goal of such a relationship, in our writer's perspective, is to share Christ's glory (2: 10), to enter God's rest (4: 11ff), to see the Lord (12: 14) and to inhabit the heavenly Jerusalem (12: 22; 13: 14).

Nevertheless, despite this emphasis on the unfulfilled aspect of the relationship with God, drawing near to God is very much a present possibility in 7: 19, 25 (cf. 4: 16; 10: 22). In one sense, believers have already 'come' to the heavenly city (12: 22, προσεληλύθατε) and entered the heavenly sanctuary (6: 19f), since Jesus has gone ahead as their forerunner and hope. The better hope by which the Christian draws near to God is not essentially something future: it is a reference to the superior high-priestly ministry of Jesus in his death and exaltation, which enables men and women to draw near to God with new directness and certainty (παρρησία) *in the present*. Thus, the perfecting of believers is not simply a future concept, equivalent to glorification,[18] though the relationship that the writer describes clearly has eternal consequences. The terminology of perfection in this cultic context, as in 9: 9; 10: 1, 14, stresses the possibility of a present realisation of God's purposes for mankind. The fulfilment of the promises of the New Covenant in the priestly ministry of Christ facilitates an access to and relationship with God that was not possible under the former covenant.

Westcott inappropriately emphasises a *moral dimension* to the concept of man's perfecting here: 'man must strive towards the perfection, the accomplishment of his destiny on earth. The Law failed him in the effort. He outgrew it. The very scope of the Law indeed was to define the requirements of life, and to show that man himself could not satisfy them.'[19] This view of the Law as defining 'the requirements of life', which man must pursue to achieve his 'destiny on earth', goes beyond our writer's view, in which the Law's purpose is to regulate man's approach to God in a cultic sense.[20] However, in an earlier discussion, Westcott rightly argues that 'the aim of a religious system is $\tau\epsilon\lambda\epsilon\iota\omega\sigma\iota\varsigma$ (7: 11), to bring men to their true end, when all the fulness of humanity in power and development is brought into fellowship with God'.[21]

(b) An earthly sanctuary and a limited Covenant (8: 1ff)

The fundamental weakness of the levitical priesthood, as presented in 7: 11ff, is the mortality of its members: they were 'prevented by death from continuing in office' (verse 23), whereas the Christian's high priest 'lives for ever'. Another aspect of this — the necessity for repeated sacrifice for sins, both for priests and people — is alluded to in 7: 27. A further weakness of the levitical system is expounded in 8: 1ff. As implied in 7: 25f, Christ has been exalted 'above the heavens' to the very presence of God and conducts his ministry in that sphere. Levitical priests, on the other hand, serve only 'a copy and shadow of the heavenly sanctuary' (8: 5).

The writer asserts that his main point ($\kappa\epsilon\phi\acute{a}\lambda\alpha\iota ov$)[22] is that we have a high priest 'who is seated at the right hand of the throne of the Majesty in heaven, a minister in the sanctuary and the true tent which is set up not by man but by the Lord' (8: 1f RSV). 'We have such a high priest' clearly points back, at least in some measure, to the argument of chapter 7, though 8: 1f cannot simply be described as a summary of the argument so far.[23] The words 'who is seated at the right hand of the throne of the Majesty in heaven' recall the affirmation of Jesus' heavenly session in 1: 3.[24] This theme is linked to that of Jesus' priesthood in 8: 1 to show how he exercises a *heavenly office*. Psalm 110: 1, which is alluded to here, thus becomes 'the only Scriptural evidence which the author adduces to prove that Jesus is in heaven: and, if he were not in heaven, he would not be a priest at all' (8: 4).[25]

When Christ is described as $\tau\tilde{\omega}v$ $\acute{a}\gamma\acute{\iota}\omega v$ $\lambda\epsilon\iota\tau ov\rho\gamma\acute{o}\varsigma$, the writer most likely uses the expression $\tau\tilde{\omega}v$ $\acute{a}\gamma\acute{\iota}\omega v$, as often it is used in the LXX, to refer to the sanctuary in general, 'without any reference to the distinction (cp. 9: 2f) between the inner and outer shrine'.[26] Although it is argued below that a distinction must be made in 9: 11f between the $\sigma\kappa\eta v\acute{\eta}$ through which Jesus passed and $\tau\grave{a}$ $\acute{a}\gamma\iota a$ which he entered, such a distinction does not seem to be appropriate here.[27] That a hendiadys is intended by 'the sanctuary and the true tent' seems obvious from the singular number of the pronoun ἥν in the relative clause that follows ('which is set up not by man but by the Lord'): 'our author could hardly have meant that the Lord set up only a heavenly holy place, especially as the focus of his attention is on the high-priestly entry of Jesus into the heavenly holy of holies' (cf. 9: 24).[28] The heavenly sanctuary is described as 'the true tent which is set up not by man but by the Lord' to anticipate the contrast of 8: 5.

Although Moses received the command from God to erect the earthly tent, and God showed him the 'pattern' or 'model' (τύπος) to follow (8: 5), it was truly a man-made sanctuary (cf. 9: 24). The Tabernacle that 'the Lord pitched' is by implication 'not made with hands', which in 9: 11 means 'not of this creation'. Furthermore, it is 'the true tent' (verse 2), of which the earthly Tabernacle is only a poor copy (verse 5).[29] Although the heavenly Tabernacle is not called eternal, ἀληθινή fundamentally means that it is eternal in character.[30] Earthly priests serve only 'a copy and shadow of the heavenly sanctuary' (verse 5). As in 9: 23, ὑπόδειγμα means 'a mere outline or copy' and the phrase ὑποδείγματι καὶ σκιᾷ is 'practically a hendiadys for "a shadowy outline", a second-hand, inferior reproduction'.[31] Moffatt notes how the idea was current in Alexandrian Judaism, under the influence of Platonism, that the earthly Tabernacle had been 'but a reproduction of the pre-existent heavenly sanctuary'.[32] Our writer is said to have been influenced by a modified form of Platonic idealism: 'above the shows and shadows of material things he sees the real order of being, and it is most real to him on account of Jesus being there'. However, although there may be certain linguistic parallels between 8: 5 and Philonic Platonism, 'there is no trace in the verse, or indeed anywhere else in the Epistle, of the fundamental attitudes or convictions which constitute Platonism either in its original or in its Philonic form. The writer of Hebrews does not use his philosophical terminology in anything approaching a rigorously philosophical way.'[33]

Despite the image of the heavenly sanctuary as something objective, virtually a part of the heavenly topography, our writer is ultimately using the terminology as 'an expression for the representation of Christ at God's right hand',[34] as the collocation of the two ideas in 8: 1f shows. The heavenly things are the eschatological realities which OT institutions only foreshadowed, and the relationship between the two sanctuaries is basically a *temporal* one.[35] The citation from Exod. 25: 40, which is used to substantiate the argument in 8: 5, certainly implies that Moses was shown some sort of model which could be reproduced on earth.[36] Nevertheless, our writer's distinction between earthly and heavenly is eschatologically controlled, rather than philosophically inspired. We may 'demythologise' the language and represent the essence of the argument thus: levitical priests served in a God-ordained, but man-made sanctuary, and in this ministry foreshadowed only superficially the definitive priestly ministry of Christ, in his death and exaltation to the very presence of God.

Christ's ministry is therefore superior to that of earthly priests because the sphere in which he serves is the heavenly sanctuary or the true Tabernacle. His ministry is also superior because it makes him the mediator of a new and better covenant (8: 6). The New Covenant itself is said to be better because it is 'enacted on better promises'.[37] Vanhoye rightly argues that the extensive citation from Jer. 31: 31–4 in the following section serves a fundamentally *negative* purpose:[38] the introductory and concluding verses (verses 7, 13) stress the imperfect and provisional character of the Old Covenant. The writer draws attention to the blame contained within the oracle itself (verses 8f) and does not deal with the positive implications of the new and better promises immediately. However, the fundamental point is made that the covenant that Jesus institutes and maintains is based on better promises and these are listed. When a second, abbreviated citation from the same prophecy concludes the central exposition of the work of Christ (10: 15–18), it is clear that the oracle is vital to our writer's thinking. Although the promises of the New Covenant are not couched in cultic terms and say nothing of a new priesthood and sacrifice, it will be shown below to what extent these promises have influenced the argument.[39]

The cleansing of the conscience

(a) A particular weakness of the Old Covenant (9: 6–10)

In 9: 1 the author announces two subjects which he then treats in reverse order, 'regulations for worship' and 'an earthly sanctuary', the latter in 9: 2–5 and the former in 9: 6–10.[40] In the first paragraph, the writer stresses the earthly nature of the Mosaic sanctuary and its ritual, and therefore its insufficiency as a means of relating to God. The description of the sanctuary as κοσμικόν (NEB 'a material sanctuary'),[41] recalls the contrast of 8: 2 ('which is set up not by man but by the Lord') and anticipates the description 'made with hands' (9: 24, cf. 9: 11). As a man-made sanctuary, it is not only transitory but also only a shadowy outline of the true, heavenly or eschatological realities (8: 5), which are now made available through the ministry of Christ (9: 11ff). As a preparation for the argument of verses 6–10, the writer seeks to 'bring out as strongly as possible the distinction and independent significance of the two chambers' in the earthly sanctuary.[42]

Worship by means of such a sanctuary is then shown to be inadequate on several grounds. The whole system allowed the people to approach God only through their representatives the priests (verse 6). The ritual of the Day of Atonement stressed that only the high priest could draw near to the inner sanctuary, symbolic of the actual presence of God, and there but once a year, with the appropriate sacrificial blood (verse 7). The very existence of such a sanctuary, with its two divisions and rigid regulations of approach, 'witnessed constantly to the aim of man and to the fact that he could not as yet attain it. He could not penetrate to that innermost sanctuary to which he necessarily looked, and from which blessing flowed' (verses 8–9*a*).[43] However, the full significance of the ritual just described has only been disclosed by the Holy Spirit in the light of the Christ-event (τοῦτο δηλοῦντος τοῦ πνεύματος τοῦ ἁγίου).[44] That significance is as follows.

As long as the 'first tent' continued to have the status of a sanctuary,[45] the way into the Holy of Holies remained unrevealed. At the literal level, our writer is referring to the outer tent (σκηνή ... ἡ πρώτη verses 2, 6), which prevented the people from seeing, let alone entering, the Holy of Holies.[46] However, the 'first tent' of 9: 8 may mean more in context: it may represent the sanctuary of the first covenant, either tabernacle or temple, meaning Holy Place and Holy of Holies together.[47] In this case, the sanctuary represented by the words τὴν τῶν ἁγίων ὁδόν is the heavenly sanctuary (8: 2), the sanctuary of the New Covenant. The παραβολή, then, is that 'the continuance of the first covenant is a function of the existence of the first tabernacle and the latter symbolises the impossibility of access to heaven, the true sanctuary'.[48] Our writer insists that 'all this is symbolic, pointing to the present time' (verse 9 NEB).[49] This refers primarily to the fact that Christ has opened the way into the heavenly sanctuary by his high-priestly ministry (10: 19f τὴν εἴσοδον τῶν ἁγίων) and inaugurated the time of eschatological salvation (9: 11f) or 'time of reformation' (verse 10). The readers are living in 'the span between the two ages',[50] in which the old order has actually been superseded by the work of Christ and will shortly disappear (8: 13). If W. Manson is correct, the message of these verses (9: 8–10) has particular bearing on the 'crisis' with which the readers were faced.[51]

A particular weakness of the Old Covenant is then emphasised (verses 9–10). In the worship of the earthly sanctuary,[52] gifts and sacrifices are offered that are not able to 'perfect the worshipper with respect to conscience' (κατὰ συνείδησιν τελειῶσαι τὸν λατρεύοντα). The following verse explains this failure in terms of the external operation of the cultus. Food laws, libations to accompany sacrifices, various rites for bodily cleansing and the sacrifices themselves can all be described as 'outward ordinances' (δικαιώματα σαρκός). This whole earth-bound system was only a temporary provision in the outworking of God's plans for his people, being in force 'until the time of reformation' (verse 10).

Turning specifically to the words κατὰ συνείδησιν τελειῶσαι τὸν λατρεύοντα, we may note firstly that all the participants in the OT cultus were disqualified in the same way. Those commentators who argue that τὸν λατρεύοντα refers to 'the priest in the act of sacrifice' (cf. 9: 6),[53] are making an unwarranted restriction of our writer's meaning. Strathmann correctly emphasises that 'the distinction between λειτουργεῖν (priestly sacrificial ministry) and λατρεύειν, which is so strict in the LXX except at 1 Esdras 4: 54, is now obliterated. For in 8: 5 and 13: 10 λατρεύειν refers primarily to the sacrificial ministry of the priests.'[54] However, it does not follow that the term is used in such a restricted sense in 9: 9 and 10: 2, where the wider, more usual LXX sense (e.g., Exod. 3: 12; 4: 23; 7: 26) is more appropriate to the context.[55] The parallel between 9: 9 and 10: 1f is instructive here. The object of the aorist infinitive τελειῶσαι is τὸν λατρεύοντα in the first case and τοὺς προσερχομένους in 10: 1, though the expression τοὺς λατρεύοντας is clearly parallel, referring to the OT worshippers in general. The particular focus of concern in 9: 9 is the perfecting of the worshipper κατὰ συνείδησιν and in 10: 2 it is the failure of the OT system to remove συνείδησιν ἁμαρτιῶν. Undoubtedly, the search for a cleansed conscience through the sacrificial system is represented as being the concern of priests and laymen together.

Thus, the perfecting so vaguely specified in the context of 7: 11, 19 is here defined as having special regard to the conscience of mankind. The nouns συνειδός and συνείδησις only appear to have come into common use in Greek literature in the first century BC. The verbal expression σύνοιδα ἐμαυτῷ had long been used to describe the process of self-reflection and self-awareness, in both a moral and a non-moral sense,[56] and the sporadic use of the nouns in the earlier period shows the language 'feeling its way towards a noun to express the moral conscience in the bad sense'.[57] In the pre-Christian usage, 'moral conscience is not primarily concerned with preparations for approaching decisions (*conscientia antecedens*) but with assessing and condemning acts already committed (*conscientia consequens*). Hence, the normal case is the bad conscience; the good conscience is an exception.'

In his *Conscience in the New Testament*, C. A. Pierce argues that συνείδησις is 'one of the few important Greek words in the NT that have not had imported into them, through use by the LXX, a colouring from the Hebrew experience and outlook of the OT'.[58] However, C. Maurer rightly argues that the OT view of man in general, and of the 'heart' in particular, must be taken into account when assessing NT teaching about the conscience.[59] The limited use of the term in the LXX certainly cannot be held responsible for this combination of 'the Greek view of man as especially a thinking being' with 'the Hebrew tradition which stresses the primacy of the Word'.[60] The Apostle Paul seems to have been a pioneer in this regard. Yet the originality and independence of Hebrews should not be overlooked. Although our writer is more sparing in his use of συνείδησις (9: 9, 14; 10: 2, 22; 13: 18) than Paul, application of the term to the area of soteriology shows how much more central it is to his thinking.[61]

Our writer links the concepts of 'conscience' and 'heart' in the following way. As in the OT, the heart in Hebrews appears to be the seat of the rational functions, planning and volition (3: 8, 10, 12 ('evil, unbelieving heart'), 15; 4: 7, 12). Since it is 'the centre of life and the epitome of the person',[62] it is the aspect of man that must be strengthened by God's grace (13: 9). On two occasions, God's promise to write his laws 'on their hearts' is cited (8: 10; 10: 16; cf. Jer. 31: 33). Although the promise to 'remember their sins and their misdeeds no more' (8: 12; 10: 17; cf. Jer. 31: 34) is clearly central to our writer's exposition of the work of Christ, the former is not forgotten. In 10: 22*a* the writer declares that it is possible to draw near to God 'with a true heart in full assurance of faith'. Westcott rightly suggests that this is 'a heart which fulfils the ideal office of the heart, the seat of the individual character towards God – a heart which expresses completely the devotion of the person to God. There is no divided allegiance: no reserve of feeling.'[63] At this point, our writer proclaims the fulfilment of the promise of Jer. 31: 33 (cf. Ezek. 36: 26f).[64] It is made possible by the fulfilment of the promise of Jer. 31: 34 (cf. Ezek. 36: 25), expressed in 10: 22*b* in terms of 'hearts sprinkled clean from an evil conscience'. There is no simple equation of heart and conscience here, yet they are clearly related. It is 'consciousness of sins' *with respect to God* that essentially concerns our writer (10: 2 συνείδησις ἁμαρτιῶν).[65] Just as the OT speaks of the burdened, smiting heart (1 Sam. 24: 5 (MT 24: 6); 25: 31; 2 Sam. 24: 10, compare Psalm 51: 3–11), so our writer speaks of a heart with 'an evil conscience', meaning a heart that is aware of God's command and authority and of having offended against these.[66] Certainly, conscience can bear witness to the holiness and sincerity of one's motives or conduct in our writer's view (13: 18 'a good conscience'),[67] but he is fundamentally concerned with conscience as a register of man's guilt before God – with the *accusing conscience*.

Hebrews therefore envisages that the promises of the New Covenant are fulfilled when a person's heart is 'sprinkled clean from an evil conscience' — that is, set free from the burden of unforgiven sins — and thus renewed in faith and sincerity towards God (10: 22; cf. Psalm 51: 10 (LXX 50: 12)). Such cleansing of the conscience is only made possible by the 'blood of Christ' (9: 13f), since the levitical sacrifices were only 'outward ordinances' (δικαιώματα σαρκός, 9: 10), unable to affect the heart. Indeed, far from removing the 'consciousness of sins' (10: 2), the Old Covenant ritual actually accentuated the problem by providing a yearly reminder of guilt before God (10: 3). Since it is impossible that 'the blood of bulls and goats should take away sin' (10: 4), it is impossible for the sacrificial system to perfect man with respect to conscience.

Clearly, there is an inner connection between τελειοῦν (9: 9; 10: 1) and καθαρίζειν (9: 14; 10: 2), yet simple identification of these two terms is not valid. Exegesis of 7: 11–19 showed that the perfecting of believers in terms of a *relationship with God* is the primary thought. In 9: 9, it is not strictly the conscience that is perfected. Man, viewed in his role as 'worshipper' (τὸν λατρεύοντα), that is as one who would draw near to God, is perfected 'in relation to conscience' (κατὰ συνείδησιν).[68] One's relationship with God cannot be perfected until conscience is cleansed from guilt and one is enabled to relate to God with that confidence which the work of Christ alone provides (10: 19f; 4: 16). Perfection in this context certainly involves purification and forgiveness, but the overall usage of τελειοῦν in relation to believers suggests that the term has a broader meaning than this. It refers to a relationship with God such as is not 'realized and established by the law but by the sacrifice of Christ and his covenant'.[69] Perfection is not synonymous with cleansing but involves the latter as a most significant element.

(b) The achievement of Christ (9: 11–14)

The argument of this section has been somewhat anticipated in the discussion above. From 9: 11 to 9: 28 the efficacy of Christ's priestly ministry is expounded: it is the liturgy of his blood (9: 12ff), the offering of himself to God (9: 14).[70] The 'time of reformation' (9: 10) has begun, since Christ appeared as 'high priest of the good things that have come' (9: 11).[71]

The work of Christ is described in terms of an extended comparison with that of Jewish high priests on the Day of Atonement. The *sphere* of his ministry is superior because he passes through 'the greater and more perfect tent, not made with hands, that is, not of this creation', to enter the heavenly sanctuary. Detailed consideration of this complicated imagery will be undertaken in a special section below. The *means* of Christ's atoning work is also superior because it is 'his own blood'. The writer has already indicated that the sacrifice of animal blood 'cannot perfect the worshipper with respect to conscience' (9: 9) and in 10: 4 he will assert that it cannot take away sins. The exposition of Psalm 40: 6–8 in 10: 5–10 will emphasise the superiority of Christ's self-offering because it is a sacrifice 'into which obedience enters, the sacrifice of a rational and spiritual being, which is not passive in death, but in dying makes the will of God its own'.[72] Such a contrast is suggested also in 9: 12 with the words 'not by means of (διά)[73] the blood of goats and calves but his own blood', indicating that this high priest willingly makes *himself* the sacrifice for sins (cf. 9: 26). By means of his own blood, Christ has entered the very presence of God ('he entered once for all into the Holy Place'). As in 8: 2; 9: 24; 10: 19, and probably 9: 8, τὰ ἅγια refers to heaven itself, and the purpose of his entry into the heavenly sanctuary is 'to appear before the face of God on our behalf' (9: 24).

Thus, finally the author is able to speak of the *issue* of Christ's atoning work as superior: 'he obtained an eternal redemption, in contrast with the limited, recurrent redemption of the yearly atonement'.[74] The eternal redemption that Christ has obtained is best understood as 'a once-for-all and standing offer of forgiveness for mankind'.[75] This seems likely in view of the comparison with the work of the high priest on the Day of Atonement and the parallel with 9: 15, where redemption from transgressions is specifically in view.[76] The latter focusses attention on the death of Christ as the means by which this remission of sins occurs and suggests that the participial clause αἰωνίαν λύτρωσιν εὑράμενος is related to the principal clause εἰσῆλθεν ἐφάπαξ εἰς τὰ ἅγια as a *precedent*, rather than as a *coincident* fact. The eternal redemption is secured by the sacrifice of the cross, which needs no repetition or renewal, but the ascension 'consecrates the eternal validity of his work'.[77]

A particular proof of the efficacy of Christ's work is then presented in the *a fortiori* argument of 9: 13f. At the same time, further indication is given as to what makes his work so absolute and final. The sacrifices of the Day of Atonement are again alluded to with the phrase 'the blood of goats and bulls' (verse 13), though a broader reference to sacrifices in general may be intended (cf. Psalm 50: 13). Our writer associates with these the occasional sacrifice of the heifer, the ashes of which were to be sprinkled with water upon any Israelite who had touched a dead body. The ceremony in question is certainly described as a 'sin offering' (Num. 19: 9), but its essential character is that of removing ceremonial defilement. It is the external nature of the latter rite that our writer emphasises here and associates it with the blood of goats and bulls to imply that all the rituals of the Old Covenant were only able to provide the participants with an outward purity, sanctifying only 'for the purification of the flesh'.[78] They were restored to fellowship with God in the sense of being able to participate in the worshipping community again, but no cleansing of the inward man or personal contact with God could be achieved by such regulations for the body.[79]

The fundamental assertion that blood 'purifies' and 'sanctifies' under the Old Covenant, even if only at a ceremonial level, provides the basis for the 'how much more' of verse 14.[80] The 'blood of Christ' is a synonym for the death that achieves deliverance from sins (9: 15): our writer refers 'not to matter or substance but to an *action*',[81] as the relative clause in verse 14 makes perfectly clear ('who through the eternal Spirit offered himself without blemish to God'). This refers to the self-sacrifice of Christ, by which he is enabled to enter the heavenly sanctuary and thus provide access for others (10: 19f). The perfection of the sacrifice has to do with the spotless nature of the victim (ἄμωμον)[82] and the voluntary and rational nature of his sacrifice. The latter theme has already been mentioned in connection with 9: 12 ('by means of his own blood') and is emphasised here by the words διὰ πνεύματος αἰωνίου. Moffatt's rendering of these words in terms of 'the realm or order of the inward spirit, not of the outward and material', leads him to conclude that 'it was because Jesus was what he was *by nature*, that his sacrifice had such final value: its atoning significance lay in his vital connexion with the realm of absolute realities'.[83] It is 'in, or in virtue of, his spiritual nature' that his sacrifice is spiritual and eternal in its effects. This rather abstruse rendering of the expression may fit into the general argument, but insufficiently captures the emphasis of the clause itself. The voluntary and rational nature of his sacrifice, 'without blemish' because it was the culmination of a *lifetime of obedience to God*, implies a power upholding and maintaining him in his office. Although the reference is possibly to 'the divine nature, the absolutely celestial nature of Christ', which 'by its powerful effect takes hold of the human nature of Christ',[84] it is doubtful that our writer presents such a developed Christology with so brief an allusion. It is more probable that the expression is a periphrasis for the Holy Spirit,[85] especially in view of the likelihood that our writer was influenced in his presentation of Christ by the Isaianic Servant theme.[86]

It was argued above that the eternal redemption that Christ secured by his death (9: 12) is a 'once-for-all and standing offer of forgiveness for mankind'. In the principal clause of 9: 14, this truth is explained in terms of its *effect* on those who receive it. The blood of Christ 'will cleanse (καθαριεῖ) our conscience from the deadness of our former ways and fit us for the service of the living God' (NEB).[87] The NEB rendering of ἀπὸ νεκρῶν ἔργων ('from the deadness of our former ways') is a fair paraphrase in the light of 6: 1f. There we find repentance ἀπὸ νεκρῶν ἔργων in a short list of the 'foundation' teachings known to the readers. In such a context, 'dead works' will be 'the moral offences from which a man had to break away in order to become a Christian at all'.[88] Not only must there be *repentance* from dead works, but also a *cleansing of the conscience* from such, if one is to 'serve the living God' (9: 14). The opposite of dead works is presumably 'good works' (10: 24). The adjective νεκρά seems to have been chosen to emphasise the fact that they have 'no principle of life in them, or that they lead to death'.[89] While it may be true that the readers needed weaning from an attachment to the levitical system, its 'works' are not such as would give a person a *guilty conscience* and therefore cannot be the dead works in question here.[90]

Summarising the contrast between 9: 9 (with 10: 1–4) and 9: 14, Du Plessis observes that:

> 'the inefficiency of sacrificial offerings is explained as inability to banish the self-indictment or consciousness of the presence of sin even after expiatory services. A continual repetition of the deed was therefore necessary. By contrast, the all-sufficient sacrifice of Christ removed the self-incrimination and realized positive self-appraisal and self-determination, one dominated by the sense of liberation from the bondage and slavery of sin.'[91]

Clearly, the power of the defiled conscience to keep a person from serving God effectively is a fundamental presupposition of our writer's teaching on the perfecting of believers.

The purpose of Christ's cleansing of the conscience (εἰς τὸ λατρεύειν θεῷ ζῶντι) is often interpreted in purely cultic terms. Our writer's use of λατρεύειν for the priestly sacrificial ministry elsewhere (8: 5; 13: 10) suggests to some that 'the Christian now has the ability to come to God, to approach him, like the priest in sacrificial ministry'.[92] Even if a particularly sacerdotal reading of this verb is not adopted, the cultic imagery of 9: 14 suggests at least that the conscience needs cleansing for 'open access to God in worship'.[93] This is consistent with the imagery and appeal of 10: 19ff, where right of access into the very sanctuary of God is provided by the blood of Christ. The readers are encouraged to draw near in the certainty that their hearts have been 'sprinkled clean from an evil conscience'. Nevertheless, the interpreter of Hebrews must probe further into our writer's use of cultic language to investigate the extent to which it has been modified and the precise way in which it has been applied. I have consistently maintained that προσέρχεσθαι and ἐγγίζειν are used to describe those invisible acts of faith by which an individual appropriates the benefits of Christ's work. Even if such drawing near to God continues to find expression in the activities of Christian assembly, that cultic application is not the ultimate meaning of the terminology.[94]

Apart from particular apologetic reasons, relating to the *Sitz im Leben* of the readers, the presentation of the work of Christ in terms of a heavenly cult is our writer's way of relating the once-for-all achievement of Christ's death to the promise of the New Covenant and the ongoing needs of believers. Within such a framework of thought, a guilty conscience certainly prevents 'open access to God in worship'. However, the concept of worship is almost certainly to be expanded in 9: 14, as in 12: 28, to include 'a manner of life which is pleasing to God and which is sustained both by gratitude and by a serious sense of responsibility'.[95] This means that the Christian's service is not restricted to prayer and praise, either individually or corporately, but involves a lifetime of acknowledging his name (13: 15) and of pleasing God in practical obedience (13: 16).[96] If the worship of God includes the total response of the believer in terms of hope, love and good works (10: 23f, 32ff; 6: 9–12), conscience must be cleansed to empower the believer to serve God in this way. Thus, although the perfecting of believers does not involve a moral development in our writer's perspective, it has its proper outworking in a life of obedience to God's will and perseverance in hope. The cleansing of the conscience leads to a decisive change in a person's heart with respect to God and enables that person to serve God as he requires.

The greater and more perfect tent

Since the imagery of 9: 11f has given rise to such a variety of interpretations, detailed discussion of those verses has been delayed until now. The symmetry of the passage may be represented as follows, in this very literal rendering of the Greek:[97]

(a) But when Christ appeared as a high priest of the good things that have come,

(+b) (then) through the greater and more perfect tent,

(−b) not made with hands, that is, not of this creation,

(−c) not by means of the blood of goats and calves,

(+c) but by means of his own blood,

(d) he entered once for all into the sanctuary, having obtained an eternal redemption.

Although there appears to be an identification of τὰ ἅγια and ἡ σκηνή ἡ ἀληθινή in 8: 2, it does violence to the syntax of 9: 11f to suggest that the greater and more perfect tent and τὰ ἅγια are one and the same thing here.[98] The apparent separation between the σκηνή as the *means* (verse 11) and the ἅγια as the *end* (verse 12) is consistent with the usage of 9: 2ff. In 9: 1 the earthly sanctuary as a whole is in view, but in 9: 2ff the two main divisions in that sanctuary are described in terms of the 'first tent' (verses 2, 6) and the 'second tent' (verse 7; cf. verses 13f). In 9: 8 the 'first tent' seems to be taken as a parable of the old aeon and of the levitical system, which actually prevented access to the heavenly sanctuary. Developing the image of the high priest on the Day of Atonement, entering the Holy of Holies by means of the Holy Place, our writer proceeds to argue that Christ has entered the heavenly sanctuary 'by means of' or 'through the greater and more perfect tent, not made with hands, that is, not of this creation'.[99] Thus far, many commentators would agree, but there is great diversity of opinion as to the actual significance of 'the greater and more perfect tent'. Interpretations fit broadly into one of two categories.

(a) The tent as the body of Christ

Chrysostom and a number of late Patristic writers argued that the greater and more perfect tent was the body assumed by the Son of God in the incarnation. This view has had a number of advocates ever since.[100] The justification for this lies in the use of ναός with respect to the body of Christ in John 2: 19–22 (cf. Mk 14: 58 'another, not made with hands'), the use of ἐσκήνωσεν with regard to the incarnation in John 1: 14, and general NT teaching about the body in 'tent' language (2 Cor. 5: 1ff; 2 Pet. 1: 13f). However, our writer's insistence that the greater and more perfect tent is 'not made with hands, that is, not of this creation' makes the identification with the incarnate body of Christ improbable. Any suggestion that the humanity of Christ was not genuine would be in total contradiction to our writer's overall presentation.[101] Furthermore, the very passages cited to support this interpretation point rather to the glorified, resurrection body of Christ or to the Church.

Thus, Vanhoye argues that the resurrection body of Christ is intended. He assumes that our writer is influenced by the primitive Christian tradition relating the death and resurrection of Jesus to the theme of the temple and that it is 'in the mystery of the resuscitated body of Christ' that access to God is granted to men.[102] The distinction between ἡ σκηνή and τὰ ἅγια in 9: 11f enables our author to 'plumb the religious significance of the resurrection of Christ'.[103] The connection between Christ's resurrected body and his blood in these verses is said to find its parallel in 10: 19f, where access to God for believers is by means of the blood of Christ and 'through the veil of his flesh'.

In some respects this is an appealing interpretation. It deals adequately with the overall structure and individual elements of 9: 11f, and its theological emphasis is consistent with that of other NT passages. Nevertheless, it is seriously to be questioned whether a knowledge of the primitive Christian tradition relating the resurrected body of Christ to the theme of the temple can be assumed in this context. Every other use of σκηνή, apart from 8: 2, relates to the earthly Tabernacle of Judaism, considered as a whole (8: 5; 13: 10) or in its two main divisions (9: 2, 3, 6, 7, 8). The expression in 8: 2 is best identified in the context with the heavenly sanctuary that was the pattern for the Mosaic sanctuary (8: 5).[104] In view of this usage, it is much more likely that σκηνή in 9: 11 has something to do with our writer's cosmology, in the sense outlined below. Furthermore, Vanhoye's emphasis on the significance of Christ's resurrection in our writer's soteriology is inappropriate. The concept of resurrection may be said to be assumed in the emphasis on Christ's exaltation, but it finds explicit mention only in 13: 20.[105] The real focus in Hebrews is on Christ's death and ascension. The complications of 10: 20 will be analysed below, but it is sufficient to remark here that the expression 'through the veil of his flesh' may be related to 'the way' or 'the curtain' and that the reference is more likely to be to the sacrifice of Christ than to his resurrection.[106]

In terms of our writer's soteriology, there may be more to commend the theory of L. Sabourin. Developing some of Vanhoye's arguments, he proposes that 'the greater and more perfect tent' is explained by the parallel phrase διὰ δὲ τοῦ ἰδίου αἵματος. It is by 'the great liturgy of the sacrifice of Christ' that he enters the heavenly sanctuary: 'he himself has become "celestial man" (1 Cor. 15: 47, Heb. 9: 23) by sacrificial transformation'.[107] However, the words 'and not by means of the blood of goats and calves, but by means of his own blood' introduce a new element into the structure of the verse instead of offering a further explanation of the expression 'through the greater and more perfect tent'. Furthermore, Sabourin is asking us to stretch the symbolic value of the greater and more perfect tent to the point beyond which the word 'tent' actually has any linguistic significance. It is not our writer's custom to use language so cryptically!

A further development of the theory that σκηνή is to be related to the body of Christ is found in the interpretation of Westcott. Arguing from the presupposition that the Tabernacle was designed to symbolise the presence of God among his people and to afford 'under certain restrictions a means of approach to him', he proposes that the heavenly Tabernacle must be the glorified Church: 'in this body, as a spiritual temple, Christ ministers. As members of this body believers severally enjoy the divine presence.'[108] Thus, Westcott connects 'redeemed humanity with the glorified human nature of the Lord'. However, as P.E. Hughes rightly observes: 'there is no way in which one can speak of his having entered into the heavenly sanctuary through the church: the church is not the means of his entry into the heavenly sanctuary, but, to the contrary, he is the means of the church's entry'.[109]

(b) The tent as the heavenly Tabernacle

The interpretation that best observes the structure of the sentence and gives the most natural reading to σκηνή maintains a close analogy between what is said about Christ in 9: 11ff and the work of the high priest on the Day of Atonement. According to Moffatt, we have here an imaginative description of Christ 'passing through the upper heavens (no hand-made, mundane forecourt this!) into the innermost presence' and it is a more detailed account of what is meant by 4: 14 ('since then we have a great high priest who has passed through the heavens').[110] The imagery of 9: 11 is also anticipated in 7: 26 ('exalted above the heavens'), which presupposes a passage *through* the heavens. It is true that the words 'not made with hands, that is, not of this creation' (9: 11) exclude the possibility that our writer is talking simply about a passage through the 'visible heavens'.[111] However, our writer seems to speak of the heavens in three different ways: the created and transitory heavens (1: 10–12; 12: 26), the heavens through which Jesus passed (4: 14; 9: 11–12) and heaven as the actual dwelling place of God (9: 24).[112] In our writer's thinking, both the greater and more perfect tent and the heavenly sanctuary exist beyond creation.[113] If it is objected that this cosmology finds no support elsewhere in the NT and gives extraordinary soteriological significance to the intermediary heavens,[114] it must be remembered that our writer is largely governed in his presentation by the ritual of the Day of Atonement. 'Good Friday and Ascension become Christianity's Day of Atonement and are retrospectively drawn together into a unity.'[115] Soteriological significance is not given to the intermediary heavens *per se*, but to Christ's passage through these, that is to his *ascension* (cf. Eph. 4: 8–10; 1 Pet. 3: 22).[116] Our high priest passed through all the supernatural spheres separating man and God, to enter the actual 'dwelling place' or presence of God, and not by means of animal sacrifices, but by virtue of his own sacrificial death, by which process he secured an eternal redemption.

It should finally be noted that the terminology of perfection is used in 9: 11 as part of our writer's ongoing comparison between Old and New Covenants. This 'tent', in contrast with the outer tent of the earthly ritual (9: 8), is 'more perfect' ($\tau\epsilon\lambda\epsilon\iota o\tau\acute{\epsilon}\rho a$) in the sense that it more perfectly fulfils its functions:[117] it actually leads Christ, and thus ultimately believers, into the presence of God. Since it is 'not made with hands, that is, not of this creation', it is 'better qualified for heavenly service'.[118] OT institutions, being earthly in their fabric and orientation, are transitory and unable to penetrate to the ultimate spiritual level. In the death and heavenly exaltation of Christ, perfection in a relationship with God is made possible since he has entered 'not that sanctuary made by men's hands which is only a symbol of the reality, but heaven itself, to appear now before God on our benalf' (9: 24 NEB).

Perfection and the New Covenant

Throughout the preceding analysis of passages relating to the perfecting of believers, it has regularly been observed that our writer's thinking in this regard is significantly related to the promise of Jer. 31: 31–4. This theory is confirmed by a detailed examination of 10: 1–18. It is generally agreed that this passage forms a climax to the central theological argument of Hebrews. An intricate transition from exposition to parenesis then occurs in 10: 19–25, based on the perspectives found in the whole section 8: 1 – 10: 18. The inability of the Old Covenant to perfect its beneficiaries is the emphasis of verses 1–4 and the promise of the New Covenant in this regard is the emphasis of verses 15–18. The two intervening paragraphs mark 'the modalities of this change':[119] the replacement of the sacrifices (verses 5–10) and the replacement of the priesthood (verses 11–14). Observing the use of $\tau\epsilon\lambda\epsilon\iota\tilde{\omega}\sigma a\iota$ (verse 1) and $\tau\epsilon\tau\epsilon\lambda\epsilon\acute{\iota}\omega\kappa\epsilon\nu$ (verse 14) in this context, we are able to trace the link between our writer's use of this terminology and his development of the contrast between the covenants and their effects.

(a) The failure of the Old Covenant (10: 1–4)

Just as the levitical priests are said to have served 'a copy and shadow of the heavenly sanctuary' (8: 5), so the Law as a whole is described as having 'but a shadow of the good things to come instead of the true form of these realities' (10: 1 RSV).[120] As argued above in connection with 8: 5, our writer does not use $\sigma\kappa\acute{\iota}a$ in the Platonic sense, as if the things referred to were unreal or even deceptive: our writer is not primarily a Platonic idealist but an eschatologist. He means that 'the new order was at hand, at the door, projecting itself on the plane of OT history, announcing its advent. The history, the law and the cultus of Israel were to this extent witnesses in advance to the Christian salvation.'[121]

Although there are aspects of the Christian salvation as yet unrealised, the expression οὐκ αὐτὴν τὴν εἰκόνα τῶν πραγμάτων does not simply suggest that the gospel offers a more exact imitation of heavenly realities than the OT. The contrast implied between Old and New Covenants by σκία ... εἰκών is more absolute. In the strictest sense, εἰκών means 'a replica', such as an artist might produce in a painting or a sculptor in a statue, yet it can also mean 'an embodiment' or 'a manifestation' of the reality in question.[122] The latter sense is more appropriate to our writer's general perspective. The most natural way to take the verse is to interpret τῶν μελλόντων ἀγαθῶν and τῶν πραγμάτων as parallel expressions and see them as a reference to the boons and blessings of the new age, from the standpoint of the Law.[123] That which was only *foreshadowed* in the OT cult, is now a reality available to men through the New Covenant. Hebrews 'does not separate rigorously between present and future, but the future becomes a living reality in the present (6: 5, 9: 11)'.[124]

Even if the Law was 'a shadow of the good things to come', in no sense was it able to perfect the worshippers (οὐδέποτε δύναται τοὺς προσερχομένους τελειῶσαι).[125] As in Exod. 16: 9; 34: 32; Lev. 9: 5 and Num. 10: 3f, προσέρχεσθαι is used to describe the Israelites in general, drawing near to God in solemn assembly. The verb λατρεύειν is surely used in a parallel sense in verse 2 and refers to the worshippers in general: the sacrificial ritual was for the benefit of all and the problem of a guilty conscience remained for all.[126] Although the verb προσφέρουσιν may make special mention of the priests in their sacrificial ministry, with τοὺς προσερχομένους 'the wider circle of the members of the congregation, for whom the sacrifice is meant, are to be understood'.[127] Our writer's development of the terminology of drawing near to God (4: 16; 7: 19, 25; 10: 1, 22; 12: 22) suggests that the Old Covenant ritual limited the extent to which the people could do this and that the glory of the New Covenant is the boldness of approach to God (παρρησία) made possible for all the people of God by the sacrificial ministry of Christ.

As in 7: 11, 19; 9: 9, we find the concept of perfection introduced in a cultic context, where the object of the verb is man in his role as worshipper, that is, as one who would draw near to God. Those who drew near to God by means of the OT cultus were seeking a cleansing which the system could not provide (10: 2). The failure of the Old Covenant in this regard is emphasised firstly by pointing to the necessity for a continual

offering (εἰς τὸ διηνεκές), year after year (κατ᾽ ἐνιαυτόν).[128] The very
provision of an annual Day of Atonement was a sign of inefficacy: the worshippers never experienced a definitive cleansing (ἅπαξ κεκαθαρισμένους),
but continued to have 'a consciousness of sins' (συνείδησιν ἁμαρτιῶν).[129]
If this sense of guilt and transgression in relation to God remained, man
could clearly not be perfected in his aim of drawing near to God with full
sincerity and confidence.

Not only is the provision for repetition of sacrifices a sign of inefficacy,
but the Day of Atonement ritual itself actually provided a 'reminder of
sin' (ἀνάμνησις ἁμαρτιῶν, verse 3). This expression speaks of more than a
personal recollection of sins: the complicated ritual itself served 'to make
sins present *in actu* as a hindrance to fellowship with God'.[130] It was an
occasion on which the people were to 'afflict' themselves (Lev. 23: 26–32)
and confess their sins (Lev. 16: 20–2) and the ritual of the high priest's
entrance into the Holy of Holies then provided a vivid reminder of the fact
that sin caused a separation between man and God. Although the bull was
prescribed as a sin-offering for the high priest and his house (Lev. 16: 6,
11–14) and the goats for the people (Lev. 16: 7–10, 15ff, 20ff), our
writer argues that such animal sacrifices could never actually 'take away
sins' (verse 4).[131] The following section goes on to argue that these
sacrifices have been replaced by the uniquely successful sacrifice of Christ.
The replacement of the former system, with its yearly rituals of atonement,
by the once-for-all offering of the body of Christ (verse 10), proclaims the
possibility of that definitive cleansing from sin which was previously
denied to mankind (verse 2).

Once again I have cause to comment on the relationship between
τελειοῦν and καθαρίζειν, since both these verbs occur together, describing
those effects that the levitical sacrifices could not produce. Our writer
maintains that the Old Covenant provided for the cleansing of 'the flesh'
(9: 13) and of all the objects used in worship (9: 21f), but not for the
cleansing of the conscience (9: 9, 14). Christ, however, having made the
necessary 'purification for sins' (1: 3, καθαρισμὸν τῶν ἁμαρτιῶν) by his
sacrificial death, will purify the conscience of believers from dead works
'to serve the living God' (9: 14). Those who draw near to God through
Christ experience the once-for-all cleansing that was not possible under the
levitical system (10: 2): that cleansing of human hearts from 'an evil
conscience' (10: 22). Such a decisive and personal assurance of God's
forgiveness is a prerequisite for drawing near 'with a true heart in full
assurance of faith'. That the perfecting of believers involves not only
cleansing but also *the consequent approach to God* seems likely from the
fact that the object of τελειῶσαι in 10: 1 is τοὺς προσερχομένους. Those

who would draw near to God are perfected as such when that directness
and openness of access that they seek is achieved. The attaining of this
goal is proclaimed a possibility in 10: 19ff, where readers are encouraged
to realise in ongoing experience the benefits already won for them by the
death and exaltation of Christ.

(b) Realisation of the better Covenant (10: 5–18)

The application of Psalm 40: 6–8 to Christ is clearly motivated by the preceding argument, since the writer of that psalm goes further than many other OT
writers in pointing to the powerlessness of sacrifices in themselves to please
God and bring about a proper relationship between God and man. The
LXX rendering σῶμα δὲ κατηρτίσω μοι[132] seems to have struck our writer
as being particularly relevant to express the idea of the pre-existent Son
becoming man, to fulfil the divine purpose for man (cf. 2: 14, 17). The
fact that these words are put into the mouth of Christ 'when he comes
into the world' (verse 5) may suggest that 'his incarnation itself is viewed
as an act of submission to God's will and, as such, an anticipation of his
supreme submission to that will in death'.[133] On the other hand, the words
'Lo, I have come to do your will, O God' (verse 9), which clearly represent
for our writer the essential utterance of Christ in the psalm, stress the
attitude of one who has already come. That attitude is one of preoccupation with doing the will of God. If obedient submission to God's will
characterised Jesus' life as a whole (cf. John 4: 34; 6: 38), it is pre-
eminently the attitude with which he faced the climax of his life and
ministry, and thus became 'the source of eternal salvation' (5: 7–9).

The Psalmist uses four terms for sacrifice, which appear to cover all the
main types of offering prescribed in the levitical ritual.[134] In our writer's
exposition of the psalm, these sacrifices are relegated to the period of the
Law in God's dealings with his people ('these are offered according to the
law', verse 8). The words, 'then I said, "Lo, I have come ... to do your will,
O God" (verse 7), are then taken to be significant in terms of salvation-
history: 'he abolishes the first to establish the second' (verse 9). The Old
Covenant, with its animal sacrifices, is set aside to make way for the New
Covenant, established by the rational and willing self-sacrifice of Christ.
W. Manson rightly notes that: 'the Christ of the psalm is not rejecting
sacrifices and offering in favour of something else, but rejecting animal
sacrifice in favour of that personal sacrifice which God has willed for him,
and for which he has prepared by appointing for him the body of his incarnation'.[135] Christ is represented as finding his duty set out in Scripture ('as
it is written of me in the roll of the book'),[136] and setting himself to carry

it out with whole-hearted obedience. The New Covenant, which provides for a writing of God's law 'on their hearts' (Jer. 31: 33; Hebrews 8: 10; 10: 16), is thus significantly established by the action of one in whom such heart-obedience was perfectly expressed (cf. Psalm 40: 8).

Although it is true that the words 'I have come to do your will' could be ascribed to Christ at any stage of his earthly experience, verse 10 indicates that our writer's focus is on Jesus' willingness to offer himself as a sacrifice in death. The ἐν ᾧ θελήματι of verse 10 interprets the τοῦ ποιῆσαι τὸ θέλημά σου of verse 7 and verse 9: the will of God, which Jesus came to fulfil, is the will 'by which we are sanctified'. God's will is for Jesus to offer himself as a sacrifice for sins and so achieve the sanctification of his people. Westcott takes 'the offering of the body of Jesus Christ once for all' (verse 10), to refer to the offering which 'slowly matured through life' and was 'consummated on the cross' — in the perfect life of the Son of Man 'each man as a member of humanity finds the realisation of his own destiny'.[137] However, this interpretation is inappropriate on several counts. The sanctification that Christ effects is elsewhere related to his *blood* (13: 12; 10: 29; cf. 9: 13f). Although 10: 10 appears to be open to a wider interpretation, the corresponding phrase in 10: 14 (μιᾷ ... προσφορᾷ) has its parallel in 10: 12 (μίαν ὑπὲρ ἀμαρτιῶν προσενέγκας θυσίαν), which is undoubtedly a reference to the death of Jesus. Furthermore, the ἐφάπαξ of 10: 10 is more likely to be related to the 'unique and definitive offering of the body of Jesus' than to the expression ἡγιασμένοι ἐσμεν.[138] The periphrastic perfect already has the effect of stressing a state of sanctification resulting from some decisive event in the past, and ἐφάπαξ is elsewhere related to the death of Christ and his entrance thereby into the heavenly sanctuary.[139] This is not to ignore the perspective of 9: 14, in which it may be implied that the obedience of a lifetime makes Christ's offering to God 'without blemish'. However, it is still the actual death of Christ that achieves sanctification, in our writer's perspective. The redemptive value of Christ's obedience — that is, its value for us — 'belongs to it not simply as obedience, but as obedience to a will of God which requires the Redeemer to take upon himself in death the responsibility of the sin of the world'.[140] Further discussion on the sanctification which Christ achieves will be undertaken below, in connection with 10: 14.

From a contrast between the two types of sacrifice, characterising the Old Covenant and the New, the writer turns to a contrast between the respective priests (10: 11–14). Some of the thoughts already expressed in 10: 1–4 are restated here: the levitical priests were involved in daily acts,[141] in which the same sacrifices were offered repeatedly, which could never take away sins. However, Christ has offered a single sacrifice for sins, which has perpetual efficacy (εἰς τὸ διηνεκές).[142] The novel emphasis in these verses is the contrast between the many priests of Judaism 'standing' at their daily sacrificial ministry (λειτουργῶν), and Christ 'sitting' at the right hand of God. Psalm 110: 1 is once more brought into connection with Christ's priestly ministry (compare 1: 3; 8: 1), to prove afresh that his sacrifice was final and completely effective: 'the rest is the sign of perfection, the "sitting" a sign of dominion'.[143] Jesus sits because his sacrifice needs no repetition and his heavenly session becomes an attestation of 'the enduring effect of the sacrifice'.[144]

The γάρ of 10: 14 links the conclusions of that verse with the preceding argument and the perfect tense of τετελείωκεν emphasises again that the sacrifice of Christ has a permanent result for believers. The εἰς τὸ διηνεκές gives further stress to the idea of ongoing effect: 'the virtue of Christ's work remains ever available as long as the need of man exists'.[145] The means by which Christ has perfected his people is his sacrificial death (μιᾷ ... προσφορᾷ, cf. verse 12).[146] The perfection that was not possible through the levitical priesthood (7: 11), the Law and its sacrifices (7: 19; 9: 9; 10: 1), is here proclaimed as an act of Christ, already accomplished by his single offering for sins. The citation from Jer. 31: 31–4 that follows, with the author's special comment in verse 18, shows that the perfecting 'for all time' is to be related to that prophecy. God's intention to 'remember their sins and their misdeeds no more' implies a once-for-all offer of forgiveness, requiring no further offering for sin (verse 18). Christ has offered that all-sufficient sacrifice (μιᾷ ... προσφορᾷ, verse 14) and thus secured that definitive forgiveness of sins.

However, the perfecting of which our writer speaks here cannot simply be identified with the forgiveness of sins or cleansing of the conscience. The promise of forgiveness in the oracle of Jeremiah is the basis of a new relationship of heart-obedience towards God on the part of his people.[147] I have already shown how our writer develops these two ideas together in 10: 22 and how 9: 9 and 9: 14 are to be interpreted in this light. Cleansing from sin is essentially a negative concept, though it makes possible a positive consecration to God: 'consecration requires as the beginning of its actual fulfilment cleansing'.[148] The definitive consecration of men to God, promised in the prophecy of Jeremiah, is accomplished by the offering of the body of Christ, once for all (10: 10), because that offering is a 'sin-offering' (περὶ ἁμαρτίας, verse 18), providing the essential assurance that God 'will remember their sins and their misdeeds no more'. Such forgiveness or cleansing from sin enables men to draw near to God, as outlined in 10: 19ff. It can thus be seen that the τετελείωκεν of 10: 14 must be understood in the light of the writer's description of its recipients as τοὺς ἀγιαζομένους. The precise relationship between these two concepts in our writer's presentation must now be discussed.

Michel argues that τελειοῦν and ἀγιάζειν must be virtually synonymous: the former implies 'that the sacrifice creates a new relationship with God in a cultic respect. That which is a once for all event (τετελείωκεν), takes place in an ongoing process (ἀγιαζομένους).'[149] Kögel also concludes that what Christ achieves once and for all by his suffering and death must be 'supplied to the different generations and conveyed to them'.[150] However, these commentators may be reading too much into the use of the present tense of ἀγιαζομένους here. Just as the present participles in 2: 11 may be taken as 'timeless designations of the two parties, taken from the part characteristic of each',[151] so in 10: 14 τοὺς ἀγιαζομένους may be a general designation of believers as the 'sanctified'. This would be more consistent with the stress on sanctification as something already effected by the blood of Christ (10: 10; 10: 29; 13: 12). Thus Riggenbach proposes:

'the timeless present participle τοὺς ἀγιαζομένους describes merely the religious result of the sacrifice, always and everywhere to be expected. The true sacrifice purifies from sin and confers the consecration which authorizes and qualifies for fellowship with God. The stress lies wholly on the words τετελείωκεν εἰς τὸ διηνεκές. What the OT priests with their accumulated sacrificial offerings were not able to achieve, Christ has brought about by his unique sacrifice, namely the perfection which suffices for ever.'[152]

The verb ἀγιάζειν is used in Hebrews with both cultic and covenantal connotations. The purely material concept of sanctification in 9: 13 ('for the purification of the flesh'), gives way to the concept of a conscience cleansed 'from dead works to serve the living God' in 9: 14. Although ἀγιάζειν is not used in 9: 14, the verse itself describes a definitive consecration to God through a cleansing that fulfils the promises of Jer. 31: 31–4. By implication, the purification effected by the blood of Christ effects a sanctification to God 'so complete that it is synonymous with perfection'.[153] This broader sense of consecration into a new relationship with God through the blood of Christ is found in 10: 29, where the blood of the covenant is said to effect such sanctification. In 13: 12 it is the purpose of Christ's death 'to sanctify the people through his own blood'. In 10: 10 we are told that it was God's will that Jesus should offer himself willingly as a sacrifice for sins and through his atoning work bring about a once-and-for-all consecration of men to God (ἡγιασμένοι ἐσμέν). Thus, Christ is the 'sanctifier' *par excellence* (2: 11 ὁ ἀγιάζων), by virtue of his atoning death.

Westcott takes the τοὺς ἁγιαζομένους of 10: 14 to refer to 'all who from time to time realise progressively in fact that which has been potentially obtained for them',[154] and implies that a moral development is involved in this by relating it to 12: 10 ('that we may share his holiness'): 'that which is true ideally has to be realised actually'.[155] Indeed, in connection with 12: 14 ('strive for ... the holiness without which no one will see the Lord'), he describes sanctification as 'an object of human effort'.[156] Riggenbach, as we have seen, does not view the present participle in 10: 14 as having such significance, but suggests that 12: 14 brings a call for the readers to 'apply themselves ethically to prove and exhibit the religious consecration which they have obtained in their fellowship with Christ (2: 11; 10: 10, 14, 29; 13: 12)'.[157] However, Michel argues that even this is a dangerous modernisation of our writer's meaning: 'the cultic thought form does not change into the ethical but subordinates the human action to the divine work'.[158] When our writer emphasises that only the consecrated will see God (12: 14), he is not saying that they must make moral progress to prove their consecration: the context indicates to Michel that 'the consecrated person himself becomes a sacrifice for others'.[159] However, this attempt to exclude any suggestion of moral development from the use of ἁγιασμός in 12: 14 is unnecessary and exaggerated (cf. 1 Thess. 4: 3f; Rom. 6: 19, 22; Rev. 22: 11). If we return to the paradigm of 9: 14 we observe that the cleansing of the conscience from dead works has in view the service of God. Such consecration to God cannot be restricted in sense to the sphere of 'worship', but includes the life of faith, hope and love, as the proper response to God's grace. 'If atonement is the basis of the Christian life, ἁγιασμός is the moral form which develops out of it and without which there can be no vision of Christ.'[160] Although the use of ἁγιάζειν itself does not lead us to imply a moral dimension to the sanctifying work of Christ, a sense of moral development cannot be excluded from 12: 10, 14.

The collocation of τετελείωκεν and τοὺς ἁγιαζομένους in 10: 14 indicates that the perfection of man is to be understood in terms of his consecration to God through the atoning death of Christ. This is the fulfilment of the relationship with God promised in the oracle of Jeremiah. However, this does not mean that τελειοῦν and ἁγιάζειν are entirely synonymous terms. When Dibelius renders τετελείωκεν in terms of the bestowal of 'the perfected consecration',[161] he not only errs in respect of the etymology of the verb but also confuses it with ἁγιάζειν. Although there is clearly overlap of meaning in our writer's use of these two verbs, the particular linguistic contribution and theological significance of τελειοῦν must not be obscured. The *consummation* of man in a direct and lasting personal relationship with God, which seemingly is the goal of all religion, is proclaimed a present possibility, through the finished work of Christ. The fact that such a relationship with God implies ultimately a face to face encounter with God (12: 14, 22ff), makes the use of this verb in 10: 14 all the more remarkable. Our writer uses τελειοῦν to stress that: 'what will first reach complete realization at the final fulfilment of all God's promises (11: 40; 12: 23), is only an unfolding of what is, in principle, even now achieved through Christ's sacrifice'.[162]

On the one hand, this can be related to the fact that Christ's death has destroyed Satan's power over death and can deliver all 'who through fear of death were subject to lifelong bondage' (2: 14–15). Christ's sacrifice opens the way to 'glory' as a certain goal, not only for himself but also for 'many sons' (2: 10; cf. 6: 19f). On the other hand, one can be described as perfected already by the sacrifice since it secures entrance to the heavenly sanctuary as a present possibility (12: 22ff). In C.K. Barrett's words, believers are 'sustained by the fact that that for which they strive has already been achieved for them, and that they have already begun to enjoy it'.[163]

Those writers who identify perfection with entrance into heaven or glorification point particularly to the use of τελειοῦν in 11: 40 and 12: 23 and the concept of Christ being glorified through suffering. However, 10: 14 presents the greatest difficulty for this approach. Käsemann says that Christians are only perfected on earth inasmuch as they are 'the sanctified': 'through consecration one becomes a member of the heavenly sphere, while still on earth'.[164] However, perfection in a true sense is a future reality – 'a final and comprehensive perfecting is still outstanding, precisely with a view to which one is consecrated'.[165] Christians are only perfected now inasmuch as they have received heavenly gifts and become partakers of the Holy Spirit (6: 4f), making them candidates for 'the complete and lasting possession of these good things'. Käsemann rightly draws attention to the unfulfilled aspects of salvation in our writer's presentation and to the fact that the sanctified have a heavenly destination. The terminology of perfection itself quite naturally suggests some eschatological or ultimate adjustment to the nature and situation of men. However, 10: 14 clearly locates this perfecting *in the past with respect to its accomplishment and in the present with respect to its enjoyment.* That the primary focus is on the accomplishment of the relationship with God foretold in the oracle of Jeremiah is indicated by the paragraph immediately following 10: 14. Of course, the establishment of the New Covenant makes it possible for those who are called to receive 'the promised *eternal* inheritance' (9: 15).[166] However, the real emphasis in our writer's development of the covenantal theme is on the 'redemption from transgressions', achieved by Christ. This brings about *a definitive consecration of man to God in the present*, as well as securing that eternal inheritance. The terminology of perfection is used by our writer here to stress the realised aspect of Christian salvation.

(c) Enjoyment of the benefits of Christ's sacrifice (10: 19–25)

As the writer moves from exposition to parenesis, we see how the preceding emphasis on the perfecting of believers by the sacrifice of Christ is meant to have its effect in their ongoing experience. The present participle ἔχοντες has two objects, παρρησίαν ... (verses 19–20) and ἱερέα μέγαν ... (verse 21), stressing the Christian's present possession of two significant blessings. This short doctrinal summary provides the basis for the first of three significant cohortatives in the present tense (verse 22 προσερχώμεθα). Further stress on the present possession of certain benefits is provided by the supporting perfect participles (ῥεραντισμένοι ... λελουσμένοι ... verse 22). Thus, the challenge of 'let us draw near ...' is to realise the benefits of Christ's high-priestly work.

Although there is clearly a subjective dimension to the παρρησία of which the writer speaks – '*boldness* in spite of the frankest recognition of our sins'[167] – the ἔχοντες and the instrumental use of ἐν with the dative (ἐν τῷ αἵματι Ἰησοῦ) suggests that παρρησία has 'a peculiarly objective character'.[168] Fundamentally, it is 'the free right to approach God, given in the sacrifice of Christ, which is the essence of the Christian faith'.[169] Consistent with the imagery of preceding chapters, this freedom of access to God is presented in terms of a freedom to enter the heavenly sanctuary (εἰς τὴν εἴσοδον τῶν ἁγίων).[170] Although the context stresses the present enjoyment of eschatological realities (cf. 12: 22ff), the imagery suggests also the promise of a share in the world to come:

'through Christ, their high priest, Christians may approach God in the sanctuary of heaven and of the world to come. In their worship they participate in the heavenly worship of the angels and of the perfect saints. Having in prayer access to God through Christ, they have already a share in the life of the new, eschatological world.'[171]

The access to the heavenly sanctuary, which is available for Christians to enjoy, is further described in verse 20 as 'the new and living way' which Christ 'opened'[172] or 'consecrated' (ἐνεκαίνισεν)[173] for us. The description 'through the curtain' suggests that Christ has passed through the veil across the entrance to the heavenly Holy of Holies.[174] However, when we seek to probe the meaning behind this imagery, we are faced with a good deal of debate amongst interpreters. Although some understand τῆς σαρκὸς αὐτοῦ in the following phrase as a 'genitive of dependence', referring back to ὁδὸν πρόσφατον καὶ ζῶσαν,[175] there are better grounds for the view that τοῦτ᾽ ἔστιν here introduces an *appositional* phrase, relating to διὰ τοῦ καταπετάσματος.[176] In reviewing these and other current theories, N.H. Young argues that if 10: 20*b* is an example of a genitive of dependence attached to ὁδόν, 'we could expect a repetition of ὁδός before τῆς σαρκός'.[177] Against the argument of Andriessen that other uses of τοῦτ᾽ ἔστιν in Hebrews do not support the appositional view,[178] Young argues convincingly that 'the grammatical grounds for taking τῆς σαρκὸς αὐτοῦ as an appositional explicative of καταπέτασμα are coercive'.[179] Following Moffatt, he then proposes that the 'flesh' of Christ here is not to be understood as a 'barrier', but rather as a 'means of access' to God's presence. The flesh of Christ:

> 'had to be rent before the blood could be shed, which enabled him to enter and open God's presence for the people. It is a daring poetical touch, and the parallelism is not to be prosaically pressed into any suggestion that the human nature in Jesus hid God from men ἐν ταῖς ἡμέραις τῆς σαρκὸς αὐτοῦ, or that he ceased to be truly human when he sacrificed himself.'[180]

In this case, we must see a gliding of thought from διά taken *locally* with τοῦ καταπετάσματος, to διά (understood) taken *instrumentally* with τῆς σαρκὸς αὐτοῦ (cf. διὰ δὲ τοῦ ἰδίου αἵματος, 9: 12).[181] Both verse 19 and verse 20 will conclude, therefore, with a reference to Christ's death as the means by which the way into the sanctuary of heaven was opened.

The picture of Jesus as 'a great priest over the house of God' (verse 21)[182] recalls the imagery of 10: 12–14, which speaks of his sacrificial work completed and forever effective. The expression 'the house of God' suggests the people of God (3: 1–6), as well as the heavenly sanctuary, which two ideas are combined in the picture of the church in 12: 22–4 (cf. 2: 12).[183] As in 4: 14–16, the fact that Jesus has 'passed through the heavens' is made the basis of an exhortation to draw near and to hold fast the Christian confession. However, since the giving of that earlier exhortation, our writer has added considerable content to the concept of Jesus as a heavenly high priest and pointed to the objective basis of the Christian's confidence to approach God, in the sacrifice of Christ. In assessing the significance of 'let us draw near' (4: 16), it was argued that the particular reference there was to confident prayer for mercy and timely help. However, seen against the background of our writer's use of this terminology in 7: 25; 11: 6; 12: 18, 22 (cf. 7: 19), the prayer of 4: 16 was to be understood as an expression of the new relationship with God in Christ, which is at the heart of the promised New Covenant. So, too, in 10: 22, προσερχώμεθα will suggest something like 'personal appropriation of salvation'.[184] There is no indication in the immediate context that prayer is the specific reference, though several writers point to the possibility that each of the three exhortations refers to the activity of Christian assembly. In this case, drawing near could mean 'the reception of the gifts of salvation in the act of divine worship and confirmation of the adopted ὁμολογία'.[185]

However, if the activity of drawing near to God finds expression in the worship of a Christian congregation, it must be remembered that the initial encounter with God in Christ, portrayed so vividly in 12: 22ff, essentially describes an act of faith and personal commitment. Thus, Michel argues: 'one draws near to the good things of salvation by first grasping the word of God, which receives through the New Covenant a particular urgency. This "drawing near" is on the one hand eschatological: we stand directly before the final perfection. On the other hand, it is present: we are bound in faith to the word.'[186] That 10: 22 is calling for ongoing expression of an existing relationship with God, is confirmed by the presence of the two perfect participles ῥεραντισμένοι and λελουσμένοι.[187] Both speak of the work of Christ applied to individuals at some decisive moment in the past. The sprinkling of the heart from an evil conscience recalls the imagery of 9: 18–22, where the sprinkling of the people with blood was associated with the inauguration of the Old Covenant. In one sense, the sprinkling of the people of the New Covenant is to be associated with Jesus' inauguration of the new way to God through his death (10: 20; cf. 9: 18).[188] However, the probable allusion to Christian baptism in the expression 'our bodies washed with pure water' points to that action as the outward sign of the application of the benefits of Christ's sacrifice to the individual's heart.[189]

If the sprinkling of Christ's blood can cleanse the conscience, the believer can continually approach God 'with a true heart in full assurance of faith'. Here is a picture of 'a heart which fulfils the ideal office of the heart, the seat of the individual character towards God — a heart which expresses completely the devotion of the person to God. There is no divided allegiance: no reserve of feeling.'[190] Thus, the writer proclaims the fulfilment of the promised 'new heart' for God's people (Jer. 31: 33; Ezek. 36: 26f),[191] made possible by the sprinkling that only the sacrifice of Christ can provide. Man is perfected in relation to God *when the promises of the New Covenant are realised in individual experience.*

The second exhortation, to be 'firm and unswerving in the confession of our hope' (verse 23) recalls 4: 14 (cf. 3: 1). While scholars debate the content and *Sitz im Leben* of this 'confession', it is well to note with V.H.

Neufeld that our writer's focus is on the necessity for the readers to 'cling to their faith as expressed in the *homologia*, which they once accepted and have openly declared'.[192] It is not so much the confession of faith in the context of Christian assembly that is in view, but rather the active *holding fast* to that confession in the face of opposition from unbelievers and personal doubts (cf. 10: 32–9).[193] Holding fast to the Christian hope is itself an act of 'confession', even though words may not be uttered. Both παρρησία and τὸ καύχημα τῆς ἐλπίδος must be held fast by those who would reach their heavenly destination (3: 6ff). The third exhortation (verses 24f 'let us consider one another ...'), concentrates on the responsibility of Christians to one another in such a situation of waiting and testing, before the consummation of God's plans for his people takes place (cf. 3: 12ff; 12: 14ff).

The ultimate perspective

(a) The promised eternal inheritance (11: 39–40)

A fitting conclusion to the argument of chapter 11 and transition to the argument of chapter 12 is provided in 11: 39f. All those whose lives have been celebrated in the preceding verses are said to have been commemorated in Scripture (μαρτυρηθέντες) because of their faith.[194] As such, they stand as examples for later generations, especially for Christians, caught up in the last great hour of testing (12: 1ff).[195] Nevertheless, none of these OT men and women of faith 'obtained the promise' (οὐκ ἐκομίσαντο τὴν ἐπαγγελίαν). Although they experienced the fulfilment of specific promises in this life (e.g., verses 11, 33), they did not obtain the ultimate promise of 'the messianic bliss with its eternal life'.[196] The parallel expression in 11: 13 (μὴ κομισάμενοι τὰς ἐπαγγελίας) views their expectation in terms of a number of promises, which were seen from afar and welcomed. However, when our writer specifically describes their goal as the heavenly 'country' or 'city', all the promises are comprehended (verses 14–16, cf. verse 10).[197]

The failure of these exemplars of faith to experience the promised eternal inheritance was through no fault of their own. In 11: 40, the writer stresses the gracious providence of God (τοῦ θεοῦ ... προβλεψαμένου),[198] who, with us in mind (περὶ ἡμῶν), had a better plan (κρεῖττόν τι). The κρεῖττόν τι here does not mean 'something better than the fathers experienced',[199] nor something better than Christians themselves have already experienced. The final clause (ἵνα μὴ χωρὶς ἡμῶν τελειωθῶσιν) is epexegetical and shows that the κρεῖττόν τι should be taken *absolutely*:

the 'better thing' is that 'the transfer of the elders to the state of perfection would not happen without us'.[200] Putting it a slightly different way, Moffatt says the 'better thing' is that 'God in his good providence reserved the messianic τελείωσις of Jesus Christ until we could share it'.[201] In short, the fact that 'these all died in faith, not having received the promise' is to be taken as a sign of God's special grace towards those living 'in these last days' (1: 2). Some of the practical implications of this interpretation will be considered below, but first it is necessary to examine the precise meaning of ἵνα ... τελειωθῶσιν in 11: 40.

It is interesting to note that a commentator like Riggenbach feels compelled to give the verb a different sense in this context. It is not to be taken 'in the religious sense of the perfection effected by Christ's death (10: 14; cf. 9: 9; 10: 1)', but the reference to the fulfilment of the promise in verse 39 shows the sense in which the perfection of verse 40 is to be understood.[202] If a precise parallelism with the concept of obtaining the promise is maintained, the interpretation of τελειοῦν in terms of the entrance into glory or into the eternal inheritance seems most likely.[203] If the parallel expression 10: 36 is noted (ἵνα ... κομίσησθε τὴν ἐπαγγελίαν), it could be argued that our writer's use of ἐπαγγελία in 11: 39 is indeed limited to the events associated with the second coming of Christ (10: 37ff; cf. 11: 35, ἵνα κρείττονος ἀναστάσεως τύχωσιν). However, Riggenbach himself rightly suggests that the promise of 11: 39 refers to the *eschatological salvation as a whole, viewed from the standpoint of OT prophecy*: we may not distinguish here between the achievement of Christ at his first coming and the fulfilment of God's promises at the second coming. Furthermore, it is hard to believe that our writer used τελειοῦν in 11: 40 in a way that differed significantly from previous applications.

The totality of the messianic salvation, in our writer's presentation, must be related to the high-priestly work of Christ in his death and heavenly exaltation. This secures for believers in the present a relationship with God which fulfils the promises of the New Covenant. Expressed in terms of the believer's access to the heavenly sanctuary, *the Christian's immediate experience of God is the earnest of his ultimate transfer to the actual presence of God, in the heavenly city.* Such is the message of 12: 22ff in particular, as will be shown below. The perfecting of believers by the sacrifice of Christ has this total perspective in view even in 10: 14, though the emphasis there is certainly on the present enjoyment of the benefits. Riggenbach himself rightly comments on 10: 14: 'what will first reach complete realization at the final fulfilment of all God's promises (11: 40; 12: 23), is only an unfolding of what is, in principle, even now achieved through the sacrifice of Christ'.[204] It would therefore be more accurate to say that the concept of perfection, as related to believers, consistently has in view the totality of Christ's work on their behalf. If 11: 40 in its context places the emphasis on the final realisation of the relationship with God and 10: 14 on the cleansing and sanctification available for believers in the present, this does not imply a dichotomy in our writer's thinking. The sacrifice of Christ achieves all that is necessary for the enjoyment of eschatological blessing (τελείωσις): cleansing, sanctification and glorification. Christians may penetrate the sanctuary of heaven by faith now, and ultimately in person, in company with believers from all ages, thanks to 'the new and living way', opened by Christ in his death and exaltation. Using different terminology, Paul expresses a similar sequence of thought in Rom. 8: 30 ('and those whom he justified he also glorified').

The close relationship between the fulfilment of the promises of the New Covenant and the securing of the eternal inheritance by Christ is clearly set forth in 9: 15. Here we are told that the death of Christ makes him 'mediator of a New Covenant', since it accomplishes a 'deliverance from sins committed under the former covenant'. By this means, those who are called may receive the promised eternal inheritance. Even though the verse makes special reference to 'sins committed under the former covenant' or 'in association with the former covenant',[205] it is clear that a wider application of the text is possible. By his death, Christ makes it possible for all the beneficiaries of the New Covenant to enjoy the promised inheritance, to share in the glory of 'the world to come' (2: 5) and to enter 'God's rest' (4: 1–10). This shows how the perfection already accomplished (τετελείωκεν, 10: 14), could include glorification, as being part of the salvation already achieved for believers by the sacrifice of Christ. 'Those who are called' (9: 15), would seem to include believers in former times, implying that 'the sacrificial death of Jesus has a retrospective value; it clears off the accumulated offences of the past'.[206] Relating this to 11: 40 we can see how the perfecting of the OT men and women of faith depended on the death of Christ: the inheritance, which from the beginning was held out to the People of God, has only become attainable since the sacrifice of Jesus.

Returning to 11: 40, therefore, I would argue that our writer's use of τελειοῦν cannot be divorced from his preceding applications of the verb. Our writer means that OT saints were denied the historical experiencing of the messianic τελείωσις as a totality. Since Christ has accomplished his work, they too will share in its benefits. However, this does not permit us to make confident assertions about the present state of these men and women of faith. On the one hand, the perfection wrought by Christ can be said to be theirs now, as it is ours (10: 14; 12: 23; cf. 9: 15).[207] Yet such an argument begs the question as to the nature of the change in their status or situation, before and after the advent of Christ. This issue is explored below, in connection with 12: 23. On the other hand, there is some logic in the argument that they are still not yet perfected: whereas we may enjoy the benefits of that perfection in anticipation now, they must wait until the resurrection (11: 35; 6: 2), to experience it at all.[208] At the same time, Michel exaggerates the significance of χωρὶς ἡμῶν (11: 40), when he suggests that the fate of the faithful from earliest times to the present is placed 'in the hands of the last generation, the Christian church'.[209] It is certainly true that the context emphasises the social dimension to salvation: 'no one is perfected for himself alone, without the others'. However, to suggest that individual Christians, by their despondency in the last struggle, may actually endanger the perfecting of the totality, is to ignore the emphasis of the verses themselves on the sovereignty and grace of God. Τελειοῦν is not used here to describe the perfecting of the 'household of faith' in the formal sense of making its membership complete.[210] It refers us back to the concept of eschatological salvation effected completely by the high-priestly ministry of Christ. Our writer seeks to impress his readers with a particular instance of the grace of God: the coming of the messianic perfection was actually deferred to allow *them* to share in it![211]

As the following chapter shows, Christians are not only the recipients of that messianic perfection in terms of their immediate experience of God but are also able to benefit from the example of these OT witnesses to faith, as they seek to run the race that is set before them (12: 1ff). The exemplars of faith in chapter 11 persevered without seeing anything like the fulfilment of God's promises that Christians have experienced. In every respect, then, Christians have greater grounds for not growing weary or fainthearted in their pilgrimage towards 'the city which is to come' (13: 14). Westcott achieves an effective balance between our writer's various perspectives when he writes:

'The consummation of all the saints therefore followed upon the completion of Christ's work, the accomplishment by him of the destiny of man, though fallen ... The fathers with a true faith looked for a fulfilment of the promises which was not granted to them. To us the fulfilment has been granted, without the trial of deferred hope, if only we regard the essence of things. Christ has already opened the way to the Divine Presence on which we can enter, and he offers us now a kingdom which cannot be shaken (12: 28). At the same time there is the thought that God looked further, even beyond our age of trial, to the end.'[212]

(b) The spirits of just men made perfect (12: 18–24)

The exhortation to endurance, which dominates the argument in 12: 1–3, takes its rise from the presentation of the preceding chapter. From 12: 14 to the end, the emphasis is on warning the readers not to lose sight of the privileges that are theirs by God's grace.[213] Such privileges demand a certain response of faith and obedience on the part of those who would 'see the Lord' (verse 14), or 'inherit the blessing' (verse 15). In particular, our writer is concerned to contrast the situation of the Israelites, assembled at Mt Sinai to meet God (verses 18–21), and Christians, assembled to meet him at the heavenly Mt Zion (verses 22–4). Since the latter are in such a favoured position before God, the challenge to respond appropriately to the one who calls them is greater (verses 25–9).

The description in verses 18–21 is designed to illustrate the awefulness of the encounter with God at Sinai: 'step by step the writer advances from the physical terrors by which it was accompanied (verses 18–20), to the confession of the Lawgiver himself (verse 21), who alone of all the prophets was allowed to speak to God face to face'.[214] God's holiness was manifested there in numerous ways, recalled by our writer from a variety of OT texts.[215] The description in verses 22–4 is also modelled to some extent on the pattern of Sinai, with its picture of angels, assembled participants, a presiding Deity, a scrutiny and a mediator:

> 'clearly the ἐκκλησία here recalls the *qehal-Yisra'el*, assembled for approval at Sinai, and the recipients are reminded that what stretches before them in prospect as God's people on the move is *eschatological acceptance into final covenant conclusion*, vividly presented in this context on striking analogies drawn from the conclusion of the old covenant. Jesus, perfected, having led many sons into glory, stands in the company of the congregation of his many brethren.'[216]

In other words, our writer presents us with a vision of the final encounter between God and his people. However, in contrast to the traditions about Sinai, every aspect of this vision provides encouragement for the recipients to approach God boldly. In fact, *the use of the perfect tense in verse 22 (προσεληλύθατε), suggests that Christians 'in their conversion'* have already, in a sense, reached their heavenly destination.[217] Although it is true that there is an overlap between the ideas of the heavenly city and the heavenly sanctuary, it is not sufficient to conclude that προσεληλύθατε is used here to describe the approach of Christians to God 'as a cultic fellowship'.[218] Even if the perfect tense points to baptism as the initial approach and Christian worship as an ongoing expression of that new relationship with God, our writer does not represent the church as essentially a cultic fellowship: 'one draws near to God by first grasping the word of God'.[219] The personal encounter with God through Christ, which lies behind our writer's use of προσέρχεσθαι, must be understood in terms of the journey motif, as in 3: 7 – 4: 11 – 'the whole Christian pilgrimage is carried out from beginning to end in view of the heavenly Jerusalem'.[220] There is a certain dialectic in our writer's presentation that is most obvious here: 'the promise is as much the goal as the basis constituted for the wandering of faith'.

Turning to an examination of the specific elements in the vision of verses 22–4, we may note firstly the *setting*. Since the earthly Mount Zion or Jerusalem came to denote the seat and city of God, as well as the community of Israel itself,[221] it is not surprising to find it at the centre of prophetic hopes for the eschatological age of salvation.[222] The expression 'heavenly Jerusalem' does not occur in Jewish apocalyptic, but like Paul in Galatians (4: 26; cf. Apoc. 21: 2), our writer derives his metaphor from that tradition.[223] In short, our writer is referring to the actual dwelling place of God, which is also the meeting point for the people of God in the age to come. It is the city towards which men and women of faith in the OT journeyed (11: 10, 13–16), and similarly the goal of the Christian's pilgrimage (13: 14; cf. 4: 1–11).

The *inhabitants* of the heavenly Jerusalem are then described. Of the five different patterns of punctuation that have been suggested for the words καὶ μυριάσιν ἀγγέλων πανηγύρει καὶ ἐκκλησίᾳ,[224] the one that seems best suited to the rhythm of the sentence is represented by the RSV ('to innumerable angels in festal gathering and to the assembly of the first-born who are enrolled in heaven').[225] In this case, the πανηγύρει is best understood as a 'circumstantial dative', relating to the preceding μυριάσιν ἀγγέλων.[226] However, strong arguments have been advanced for relating πανηγύρει to the following clause, as the translators of the NEB have done ('before myriads of angels, the full concourse and assembly of the first-born citizens of heaven').[227] To attach πανηγύρει to ἀγγέλων would seem to some 'tautologous in depicting a scene of this character, for one would imagine that their heavenly character is always that of a "festal gathering"'.[228] To add πανηγύρει to ἐκκλησίᾳ would give the latter much more of the sense of a cultic gathering than it has in LXX or extra-Biblical literature. Yet, the citation of Psalm 21: 23 LXX in 2: 12 has already anticipated the use of ἐκκλησία in 12: 22, as a description of the people of God, gathered to worship. Furthermore, if our writer is emphasising the contrast between the role of angels at the giving of the Law (2: 2; cf. Deut. 33: 2; Acts 7: 38, 53; Gal. 3: 19) and their role in the eschatological encounter with God, the description of them as being 'in festal gathering' seems most appropriate.[229]

Careful attention must be paid to the various interpretations of 'the assembly of the first-born who are enrolled in heaven' that have been offered. Against the view that the clause refers to the elect angels,[230] it has been argued that 'the idea of enrolment in the heavenly book is regularly associated with men', and not angels, and that 'all the people of Christ are the "first-born" children of God, through their union with him who is The Firstborn *par excellence*'.[231] In 2: 12, the ἐκκλησία in whose midst Christ leads the worship of God can be none other than the assembly of 'the brothers' he came to sanctify (2: 11ff). Against the view that the assembly of the first-born refers properly to faithful Israelites (compare Exod. 4: 22ff; Sir. 36: 11),[232] it has been argued from 11: 40 that they are not yet perfected.[233] However, this is not a decisive objection if it is acknowledged that the vision in 12: 22−4 is of *the ultimate, completed company of the people of God, membership of which is now enjoyed by faith.* Nevertheless, against all views restricting the privileges of the first-born to some special group, it is likely that 'the "Firstborn" and the "firstborn" belong closely together, even as the "Son" and the "sons" do (Rom. 8: 29)'.[234] The reference must be to *all* who will ultimately enjoy the privileges of the sons of God (cf. 12: 5ff), namely 'the whole communion of saints'.[235]

Westcott observes that there are two constituent bodies here in the 'divine commonwealth', the heavenly element (angels), and the earthly element (men):[236] 'men are described as a "church", a "congregation", gathered for the enjoyment of special rights, even as the angels are assembled for a great festival; and they are spoken of as "firstborn" enjoying all the privileges not only of sons but of firstborn sons'. However, it is only correct to say that this congregation is earthly in regard to the origin of its participants. The setting in 12: 22ff clearly shows that the assembly in view is *an eschatological or heavenly entity.* In coming to Christ, who is in the midst of this heavenly assembly as mediator of the New Covenant (verse 24), men and women become members by faith, with the promise of one day enjoying the full rights of citizenship in the heavenly city, as the inheritance of the first-born (cf. verse 16).

If it is now argued that the expression πνεύμασι δικαίων τετελειωμένων describes the same group of people from a different point of view, the intervening phrase (κριτῇ θεῷ πάντων) will indicate why our author thought it necessary to refer to them as such. When it is asserted that Christians have approached the 'God of all as judge',[237] it is clear that our writer views this heavenly assembly as in some sense met for scrutiny or judgement. The warnings of 2: 2f; 4: 13; 6: 8; 9: 27; 10: 26−31; 13: 4, focus the readers' attention on the prospect of such an encounter with God. Similarly here too 'it is implied that he is no easy-going God. The contrast is not between the mere terrors of Sinai and the gracious relationship of Sion, but between the outward sensuous terror of the former and the inward intimacy of the latter – an intimacy which still involves awe' (verses 25–9).[238] However, πανηγύρει (verse 22), with its festive associations (cf. Hos. 2: 13; 9: 5; Ezek. 46: 11; Amos 5: 21 LXX), suggests a judgement with positive results for the assembled multitude. For the person who has 'spurned the Son of God and profaned the blood of the covenant by which he was sanctified' there remains only a 'fearful prospect of judgement, and a fury of fire which will consume the adversaries' (10: 26ff). However, for those who have been perfected by the sacrifice of Christ and hold fast their first confidence firm to the end (3: 14), not forfeiting the grace of God (12: 15), there remains the prospect of eschatological acceptance.[239] Set between the description of God as judge and Jesus as mediator of a New Covenant, the words '... and to the spirits of just men made perfect' are a further expression of the truth expounded in 10: 14.

According to apocalyptic tradition, the dead are πνεύματα (e.g., 1 Enoch 22: 3ff; 103: 4), or ψύχαι (e.g., 1 Enoch 9: 3, 10; 102: 4f; 103: 3, 7f). The 'souls of the righteous' and the 'souls of sinners' lie together in Sheol (1 Enoch 102: 4ff), but in different divisions (22: 9–14). However, there is considerable confusion in the material about the state of the dead and their separate destinies. For our purpose, it is important to note that the righteous are sometimes described as being asleep, as they await the resurrection (e.g., 1 Enoch 91: 10; 92: 3). 'All goodness and joy and glory' are prepared for them, 'abundantly beyond the lot of the living' (103: 3f), though it is sometimes difficult to decide whether these blessings are to be enjoyed in Sheol or in 'the spiritual theocracy set up after the final judgement'.[240]

The expression πνεύμασι δικαίων in Hebrews 12: 23 leaves Westcott feeling that 'something is yet wanting to the blessedness of the blessed', though they are essentially 'made perfect', having realised 'the end for which they were created in virtue of the completed work of Christ'.[241] Yet it is hard to believe that those so described are in some sort of intermediate state, since they are enjoying the presence of God in the heavenly city itself, which is the stated destination of the saints under both covenants (11: 10, 13–16; 13: 4). Although resurrection of the dead is clearly part of our writer's expectation (6: 2; 11: 35), it is not at all clear how we are to relate this to 'the spirits of just men made perfect'. It may be that Apoc. 6: 9ff provides something of a parallel, and that our writer is suggesting that the 'final event in the great eschatological drama has not yet taken place – the New Jerusalem has not yet descended'.[242] On the other hand, if πνεύμασι is used to stress the 'spiritual and immaterial nature of the new order of existence',[243] it may well be that he understands this to include 'the better resurrection' (11: 35).[244] At all events, the use of τετελειωμένων, and the very context in which these 'spirits' are found, suggest that nothing is lacking in their situation.

Michel is strongly inclined to the view that δικαίων τετελειωμένων reflects the Jewish idea of 'the perfect righteous' who are promoted to a special state of waiting, having 'obtained the witness that they are righteous'.[245] However, the use of the perfect passive participle, instead of the adjective (τελείων), *points to preceding applications of τελειοῦν as the key for interpreting the expression here.*[246] Our writer is speaking of all who have been perfected by the sacrifice of Christ (10: 14). There seems little point in restricting the 'spirits of just men made perfect' to 'believers of pre-Christian days'.[247] The citation from Hab. 2: 3f (LXX) in 10: 37f makes it clear that these 'righteous' are characterised by faith ('... but my righteous one shall live by faith', compare 11: 4). Yet this is precisely the way our writer would describe Christians (10: 39), suggesting that the righteous of 12: 23 would include *all who have died manifesting true faith.* The fact that few Christians would have died up to the point at which Hebrews was written does not negate this argument. On the other hand, it seems equally wrong to restrict 'the spirits of just men made perfect' to Christian dead, as Michel does. Arguing from 11: 40, he implies that OT men and women of faith must wait until the very last Christian has been perfected, before sharing in the same blessings.

If 12: 22–4 is indeed a picture of the ultimate, eschatological encounter with God, 'the spirits of just men made perfect' will refer to the saints of all ages as those who have been perfected by the work of Christ. Looked at in this light, 12: 23 speaks of the fulfilment of 11: 40, so that believers of pre-Christian days and Christians together enjoy the consummation of their hopes. Christians enjoy the blessings of the New Covenant in this life, but OT saints must wait until their transfer to the heavenly city for this. Does this mean that pre-Christian believers do not experience the messianic perfection until the resurrection? Riggenbach suggests that 'God's saving interventions have already been experienced by the spirits of the righteous, who lie waiting for it in the bodiless existence of resurrection, so that they have been brought to perfection.'[248] If he means by this that there was an immediate change in the situation of the dead when Christ accomplished his saving work, I can find no NT parallels to support such a theory.[249] Westcott proposes that 'when the Son bore humanity to the throne of God

— the Father — those who were in fellowship with him were (in this sense), perfected, but not till then'.[250] This is valid as long as one is thinking in ideal or representative terms. All the people of God in every age — past, present and future — were perfected when Christ was perfected. Yet, if we seek to specify precisely *when* believers of pre-Christian times actually experience the benefits of Christ's saving work, we have insufficient evidence to speak with certainty. If transfer to the heavenly city and 'the better resurrection' are identical concepts, it may be that our writer envisaged all the people of God entering this eternal inheritance together, at the time of Christ's second coming (cf. 9: 28, εἰς σωτηρίαν). If transfer to the heavenly city is experienced by Christians immediately upon death, to exclude believers of pre-Christian times from this present reality, as Spicq does,[251] seems to deny the fundamental assertion of 11: 40 that 'they should experience the substantiation of their hope not in separation from but in union with us'.[252] However, to suggest that OT saints could experience the messianic perfection immediately upon death also seems to contradict 11: 40.

Käsemann observes here that 'the perfecting of the righteous, as the OT witnesses of faith, occurs through entrance into heaven'.[253] However, I have already shown that the restriction of δίκαιοι here to OT believers is unwarranted. Furthermore, when he goes on to assert that 'perfection and perfecting are exclusively coordinated with heavenly existence', he is also restricting the scope of our writer's reference. Käsemann seeks to relate his concept of perfection through glorification to the achievement of Christ's sacrifice. Yet his argument is weakest when he seeks to explain how believers can be said to be perfected already (10: 14). I have not denied that glorification is an essential element in our writer's concept of perfection. However, the emphasis in previous passages falls on the realisation of the New Covenant relationship between man and God. This is something to be experienced by believers in this age, with glorification as its logical outcome. That the emphasis in 12: 23 is similar, is indicated by the terminology of 12: 24. Here, as in 10: 14ff, the relationship between Jesus' death and the establishment of the New Covenant is in view.[254] As the believer looks towards his heavenly destination, he is invited to hear the blood of Christ continually 'speaking'.[255] Whereas the blood of Abel cried for vengeance, the blood of Christ 'has better things to tell than the blood of Abel'.[256] It speaks of acceptance and forgiveness, perpetually available to those who draw near to God through Christ (cf. 7: 25; 4: 16). It speaks of the opening of the heavenly sanctuary for immediate encounter with God (10: 19ff) and as a hope to be grasped for the future (6: 18–20).

If 12: 24 locates the blood of Christ in the heavenly sanctuary, pursuing the imagery of the Day of Atonement ritual, 10: 14 stresses the effect of that blood-sprinkling on the lives of believers (cf. 10: 22, 'with our hearts sprinkled clean from an evil conscience'). The assurance that believers have been perfected by the one sacrifice of Christ (10: 14; 12: 23) and that Christ's blood continually avails for the forgiveness of sins (12: 24) means that Christians on the march to the heavenly city have the greatest encouragement to hold fast the confession of their hope without wavering. Instead of throwing away their confidence, which carries with it 'a great reward' (10: 35), they have every reason to hold it fast (3: 6). Our writer says nothing about the work of the Holy Spirit in the believer as 'pledge' of the future inheritance (cf. 2 Cor. 1: 22; 5: 5; Eph. 1: 14). However his teaching about the perfecting of believers fulfils a similar function. *The relationship with God that believers may now enjoy, by virtue of Christ's finished work, involves as its implied end the transfer of believers to the heavenly city.* Whereas Paul develops the theme of the New Covenant largely in terms of the work of the Spirit (especially in 2 Cor. 3), our writer develops it in terms of a heavenly cult. The approach to God in his heavenly sanctuary, which is a present possibility for Christians by faith, becomes the means of entering the actual presence of God in the age to come.

Conclusion

An examination of the first context in Hebrews in which the perfecting of believers is mentioned revealed that it has to do with *'the better hope' through which Christians draw near to God* (7: 19). Neither the levitical priesthood (7: 11) nor the Law (7: 19) was able to facilitate the directness of approach and permanency of fellowship with God that Jesus provides by means of his death and heavenly exaltation (7: 24–5). The concept is not, as Dey suggests, one of 'unmediated access' to God,[257] but of *the complete facilitation of mankind's approach to God through the high-priestly mediation of Jesus Christ.*

The object of the verb in 9: 9 and 10: 1 suggests that τελειοῦν was being applied to believers in a 'vocational' sense: they are perfected as would-be worshippers, as those who would draw near to God, through the work of Christ. The better hope through which Christians draw near to God has to do specifically with *a definitive cleansing of the conscience.* The gifts and sacrifices of the Old Covenant were not able to provide this (9: 9f; 10: 1ff). However, by virtue of his once-for-all sacrifice and entrance into the heavenly sanctuary, Christ has secured 'an eternal redemption' (9: 11f), which makes it possible for consciences to be cleansed from 'dead works' and for men and women to 'serve the living God' (9: 14).

The definitive consecration to God that the work of Christ makes possible (9: 14; 10: 10) is clearly related by our writer to the fulfilment of the promises of Jer. 31: 31–4. The sacrifice of Christ is the sin-offering that provides the essential assurance that God 'will remember their sins and their misdeeds no more'. Such forgiveness enables believers to draw near to God with the confidence outlined in 10: 19ff.

Although there is clearly overlap of meaning in our writer's use of τελειοῦν and ἁγιάζειν, the particular linguistic contribution and theological significance of the former must not be obscured. The *consummation* of men and women in a direct and lasting personal relationship with God is now a present possibility, through the finished work of Christ (10: 14, τετελείωκεν εἰς τὸ διηνεκές). The terminology of perfection itself quite naturally suggests some eschatological or ultimate adjustment to the nature and situation of man. However, 10: 14 clearly locates this perfecting *in the past with respect to its accomplishment and in the present with respect to its enjoyment.*

The access to the heavenly sanctuary that is available for Christians to enjoy in the present (4: 16; 7: 25; 10: 19ff) is the earnest of their ultimate transfer to the actual presence of God (6: 19f; 12: 22ff). The sacrifice of Christ achieves all that is necessary for the enjoyment of eschatological blessing: cleansing, sanctification and glorification (2: 10; cf. 9: 15). Christians may penetrate the sanctuary of heaven by faith now, and ultimately in person in company with believers from all ages, thanks to 'the new and living way' opened by Christ in his death and exaltation.

In 12: 22ff, there is an overlap between the ideas of the heavenly city and the heavenly sanctuary. Christians in their conversion have already, in a sense, reached their heavenly destination. However, the heavenly city is still the goal of the Christian's pilgrimage (13: 14; cf. 4: 1–11). The vision in 12: 22–4 is of the ultimate, completed company of the people of God, membership of which is now enjoyed by faith. Men and women of faith in OT times were denied the historical experience of the perfection brought by Jesus Christ (11: 39f). However, they are included amongst 'the spirits of just men made perfect' (12: 23): it is the sacrifice of Christ that makes it possible for them to receive 'the promised eternal inheritance' (9: 15).

7

PERFECTION AND THE PURPOSE OF HEBREWS

Enduring with Christ

An examination of the last context in Hebrews in which the terminology of perfection occurs,[1] provides us with the opportunity of assessing the relationship between the perfecting of Christ and the perfecting of believers. Continuing the theme of perseverance in faith, which is implicit throughout chapter 11, the writer contrasts 'us' ($\kappa\alpha\grave{\iota}\ \dot{\eta}\mu\epsilon\hat{\iota}\varsigma$, 12: 1ff), with 'all these' ($\kappa\alpha\grave{\iota}\ o\dot{\upsilon}\tau o\iota\ \pi\acute{\alpha}\nu\tau\epsilon\varsigma$, 11: 39).[2] As Westcott puts it,[3] 'Christians in one sense had entered on the inheritance of the promises for which the fathers had waited (11: 39); but the full enjoyment of possession was still delayed. In such a case the example of the earlier heroes of faith was of prevailing power.'

As a climax to his presentation of the great heroes of faith, the writer recalls the example of Christ (12: 2) and relates it specifically to the situation of the readers (verses 3–4). The example of Christ's triumph through suffering then leads to a consideration of the purpose of suffering in the life of a Christian (verses 5–11), before the final appeal is made for endurance in the struggle, with a proper concern for the weakest of their number (verses 12–13). It may be argued that the overall theme of this section is 'the necessary endurance',[4] and that it serves as an expansion of the exhortation in 10: 32–9. On the other hand, it may be more precise to say that *faith* continues to be the underlying theme, as it is actualised in *endurance* and *submission* under discipline.[5]

(a) The pioneer and perfecter of faith (12: 1–4)

The Christian is called to endure a contest and do everything necessary to see that he is unhindered in this task. Although the word $\dot{\alpha}\gamma\acute{\omega}\nu$ originally meant a 'place of assembly', then a 'place of contest' or 'stadium', it came to be used for the 'contest' itself (including litigation and debate) and finally for 'any kind of conflict'.[6] That the image of an athletic contest, and more specifically a foot-race, is intended by Hebrews 12: 1, is shown from the use of τρέχωμεν.[7] However, the suggestion of *antagonists* and of a conflict involving even *bloodshed* lies close at hand (verses 3–4), suggesting a parallel with the portrayal of the Jewish martyrs in 4 Maccabees.[8]

Pursuing the image of the athletic contest, the writer points to the necessity of putting off 'any encumbrance that handicaps us'.[9] By using the adjective πάντα he shows that he had nothing explicitly in mind with ὄγκον.[10] The Christian is thus encouraged to free himself from 'associations and engagements which, however innocent in themselves, hindered the freedom of his actions'.[11] Furthermore, there is the challenge to put off 'the sin which clings so closely' (καὶ τὴν εὐπερίστατον ἁμαρτίαν).[12] The use of the singular here should warn us against understanding a simple moralism or call to asceticism: our writer is concerned with *sin itself*, rather than with specific sins.[13] Käsemann rightly observes that 'as faith finds its essential character in holding on, so sin in falling away',[14] but exaggerates when he asserts that 'with the people of God sin can only ever be apostasy'.[15] While it is true in the present passage, as elsewhere in Hebrews, that the warning is to keep one's eyes fixed on the person and work of Christ and not to miss out on the heavenly inheritance, it is too simplistic to equate sin with apostasy. The latter is the ultimate expression of unbelief and disobedience and the terminology is restricted in this way by our writer's own usage (6: 4–6; 10: 26–31).

The first encouragement to press on in faith and obedience towards the final goal is the certainty of being 'surrounded by so great a cloud of witnesses'. Although it is tempting to interpret this terminology in terms of 'the image of the amphitheatre with the rising rows of spectators',[16] it is 'what we see in them, not what they see in us, that is the writer's main point'.[17] These are those who have received witness or acknowledgement from God because of their faith (11: 2; cf. 11: 4, 5, 39). They stand *in Scripture* as a witness to the nature and possibilities of faith for later generations. Indeed, a μάρτυς is never a 'mere observer' (θεατής), but 'always an eye and ear witness, who makes known his observation and stands up for it with his person'.[18] In this way, the writer indirectly asserts again that Scripture speaks with a living voice to believers in all ages (cf. 3: 7ff; 4: 12f; 10: 36ff; 12: 5ff).

However, in addition to the encouragement to be had from these witnesses, the Christian has the supreme encouragement that springs from contemplating Christ. The words ἀφορῶντες εἰς suggest the same concentrated attention as ἀπέβλεπεν ... εἰς (11: 26) and imply 'with no eyes for anyone or anything except Jesus'.[19] The use of the name Jesus suggests that the focus should be on his experiences as a man (cf. 2: 9; 3: 1). Such concentrated attention on the person of Jesus and his achievement on behalf of his 'brothers' epitomises the fundamental challenge of Hebrews.

The nature of Christ's experience is indicated in the rest of verse 2 and in verse 3. The similarity between verse 2b and Phil. 2: 6ff has often been noted. In both cases 'the way of the Incarnate One is described as the way to the *cross*, whereby the death on the cross is understood from the viewpoint of humiliation, as the embodiment of shame and disgrace'.[20] In both cases, the 'manifestation of the eschatological glory of God in the exaltation of the crucified Jesus Christ'[21] is celebrated, though in Hebrews this is especially linked with the idea of enthronement from Psalm 110: 1. Here we see a restatement of the theme first announced at 1: 3 and expanded in 2: 5–9 and 10: 12f. For all that, it does not seem suitable to the context to render ἀντὶ τῆς προκειμένης αὐτῷ χαρᾶς as 'instead of the joy that was set before him', relating this to Phil. 2: 6f.[22] The ἀγών that Christians must endure has at its end a participation in the joy of the exalted Christ.[23] Christ endured the shame and suffering of his ἀγών 'for the sake of' or 'because of the joy that was set before him',[24] and the implied challenge is for the readers to have the same perspective on their struggle.

The fact that Jesus 'despised the shame' of the cross and 'endured from sinners such hostility against himself'[25] will have its own particular relevance for the readers, in view of their past experience (10: 32–4), and what they may reasonably have expected again (10: 35ff; 13: 13). Nevertheless, the writer insists that Jesus had to suffer more disgrace and opposition than anything yet experienced by the readers (verse 4). Their struggle has not yet been μέχρις αἵματος, which could be taken figuratively to mean 'you still have not done the utmost' but is more likely to imply that no blood persecution has yet overtaken them.[26] The 'struggle against sin' (verse 4), suggests a conflict with 'a hostile power standing against the church', a periphrasis for 'sinners' in view of verse 3, rather than an expression of the inward struggle against sin as in verse 1.[27] The writer is not *blaming* them for their failure to resist to the point of bloodshed but *shaming* them: their sufferings are much less than Jesus had to bear, and they are apparently ready to 'lose heart and grow faint' (verse 3 NEB).[28]

Thus, the contest of Jesus is compared with the contest set before believers, with particular focus on his attitude under suffering and in the face of shame and disgrace. Furthermore, Jesus' *heavenly session* is related to the race of faith that he has already finished and his brothers must still run.[29] Jesus has entered God's rest and believers are summoned to 'guide their pilgrimage by looking to Jesus, considering both his earthly career and his celestial glory. Their conduct should be modeled on his earthly perseverance; but they are also to meditate on his SESSION, the reward of the perseverance.'[30]

Within this context I must now consider the key expression τὸν τῆς πίστεως ἀρχηγὸν καὶ τελειωτὴν Ἰησοῦν. With regard to ἀρχηγός, it was argued that, in view of the LXX background and the particular context at 2: 10 (τὸν ἀρχηγὸν τῆς σωτηρίας αὐτῶν), the primary sense of 'leader' or 'pathfinder' was to be understood there. However, suggestions that the word also conveyed something of the sense of 'originator' or 'initiator' were also entertained, as being relevant to the context. The athletic metaphor and the comparison of Jesus' experience with that of believers in 12: 1–4 suggests the primacy of the leadership motif again: Christ is 'forerunner' and 'example' for his people in the life of faith. It remains to be seen whether the sense of 'author' or 'source' is also present.[31]

The fact that no definite article precedes τελειωτήν indicates that τῆς πίστεως relates equally to both the following nouns and not simply to ἀρχηγόν (Vulgate: *in auctorem fidei, et consummatorem Iesum*). Furthermore, 'faith' should be understood here with reference to the preceding chapter, as something exercised by the 'cloud of witnesses' and preeminently by Jesus himself.[32] The writer does not strictly speak of Jesus as 'the Pioneer and Perfecter of *our* faith' (RSV), as if to say that our faith finds its beginning and final development in Christ, or as if to refer to the substance of the Christian creed. The faith in question is 'faith in its absolute type, of which he has traced the action under the Old Covenant'. Thus, Westcott takes the expression as a whole to refer to Jesus as 'the perfect example – perfect in realisation and in effect – of that faith we are to imitate, trusting in him'.[33] Similarly, Moffatt says it points to Jesus as 'the perfect exemplar of πίστις in his earthly life (cp. 2: 13), as the supreme pioneer ... and the perfect embodiment of faith ... He has realized faith to the full from start to finish.'[34]

With τελειωτής we have a word not found in classical literature or elsewhere in the Greek Bible. It is used by Origen as a description of God working in natural events,[35] by Pseudo-Methodius of God as the perfecter of those initiated into Christian Mysteries,[36] and by Gregory Nazianzen of the minister who accomplishes baptism and makes the candidate τέλεως.[37] Delling suggests that, in view of this very different usage 'one may suspect formation of the *nomen agentis* from the verb, and Hebrews 12: 2 did not have to be pioneer in this'.[38] Most interpreters take τελειωτής in Hebrews formally. As 'the perfecter of faith', Jesus is the one in whom faith has reached its perfection: 'he goes ahead of all others in faith and enables them to follow his example'.[39] Ἀρχηγός thus obtains its meaning through τελειωτής, implying priority or leadership in the exercise of faith because of his supremacy in realising it to the end. This accords well with the perspective of 2: 13, 3: 2 ('faithful to him who appointed him') and 5: 8f (cf. 10: 5–10).

For all that, Du Plessis is right to question whether there is only a *quantitative* difference implied between the steadfastness of OT heroes of faith and that of Jesus: 'his very supremacy over them infers a qualitative distinction. A pedagogical motivation seems a flimsy explanation for the application at this point of so poignant an expression, which elsewhere (2: 10) is one of considerable soteriological weight.'[40] He argues that there is a correlation between the perfecting of Christ and his function as perfecter: 'by his achievement he secured the τελείωσις for all who believe in and obey him'.[41] The τῆς πίστεως is to be taken absolutely and 'not as the subjective act of Christ in the individual, as if he is confessed as the Generator of personal faith'. On the other hand, 10: 19ff is said to emphasise that 'faith reached its full dimension, or in other words, that it was only made possible in the full sense of the word with the coming of Christ'.[42] Thus, as ἀρχηγός and τελειωτής he constitutes 'the new ground, content and possibility of true realization of faith in God. By his work he created a new dimension and channel for the fusion of obedience, confidence, hope and fidelity, because he pioneered this road.' Delling similarly argues that Christ is set forth in 12: 2 as 'the One who has "brought" believing "to completion" ... i.e., given it a perfect basis by his high priestly work'.[43] Michel goes further and describes the expression in 12: 2 as a liturgical 'messianic redeemer designation', adopted by the writer to describe Christ's 'perfecting work on his church'.[44] The Redeemer himself has 'gone ahead in the history of this way of faith and made it possible'.

It is certainly correct to relate the Christology of 2: 10; 5: 9 and 6: 20 to 12: 2. The terminology itself suggests this and the relative clause in 12: 2*b* recalls the process by which Christ himself was perfected, thus becoming 'the source of eternal salvation to all who obey him'. Nevertheless, care must be taken to relate 12: 2*a* to the surrounding argument as a whole and not to confuse τῆς πίστεως with the τῆς σωτηρίας αὐτῶν of 2: 10. I judge those commentators correct who see the primary reference here to *the exercise of faith by Christ himself*. However, this is not simply offered as a further example to encourage the readers to persevere in faith. 12: 2*b* reminds us that Christ's passage through suffering and shame to the glory of the Father's right hand opened the way for us to follow in his footsteps. He himself was perfected and obtained perfection for us by his unique self-offering to God (10: 5–10, 14). Although the emphasis in 5: 7–9 was on the uniqueness of Christ's work on behalf of his people, it was noted in connection with the words 'to all who obey him' that there was a hint of the need for those who would benefit from his salvation to follow in his footsteps, at least in some measure. That latter emphasis is made explicit in 12: 1–4, but the preceding emphasis on the uniqueness of his personal achievement is not forgotten. Indeed, because Christ has given faith 'a perfect basis by his high-priestly work', his faith, and what it achieved both for himself and for others, becomes *a greater incentive for faith on our part than the faith of OT saints*. His faith is thus 'qualitatively' and not just 'quantitatively' greater than theirs.

(b) Submission under discipline (12: 5–11)

The links between this section and the preceding one are important to observe. The contest that Christians are called to endure has been compared with the earthly experience of Christ. Believers are, to a certain extent, engaged in the same struggle that he was (verses 3–4). When our writer turns to consider these experiences as the discipline of God, he primarily has in view the hostility and suffering encountered because of identification with Christ. In a sense, he is seeking to justify and explain the significance of events such as the readers had previously experienced (10: 32–4).[45] He questions whether they had forgotten the sort of exhortation with which God addresses his people in Prov. 3: 11–12.[46] In that passage μὴ ὀλιγώρει means 'do not make of little account' the discipline of God; 'do not neglect to consider its real scope and end'.[47] The citation also challenges not to 'lose heart' (μηδὲ ἐκλύου) in the face of such testing and it would seem from 10: 35–9; 12: 3 and 12: 12–13, that this was even more directly relevant to their situation. Whether in prospect or present experience, the suffering and abuse involved in identification with Christ was apparently causing some of their number to collapse weakly and 'shrink back' (10: 38b–9).[48]

Addition of the word μου to the conventional wisdom formula Υἱέ (verse 5), together with the ὡς υἱοῖς of verses 5, 7, suggests to Bornkamm that the writer of Hebrews has taken Prov. 3: 11–12 as God's personal word to those who are his 'sons' in the New Covenant sense.[49] The aim is to stress 'the positively wonderful, eschatological position of grace in which believers stand, which makes them sons', through the mediation of the Son. Thus, we find an eschatological orientation to the discipline of God here. Far from discouraging them, the discipline they experience should stimulate 'the confidence and pride in our hope' that were declared so important in 3: 6. The very fact that Christians suffer for their faith, if rightly regarded, is *an assurance of sonship*. 'You can recognise in it the dealing of a Father':[50] 'God is treating you as sons' (verse 7). Thus,

Christians are called to 'endure for the sake of discipline' (εἰς παιδείαν ὑπομένετε),[51] and this has the effect of *proving their sonship* and strengthening their resolve to persevere further. Using a human analogy, the writer points out that lack of discipline is the sign of abandonment by a father (verse 8).

A second purpose for discipline at the hands of 'earthly fathers' is the teaching of due respect (verse 9). The respect and submission owed to God as 'spiritual Father' (τῷ πατρὶ τῶν πνευμάτων),[52] is so much greater, making divine discipline all the more necessary than ordinary parental discipline. The result of such subjection is nothing less than 'life' in the fullest sense (καὶ ζήσομεν, cf. 10: 38).[53] Thus, the discipline of God is related again to the enjoyment of eschatological salvation and this theme is repeated in verse 10 with the expression 'that we may share his holiness'. The rare term ἁγιότης points to the holiness which is the essential attribute of God and which Christians are to share.[54] Although it may be argued that this is not experienced until men actually 'see the Lord' (verse 14), there is an anticipation of it in 'the peaceful fruit of righteousness' (verse 11). Peace and righteousness are gifts of eschatological salvation that 'point to the new age and the future perfection',[55] but there is no need to restrict the enjoyment of these benefits to the future: 'The man who accepts discipline at the hand of God as something designed by his heavenly Father for his good will cease to feel resentful and rebellious; he has "stilled and quieted" his soul, which thus provides fertile soil for the cultivation of a righteous life, responsive to the will of God.'[56]

Following the human analogy again, the writer asserts that the period of discipline, however brief, seems painful rather than pleasant. Yet there is a period of joy that follows, in this case linked with the immediate enjoyment of the fruit of righteousness and the ultimate enjoyment of God's character and presence. This recalls the picture of Jesus in verse 2, who endured suffering with his eye fixed on the ultimate joy. Both the Jesus-tradition and the Scriptural exposition (verses 5–11) challenge the readers to respond appropriately to the joy set before them and the divine discipline that may be entailed beforehand.

(c) The perfecting of Christ and the perfecting of believers

This brings me to consider how closely the writer draws the parallels between the experience of Christ and the experience of believers. More particularly I shall be concerned to see how the perfecting of Christ through suffering relates to the perfecting of believers. Although I have indicated that the expression 'Pioneer and Perfecter of faith' expresses some clear differentiation of function and status on the part of Christ,[57] the parallelism between the experience of Christ and that of his people is most explicitly drawn in this passage. Allen Wikgren argues that, for believers,

> 'the end, though in a sense proleptically possessed, is neither fully nor automatically attained; its achievement involves struggle and suffering, a sharing, in fact, in the sufferings and in the death of Jesus himself (13: 13). This imitation and participation consequently implies more than an ideal or abstract good; the ideal has been objectified, made incarnate in Jesus Christ and the believer should be prepared through faith to share objectively in his experiences.'[58]

The suffering of Christ in our writer's presentation is primarily regarded in its *redemptive* role, Christ achieving for others the salvation that they could not achieve for themselves (1: 3; 2: 9, 14–15, 17; 5; 9; 9: 12, 14, 15, 26, 28; 10: 10, 12, 14, 19–20; 12: 24; 13: 12). The perfecting of Christ refers primarily to his vocational qualification. This takes place διὰ παθημάτων because of that redemptive role he is called to play. Allied to this is the need for him to experience temptation under suffering, so that he might minister sympathetically to his brothers as they proceed on their way as the pilgrim people of God (2: 18; 4: 15f).

The perfecting of believers can also be considered as a vocational qualification when it is noted that they are perfected as worshippers or as those who would draw near to God. However, although the perfecting of Christ is a process, necessitating his learning obedience through suffering, his death and exaltation, a simple parallel cannot be argued with respect to the perfecting of believers. They are perfected by *the very actions and accomplishments that perfect Christ*, not by any actions of their own. *Believers are perfected by the perfecting of Christ.* Nowhere does our writer suggest that Christians must be perfected διὰ παθημάτων because their perfection is *already accomplished by Christ* (10: 14). Nevertheless, suffering has an important role to play in enabling the Christian to reach his heavenly destination and the full enjoyment of the perfection achieved for him by Christ. The discipline of God serves as an encouraging proof of sonship, as a means of developing the appropriate subjection to the person and will of God, and as a process by which God gives men a 'share in his holiness' and 'the peaceful fruit of righteousness'.

To what extent can it be said that the sufferings of Christ were an expression of the discipline of God? 'Son though he was' in 5: 8 implies that his learning obedience through the things that he suffered was something totally unexpected. As the pre-existent Son of 1: 1f, it might be thought that he had no need of such experiences, whereas believers should expect divine discipline *because they are sons* (12: 5ff). Our writer emphasises in 5: 8f that Christ's sufferings were necessary for our sake, so that he might become the source of eternal salvation and a perfectly sympathetic high priest. Both 5: 9 and 12: 2f suggest also the significance of his *example for believers*, as he exhibited steadfast faith and perfect submission to the will of God in the face of suffering. The experiences that he had may well have served as a proof of sonship for him, but our writer makes nothing of this. Those experiences undoubtedly served to teach him what it was like to be subject to God in the human situation and to prepare him for his final great act of submission, but our writer nowhere suggests that he needed to learn submission to God because of disobedience. Furthermore, there is no suggestion that he needed to suffer in order to receive the peaceful fruit of righteousness. On the contrary, Christ is presented as 'tempted as we are, yet without sin' (4: 15). Thus, when we analyse the function of suffering in his experience and ours, as presented by the writer, it is clear that we cannot draw the parallels too closely.

Perfection and maturity

The hortatory preamble to the central doctrinal section of Hebrews offers both warning of the most severe kind (5: 11 – 6: 8), and encouragement (6: 9–20).[59] Not only does this passage reveal to us something of the situation of the recipients but it also employs terminology related to the main issue of this study (5: 14 $\tau\epsilon\lambda\epsilon\iota\omega\nu$; 6:1 $\tau\dot{\eta}\nu$ $\tau\epsilon\lambda\epsilon\iota\dot{o}\tau\eta\tau\alpha$). As a prelude to the detailed exposition of Christ's high priestly work, towards which the writer has been steadily moving (2: 17f; 4: 14ff; 5: 10), he insists on 'the strenuous labour which believers must undertake that they may rightly enter into it'.[60] Yet, his purpose is not merely speculative or intellectual, but practical (6: 11–12): 'to lead his hearers from superficial apprehensions of the life to which they are as Christians committed, by asking them to follow up in appropriate action'.[61]

(a) The situation of the recipients (5: 11–14; 6: 4–12)[62]

A major issue that divides the commentators is the question of balancing what the writer has to say in 5: 11–14 and 6: 4–8 with 6: 9–12. Where does his emphasis really lie and what, in fact, is the situation of the readers? Are we to conclude that they are 'sluggish' ($\nu\omega\theta\rho\sigma\acute{\iota}$), or not? This would seem to be the case from 5: 11, but in 6: 12 the writer is concerned lest they 'become sluggish'. Are we to conclude that they are immature or not?

The argument in 5: 12—14 would suggest as much, but 6: 10 commends them for past and present expressions of Christian commitment (note the present tense of διακονοῦντες), in words as complimentary as Paul's in 1 Thess. 1: 3. Are they really on the verge of apostasy, as 6: 1—8 might imply, or can we dismiss this section in the light of 6: 9—12 as a 'rhetorical hyperbole'[63] or 'theoretical case',[64] designed to motivate the readers to respond appropriately to the difficult teaching that is to follow?

P. Andriessen argues that 5: 11—14 is the only passage where the writer could actually be described as *blaming* the readers for spiritual lethargy.[65] If, however, the conjunction ἐπεί in 5: 11 is translated in an 'elliptical' sense to mean 'otherwise', rather than 'since', any suggestion of remonstrance is removed from this section and it becomes parallel in meaning to 6: 9—12. Thus, he would have us translate as follows: 'on this subject, permit us to give you a detailed and difficult exposition. *Otherwise*, you will have become slothful of hearing and although, in view of the time, you ought to be teachers, you will need again someone to teach you.' As Andriessen points out, this translation not only resolves the questions raised above but also removes the difficulty of the translation in 6: 1 (Διό): since the readers are in fact regarded by the writer as being among the mature, it is logical for him to go ahead and expound his detailed and difficult theme to them. However, Andriessen's rendering pays scant regard to the syntax of our text.[66] In addition there are important verbal parallels to the charge of being dull of hearing in hortatory passages preceding 5: 11—14, suggesting that 5: 11 does not stand on its own but makes the previous challenges even more explicitly personal and relevant to the readers.[67]

Setting 5: 11 in this broader context, I would maintain that 'dull of hearing' means more than an unwillingness to progress to a higher stage of understanding the Christian message,[68] though this is clearly present. There appears to be a certain unresponsiveness to the gospel already received: an unwillingness to work out its deeper implications and respond with faith and obedience.[69] The basic meaning of νωθρός in the LXX, as in extra-Biblical literature, is 'sluggish' or 'obtuse',[70] and the word appears to be used in this broader, literal sense in 6: 12. There, the opposite of νωθροί is clearly to become 'imitators of those who through faith and patience inherit the promises'. The qualifying phrase ταῖς ἀκοαῖς in 5: 11 puts the emphasis on their sluggishness in *receptivity* or *hearing*. Balancing the two passages together we may say that their present manifestations of unresponsiveness, if not checked, will lead to a total spiritual inertia and complete loss of faith and hope: that is how serious the situation appears to be. As Westcott puts it: 'if hope failed to have her perfect work the dullness which had already come over their powers of spiritual intelligence would extend to the whole of life'.[71]

There are three further descriptions of the readers in 5: 12–14, which may be related to the general charge of spiritual immaturity, and provide the necessary background for understanding the challenge of 6: 1–3.

(i) Unwillingness or inability to teach others

The words 'though by this time you ought to be teachers' (5: 12), can scarcely be taken as evidence that the original recipients were some special group within the wider church.[72] The writer refers to 'spiritual teaching capacity on the basis of the Word, not to the filling of church offices'.[73] The exhortation is addressed to all of his readers and διδάσκαλοι is used quite informally. The phrase διὰ τὸν χρόνον supports this interpretation, suggesting their failure to progress to what he considers a mature stage of development, where 'anyone who is instructed in his faith may be expected to be able to explain it to others (1 Pet. 3: 15; Rom. 2: 21)'.[74]

Although 5: 12 suggests that the problem is fundamentally one of *retardation*, the warning of 10: 32–9 indicates a certain *regression* from a former state of boldness and faith in confrontation with public hostility.[75] Particularly in 10: 35, the readers are exhorted not to discard the confidence that they had received and manifested in the past. I have observed in connection with 4: 16; 10: 19 that παρρησία refers to the 'free right to approach God, given in the sacrifice of Christ, which is the essence of Christian faith'.[76] At 10: 35 (and possibly 3: 6), the reference is rather more to the 'open confession of this faith, which is an unshakable hope', especially in the face of opposition and discouragement. The rebuke of 5: 12 may be related to this tendency to withdraw from confrontation with the world and the loss of certainty that this presupposes. In this case, διδάσκαλοι may refer specifically to the idea of communicating the faith to outsiders.

(ii) They want 'milk' rather than 'solid food'

'You need someone to teach you again the first principles of God's oracles' (5: 12a), is generally taken to be a judgement of the writer on the situation of his readers. However, this interpretation is hard to reconcile with his decision to move them on to solid food (6: 1, 3). It is much more satisfactory to suppose that 5: 12a reflects *their own expressed need* for someone to teach them again 'the ABC of God's oracles' (NEB) — 'with some such phrase they had perhaps been excusing their failure to take the bold step he demands'.[77] Here we may see another symptom of their with-drawal, which the writer characterises as a sign of immaturity with the rebuke 'you need milk, not solid food' (5: 12b). This assumes, with most commentators, that 'milk' is a figure for 'the first principles of God's oracles' (τὰ στοιχεῖα ... τῶν λογίων τοῦ θεοῦ), and 'the elementary doctrine of Christ' (τὸν τῆς ἀρχῆς τοῦ Χριστοῦ λόγον), described in 6: 1f.[78]

In this context τὰ στοιχεῖα means 'first principles', with perhaps a 'slightly derogatory nuance', a sense that is 'strengthened or brought to expression by τῆς ἀρχῆς'.[79] In the LXX, τὰ λόγια τοῦ θεοῦ is a term which in several contexts has become 'a vehicle for the Biblical conception of revelation by Word',[80] and is plainly so used in Acts 7: 38 to refer to the OT revelation at Sinai, received by Moses, and in Rom. 3: 2 to refer to the OT revelation as a whole. Thus, Westcott assumes it is most natural to take the phrase in Hebrews 5: 12 as a reference to 'the collected writings of the OT which the Hebrew Christians failed to understand and so, through mistaken loyalty to the past, were in danger of apostasy'.[81]

Westcott's interpretation is certainly appropriate to the general context of Hebrews, in which the writer is at pains to give the readers a Christian interpretation of the OT and point out the importance of Jesus as the climax to, and key to, the interpretation of these λόγια that God spoke 'by the prophets' (1: 1f). However, when he equates the expression in 5: 12a with τὸν τῆς ἀρχῆς τοῦ Χριστοῦ λόγον in 6: 1 and describes the latter as 'the fundamental explanation of the fulfilment of the Messianic promises in Jesus of Nazareth',[82] this hardly fits the context. The six items in 6: 1f, which appear to be descriptive of 'the elementary doctrine of Christ', are more like a primitive Christian catechism – especially in view of 'instruction about ablutions (and) the laying on of hands' – than a set of principles for interpreting the OT Scriptures.[83] This suggests the correctness of rendering τὰ στοιχεῖα τῶν λογίων τοῦ θεοῦ as 'the ABC of God's oracles' (NEB), or 'the rudimentary principles of the divine revelation'.[84]

J.C. Adams has recently questioned this whole line of exegesis by a reassessment of the elements of the so-called primitive Christian catechism in 6: 1f. 'The first problem is that in none of these six things is there any reference to anything specifically Christian. They are in fact all part of the faith of a Jew.'[85] Secondly, 'in these six "fundamental articles" of the Christian faith no mention is made of that which many scholars think to be one of the most fundamental of all, namely the confession "Jesus is Lord",' and this is most remarkable in the context of Hebrews where the writer transfers the title κύριος to Jesus without hesitation. The third difficulty is the injunction to 'leave behind' these 'rudiments of

Christianity' (NEB), if such they are, and the fourth difficulty that of making sense of the Διό of 6: 1.

Adams goes on to propose that the τοῦ Χριστοῦ in 6: 1 should be taken as a subjective genitive to give the sense: 'wherefore, let us leave on one side *Christ's original teaching* and let us advance towards maturity'.

> 'What the writer is calling upon them to "leave behind" is not the basic elements of the Christian faith, but a preoccupation with the content of Christ's own teaching. He is calling upon them to grasp more deeply the significance of his person and work (the whole of the theology of the Epistle is concerned explicitly with the significance of Jesus). This is the "solid food" of which the author speaks (verses 12, 14).'[86]

It is certainly odd that the statement of fundamentals in 6: 1f contains no specific mention of Jesus as Lord and Christ. If the writer is quoting from some primitive catechism or list of teachings familiar to the readers, it may well be that he sees this as a particular deficiency and sets out to correct it with his teaching about the person and work of Christ.[87] Adams is right to draw attention to the emphasis on Christology in Hebrews as a key to understanding the theological needs of the readers. However, when he suggests that 'they have accepted the message of Jesus, but not his person and work' or that 'their faith is in what he said, not what he did',[88] he is setting up an unreal situation. Could such a 'gospel' be sufficient to motivate the readers to make the stand for Christ described in 10: 32–4, in the teeth of such opposition? Would such a 'gospel' have given them the παρρησία (10: 35), which the writer begs them now not to throw away?

The observation that all six points listed in 6: 1f are part of the synagogue teaching, and therefore would have been known to the Jewish Christians who emerged from the synagogue, has often been made.[89] It is the very similarity of the items in this list to the creed of a contemporary Pharisaic or non-conformist Jew that has led many commentators to the conclusion that the readers were, in fact, Jewish converts to Christianity faced with a unique problem of identity: *what indeed is the difference that the coming of Christ makes to such a confession?* It is evident from 10: 35–9 that the delayed return of Jesus posed serious questions for the readers and was becoming a test of their commitment. It is reasonable to suppose that they were yielding to pressure particularly from Jewish sources to 'give up more and more those features of faith and practice which were distinctive of Christianity, and yet to feel that they had not abandoned the basic principles of repentance and faith, the realities denoted by religious ablutions and the laying on of hands, the expectation of resurrection and the judgement of the age to come'.[90]

(iii) They are 'unacquainted with teaching about righteousness'

It must be admitted that the writer does not directly charge them with this, but simply asserts that the one whose only food is spiritual 'milk' (ὁ μετέχων γάλακτος) remains ἄπειρος λόγου δικαιοσύνης. By implication, this includes the readers and helps to explain further why the writer's message is 'hard to explain'.[91]

Some German commentators take ἄπειρος λόγου δικαιοσύνης in the formal sense 'incapable of understanding correct, normal speech'.[92] Although this translation may be related to the words which follow ('for he is a child'), describing a characteristic of immaturity and thus of the readers who are unable to respond to mature speech, linguistically such a use of δικαιοσύνης is not well founded and this is not the most natural reading of the expression as a whole. Based on the similarity of the language in 5: 11–14 to the schemes of philosophical education advocated by Philo and the Stoics, some commentators argue that the expression means 'unskilled in moral truth'[93] or 'lacking a principle of righteousness'.[94] However, it is seriously to be questioned whether the writer gives evidence of a *moral* stagnation preventing the readers from advancing in the Christian way. It is rather a question of general spiritual lethargy, with a definite disinclination to explore more deeply the implications of their Christian position, that our writer reveals. This is certainly a condition 'likely to have serious moral consequences, as being likely to lead to an act of apostasy on their part',[95] but the moral element appears to be secondary in the context. The mature are certainly described as those who have 'their faculties trained by practice to distinguish good from evil' (verse 14),[96] but our writer seems to imply a power of spiritual discrimination by these words, and not simply moral discernment.[97] Thus, R. Williamson appears to be justified in his conclusion that Hebrews uses the language of the ethical teachers only as a means by which to 'draw attention effectively to the theological backwardness of his readers'.[98]

It seems best to render λόγου δικαιοσύνης with Westcott as 'teaching of righteousness' and to understand that the readers are 'unprepared by past training to enter upon the discussion of the larger problems of Christian thought'.[99] Since the absence of definite articles makes a simple equation with the gospel a difficulty, Westcott proposes a more general reference to 'teaching which at once deals with the one source of righteousness in Christ and the means by which man is enabled to be partaker of it. The doctrine of Christ's priestly work is based upon these conceptions, which belong to the "solid food" of the mature believer.' That which follows in Hebrews may be described as 'teaching about righteousness' insofar as it emphasises the righteousness of Christ and the finished nature of his redemptive work, thus encouraging the sort of faith which 'works righteousness' (11: 33) and, by the appropriate response to the discipline of God, receives 'the peaceful fruit of righteousness' (12: 11).[100]

If the readers continue on their diet of 'milk', they will remain 'unacquainted with' or 'unaccustomed to' (ἄπειρος)[101] the teaching which alone can motivate them to righteousness and give them that discernment which is the mark of spiritual maturity (5: 14).[102] Although the writer makes a rigid distinction between the spiritual νήπιοι who feed on milk and spiritual τέλειοι who feed on solid food, it is clear from what follows (6: 1ff, Διό ...), that he envisages only one way of moving his readers into the second category, namely by feeding them solid food.[103]

Du Plessis observes that τέλειοι here 'corresponds manifestly with διδάσκαλοι (5: 12), without being wholly identical'.[104] The community of believers 'can only act as preceptors in Christian kerygma and dogma if their own Christian constitution or being is sound and maturely developed'. This assessment is valid only if we remember that their inability to teach others is symptomatic of a wider problem: they need σπουδή (6: 11), παρρησία (10: 35) and ὑπομονή (10: 36), that is, 'the power to translate Christianity into action'.[105] The challenge to respond favourably to the solid food that the writer will dispense has a practical end in view. In the light of 6: 4–8 it is to rescue them from the danger of apostasy, but in the light of 6: 9–12 it is the more positive aim of encouraging them to a renewal of their former zeal.

This faces us with the problem of relating the warning passage in 6: 4–8 with the very positive things said about the readers. P.E. Hughes rightly argues that 'the confidence expressed in 6: 9 and 10: 39 arises from the certitude that a true work of God has taken place in their midst; but this does not exclude the possibility that some of their number are rebellious at heart and, unless there is a radical change, will find that they have reached the point of irremediable apostasy'.[106] This emphasis on 'some of their number' failing to show spiritual progress and slipping away, possibly even into reprobation, accords well with the words 'each of you' in 6: 11, and the various other suggestions throughout Hebrews that the mighty confirmation of the gospel in their midst (2: 4) had not touched each of them with the same conviction.[107]

I might also note that the writer addresses his encouraging words to them in 6: 9 using the expression τὰ κρείσσονα. It is best to see this as a reference back to the two types of soil in the parable of verses 7–8 and to translate with NEB 'you, my friends, are *in the better case*'.[108] In terms of the stark contrast presented there – the fruitful soil about to receive a blessing from God and the useless soil about to be cursed – he must certainly classify them as a group in the first category. He provides no middle ground for the sluggish and disobedient. But surely the point of 6: 4–8; 10: 26–31 and 12: 15–17 is that one who appears to be in the first category can drift into the second.

The writer's persuasion about the reality of their commitment as a group (6: 9), is based particularly on the recollection of their behaviour on some well-known occasion in the past (suggested by the aorist tense of ἐνεδείξασθε). Most commentators agree in identifying this with the events described in some detail in 10: 32–4. Even though the present participle (διακονοῦντες) stresses that in some sense their exemplary love for one another, shown on that previous occasion, is continuing, the real emphasis of 6: 10–11 is on *renewing their past zeal*.[109] Reading 6: 10 in the light of 10: 32–4, I would argue that καὶ τῆς ἀγάπης is not epexegetical of τοῦ ἔργου ὑμῶν, as if the verse was only speaking of manifestations of mutual love: their 'work' refers to the overall faithfulness to Christ that they exhibited previously, including their great boldness before persecutors, and cheerful acceptance of the seizure of their property. The exhortation of 6: 11 is not simply to 'show the same zeal in other directions as they showed in works of love',[110] nor 'to complete their brotherly love by a mature grasp of what their faith involved'.[111] Clearly their faithfulness to Christ and practical concern for one another on that past occasion was inspired by a compelling hope (10: 34). It is a renewal of their former zeal in every respect that the writer calls for – faith, hope and love – when he uses the expression πρὸς τὴν πληροφορίαν τῆς ἐλπίδος ἄχρι τέλους. '*The full scope of hope* is what they should realize, and the urgent entreaty "to be imitators of those who through faith and patience inherit the promises" (verse 12b), stresses its historical character'.[112] When hope is realised in daily living, as the record of chapter 11 will show, patience, obedience, faithfulness and love are the result.

(b) The writer's challenge (6: 1–3)

I have already observed that the rather unexpected 'wherefore' (Διό), of 6: 1 implies that the immature can only mature when they are fed and learn to assimilate solid food.[113] Those who stay on milk cannot develop a taste for solid food and acquire that maturity of spiritual discernment which is the mark of the mature. The writer does not call upon them to abandon in an absolute sense one aspect of Christian teaching for another. The challenge is to build upon the foundations already laid or work out the further implications of the teaching already received. 'Not laying again a foundation' explains in a negative fashion what the positive injunction (ἀφέντες) means.[114] The solid food that the writer goes on to give his readers is intimately related to the milk, which is a figure for the 'rudiments of Christianity' (NEB), listed in 6: 1f. The solid food is in fact a development of the themes of repentance and faith, resurrection from the dead and eternal judgement in the light of our writer's novel exposition of the high priesthood of Christ.[115] Even the subject of ablutions comes up for further consideration in the exposition which follows (9: 10; 10: 22; cf. 9: 13f).

The plural φερώμεθα is not the literary plural of 5: 11 but an indication that 'the writer wishes to carry his readers along with him'.[116] The passive here suggests the need for 'personal surrender to an active influence',[117] rather than personal striving for a goal, and it is remarkable that the English versions do not adequately convey the sense of the Greek. Westcott regards ἐπὶ τὴν τελειότητα as meaning 'for the readers full maturity of spiritual growth, opposed to νηπιότης (5: 13); and for the writer the teaching which corresponds with maturity'.[118] Moffatt would restrict τελειότης to 'the mature mental grasp of the truth about Christ as ἀρχιερεύς, a truth which the writer is disappointed that his friends still find it difficult to understand'.[119] Some would restrict the meaning even further to 'the perfection of Christian doctrine', or even to 'the question or subject of perfection'.[120]

Du Plessis, who proposes the last rendering, argues that τελειότης is nowhere used in the literature simply to express 'maturity': 'by its very nature of abstraction and indication of totality of aggregates it is not equipped to convey the notion thus being forced upon it. If the author had a dynamic progressive capacity in mind — which is required if one wishes to entertain the notion of spiritual ripening — he would have had to employ τελείωσις.'[121] It is certainly true that τελειότης is generally used in an abstract and formal sense in the limited range of examples that can be found.[122] Yet Du Plessis does not consider the evidence from Philo at this point, even though the latter uses τελειότης thirty-five times. The formal and abstract qualities of this noun are obvious when Philo writes of the Creator employing 'every form that tends to perfectness' (πάσαις ταῖς πρὸς τελειότητα ἰδέαις),[123] or of God giving the graces of teaching, nature and practice to mankind 'for perfecting its life' (πρὸς τελειότητα τοῦ βίου).[124] However, when he writes of 'the perfection of the soul', it is clear that he has a particular τέλος in view. Through the faculties of his soul, a man can 'make a beginning, make progress, and reach perfection in praiseworthy things' (τελειότητας ἐν πράξεσιν ἐπαινεταῖς).[125] This special application of the noun to the concept of spiritual and moral development is clearly related to Philo's use of τελειοῦν in such contexts. The three natural orders 'teaching, perfection, practice' are said to be symbolised in the Biblical records of Abraham, Isaac and Jacob.[126] Yet perfection is not a purely ethical concept here, since the highest stage of humanity is reached with *the vision of God.*[127]

I am not suggesting a simplistic equation of our writer's use of τελειότης with that of Philo. However, Philo's application of the term to men in a moral and spiritual sense, within the general context of νήπιοι– τέλειοι thinking, shows that our writer could well have been using it in contrast with his own measure of νηπιότης. H.P. Owen rightly observes that Philo's solid food is 'an advanced form of intellectual vision approximating to union with the Godhead. The author of Hebrews on the other hand appears deliberately to avoid construing his στερεὰ τροφή in intellectualist terms.'[128] Owen argues that Hebrews aims to 'remedy moral inertia by religious vision' and that 'this intention is conditioned throughout by an eschatological setting'.[129] I have questioned the assumption that moral inertia was the fundamental problem with which the writer had to deal. It was rather a general spiritual lethargy, involving loss of zeal, lack of confidence and faltering hope, that he sought to overcome. His method was to present *a vision of Christ, perfected through suffering and opening 'the new and living way' for mankind into the sanctuary of heaven.*

The τελειότης of 6: 1 does not simply refer to the moral maturity that the solid food will confer,[130] but more generally to that spiritual maturity of which the context gives general indication. In response to Du Plessis, I would argue that this maturity is to be viewed as a *goal* rather than as a *process*, hence the choice of the term. It also seems likely that τελείωσις was avoided to prevent confusion with the concept of perfection in a relationship with God, achieved through the perfecting of Christ. The term in 6: 1 refers neither to 'vague spiritual efficiency' nor simply to a 'maturity of apperception in pedagogical or tutorial respect'.[131] Maturity for our writer involves a spiritual receptivity and responsiveness to the truth of God, issuing in certain practical responses. If the practical response specifically indicated in 5: 12 is an ability to communicate the faith to others, the broader challenge of 6: 11ff links the passage to the emphasis of Hebrews as a whole. There, as we have seen, the call is for a renewal of their zeal in every respect, with a view to realising the 'full scope of hope' in patient faith, love and good works.[132]

It cannot be denied that 5: 11 – 6: 3 puts the emphasis on progress in understanding the Christian faith as the pathway to maturity. However, to understand τὴν τελειότητα as the 'perfection of Christian doctrine' or 'the subject of perfection', in strict contrast with 'the elementary doctrine of Christ', suggests that such teaching is an end in itself. This falls short of our writer's stress in the passage as a whole. Furthermore, it involves the assumption that τελειότης is a pregnant expression for λόγος τέλειος, although no real precedent for such usage has been offered to justify such an interpretation.[133]

For all that, it is important to observe that the writer's teaching about the perfecting of Christ and the perfecting of believers is central to the solid food that he seeks to impart to his readers. Properly understood, this provides the greatest encouragement to faith and zeal. Teaching about perfection is not only for the mature (5: 14), to sustain them in their earthly pilgrimage, but also the best means of drawing the immature along the pathway to maturity. Our writer's emphasis on the perfecting of believers by Christ is designed to encourage *confidence about their relationship with God* and to encourage them *to persevere in that confidence*, even in the face of hostility and suffering. Although in a sense there is a journey of faith to be completed towards the final goal, the end is already experienced and *enjoyed as a gift from God* (12: 22–4, 28).

Conclusion

I have argued that the writer of Hebrews was seeking to deal with a problem of spiritual lethargy on the part of his readers, involving loss of zeal, lack of confidence and faltering hope. Certainty about the factors contributing to this situation is not possible, though persecution or the threat of further suffering for the sake of Christ seems to have been a significant factor. It is most likely that the original recipients were Jewish Christians, tempted to slip back into a form of Judaism in order to escape the hostility and suffering associated with being Christian.

Fundamental to the problem of the readers is an inadequate grasp of the person and work of Christ. The writer's message could be summarised as a call to 'consider Jesus, the apostle and high priest of our confession' (3: 1). Put another way, it is a call to concentrate attention on the person of Jesus and his achievement on their behalf. They are to remember the whole process by which he was perfected as their saviour and high priest in order to appreciate *the help he can give for running the race that is set before them* (12: 1ff). His life of obedience, his sacrificial death and heavenly exaltation are the means by which he was perfected. Believers in turn are perfected by the very actions and accomplishments that perfect Christ.

Such a presentation of the person and work of Christ provides the readers with the certainty that he is ever able to apply to them the benefits of his salvific work and thus bring them to their heavenly destination.

However, the focus is not simply on Christ's unique achievement nor on his qualification to act in the present on behalf of his people. The perfecting of Christ 'through suffering' provides a pattern for Christian discipleship. Christians share to a certain extent in the same struggle or contest that Christ endured and, because he pioneered the way, they have the prospect of enjoying his victory if they share his faith and manifest the same sort of perseverance in the face of hostility and suffering.

The teaching about the perfecting of Christ and the perfecting of believers is clearly *more central to the argument of Hebrews than many commentators have allowed.* It is not simply the writer's way of presenting 'a kind of philosophy of history'.[134] It is central to his exhortation for a group of Christians in danger of growing weary and fainthearted in the journey of faith. There is no real evidence that the writer's use of the terminology of perfection was part of a special polemic against a form of perfectionism being expounded to or by the readers. In 7: 11–19 the terminology is clearly related to the writer's general argument about the surpassing worth of the New Covenant. However, this does not prove that the readers were themselves asserting that perfection was attainable through the levitical priesthood and the Law of Moses. It is best to conclude that the writer adopted this terminology as a means of expressing the absolute effectiveness of Christ to fulfil the divine plan of bringing 'many sons to glory'.

APPENDIX A: THE SINLESSNESS OF CHRIST AND HIS PERFECTING

In a contribution to *Expository Times*, Ronald Williamson raises again the question of Jesus' sinlessness, which has so exercised the minds of thinkers throughout the centuries. Whereas the writer of Hebrews stresses, both in the first part of 4: 15 and elsewhere, that Jesus' humanity was total and authentic, 'yet what seems to be implied by the phrase χωρὶς ἁμαρτίας contradicts this emphasis on the unimpaired genuineness of the humanity'.[1] Having stated the problem in these terms, Williamson sets out to question the traditional assumption that 'without sin' in 4: 15 means that Jesus was 'perpetually sinless, sinless from the beginning'. He suggests that 'Jesus' sinlessness was achieved only after a struggle in which it is not inconceivable that he actually sinned.' In particular, he argues that Hebrews pictures Christ achieving the state of sinlessness at 'the moment of his self-sacrificial death, when "through what he suffered", the process of learning obedience, of being made perfect, was consummated'. Following G. W. Buchanan's interpretation of 7: 27,[2] Williamson proposes that Jesus offered a sacrifice both for his own sins and the sins of all men and suggests that our writer's presentation of the humanity of Christ is therefore consistent. Thus, 'the sinlessness of Jesus was achieved and not innate. It was not something he possessed when he began his struggle with temptation, a kind of built-in pre-disposition against sin which would have infringed the reality of his humanity.'

It is certainly much more in keeping with our writer's overall presentation of the person and work of Christ, to view the 'without sin' of 4: 15 as descriptive of the *issue of Jesus' temptations*, rather than as a qualification of his likeness to us or to our temptations (καθ' ὁμοιότητα). Westcott favours the latter course when he argues that Christ was *not tempted by previous sin*, as we are: 'there is no sin in him to become the spring of trial'.[3] Moffatt also acknowledges the possibility that 'without sin' excludes some temptations — 'since a number of our worst temptations arise out of sins previously committed' — but concludes that this was 'not in the writer's mind at all', the expression meaning simply 'without yielding to sin'.[4] Michel similarly insists that the sinlessness of Jesus is a 'happening' (*Ereignis*) but not a 'condition' (*Zustand*): 'it must not be viewed as an attribute or quality of his nature. "Sinlessness" occurs as the beginning of a new actuality, but one does not "have" it.'[5]

While it is true that the concept of Jesus' sinlessness must not be divorced from the idea of his overcoming temptation, it also seems valid to argue that the judgement 'without sin' could be made about Christ, at *every stage of his earthly struggle*. Williamson rightly draws attention to the centrality of the sin of apostasy in Hebrews and suggests that this is 'the sin which Jesus presumably had to overcome when he was learning obedience'. If this is so, the cross will certainly be the consummation of his learning obedience and the final expression or achievement of 'sinlessness'. However, to define the essential sin that Jesus had to overcome as apostasy necessitates the conclusion that he was 'without sin' in this respect throughout his life and ministry. Apostasy, as our writer defines it (3: 12; 6: 6; 10: 26−8), involves a definitive act of rebellion against the living God and his revealed will. Jesus could not have sinned in this way without destroying his whole mission and we must conclude that he remained 'without sin' in this regard, until he had perfected the Father's work and was thereby perfected in his role as messianic high priest. It is not logical to say with Buchanan that the expression in 4: 15 refers to 'the crucifixion alone, and not to Jesus' entire life',[6] if apostasy is the sin in view.

Williamson suggests that Jesus' holiness, blamelessness, stainlessness and separation from sinners (7: 26), 'were achieved only after a lifetime's struggle'. The expression 'separated from sinners' certainly implies that 'a process of separation had taken place, which in turn implies that there was a time in Jesus' life when he was not separated from sinners', but it does not follow that at that time 'the term "sinner" could without injustice be applied to him'. If 'separated from sinners' in 7: 26 is parallel, at least in some respects, to 'exalted above the heavens' it simply asserts that Jesus' life among 'sinners' ceased with his ascension. The reason for Christ's exaltation is his perfect sacrifice (verses 27f), which is clearly associated in this context, as in 9: 14, with the perfection of the victim. The adjectives 'holy, blameless, unstained' refer to the perfect obedience of Christ, proved through the struggles of his human existence.

If 'without sin' refers simply to Jesus' faithful fulfilment of his messianic calling, is it conceivable that he actually sinned in other respects while carrying out his mission? May we not see indications of this in the evidence of the Gospels that he 'was angry, he was harsh to his mother, he evaded his enemies, he broke the law of his people, he stirred up revolt against the rulers and religious men of his country'?[7] This can hardly have been our writer's view when he wrote that Jesus 'offered himself without blemish to God' (9: 14), which suggests that Jesus was blameless when he offered himself to God. Westcott rightly observes that 'the connexion in which ($\overset{"}{\alpha}\mu\omega\mu\omega\varsigma$) stands shews that it refers to the conditions and issues of the Lord's earthly life',[8] not simply to the blameless way in which he actually made himself a sacrifice for sins. It would be a strangely limited use of $\overset{"}{\alpha}\mu\omega\mu\omega\varsigma$ anyway, if our writer meant it to refer only to the final act of obedience by Christ! If the writer genuinely believed that Christ needed to offer for his own sins first and then for the sins of the people (7: 27), it would be hard to reconcile that view with the insistence of 9: 14 that it was *as a spotless victim* that he offered himself to God in death.

Every attempt to limit 'without sin' to the last events of Christ's life or to the fulfilment of his Messianic mission alone ignores the force of $\kappa\alpha\tau\grave{\alpha}$

πάντα καθ᾽ ὁμοιότητα in 4: 15. It is not necessary to assert that Christ experienced literally every form of temptation known to man. On the other hand, it is not valid to restrict the κατὰ πάντα to temptations experienced in connection with suffering or with apostasy. Our writer's focus is certainly on such temptations, both with respect to Christ and the readers, but the κατὰ πάντα καθ᾽ ὁμοιότητα allows for a wider experience of temptation. 'Without sin' must logically be interpreted with reference to the full scope of human temptation, even if the Gospel records illustrate only the testing experienced by Christ with regard to his mission.[9]

I judge, therefore, that our writer wished to emphasise the breadth of Jesus' experience as a man, 'who in every respect has been tempted as we are' (RSV), or who 'because of his likeness to us, has been tested every way' (NEB). When he added the words 'without sin' it was to assert the victory of Christ over sin in every respect. This does not mean that he had 'a kind of built-in pre-disposition against sin which would have infringed the reality of his humanity'. Our writer emphasises the *struggle* that was involved for Jesus in overcoming sin and fulfilling the Father's will (5: 7f; 12: 2ff). Yet 'without sin' certainly implies a difference in the humanity of Jesus. We cannot say that it was *metaphysically* impossible for Jesus to sin, yet Hebrews presents him as having the freedom not to sin. In this respect he is certainly a man with a difference.[10]

Williamson asks 'how could Jesus in any sense save sinners if he had not fully shared himself in the human condition, as the author of Hebrews insists that he did, including actual participation in the experience of sinning?'[11] However, Hebrews does not simply present Christ as an example to believers in their 'struggle against sin': his salvific role is a unique function on behalf of others, involving a life of perfect obedience to the will of God and culminating in his redemptive death. Sinlessness is nowhere held out as a possibility for Christians, but sin can be defeated in the ongoing struggle by reception of the 'mercy' for past failures and 'timely help' that Christ alone can offer (4: 16). This puts Christ and his people into different categories, as Redeemer and redeemed respectively, in this matter of overcoming sin. Such an emphasis on the uniqueness of Christ's person and work must not be exaggerated to the point of docetism, since that is plainly contrary to the author's presentation. On the other hand, Christ's likeness to us is certainly qualified when the judgement 'without sin' is passed on his life.

In 2: 5ff the uniqueness of Christ's achievement as a man is presented in terms of his fulfilment of Psalm 8: 4–6. The dominion that he exercised over sin, death and the Devil culminated in his becoming 'heir of all things' (1: 2). It is possible that our writer viewed the manhood of Jesus as comparable to that of Adam before the Fall, Christ achieving that dominion that Adam lost through sin. If we speak of humanity as we know it empirically, sinlessness is indeed impossible. Yet Scripture confronts us with the picture of Adam as one who had no history of sin before he was tempted and fell. Our writer's Adam Christology may not be as explicit as Paul's, but it is reasonable to suppose that he saw Christ as the Man who fulfils the ideal of manhood, thus enabling his people to share in his dominion and glory.

APPENDIX B: WHEN DID JESUS 'BECOME' HIGH PRIEST?

This issue, which is often discussed in the commentaries, concerns not only the nature of Christ's priesthood but also the nature of his perfecting. As raised by the Socinians of the sixteenth century, it was part of a larger question as to whether the death of Christ was truly an atoning sacrifice for sins. Socinus distinguished between Christ's 'bloodletting' – his death on the cross which was 'a necessary preparation for the exercise of priestly service, but of itself possessed no expiatory power'[1] – and his sacrifice proper. The latter is said to have taken place in the heavenlies, being 'the presentation of the fruit of Christ's passion to the Most High'. Thus, we are told that:

> 'Christ did not offer himself to God on the cross but only in heaven itself. This is amply supported by the fact that Christ was not properly inaugurated to priesthood until after his death, indeed until after his ascension to heaven ... Christ was not truly priest before he had attained to the glorification of his body and to immortality.'[2]

As raised by commentators today, the question is not fundamentally whether the death of Christ was an atoning sacrifice for sins, but relating the death of Christ to the concept of his heavenly ministry is still the heart of the matter. When our writer speaks of Christ offering himself as a sacrifice for sins (7: 26; 9: 14, 26; 10: 10), it is natural to think of his death on the cross as a high-priestly action, and yet our author explicitly states that Christ's high-priestly ministry is essentially heavenly in its *locus*, rather than earthly (7: 23–6; 8: 1–6; 9: 11ff). Indeed we are told 'if he were on earth, he would not be a priest at all, since there are priests who offer gifts according to the law' (8: 4). The assertion of 7: 16 that Christ became a priest 'by the power of an indestructible life' points to the significance of his resurrection–ascension in the establishment of his heavenly ministry, as I have argued.[3] Are we, then, to locate the moment of his becoming high priest at the resurrection–ascension and, if so, how are we to relate his death to his heavenly priesthood?

The emphasis on Christ's ascension in Hebrews is well known, and the presentation of this theme typologically in terms of Christ's entrance into the heavenly sanctuary is unique in the NT (6: 19f; 8: 1f; 9: 11ff, 24ff). However, it is important to remember, as A. B. Davidson stresses that:

> 'the slaying of the victim and the entrance of the high priest into the holiest with the blood constituted one act of sacrifice. The sacrifice

was not merely an offering, it was the realizing through the offering of the continued covenant relation of the Lord and the People. This was shown in the entering of the high priest, the representative of the people, with blood into the holiest, the very presence of God.'[4]

In his use of the imagery of the Day of Atonement, our writer stresses the entrance of Christ into the heavenly sanctuary, but this cannot be divorced from the preceding sacrifice, as if only the entrance could be considered heavenly. Indeed, I would argue that the writer's aim in his use of this symbolism is to stress the heavenly nature of Christ's sacrifice on the cross. Just as the sacrifice in Lev. 16: 15 was performed outside the earthly sanctuary, with a view to ministry in that sanctuary, so our writer shows that *the sacrifice of the cross in its intrinsic nature was a heavenly act*. It was a sacrifice performed with respect to the heavenly sanctuary, and as such was 'an act which fell in the sphere of the αἰώνιον'.[5] The resurrection— ascension is important to our writer because it indicates the permanency of Christ's high-priesthood (7: 23ff) and the eternal or heavenly significance of his sacrifice (9: 11−14, 23−6; 10: 12−14, 19ff). Nowhere does the writer formally touch upon the question as to whether Christ was ever priest on earth, but the use of the imagery of the Day of Atonement ritual stresses that both his sacrifice and entrance into the heavenly sanctuary are part of the same priestly action (cf. 13: 12−13).

Westcott argues in connection with 6: 20 and 7: 27 that 'the offering of Christ upon the cross was a high-priestly act, though Christ did not become "High-priest after the order of Melchizedek", that is, royal High-priest, till the Ascension'.[6] This is based on the assumption that the γενόμενος in 6: 20 implies entrance into the new order after his exaltation to the throne of God, though it is clear that the participle could also mean that he was invested with his priesthood prior to, or simultaneously with, his entrance into the heavenly sanctuary. Westcott sees the necessity for viewing Christ's death and entrance into the heavenly sanctuary as a single sacerdotal action and thus speaks of him 'fulfilling the type of Aaron'.[7] However, when he goes on to suggest that Christ's investiture to the royal high-priesthood of Melchizedek is subsequent to that, he is making an artificial distinction between the representations of the priesthood of Christ in Hebrews. The same could be said for the argument of J.H. Davies that Christ's becoming high priest could be related to the 'bestowal' (5: 10, προσαγορευθείς), which he takes to be the climax of the sequence in 5: 7−10, and synony- mous with the invitation in Psalm 110: 1 ('sit at my right hand').[8]

With regard to the latter argument, there is no need to restrict this bestowal or designation of Christ with the priesthood after the order of Melchizedek to his session at God's right hand. Our writer could simply be referring to the fact that Christ is appointed to this priesthood by God *in the psalm*, with no particular regard for the time of that appointment. If, however, the writer intends us to associate this with God's invitation to the Son to sit at his right hand, by the link with Psalm 110: 1 and the combination with Psalm 2: 7 in 5: 5f, we must interpret that investiture on the analogy of his sonship. Son though he was, in his earthly ministry (1: 2; 5: 8), his enthronement marks the consummation of his messianic work, the proclamation of his sonship to all and the moment when the

Son begins to enter into his inheritance (1: 2; 10: 12f). If the enthronement marks also the proclamation of his eternal high-priesthood at the Father's right hand, this new representation of Christ cannot be divorced from his previous work as high priest but must be viewed as its consummation. Davies speaks of Christ's oblation of his life, his death and entry into heaven as the cause of his investiture with the Melchizedek priesthood, and 'thus the ground of Christ's ministry of intercession'. Davies does not explain how the oblation can be the ground for subsequent priestly ministry if Christ was not a priest until his heavenly session. If Christ's priesthood is viewed in terms of two different 'orders', we are brought to the extraordinary conclusion that 'the high priest who, abiding before the face of God for us, is surety of the eternal covenant, is of a different order from the high priest who, in his entrance before God, realized this covenant'.[9]

It is much more satisfactory to argue that Christ fulfills the type of Aaron's high-priesthood *as priest after the order of Melchizedek*, and to conclude that 'the nature of his person alters the character of these acts, and makes them, instead of being fleshen and figurative, spiritual and possessing ideal validity'.[9] It is unwarranted literalism to restrict the exercise of Christ's priesthood 'after the order of Melchizedek' to his heavenly session and intercession — 'Christ is always, from the moment he was priest at all, a priest after the order of Melchizedek.'[10] Only such a position as this can make a satisfactory link between the two representations of Christ's priesthood and show how the present ministry is in fact based on the fulfilment of his sacrifice and entrance into the heavenly sanctuary.

If we ask, then, precisely *when* Christ became high priest, we have to admit that our author gives us no clearcut answer. His death on the cross must be included in our view of his priestly work, though our writer nowhere explicitly states this. Can we go further back and assert with the majority of Catholic commentators that Christ is 'consecrated priest at the very moment of his incarnation, when his human nature is created and at the same time united with the divine in the person of the Son of God'?[11] This is based on the assumption that 'a perfect priest will be one who is perfectly one with his fellow men and perfectly one with God', and the conclusion that 'the personal union of the two natures in Christ lays the foundation for his priesthood'.[12]

The essence of high-priesthood in our writer's view is the offering of 'gifts and sacrifices for sins' (5: 1) and the associated task of dealing appropriately with the people who need that mediatorial work (5: 2). The incarnation is therefore shown to be necessary for Christ on both counts. His experience of suffering and temptation was to make him 'a merciful and faithful high priest in the service of God' (2: 17f), both with respect to the offering of a perfect sacrifice 'to expiate the sins of the people', and to enable him to exercise his heavenly ministry of sympathy and timely help (4: 15f; 7: 25). It is true that our writer envisages the words of Psalm 40: 6–8 being placed in the mouth of Christ 'coming into the world', and it is therefore tempting to argue that the offering of Christ includes his death *and* the preceding life of obedience through suffering and temptation, of which it is the climax. Nevertheless, the writer's own interpretation of the Psalm citation in 10: 5−10 concludes with the clear reference to the 'offering of the body of Jesus Christ once for all' as the means by which the people are sanctified. The use of ἐφάπαξ here suggests that the writer is giving 'central place to the crucifixion' (7: 27; cf. 13: 12),[13] and the immediate context confirms this by emphasising the role of blood in the taking away of sins (10: 4) and the clear reference to the death of Christ as the 'single sacrifice for sins', which leads to his exaltation to the right hand of God (10: 12). For this reason, it is more accurate to say that our writer envisaged Christ's life of obedience as a *preparation* for the great act of self-sacrifice and subsequent ministry of the benefits of that sacrifice, rather than to say that the life of obedience is viewed as a priestly ministry or offering in itself.[14]

The comments of G. Schrenk in this regard are helpful:

'5: 1−10 shows how he becomes High-priest (γενηθῆναι verse 5), namely, by fidelity to the One who has appointed him in his incarnation, 3: 2, by learning obedience through suffering, 5: 8, by enduring the severest tests with εὐλαβεία with holy fear, 5: 7, and therefore by being made perfect in obedience, 5: 9. Τελειωθείς implies both that he has proved himself to be the victor through obedience ... and also that he is exalted to all eternity υἰὸν εἰς τὸν αἰῶνα τετελειωμένον 7: 28. He thus becomes High-priest by proving and accrediting himself as the Son.'[15]

In his article, Schrenk insists that 'the crucifixion belongs to the high-priestly office of Christ as well as his present rule in the sanctuary. His office comprises both the penetrating movement of his saving action and the lofty calm of his constant giving'.[16] A. B. Davidson reaches a similar conclusion when he suggests that 'the Son exhibited and authenticated himself as a priest in the performance of his priestly functions',[17] namely in his sacrificial death and exaltation. This is as much as we can say with regard to *when* Christ became high priest. To base the interpretation of the priesthood of Christ in Hebrews on the doctrine of the two natures in Christ is to place the emphasis where our writer does not. Perfect mediation between man and God in his view is not achieved simply by the incarnation but by a perfect sacrifice and the entrance of Christ into the heavenly sanctuary. Even to speak of the union of two natures in Christ as 'the foundation for his priesthood' and the perfection of his priesthood 'when his priestly human nature has reached the celestial place of divine power and glory',[18] is to obscure the centrality of *making expiation for the sins of the people* in our writer's presentation of the high-priesthood of Christ. Such an emphasis on the perfection of Christ's humanity through glorification brings to the forefront a concept that is, at best, only secondary in Hebrews.

Relating our conclusions to the concept of Christ's perfecting I would stress that the latter is a reference both to the *preparation* for his high-priestly ministry and to the *carrying-out* of that ministry in death and heavenly exaltation. The whole process by which Christ is consummated as 'the leader who delivers them' (2: 10), 'the source of eternal salvation'

(5: 9) and 'Son' (7: 28), includes the fulfilment of the type of Aaron's high-priesthood, but is not simply synonymous with that. Furthermore, if the perfecting of Christ includes the fulfilment of the high-priestly role with respect to the heavenly sanctuary, that perfecting cannot be described as his 'consecration' to heavenly high-priesthood. We may infer that Christ was consecrated to his priesthood in the very act of offering himself as a sacrifice in death, but his perfecting is a broader concept, as I have consistently argued.

NOTES

1 The hermeneutical issues

1 The abbreviation 'Hebrews', rather than 'the Epistle to the Hebrews', is used because I am convinced that the document is best described as a 'homily in written form, with some personal remarks at the end' (F.F. Bruce, *Commentary on the Epistle to the Hebrews* (London–Edinburgh, 1964), p. 413). Cf. J. Swetnam, 'On the Literary Genre of the "Epistle" to the Hebrews', *NovT* 11 (1969), 261–9.

2 O. Michel, 'Die Lehre von der christlichen Vollkommenheit nach der Anschauung des Hebräerbriefes', *Theologische Studien und Kritiken* 106 (1934–5), 333–5 (citation from p. 333).

3 P.J. Du Plessis, ΤΕΛΕΙΟΣ: *The Idea of Perfection in the New Testament* (Kampen, 1959), p. 212.

4 J. Kögel, 'Der Begriff τελειοῦν im Hebräerbrief im Zusammenhang mit dem neutestamentlichen Sprachgebrauch', *Theologische Studien für M. Kähler* (Leipzig, 1905), pp. 37–68.

5 The title 'Son' is said to be used in 7: 28 *messianically* and to point to 'the vocation which Jesus has'.

6 Kögel leaves the detailed consideration of Jesus' trials and 'inner development' for K. Bornhäuser, whose article ('Die Versuchungen Jesu nach dem Hebräerbriefe') follows his own (pp. 69ff).

7 Michel, 'Vollkommenheit'.

8 He quotes Rabbinic sources to show that a person becomes *tāmîm* through God himself, through his word and command. Thus Abraham became *tāmîm* through circumcision when God declared him such, and Israel through God's declaration at Sinai. It depends on 'God's pleasure and man's obedience' (p. 341). On the other hand, Philo concludes that men of the OT are τέλειοι 'because they are wise and fulfil the ideal of a human ethic'.

9 This perfecting may happen after death, when one becomes a member of the heavenly city (12: 23), or with the Parousia of Christ, when the Christian reaches 'with Christ the goal which God has set for him' (p. 355).

10 E. Käsemann, *Das wandernde Gottesvolk* (Göttingen, 1961; first published 1939), especially pp. 82–90 and 140–5.

11 Since the antithesis τέλειοι–νήπιοι (5: 11ff) is a *metaphysical* one in his view, between the 'enlightened' and the 'ignorant', the

perfection or maturity in view has nothing to do with moral or spiritual maturity.

12 'Die Versuchungen Jesu nach dem Hebräerbriefe', *Theologische Studien für M. Kähler* (Leipzig, 1905), pp. 69ff.

13 Th. Häring, 'Über einige Grundgedanken des Hebräerbriefs', *Monatsschrift für Pastoraltheologie* 17 (1920–1), 260–76.

14 However, Herodotus III. 86 is said to offer a limited example, referring to the 'certifying consecration' of Darius as king (p. 266).

15 He draws attention to the cultic sense of τελειοῦν in early Christian literature for what he describes as the 'baptism' of the martyr's death, and the less infrequent use in relation to ecclesiastical rites. On these texts see my discussion in chapter 2.

16 Τελειότης (6: 1) and τελειωτής (12: 2) are not interpreted in a cultic way.

17 E. Riggenbach, 'Der Begriff der τελείωσις im Hebräerbrief. Ein Beitrag zur Frage nach der Einwirkung der Mysterienreligion auf Sprache und Gedankenwelt des Neuen Testaments', *NKZ* 34 (1923), 184–95.

18 Philo's interpretation of the Pentateuchal data shows that for him the installation of the levitical priests was an act of consecration similar to that of the Mystery religions (pp. 187f. Cf. *Vit. Mos.* II. 143–53). However, Philo uses τελεῖν and does not employ τελειοῦν, τελείωσις or τέλεος in the technical sense of 'consecration to the Mysteries'.

19 He argues that τὰς χεῖρας can only be 'an accusative of relation'.

20 Häring's brief reply to Riggenbach is in *NKZ* 34 (1923), 386–9.

21 M. Dibelius, 'Der himmlische Kultus nach dem Hebräerbrief', in *Botschaft und Geschichte*, vol. II (Tübingen, 1956), pp. 160–76 (originally in *Theologische Blätter* 21 (1942), 1–11).

22 From what he says on the 'consecration' of Christ through his sufferings, it is clear that Dibelius views τελείωσις as a prerequisite for 'entrance into the heavenly sanctuary' (p. 170). He thus differs from Käsemann, who identifies it with the heavenly passage itself.

23 However, he allows that 5: 14; 6: 1 and 9: 11 are to be understood differently (p. 167 note 10).

24 Dibelius observes even characteristics of the OT high priest in 5: 1–4, which are then applied to Christ in 5: 5–10. Christ performs actions that take the place of sacrifice and are counted by God as such (p. 169): he offers prayers for himself (verse 7) and offers himself for the people (verse 8). The 'last act' is not included at 5: 1–10 because the parallel with OT priesthood could not be taken that far: no one was brought into the earthly tabernacle by the earthly priests in the way that Christ introduced believers into the heavenly sanctuary.

25 C. Spicq, *L'Épître aux Hébreux*² (Paris, 1953), vol. II, pp. 214–25 (Excursus VI, 'La perfection chrétienne').

26 Against Kögel, Spicq argues that the usage of Hebrews is rooted in the OT (p. 251, especially note 1). The LXX rendering of *tāmîm* and *šālēm* by τέλεος, with its double application to cultic

and moral perfection, is what lies behind the use of the terminology in Hebrews. On no account can it be argued that the Mystery religions have inspired this usage (p. 218, note 2).

27 In vol. I (p. 282) Spicq stressed that this is not a 'progress in virtue', but the means by which he is consecrated high priest. He was already priest from his incarnation, but 'the consecration of Christ is renewed or better solemnised in a definitive manner by his entrance into the Holy of Holies'.

28 B. Rigaux, 'Révélation des mystères et perfection à Qumrân et dans le Nouveau Testament', *NTS* 4 (1957–8), 237–62.

29 M. Black (*The Scrolls and Christian Origins* (London, 1961), p. 170) describes the sect as 'a perfectionist "mystery" cult'. This view is confirmed by A. R. G. Deasley ('The Idea of Perfection in the Qumran Texts' (unpublished Ph.D. thesis, University of Manchester, 1972), p. 330).

30 Deasley ('The Idea of Perfection', p. 330) describes this perfection as 'a fusion of the ritual and the moral, the legal and the spiritual, the outward and the inward, so intimate that neither was complete without the other'.

31 H. K. LaRondelle (*Perfection and Perfectionism. A Dogmatic–Ethical Study of Biblical Perfection and Phenomenal Perfection* (Kampen, 1971), p. 174) describes their 'arbitrary, spiritualistic–allegorical way of interpreting the OT Scriptures, with the tendency towards an increasing liberty from the letter of the Torah' as 'an essential form of religious–theological perfectionism'. At Qumran, it is essentially 'apocalyptic perfectionism'.

32 For Paul and the Qumran Sect 'the τέλειος is a member of the eschatological community, but the observance of the law and sanctification play a much greater part in the perfection of Qumran than that of Paul. The Apostle has in view a totality of supernatural intelligence given by the Spirit' (p. 252 note 1).

33 However, the writer of Hebrews is said to function as 'un docteur' (p. 260), in a manner somewhat similar to that of the Teacher of Righteousness (pp. 245ff). Rigaux stresses that Paul makes the Holy Spirit, by the mediation of the apostles and prophets, the revealer of divine mysteries to believers (pp. 261f). However, in Hebrews the Holy Spirit apparently functions more directly in revealing the mysteries of Scripture to 'the perfect'.

34 A. Wikgren, 'Patterns of Perfection in the Epistle to the Hebrews', *NTS* 6 (1959–60), 159–67.

35 This is essentially the position of B. F. Westcott (*The Epistle to the Hebrews*[3] (London, 1914), pp. 64–8), who argues in terms of the destiny of man being fulfilled by Christ through suffering and glorification. This must be progressively realised by man in Christ.

36 He compares that ambivalence in the Qumran literature: whereas all the covenanters are ideally expected to live a blameless life, as they stand in the glow of the 'perfect light', there is a realistic recognition of the fact that the ideal community is still a future hope and expectation (p. 162).

37 L.K.K. Dey, *The Intermediary World and Patterns of Perfection in Philo and Hebrews*, S.B.L. Dissertation Series 25 (Missoula, Montana, 1975).
38 'Being in touch with the angels – a sign of divine intervention in apocalyptic Judaism (cf. Tobit 12) – is in Philo a lack of immediacy to God and hence an inferior status' (p. 93).
39 Wis. 11: 9f; 12: 22; 2 Macc. 6: 12, 16, 27f, 31; 4 Macc. 10: 10f.
40 3 Macc. 1: 16; 5: 7, 25; Philo's *Quaest. in Gen.* IV.233; *Quod Deus* 115.
41 'Any satisfactory interpretation of Hebrews must explain this odd feature, namely, that Jesus himself needed to be saved/perfected' (pp. 224f). Dey considers that no one has advanced beyond Käsemann's interpretation in this respect, prior to Dey's own interpretation.
42 In Philo's *Leg. All.* III.129–35; *Jos.* 26 and 4 Macc. 13: 22ff, 'sympathy and brotherly love belong to the level of training and progress'. However, Hebrews reinterprets this tradition to assert that Jesus is a superior high priest because he continues to bear a *pathos* for his brothers, even in his perfected state (pp. 225f).

2 The linguistic background

1 Τέλειος (5: 14; 9: 11); τελειότης (6: 1); τελειωτής (12: 2); τελείωσις (7: 11); τέλος (3: 14; (3: 6?); 6: 8, 11; 7: 3); συντελεῖν (8: 8); συντελεία (9: 26); ἐπιτελεῖν (8: 5; 9: 6).
2 Du Plessis (ΤΕΛΕΙΟΣ, pp. 45ff) has a study of the word in classical Greek and LXX usage.
3 As in Herodotus IV.79 (Διονύσῳ ... τελεσθῆναι) and Plato, *Phaedo* 69c.
4 Du Plessis, p. 120. Delling (*TDNT*, vol. VIII, pp. 79f) describes τελειοῦν (τελεοῦν always in Herodotus and the prevailing form in Attic prose) as *factitive*, meaning 'to make τέλειος', or in the passive 'to become τέλειος'. He concludes that the verbs τελεῖν and τελειοῦν coincide in the NT, especially in the sense 'to carry through', 'to complete' (p. 84). However, 'the thought of totality is stronger' in the case of the latter, since it carries the meanings of τέλειος ('whole', 'complete', 'perfect') in many contexts. Cf. J. Kögel, 'Der Begriff τελειοῦν', pp. 40f.
5 *Nemean Odes* IV.41–3.
6 *Oedipus Coloneus* 1089 (lyr).
7 *Politicus* 272d. Cf. G. Delling, *TDNT*, vol. VIII, p. 80.
8 *Ethica Nicomachea* 1174b. 23.
9 So Aristotle, *De generatione animalium* 776a. 31.
10 So Plato (*Republic* 487a): the State should only be entrusted to such as are 'matured by education and years' (τελειωθεῖσι τοῖς τοιούτοις παιδείᾳ τε καὶ ἡλικίᾳ). Cf. *Symposium* 192a; *Republic* 466e.
11 Stobaeus, *Ecloge* II.65.7W, in H. von Arnim, *Stoicorum veterum fragmenta*, vol. I, p. 129, 20 (see also vol. III, p. 136, 9 and p. 48, 6).

12 III.86 (translation of J. Enoch Powell, *Herodotus*, vol. I (Oxford, 1949), p. 241). E. Riggenbach ('Der Begriff τελείωσις', pp. 189f) rightly criticises the attempt of Th. Häring to give the verb a cultic meaning here ('in ein Amt einweihen').

13 Translation of H.G. Liddell and R. Scott, *A Greek–English Lexicon*, revised by H.S. Jones (Oxford, 1940).

14 So Herodotus V.11, τελεωθέντων ἀμφοτέροισι ('when both men had (their wishes) carried our fully') and I.120, ὁ δὲ πάντα, ὅσα περ᾽ οἱ ἀληθεί λογω βασιλέες, ἐτελέωσε ποιήσας ('and he did perfectly everything that real kings do' – translation of J.E. Powell, p. 63).

15 Delling, *TDNT*, vol. VIII, p. 57.

16 Cf. Du Plessis (pp. 69–72) for a survey of the technical use of τελεῖν.

17 Delling, *TDNT*, vol. VIII, p. 69. Cf. Du Plessis (p. 80) and my discussion below on the use of the terminology by Philo and in early Christian literature.

18 Jer. 13: 19 ('a total carrying away'); Psalm 139 (138): 22 ('perfect hatred'); 1 Chr. 25: 8 ('the practised', in contrast with those who are still learning); Cant. 5: 2; 6: 9 (the bride who is 'perfect' in the eyes of her husband); 2 Esd. (Ezra) 2: 63 (an attempt to interpret the Hebrew expression 'for Urim and Thummim'). Cf. Jdg. 20: 26; 21: 4 (B text only in both cases).

19 Elsewhere ἄμεμπτος (e.g., Gen. 17: 1; Job 1: 1, 8; 9: 20; 12: 4), ἄμωμος (e.g., 2 Kgs (2 Sam.) 22: 24, Psalms 17 (18): 23; 18 (19): 13; Prov. 11: 5; Ezek. 28: 15), and various terms 'expressive of personal qualities' (Du Plessis, p. 96). Cf. *TDNT*, vol. VIII, p. 72 note 22.

20 Du Plessis (pp. 96f, 99–102) develops the idea of 'wholeness' in a relationship with God as the interpretative key, observing the use of related terminology and its setting within the context of OT covenant theology. For a fuller exposition of this position see LaRondelle, *Perfection and Perfectionism*, pp. 98–158. He proposes that perfection in the OT is 'the religious–cultic walk with the covenant God, manifested in the socio-ethical walk with the fellow man, in wholehearted moral obedience to the covenant of Yahweh' (p. 137). Contrast Dey, *The Intermediary World*, pp. 111–18.

21 The same Hebrew verb (*kālâh*) is translated by ἐτελείωσεν (A text only) in 2 Chr. 8: 16, where Solomon's bringing of the work on the house of the Lord to its end is in view.

22 Sir. 7: 25, ἔση τετελειωκώς (S¹ only. A, B, and S² have τετελεκώς, which illustrates again the easy interchange between τελειοῦν and τελεῖν.). RSV ('you will have finished') is too bland in this context, even if τετελεκώς is to be read.

23 Sir. 7: 32 (cf. 7: 35, 'because of such deeds you will be loved'). The injunction of Deut. 14: 28f, with its attached promise of the Lord's blessing, could be in view here.

24 In parallel with ἕως συντελεσθῇ κόσμος κυρίου we find καὶ τὴν

λειτουργίαν αὑτοῦ ἐτελείωσεν. See *TDNT*, vol. VIII, pp. 62f on the use of συντελεῖν and my comments on its application by Luke below.

25 ὡς ἂν τελειώσω αὐτό; ('How shall I complete it/carry it through?') is a very loose paraphrase of the MT.

26 τελειῶσαι τὰ ἐπιτηδεύματά σου. She, for her part, promises to go out and 'accomplish the things about which you spoke to me' (εἰς τελείωσιν τῶν λόγων) in verse 9.

27 3 Kgs 7: 10 (A text) καὶ ἐτελειώθη τὸ ἔργον τῶν στυλῶν (1 Kgs 7: 22 MT 'the work of the pillars was finished') and 3 Kgs 14: 10 (A text) ἕως τελειωθῆναι αὐτόν (1 Kgs 14: 10 MT. The destruction of the house of Jeroboam will be as complete as when 'a man burns up dung, until it is all gone' − 'aḏ tummô).

28 Cf. M. Hadas, *The Third and Fourth Books of Maccabees* (New York, 1953), p. 185.

29 Dey (*The Intermediary World*, pp. 78f) argues that 4 Macc. 7: 15 speaks of religious perfection as 'unmediated access to God', in a way that parallels Philo's use of the terminology. His treatment of the evidence from Philo will be discussed in more detail below. Although the preceding verse here suggests that Eleazar received strength for martyrdom through '*an Isaac like reasoning* (ref. to Gen. 22)' (Dey, p. 58), there is no justification for reading anything more into the use of ἐτελείωσεν than I have suggested. See further below under 'Early Christian Literature' (pp. 45f).

30 Michel, 'Vollkommenheit', pp. 337f.

31 The MT of Psalm 18: 26 is the same, but the LXX (Psalm 17: 26) has μετὰ ἀνδρὸς ἀθῴου ἀθῷος ἔσῃ.

32 LaRondelle (*Perfection and Perfectionism*, p. 101 note 14) rightly reminds us that '*tāmîm* is continually associated with *hālak* as the hermeneutical key for the understanding of the Biblical realism of perfection' (see further pp. 35−158).

33 *Ibid.*, p. 38. A. Weiser (*The Psalms* (ET London, 1962), p. 193) comments: 'God remains faithful to his nature, but that faithfulness operates differently according to the way in which man responds to it.'

34 Delling (*TDNT*, vol. VIII, p. 80 note 7) argues that τελειῶσαι ὄπισθέν σου (verse 40d) is 'originally a marginal gloss on verse 40b, hence a material par. to ἐξιλάσαι ὄπισθέν σου here' and therefore means 'to make free from stain'. There is no doubt that the sacrifice of 'a contrite heart and a humble spirit' is what will be offered to God as a substitute for burnt offerings (verse 39), and this is further explained in verse 41 as following after God 'with a whole heart' etc. However, far from being a marginal gloss, τελειῶσαι ὄπισθέν σου takes up this idea of wholehearted seeking after God and his will from the context and explains that this is the way God's mercy is to be found (θ[1] has the variant ἐκτελέσαι ὄπισθέν σου).

35 J.A.F. Gregg, *The Wisdom of Solomon* (Cambridge, 1922), p. 39. He compares Eusebius, *Hist.* III.35 and VII.15.

36 Dey, *The Intermediary World*, p. 79 and G. Delling, *TDNT*, vol. VIII, p. 81. Both note that the outcome of the righteous man's death is 'rest' (verse 7), and compare Philo, *Leg. All.* III.45, where Aaron's death is described as his 'perfection'. Dey therefore argues that there is a tradition in Hellenistic-Jewish literature associating perfection with death (he includes 4 Macc. 7: 13–15 and Philo, *Quaest. in Gen.* I.86).

37 G. L. W. Grimm, *Das Buch der Weisheit* (Leipzig, 1860), p. 105; S. Holmes, in R. H. Charles, *Apocrypha and Pseudepigrapha of the Old Testament in English* (Oxford, 1913), vol. I, p. 541; J. Reider, *The Book of Wisdom* (New York, 1957), p. 86 and A. T. S. Goodrick, *The Book of Wisdom* (London, 1913), p. 146. Goodrick observes that τελειωθείς here is not a synonym for death, but 'obviously implies completion in contrast to τέκνα μοιχῶν ἀτέλεστα (3: 16 "the children of adulterers shall not come to maturity"), κλῶνες ἀτέλεστοι (4: 5 "branches ... before they come to maturity")'.

38 Against the identification of perfection with death here, it should be noted that 'he fulfilled long years' clearly follows τελειωθείς (the latter can hardly be concessive) and is not naturally an expression for life after death.

39 Cf. Num. 25: 5; Psalm 105: 28 (LXX); Hosea 4: 14; Deut. 23: 18 and the use of τελετή at 3 Kgs 15: 12 and Amos 7: 9. See also Philo's comment on Num. 25 (*Vit. Mos.* I.303).

40 It could be, as Du Plessis suggests (p. 72), that the 'complete disregard by LXX translators to employ (*sic*) τελεῖν (or for that matter also the compounds) when referring to consecration to the Levitic priesthood' was due to 'aversion to heathen cults'. It is interesting to note that Philo had no such reserve. Commenting on Exod. 29 and Lev. 8 (*Vit. Mos.* II.150), he speaks of those 'who were being admitted to the priesthood' (τῶν τελουμένων ἱερέων). Cf. II.153.

41 Exod. 29: 9, 29, 33, 35; Lev. 8: 33; 16: 32; Num. 3: 3 and see note 55 below regarding the use of τελείωσις in this connection.

42 Jdg. 17: 5, 12 (B text of LXX); Exod. 32: 29; Num. 7: 88 (LXX only); 3 Kgs (1 Kgs) 13: 33; 1 Chr. 29: 5; 2 Chr. 13: 9; 29: 31 and Sir. 45: 15. See also Ezek. 43: 26 (πλήσουσιν χεῖρας αὐτῶν). The use of πιμπλάναι with τὰς χεῖρας in Lev. 9: 17; 16: 12 and 4 Kgs (2 Kgs) 9: 24 is of marginal interest but certainly shows how literally the 'filling of the hand' must be taken in the majority of cases, both in MT and LXX.

43 R. De Vaux, *Ancient Israel, its Life and Institutions* (ET London, 1961), pp. 346f. Cf. Jdg. 17: 12; 18: 4 on this particular point. W. R. Arnold (*Ephod and Ark*, HTS 3 (Cambridge Mass., 1917), p. 134) argues for the filling of the priest's hands with the sacred lots.

44 *Ibid.* p. 347. This would mean that 'the priest was given the right to a part of the revenues accruing to the sanctuary and to a share of the offerings made there. This would be the priest's right

mentioned in 1 Sam. 2: 13 and later defined in greater detail by the priestly laws.' Cf. L. Sabourin, *Priesthood: a Comparative Study* (Leiden, 1973), pp. 137f.

45   G. Buchanan Gray, *Sacrifice in the Old Testament* (Oxford, 1925), pp. 249f.

46   Philo (*Spec. Leg.* I.79) interprets this incident to mean that the Levites received their consecration as a reward for their godly zeal (cf. III.125f and *Vit. Mos.* II.160f).

47   Delling, *TDNT*, vol. VI, p. 287. Thus, for Jdg. 17: 5, 12; 1 Kgs 13: 33 and 2 Chr. 13: 9 he proposes that the basic idea of being a priest is 'to receive sacrifices for presentation', and hence to appoint someone as priest is literally 'to fill his hands with offerings'.

48   'They shall make atonement for the altar and purify it, and so consecrate it' (πλήσουσιν χεῖρας αὐτῶν (αὐτῆς A⁺) for *ûmil'û yāḏāw*). Both LXX and Syriac, in reading 'their hands', the equivalent of *yāḏām*, may be attempting to connect the strange expression in the MT with the ceremony for installing the priests, which normally coincided with consecration of the altar.

49   The MT reads 'this was the dedication offering for the altar, after it was anointed' (*'aḥarê himmāśaḥ 'ōṯô*). LXX renders the last clause μετὰ τὸ πληρῶσαι τὰς χεῖρας αὐτοῦ καὶ μετὰ τὸ χρῖσαι αὐτόν.

50   De Vaux, *Ancient Israel*, p. 346 and M. Noth, *Exodus* (ET London, 1962), p. 230.

51   Noth, *Exodus*, p. 231.

52   *Ibid.* p. 232.

53   Noth describes this as having the character of 'a peace offering or a community offering, though with a number of peculiarities to fit the special circumstances of an ordination to the priesthood' (pp. 231f). De Vaux (p. 347) and J.P. Hyatt (*Exodus* (London, 1971), p. 288) rightly argue that it is more appropriate to speak of these priests being 'installed' in office (so NEB), rather than 'ordained' (so RSV).

54   De Vaux, p. 346. Cf. Delling's comment in my note 47 above.

55   The 'perfecting' or 'qualifying' of the priests for their office is particularly suggested by the use of τελείωσις (for *millu'îm*), without τὰς χεῖρας, in Exod. 29: 22, 26, 27, 31, 34; Lev. 7: 27 (LXX 37); 8: 21 (22), 25 (26), 28 (29), 31, 33. However, it is most obvious from a reference like Lev. 8: 33 that τελείωσις is a short-hand way of referring to the ceremony described by the full phrase τελειοῦν τὰς χεῖρας. Elsewhere in the LXX τελείωσις has the sense of 'completion' (Sir. 34: 8 and probably 2 Chr. 29: 35), 'accomplishment' (Judith 10: 9) and 'maturity' (Jer. 2: 2). Although some argue for 'consecration' in 2 Macc. 2: 9, Delling rightly reads the usual sense (*TDNT*, vol. VIII, p. 85), as does RSV ('sacrifice for the dedication and *completion* of the temple'). Cf. my discussion on a similar use of the terminology in Patristic literature below (p. 45).

56 Summarised above on pp. 8f.

57 Lev. 4: 5; 16: 32 and Num. 3: 3. So Delling, *TDNT*, vol. VIII, p. 81 note 11.

58 See above p. 10. The fact that Philo views the ceremony as 'initiation into sacred mysteries' (cf. note 40 above) and a 'sanctifying purification for their full perfection' (εἰς τὴν ... παντέλειαν) shows that he saw special significance in the LXX use of τελείωσις but says nothing about the original intention of the LXX translators themselves (cf. *Vit. Mos.* II.149–50, 153).

59 *TDNT*, vol. VIII, p. 81. See also note 34 above, where I argue against his suggestion that the verb means 'to make free from stain' in Daniel 3: 40 (LXX). However, there is nothing to be said against his final assessment of τελειοῦν τὰς χεῖρας as indicating that the priest is able 'to practise the cultus'.

60 *Ibid.* p. 82. In note 17 he observes: 'it is obvious why Hb no longer has τὰς χεῖρας; the way had been prepared for dropping this cf. Lev. 21: 10'. Many writers draw attention to this verse as a possible source of influence on the usage of Hebrews. Cf. Du Plessis, p. 213.

61 M. Silva, 'Perfection and Eschatology in Hebrews', *Westminster Theological Journal* 39 (1976), 61 note 3. However, he rightly acknowledges that 'we cannot assume that a "head word" may in any situation acquire the sense of the whole phrase; we need to prove it by adducing examples where the usual meaning of the word no longer makes sense'. This condition is hardly satisfied in the case of Hebrews, as his own study illustrates.

62 James Barr, *The Semantics of Biblical Language* (Oxford, 1961), p. 222. The semantic unit πληροῦν τὰς χεῖρας remains as the technical term for the installation of priests in later Jewish literature (e.g., Sir. 45: 15 and *Test. Lev.* 8: 10, where the expression is used in a literal but adapted sense, 'he filled my hand with incense, that I might serve as priest to the Lord God').

63 *Ibid.* p. 159 (my emphasis).

64 Τελεῖν is used twenty-four times, τελείωσις thirty-two times and τελειότης thirty-five times. Cf. G. Mayer, *Index Philoneus* (Berlin, 1974).

65 *Op. Mund.* 89. The translation of F.H. Colson and G.H. Whitaker in the Loeb edition (London, 1929–62) is followed in all the following references, unless otherwise indicated. Cf. *Leg. All.* I.6 and *Conf. Ling.* 89.155 (twice).

66 *Leg. All.* II.61.

67 *Spec. Leg.* IV.209; *Virt.* 157; *Praem.* 127–8, 131.

68 *Leg. All.* I.10, where τελείωσις is specifically defined as 'the power of reproducing his like'. Cf. *Aet. Mund.* 71.

69 *Vit. Mos.* I.283. Cf. *ibid.* II.275 (the prophetic word of the high priest), Josephus *Ant.* XV.4; John 19: 28; Hermas *Man.* IX.10. *Abr.* 62 has the idea of 'carrying out' a divine direction.

70 *Cher.* 35.

71 Dey, *The Intermediary World*, p. 58. In *Som.* II.231–5 Aaron is

characterised as the 'progressing one' when he is outside the Holy
of Holies, but whenever he goes in he is 'perfect, being neither
man nor God', holding the 'middle order' until he comes out of
the inner sanctuary 'to the realm of body and flesh' (Dey p. 59).

72 *Leg. All.* III.44. Cf. II.91.
73 *Ibid.* III.74.
74 Dey, p. 32 (based on *Conf. Ling.* 145–8). He is critical of E.R.
    Goodenough (*By Light, Light* (New Haven, 1935), p. 95) for not
    observing that 'the logos is a revelation inferior to a direct
    intuition of God' (Dey, p. 31 note 1).
75 *Ibid.* pp. 44f.
76 *Ibid.* p. 68 (see his helpful summary on pp. 69ff). Philo effectively
    summarises his own position in *Abr.* 52–3 when he describes
    Abraham, Isaac and Jacob as 'symbols of virtue acquired
    respectively by teaching, nature and practice ... Each possesses
    the three qualities, but gets his name from that which chiefly
    predominates in him.'
77 E.R. Goodenough, *An Introduction to Philo Judaeus*² (Oxford,
    1962), p. 147 (my emphasis).
78 *Ibid.* p. 148.
79 *Gig.* 54–5 (Goodenough's translation). Philo uses τελεῖν for
    initiation into the Mysteries but not τελειοῦν (in *Vit. Cont.* 25
    the two verbs are used together, but in different ways).
80 Dey, pp. 80f. Note his progressive criticism of Goodenough's
    position (p. 31 note 1; p. 74 note 10; p. 79 note 14).
81 He seems to deny with W. Völker (*Fortschritt und Vollendung
    bei Philo von Alexandrien* (Leipzig, 1938), pp. 283–8) and A.
    Festugière (*La révélation d'Hermès Trismégiste* (Paris, 1950–4),
    vol. II, p. 584 note 1) that this 'mystical' union with God has its
    roots in Mystery religion, and proposes that the language of
    ecstasy in Philo is purely literary. He calls for further study in this
    area (p. 75 note 11). Du Plessis (pp. 67–9; 115–18) largely
    follows Völker and argues that Philo maintains 'a twofold τέλος
    conception, motivated by theocentric considerations: σοφία and
    ἀρετή, which lead to intellectual and moral perfection'.
82 pp. 222ff.
83 R. Williamson, *Philo and the Epistle to the Hebrews* (Leiden,
    1970). He does not deal specifically with the concept of perfection
    but concludes from a detailed comparative study that 'the Writer
    of Hebrews had never been a Philonist, had never read Philo's
    works, had never come under the influence of Philo directly or
    indirectly' (p. 579).
84 Ἐκτελεῖν is used in Lk. 14: 29, 30 and ἀποτελεῖν in Lk. 13: 32.
85 Du Plessis, p. 173. He argues that there is an 'indiscriminate use'
    of these verbs in John as well as in Luke–Acts (p. 174). Delling
    (*TDNT*, vol. VIII, p. 59 note 6) suggests that πληροῦν is 'parallel
    in use but not synonymous by origin or specific content' with
    τελεῖν in the NT (cf. *TDNT*, vol. VI, p. 292). Cf. C.F.D. Moule,
    'Fulfilment Words in the NT: Use and Abuse', *NTS* 14 (1967–8),
    293–320 (especially p. 315).

86   Whether or not there is any significant difference in meaning between the simplex and the compounds of τελεῖν is discussed below (pp. 40f). Decisive accomplishment or fulfilment seems to be implied in Rom. 9: 28 (Isa. 10: 23); Mk 13: 4 and Hebrews 8: 8 (where the LXX of Jer. 31: 31 is altered).

87   Du Plessis, p. 161.

88   Delling, *TDNT*, vol. VIII, p. 84 note 33. However, I disagree with his argument that there is no reference to the end of the life of Jesus in verse 32.

89   It is significant that 12: 50; 13: 32−3 and 22: 37 are 'special Luke' material and 18: 31 is a Lucan addition to the common tradition.

90   So J. Reiling and J. L. Swellengrebel, *A Translator's Handbook of the Gospel of Luke* (Leiden, 1971), pp. 317−18 (TEV 'I shall finish my work').

91   V. Taylor, *Jesus and his Sacrifice* (London, 1959), pp. 170f (see the whole section on pp. 167−71). The words 'and the third day' suggest a strong contrast between the work of Jesus in progress and what is to come, but no allusion to the resurrection specifically is to be discerned.

92   *Ibid.* p. 168. Taylor argues convincingly against Wellhausen's conjecture (followed by J.M. Creed) that 'and the third day I am perfected' (verse 32) and 'today and tomorrow' (verse 33) are glosses and concludes: 'while Wellhausen's reconstruction provides a smoother text, it does so at the expense of the originality of the saying' (p. 171).

93   So B.S. Easton, *The Gospel According to St. Luke* (Edinburgh, 1926), p. 222.

94   E.g., Luke's addition to the Transfiguration narrative (9: 31, where they spoke of his ἔξοδος, 'which he was to accomplish at Jerusalem'), the words that preface the last journey to Jerusalem (9: 51, 'when the days drew near for him to be received up'), the association of 13: 32−3 with the prediction of the city's destruction and Jesus' triumphant return in 13: 34−5 (cf. Matt. 23: 37−9), and the wording of the final commission (24: 46−9).

95   Taylor, *Jesus and his Sacrifice*, p. 169.

96   E. Earle Ellis, *The Gospel of Luke* (London, 1966), p. 189.

97   M. Black (*An Aramaic Approach to the Gospels and Acts*[3] (Oxford, 1967), p. 233) argues for a form of *cll* behind τελειοῦμαι, meaning 'to be crowned with martyrdom'. 'There is no passage hitherto adduced from Palestinian Aramaic for the use of *cll* with this meaning', but Lk. 13: 32 makes it 'very probable that the verb was so used in the Aramaic of first-century Palestine and by Jesus himself'. Πορεύεσθαι ('"I pass on", i.e., I die') is taken as a parallel (cf. pp. 206f). However, I would argue that this verb simply refers to the ongoing ministry of casting out demons and performing cures, which culminates in Jesus' death in Jerusalem. More than martyrdom is involved in that death in Luke's presentation.

98   C.K. Barrett, *The Gospel According to St. John* (London, 1967), p. 222.

99   *Ibid.* p. 201.

100   R. Bultmann, *The Gospel of John* (ET Oxford, 1971), p. 194 note 3. He cites *Acts of Thomas* 167, 282 and also gives examples to show how 'the assurance that the messenger has fulfilled his commission is also found in similar places in the Gnostic myth' (p. 495 note 8).

101   R.E. Brown, *The Gospel According to John* (London, 1971), vol. II, p. 742.

102   Bultmann, p. 675.

103   Brown, vol. II, pp. 908f. He points out that πληροῦν is used in verses 24 and 36. Cf. C.F.D. Moule, (note 85 above), p. 318, and my note 69 above for similar usage.

104   Bultmann, p. 674 note 1. Psalm 69: 21 (LXX 68: 22) is usually suggested. Clearly this is not the last reference by John to the fulfilment of Scripture in Jesus' career (cf. verses 36–7). Barrett inappropriately suggests 'a special reference to the complete fulfilment of Scripture, with the note that one prophecy remains to be enacted' (p. 459). The reconstruction of G. Bampfylde ('John 19: 28. A Case for a different translation', *NovT* 11 (1969), 247–60) is forced.

105   Bultmann, p. 673 note 6. Against Du Plessis (p. 161) I would argue that John 13: 1 is not simply referring to the foot-washing but the aorist is a summary or constative, referring to all the events that culminate in Christ's death.

106   Du Plessis, p. 174.

107   Bultmann, p. 675 note 2.

108   C.H. Dodd, *The Interpretation of the Fourth Gospel* (Cambridge, 1963), p. 437.

109   Brown, vol. II, p. 908.

110   Bultmann, p. 516 note 3. On 17: 13 (p. 506 note 1) he says πληροῦν does not mean 'fulfilled', in the sense of Scripture or time, but 'brought to the eschatological consummation' – 'brought to its culmination' – 'the culmination of the joy which the disciples already have, as disciples'. While something of this sense may be conveyed by the context, it is hardly conveyed by the verb itself.

111   Barrett, *The Gospel according to St. John*, p. 428 (NEB 'may they be perfectly one').

112   So A.E. Brooke (*The Johannine Epistles* (Edinburgh, 1912), p. 32) and F.F. Bruce (*The Epistles of John* (London, 1970), pp. 51f), who says: 'as our *knowledge* of God is to be tested by our obedience, so too is our *love* for him – in fact, obedience is the full flowering of our love for him' (cf. 1 John 5: 3).

113   B.F. Westcott, *The Epistles of John* (London, 1883), p. 49 (my emphasis). This view is comparable to that of R. Schnackenburg (*Die Johannesbriefe* (Freiburg, 1979), p. 103). The divine initiative in love is stressed in 1 John 4: 9, 19.

114 R. Bultmann, *The Johannine Epistles* (ET Philadelphia, 1973),
     p. 25. He quotes as parallel 'love one another in faithfulness and
     bring your love to perfection' (*Ginza R.* I.20 (p. 22)).

115 *Ibid.* p. 68.

116 Westcott, *The Epistles of John*, p. 144.

117 Bultmann, *Epistles*, p. 72.

118 *Ibid.* p. 73 (my emphasis). It might be argued, as Bultmann
     suggests, that the fear—love contrast compels us to understand
     'love' as 'the love of man for God'. But the chapter as a whole
     encourages us to conclude that the sense is this: 'there can be no
     fear for those who know themselves to be endowed with God's
     love'.

119 Τελεῖν in Rom. 2: 27; 13: 6; 2 Cor. 12: 9; Gal. 5: 16; 2 Tim. 4: 7;
     ἐπιτελεῖν in Rom. 15: 28; 2 Cor. 7: 1; 8: 6, 11 (twice); Gal. 3: 3;
     Phil. 1: 6; συντελεῖν in Rom. 9: 28.

120 So A.F.J. Klijn, 'Paul's Opponents in Philippians 3', *NovT* 7
     (1964), 278—84. However, Paul 'nowhere debates with Jews as
     though they presented a menace to the peace and unity of the
     church' (R.P. Martin, *Philippians* (London, 1976), p. 24, following
     Gnilka).

121 J.B. Lightfoot, *St. Paul's Epistle to the Philippians*[2] (London,
     1869), p. 149.

122 *Ibid.* p. 129.

123 F.W. Beare, *A Commentary on the Epistle to the Philippians*
     (London, 1959), p. 109. Yet, Beare describes the opponents on
     p. 103 as *Jewish missioners*, who 'prowl around the Christian
     congregations, seeking to win·Gentile converts over to Judaism'.

124 *Ibid.* p. 129.

125 H. Koester, 'The Purpose of the Polemic of a Pauline Fragment',
     NTS 8 (1961—2), 321f.

126 W. Schmithals, 'The False Teachers of the Epistle to the
     Philippians', in his *Paul and the Gnostics* (ET Nashville, 1972),
     pp. 65—122.

127 Koester, 'A Pauline fragment', pp. 323f. This is said to be an early
     form of Christian Gnosticism, developed from 'elements of late
     Jewish theology which they radicalized by means of a misunder-
     stood Christian message'.

128 *Ibid.* p. 331.

129 R. Jewett, 'Conflicting movements in the Early Church as
     Reflected in Philippians', *NovT* 12 (1970), 362—90. Martin
     (*Philippians*, pp. 28ff), who follows this line, adds that 'the
     Philippian intruders denied an understanding of the Christian
     vocation as a commitment to lowliness and suffering that Paul is
     championing as a rebuttal of them'.

130 Schmithals (*The False Teachers*, p. 97) suggests that Paul is
     intentionally vague and leaves the object unexpressed because his
     opponents claimed to have attained everything. Klijn ('Paul's
     Opponents', pp. 281f) is certainly not to be followed when he
     suggests that 'righteousness' is the object to be understood after

ἔλαβον and that τετελείωμαι is the equivalent of γενόμενος ἄμεμπτος (verse 6). This leads him to the unPauline conclusion that 'Paul is speaking about a perfection attained by strict observance of the law. He himself is only hunting for this perfection.'

131 Against Du Plessis (p. 195), who argues that the emphasis in ἔλαβον is 'not on the aorist but on the 1st person singular'. Paul is stressing that 'all the praiseworthy possessions he had just described were not personal achievements or achieved by his own endeavours'. This reading would only be suggested if a personal pronoun was found in the text.

132 Martin, *Philippians*, p. 137. The κατελήμφθην ὑπὸ Χριστοῦ of verse 12 refers to Paul's conversion encounter, 'in which he was forcefully arrested and his life set in a new direction'.

133 V.C. Pfitzner, *Paul and the Agon Motif* (Leiden, 1967), p. 150. He seeks to show that the perfection which is the goal of Paul's striving 'dare not be reduced to moral perfection, but must rather be understood as the culminating point of his apostolic ministry and his life "in Christ"' (p. 139). However, Pfitzner exaggerates the extent to which Paul is countering an attack on his apostolicity in this chapter.

134 Beare, *Commentary*, pp. 130f. Compare Lightfoot (*St. Paul's Epistle to the Philippians*, p. 151) who assumes that Paul is taking up his opponents' term here with 'the same reproachful irony' as in 1 Cor. 8: 1; Rom. 15: 1.

135 Du Plessis, p. 160. The clause cannot really be translated in a different way from RSV ('I have finished the race') or NEB ('I have finished the course'). However, it is clear from the broader context (verses 1–8) that Paul's reference is to satisfactory fulfilment of his ministry, not just to the conclusion of his work.

136 The use of τελεῖν in a context where one would normally expect τελειοῦν apparently led scribes to substitute the latter (in Aleph[c], D[c], E, K, L, P and almost all minuscules) for the former (in Aleph*, A, B, D*, F, G, 623).

137 P.E. Hughes, *Paul's Second Epistle to the Corinthians* (London, 1961), p. 451.

138 A. Plummer, *The Second Epistle of St. Paul to the Corinthians* (Edinburgh, 1915), p. 354.

139 Cf. G. Stählin, *TDNT*, vol. I, p. 491. The μου is probably a secondary reading, but the context makes it clear that 'God's power' is the subject and EVV should convey this (NEB has the pedantic reading 'power comes to its full strength in weakness').

140 Du Plessis, p. 132. Cf. LaRondelle (*Perfection and Perfectionism*, pp. 184–6) for a restatement of this argument in the light of criticism by K. Prümm (in a review of Du Plessis' work in *Biblica* 44 (1963), 84f).

141 J.H. Moulton, *A Grammar of New Testament Greek, Prolegomena* (Edinburgh, 1908), p. 112. Cf. Du Plessis, pp. 72f and p. 124.

142 Du Plessis, p. 124. Despite this cautionary remark, he pushes the distinction too far in some examples.

143 W. Sanday and A.C. Headlam (*The Epistle to the Romans*[5] (Edinburgh, 1902), p. 265) render this 'a sentence conclusive and concise'. They note the inability of the LXX translators adequately to convey the Hebrew ('a final work, and a decisive').

144 Du Plessis, p. 240 (cf. pp. 233–40).

145 E.g., Ignatius, *Smyrneans* VII.2; *Barnabas* XIV.5; Clement, *Stromateis* I.21.

146 Thus, the *Martyrdom of Polycarp* XVI.2; Hermas, *Similitudes* IX.26, *Visions* IV.1.3; *1 Clement* XXIII.5.

147 Translation of Kirsopp Lake, *The Apostolic Fathers* (London, 1912), vol. I.

148 Translation of C.C. Richardson, *Early Christian Fathers* (London, 1953). Cf. 9: 2 ('let us fasten our eyes on those who have served his magnificent glory to perfection' and are now dead). The aorist in 49: 5 will be constative or summary, referring to the attainment of perfection through a lifetime of love and obedience. The idea of Christ's death as an example of humility and love to be imitated is found at 16: 17 and 19: 1–3, and also seems to be in focus in the present context.

149 See the excellent summary in LaRondelle, *Perfection and Perfectionism*, pp. 275–95.

150 *Ibid.* p. 296. He notes the comment of W. Völker: 'in the teaching about the image of God in man, Clement stands on Philo's shoulders and is the mediator between Philo and Origen' (his note 260, my translation).

151 *Stromateis* I.5. The translation of each quotation from this work is by F.J.A. Hort and J.B. Mayor (London, 1902).

152 *Paidagogos* I.6.25–6. Translation by LaRondelle, p. 296.

153 LaRondelle (p. 296), alluding to *Stromateis* VI.14. Clement speaks of degrees of glory in heaven.

154 *Stromateis* VII.3. The similarity of these ideas with Hebrews 4: 14; 7: 25 and 10: 19ff is clear.

155 *Ibid.* VII.10. Contrast Jas 2: 22.

156 LaRondelle, p. 297. He acknowledges that there are some apparent inconsistencies in Clement's writings on this subject.

157 *Ibid.* p. 299.

158 *Ibid.* p. 301. In this regard he is also the precursor of Pseudo-Dionysius (the 'Areopagite') and Augustine.

159 R. McL. Wilson, *Gnosis and the New Testament* (Oxford, 1968), p. 4.

160 LXV.1ff, translated by R. McL. Wilson (in W. Foerster, *Gnosis: a collection of Gnostic Texts* (ET Oxford, 1972) vol. I, p. 118).

161 Irenaeus, *Adv. Haer.* I.6.1.

162 *Ibid.* I.6.2.

163 *Ibid.* I.6.4.

164 Clement, *Stromateis* III.1.

165 Hippolytus, *Refutatio Omnium Haeresium* V.24 (translation of J.H. McMahon in *Ante-Nicene Christian Library*, vol. VI, p. 183).

166 Clement, *Paidagogos* I.6 (translation of W. Wilson, *The Writings of Clement of Alexandria* (Edinburgh, 1871) vol. I, pp. 131f).

167 *De Vita Constantini* IV.62 (κωνσταντῖνος Χριστοῦ μαρτυρίοις ἀναγεννώμενος ἐτελειοῦτο).

168 *Orationes* XLI.4 (ἐν ἑπτὰ μὲν ἡμέραις ὁ ἱερεὺς τελειούμενος).

169 *De Ecclesiastica Hierarchia* V.2 (Migne, *PG* 3.5098), where τελεῖν is used synonymously. The writer is dated at 'about the turn of the fifth to the sixth century' by H. von Campenhausen (*The Fathers of the Greek Church* (ET London, 1963), p. 174).

170 *Ibid.* II.2 (396C). Cf. IV.1 (472C) for the 'consecration' of chrism.

171 *Patristic Greek Lexicon* (Oxford, 1961). In *Apologia ad Constantium* 14, Athanasius answers a charge that Holy Communion was held in the great church πρὶν αὐτὴν τελειωθῆναι. Here, 'dedicated' or 'consecrated' seem just as possible as 'completed', as renderings of the verb. However, in *ibid.* 18 the verb is definitely used for the 'completion of the work' (τελειώσαντες τὸ ἔργον) and as a parallel to τελεῖν in the phrase ὅτε τετέλεστο πᾶς ὁ οἶκος ἐποίησας τὰ ἐγκαίνια. See my note 55 above.

172 R. Bultmann, *The Gospel of John* (ET Oxford, 1971), p. 516 note 3.

173 *De Vita Constantini* III.47.

174 *Vita St. Antoni* 90 (Migne, *PG* 26.968C). Cf. *Acta Barnabae* 9.

175 *Ibid.* 46 (909C).

176 Eusebius, *Historiae Ecclesiasticae* VI.3.13 (cf. VI.2.12). In such a context as V.16.22, τελειοῦνται will mean death by martyrdom because of the associated expression μαρτύριον κληθέντες ('those called to martyrdom'). However, the fundamental meaning of the verb in such contexts is that of being 'fulfilled' or 'completed' by death, whether it be by martyrdom or not.

177 *De Incarnatione Verbi* XXV.5, as translated by A. Robertson (*Nicene and Post-Nicene Fathers*, vol. IV, 2nd series (Grand Rapids, Michigan, 1957), eds. P. Schaff and H. Wace).

178 *Ibid.* XXXVII.1, as translated by A. Robertson (see previous note).

179 Du Plessis, p. 212. He actually proceeds to interpret the perfecting of Christ in Hebrews in terms of vocational 'consummation', allowing only for the influence of LXX cultic associations on the writer's use of the verb.

3 The Perfecting of Christ: the Broad Perspective

1 Although the aorist τελειῶσαι would not naturally of itself describe a *process*, I contend that the context points to a process. I should then describe the aorist here as constative or complexive (Cf. BDF para. 318).

2 A. Vanhoye, *La structure littéraire de l'épitre aux Hébreux* [2] (Paris, 1976), pp. 65ff. Most reviewers describe Vanhoye's work as a notable advance because of its focus on objective criteria to reveal the structure of the author's composition. However, J. Bligh

(*Heythrop Journal* 5 (1964), 170–7) rightly questions whether literary patterns are always a safe indication of the structure of the argument and whether the word 'inclusion' should be applied to every passage that has the same word or phrase at its beginning and end, whether the intervening text is a literary unit or not. Similarly, J. Swetnam (*Biblica* 53 (1972), 368–85) points out that 'if form is too much divorced from content it can lead to a distortion of content, not clarification'. Both reviewers suggest important modifications to Vanhoye's work. Vanhoye discusses criticisms in *Biblica* 55 (1974), 349–80.

3 *Ibid.* pp. 69ff.

4 Bligh, Review of *La structure littéraire*, p. 174. See also his *Chiastic Analysis of the Epistle of the Hebrews* (Oxford, 1966).

5 O. Hofius (*Der Christushymnus Philipper 2: 6–11* (Tübingen, 1976), pp. 80ff) relates the language of Hebrews 1: 3 specifically to that of Phil. 2: 6–11 and shows that the idea of God establishing his eschatological kingly glory in the exaltation of the crucified Christ appears again in Hebrews 2: 5–9 and is also the background of 10: 12f and 12: 2 (pp. 15, 75).

6 The suddenness with which the author introduces the comparison between Christ and the angels (1: 4), and the extent of his argument, call for some explanation. There is insufficient evidence to support the view of T. W. Manson (*Studies in the Gospels and the Epistles* (Manchester, 1962), pp. 242ff) that the recipients were tempted to angel-worship. Y. Yadin ('The Dead Sea Scrolls and the Epistle to the Hebrews' in *Scripta Hierosolymitana*, vol. IV (Jerusalem, 1965) pp. 36ff) is one of a number of scholars who compare the teaching of Qumran about the subordination of the Messiah(s) to the supreme figure of the archangel Michael, and thus the subordination of the world to come to angelic authority (contrast Hebrews 2: 5), and suggest that Hebrews was reacting against such views. Dey (*The Intermediary World*, pp. 145ff) suggests that

> 'Jesus' identity with logos and wisdom in primitive Christianity was itself the basis of the problem, in that he could be identified with a series of intermediary figures as was true later in the church ... It was therefore crucial for the author to show that Jesus is superior over all intermediaries and the salvation which he effected is superior as well' (p. 154).

The question of a special polemic at this point in our writer's argument can only be satisfactorily resolved by consideration of the wider issue of the *Sitz im Leben* of Hebrews. It is extremely probable that in Jewish-Christian circles the inclination to view Jesus merely as a member of the angel-world existed (so Michel, pp. 131f). At all events, to establish the *absolute transcendence* of Christ, nothing would have been more suitable in a Jewish context than a comparison with the situation of angels: 'those creatures who occupy the most elevated position and are the closest to divinity' (Spicq, vol. II, pp. 50f). Furthermore, Hebrews

2: 2 reflects popular Jewish beliefs about the role of the angels in communicating the Law (Michel, pp. 125f, Spicq, vol. II, pp. 52ff). The author wishes to stress that the revelation mediated by the Son is of greater significance than the revelation mediated by the angels and carries with it heavier penalties for neglect. This is so even though this revelation was mediated by the Son in his incarnate state (1: 2), when he was 'for a little while made lower than the angels' (2: 9).

7   G.W. Grogan ('Christ and his People: an exegetical and theological study of Hebrews 2: 5–18', *Vox Evangelica* 6 (1969), 56) discusses the function of γάρ in 2: 5 and argues that 'the author will now show that our Lord's eschatological (and present) supremacy is human as well as divine. He neither affirms nor denies the notion that the present world, as distinct from the world to come, is under the control of angels, for this does not come within the scope of his discourse.'

8   The headings used in this exegesis are those of Grogan, *ibid.*

9   J. Moffatt, *A Critical and Exegetical Commentary on the Epistle to the Hebrews* (Edinburgh, 1924), p. 23. NEB renders αὐτῷ (verse 8*b*) 'to man'.

10   Westcott, p. 45.

11   Michel, p. 138.

12   David M. Hay (*Glory at the Right Hand: Psalm 110 in Early Christianity* (Nashville, 1973), p. 124) suggests that Psalm 110: 1 must have seemed invaluable to the Apostle precisely because he could find in its 'until' a 'clear scriptural prophecy of a time gap between the onset of Christ's reign and the consummation'. Such an idea was lacking from Psalm 8: 6, though Paul cites it 'because of its authoritative assurance that *all* powers will be put beneath Christ's feet'.

13   B. Lindars, *New Testament Apologetic* (London, 1961), p. 48 and Delling, *TDNT*, vol. VIII, p. 42.

14   Michel, p. 138. There is no other OT citation between Hebrews 1: 13 and 2: 6, suggesting that Psalm 8 is used as an extension or development of the theme of Christ's dominion proclaimed in Psalm 110: 1.

15   The most recent attempts to argue that our writer gave the title 'Son of Man' to Jesus when he quoted from Psalm 8 are those of G.W. Buchanan (*To the Hebrews* (New York, 1972), pp. 38–51) and P. Giles ('The Son of Man in the Epistle to the Hebrews', *ExpT* 86 (1975), 328–32). The latter rightly argues that Psalm 8 was used 'not so much with the christological title Son of Man in mind as with the representative ministry of Christ which in turn is very closely connected and introductory to our author's High Priestly Christology' (p. 330). However, she then seeks to establish from the conflation of Psalm 110: 1 with Daniel 7: 13 (Mk 14: 62 = Matt. 26: 64; Acts 7: 55f) and the use of that psalm text in association with Psalm 8 (1 Cor. 15: 25ff; Eph. 1: 20ff; 1 Pet. 3: 22) that, in quoting Psalm 8 after Psalm 110: 1, 'our author gave

the title "Son of Man" to Jesus' (p. 331). This argument makes the unwarranted assumption that the christological interpretation of Psalm 8 developed because that text was related to Daniel 7: 13. However, the christological interpretation of Psalm 8 may simply be attributed to its association with Psalm 110: 1 in the contexts I have noted. R. Scroggs (*The Last Adam* (Oxford, 1966), pp. xv–xvii, 102) has argued convincingly against the view that Paul's Christology of the Last Adam is really a Son of Man Christology. Jewish thought about Adam explains Paul's theology here, not Son of Man speculation. There is similarly no ground for arguing that the use of Psalm 8 in Hebrews betrays a Son of Man Christology.

16   Michel, p. 137. In *TDNT*, vol. V, pp. 157ff, he notes how the cosmopolitanism of later Hellenistic culture, with its philosophical understanding of human society, used οἰκουμένη to convey the idea of 'a generally binding human society'. The philosophical and cultural use of this word fused with the political and legal structure of the Roman Empire in Roman times to describe the dominion of Rome (cf. Lk. 2: 1). However, most often in the NT it has the sense of 'the inhabited earth' (so Matt. 24: 14; Lk. 4: 5; Acts 11: 28; 17: 31 etc.).

17   *Ibid.* Thus also Westcott:
       'the phrase is not to be understood simply of the "future life" or more generally "heaven". It describes, in relation to that which we may call its constitution, the state of things which, in relationship to its development in time, is called "the Age to Come" ... and, in relation to its supreme Ruler and characteristics "the Kingdom of God" or "the Kingdom of Heaven", even the order which corresponds with the completed work of Christ' (p. 42).

18   A. Vanhoye, *Situation du Christ: Hébreux I et II* (Paris, 1969), p. 260.

19   Moffatt, p. 21. The clause 'of which we are speaking' (2: 5) possibly refers back to the prior mention of τὴν οἰκουμένην in 1: 6. Commentators are divided as to whether the expression there ('when he brings the first-born into the world') refers to the incarnation, the second coming or to the ascension—enthronement of Christ. Michel and Vanhoye, among others, argue that the last alternative fits best with the context and the writer's Christology. Vanhoye points out the necessity of distinguishing Christ's entrance into the κόσμος (10: 5) from his introduction into the οἰκουμένη (1: 6): 'the first is abasement below angels (2: 7, 9), the second is exaltation above them (1: 4, 6)' (*Situation*, p. 157). It seems best to conclude with such writers that 'the world' into which the first-born is introduced in 1: 6 is 'the world to come' of 2: 5, which has been '*inaugurated* by Christ's enthronement, although it is not yet present in its fulness' (F.F. Bruce, p. 17 note 78 and p. 33).

20   Westcott insists that βραχύ τι is used here 'of degree (compare

2 Sam. 16: 1) and not of time (Isa. 57: 17 LXX "for a little while"). The Hebrew is unambiguous, and there is no reason to depart from the meaning of the original (either in verse 7 or verse 9)' (p. 44). So also Vanhoye (*Situation*, p. 272). However, most modern commentators and EVV follow the sort of argument put forward by Moffatt: 'in applying the psalm ... our writer takes βραχύ τι in the sense of "temporarily" rather than "slightly" and so has made the "inferiority" and "exaltation" two successive phases in applying the description to Jesus' career' (pp. 22f; cf. Michel, p. 139).

21 Some manuscripts add the words 'and did set him over the works of your hands' to 2: 7. If the shorter reading is original, as seems likely, the longer reading will be an attempt to harmonise with the LXX of Psalm 8: 7. Most significant is the omission from all manuscripts of Hebrews 2: 8 of the words of Psalm 8: 8 LXX ('all sheep and oxen' etc.). Perhaps the writer stopped quoting at this point because the next verse of the psalm refers too specifically to man's dominion over the animals to allow the breadth of application implied by Christ's dominion.

22 Spicq, vol. II, p. 32. This would give special point to the exhortation of 10: 35–9 (compare 12: 12f).

23 Michel, pp. 138f.

24 There is a tradition of exegesis, epitomised by A. Nairne (*The Epistle of Priesthood* (Edinburgh, 1913), p. 70) that argues that 'the crowning with glory and honour must on any natural reading of the Greek precede the death'. Moffatt provides a convenient summary and critique of such interpretations, the variety of which indicates how much uncertainty there is as to what event *prior* to the death of Jesus could be meant. However, it is clear that Hebrews stresses the ascension—enthronement of Christ at God's right hand as the great *consequence* of his saving death (1: 3; 10: 12f; 12: 2), there to exercise the dominion promised in Psalms 110 and 8. Thus, our writer reflects the frequent NT theme that the glorification of Christ is the result of his suffering and not something prior to it (Mk 8: 31; Lk. 24: 26; Phil. 2: 8–11; 1 Pet. 1: 11, 21); his resurrection, ascension and enthronement are his 'crowning with glory and honour'. We may note further that 'glory' is the final destination of believers (2: 10), because Christ has already entered into that glory through suffering.

25 Westcott, p. 43. He goes on to argue that παρ' ἀγγέλους (LXX) is a perfectly reasonable rendering of *me' elōhîm* (MT), given that the Targum and Syrian and Jewish commentators took the Hebrew as *plural in sense*, not just in form, meaning 'divine beings', as in Psalms 82: 6; 29: 1 (p. 44).

26 Those commentators are surely to be followed who read διά with the accusative as expressing the *ground* and not the *object* of the crowning. All attempts to force a telic meaning for the preposition by arguing from the awkward syntax must be rejected. The 'suffering of death', however, is clearly the climax and goal of the

incarnation in 2: 14f, 17; 5: 8f; 10: 5–10 and here by implication.

27 Hofius, *Der Christushymnus*, pp. 16f, 63f. He agrees with M. Hengel (*Der Sohn Gottes* (Tübingen, 1975), p. 135) that Hebrews as a whole could be considered as 'a marvellous development of the christological theme already set out in the Philippian hymn'.

28 Westcott, p. 41.

29 Michel, p. 139.

30 P.E. Hughes, *A Commentary on the Epistle to the Hebrews* (Grand Rapids, Michigan, 1977), pp. 90f. Moffatt (p. 24) argues similarly: 'ὅπως ... θανάτου explains and expounds the idea of τὸ πάθημα (which consists in) τοῦ θανάτου, gathering up the full object and purpose of the experience which has just been predicated of Jesus.'

31 Vanhoye, *Situation*, p. 295. P.E. Hughes (pp. 90f) offers a critique of Spicq's approach.

32 Westcott, p. 46. So also F.F. Bruce, p. 39.

33 Despite the strong support for χάριτι θεοῦ, a significant number of Fathers, both Eastern and Western, as well as 0121*b*, 424[c], 1739*, vg[ms], syr[pmss], read χωρὶς θεοῦ. The former reading is preferred by most commentators, but Michel argues that the latter has to be the original: 'God leads Christ in suffering, but intensifies this suffering at the same time with the test of God-forsakenness (Mk 15: 34)' (pp. 141f). See also J.C. O'Neill (*JTS* 17 (1966), 79–82) and the more convincing article by J.K. Elliott (*ExpT* 83 (1972), 339–41). As *lectio difficilior*, the reading 'apart from God' perhaps ought to be preferred, and it is easy to see why copyists would change to the less controversial 'by the grace of God'. On the other hand, Vanhoye (*Situation*, p. 298) rightly asks if our writer wished to express the idea of God-forsakenness whether he would have been content with a formula 'so enigmatic in its brevity'. See B.M. Metzger (*A Textual Commentary on the Greek New Testament* (London–New York, 1971), p. 666) for an explanation of how the procedure may have worked the other way.

34 But note Matt. 3: 15 (πρέπον), with reference to Jesus, and the use of ἔπρεπεν in Hebrews 7: 26, with reference to 'us'. Cf. Philo, *Leg. All.* I.48 and Josephus, *Ap.* II.168.

35 W. Manson, *The Epistle to the Hebrews* (London, 1951), p. 102.

36 Westcott, p. 48. W.C. Linss ('Logical Terminology in the Epistle to the Hebrews', *Concordia Theological Monthly* 37 (1966), 365–9) argues that the fitness follows simply from the nature of the case.

37 Moffatt (p. 29) notes that in Aristotle (*Eth. Nic.* IV.2.2) 'fitness' has reference to 'the person himself, to the particular occasion and to the object'. Cf. J. Denney, *The Death of Christ* (London, 1964), pp. 122f.

38 A. Snell, *New and Living Way* (London, 1959), p. 65.

39 Käsemann (p. 89), who cites Delling (*TDNT*, vol. I, p. 488 note 3): Christ 'has begun to lead (ingressive aorist) by his activity up

to the cross'. Du Plessis (p. 219) takes the participle ἀγαγόντα quite illegitimately (from the syntactical point of view) as a title for Christ, co-ordinate with ἀρχηγός (viz., 'the Conductor and Author of our Salvation').

40 E.D. Burton, *Syntax of the Moods and Tenses in New Testament Greek* (Edinburgh, 1894), p. 41.

41 F.F. Bruce, p. 40 note 49. Cf. Burton (p. 149) on the use of the aorist participle adverbially to denote 'an action evidently in a general way coincident in time with the action of the verb, yet not identical with it. The choice of the aorist participle rather than the present in such cases is due to the fact that the action is thought of not in progress, but as a simple event or fact.' H. Windisch (*Der Hebräerbrief* (Tübingen, 1931), p. 21) also stresses that the time reference of the participle here must be left indistinct.

42 Hughes, p. 102. He comments:
'as the glorification of the "many sons", though yet to be experienced, is inseparably bound up with the glorification of him who is uniquely the Son, which has already been realized, the bringing of many sons to glory is more than assured, it is to all intents and purposes a reality now because of their union with him who is crowned with glory and honour.'

43 Michel, p. 149. He agrees with Bleek that the expression 'bringing many sons to glory' may be a divine epithet or a reference to God's purpose (p. 147).

44 Moffatt, p. 31.

45 Grogan, 'Christ and his people', p. 65. See his whole discussion on the scope of Christ's solidarity with men.

46 The universalism suggested by 2: 9 may be compared with that of 1 Tim. 2: 6 and 1 John 2: 2, but the effectiveness of that salvation for 'all' is only a potential effectiveness, until it is appropriated by faith (Hebrews 3: 6, 14; 4: 1). See below note 61.

47 A. Weiser, *The Psalms* (ET London, 1962), p. 144. The view of Vanhoye (*Situation*, pp. 273f) and Snell (pp. 62f) that 'crowned with glory and honour' suggests also the institution to a priestly role is both unnecessary and inappropriate in this context. The focus is on Christ receiving the glory of royal authority, from which the writer later derives sacerdotal significance.

48 G. Kittel (*TDNT*, vol. II, p. 246) notes the Rabbinic view that the first man 'had a part in God's *kabod* ... and that this radiance was taken from him after the fall ... The unfolding of salvation history aims at a restoration.' In later passages it is said that God will give the Messiah 'a share in his *kabod*, and that he will thus invest him with his own raiment ... He it is, who with five other things, restores the radiance lost by the first man' (p. 247). See also his notes on these ideas in Jewish Apocalyptic.

49 *Ibid.* p. 250. True blessedness in Rabbinic and Apocalyptic literature, as in OT Eschatology, is contemplation of the glory of the *shekinah*. In Hebrews 12: 14 this is a future prospect, while in

12: 18–24 it is implied that Christians already enjoy a more direct participation in the glory than the Israelites at Mt Sinai. Hebrews maintains a tension between the 'now' and the 'not yet', with regard to sharing in the glory of God (compare 2 Cor. 3: 18 with Rom. 5: 2; 8: 18–25). However, Hebrews falls short of the total perspective of Paul in this matter: nowhere is it stated explicitly that believers are being transformed into the image of Christ. This may be implied in 2: 10 (εἰς δόξαν) but it is more likely that the writer is emphasising there that man's *dominion* will be restored to him. The focus on sonship and brotherhood with Christ (2: 10–13) refers to 'a oneness in relation to God, as a covenant standing' (G. Vos, *The Teaching of the Epistle to the Hebrews* (Grand Rapids, Michigan, 1956), p. 96), but not necessarily metamorphosis 'into his image' (cf. 2 Cor. 3: 18).

50 E.K. Simpson, 'The Vocabulary of the Epistle to the Hebrews I', *EQ* 18 (1946), 35f. Compare Delling, *TDNT*, vol. I, pp. 487f.

51 Moffatt, p. 31.

52 Westcott, p. 49. T. Ballarini (ARCHEGOS (Acts 3: 15; 5: 31; Heb. 2: 10; 12: 2): autore o condottiero?', *Sacra Doctrina* 16 (1971), 535–51) notes how both Acts and Hebrews draw a parallel between Moses and Jesus as liberators and guides of the faithful into their inheritance. Ἀρχηγός seems to be a primitive title for Christ, both Acts and Hebrews drawing on a common Palestinian source of tradition.

53 Num. 13: 3 (2); 16: 2. Cf. Michel, pp. 144f.

54 Jdg. 5: 15 (B); 1 Chr. 26: 26; Neh. 2: 9; Isa. 30: 4.

55 Exod. 6: 14; Num. 13: 4 (3); 14: 4; 25: 4; Deut. 33: 21; Jdg. 9: 44 (A has ἀρχαί); 1 Chr. 5: 24; 8: 28 (B has ἄρχοντες); 12: 20; Neh. 7: 70, 71 (11: 16–17); Lam. 2: 10.

56 P.G. Müller, ΧΡΙΣΤΟΣ ΑΡΧΗΓΟΣ: *Der religionsgeschichtliche und theologische Hintergrund einer neutestamentlichen Christusprädikation* (Frankfurt, 1973) pp. 141–8. Note his treatment of the theme in the Qumran literature (pp. 149–71), other Jewish literature (pp. 172–212), in Gnostic texts (pp. 213–47) and in the NT (pp. 248–352).

57 So Käsemann, pp. 79–82.

58 Müller, p. 301. *Contra* Käsemann (p. 89), who envisages that Christ acted as ἀρχηγός even in his earthly ministry.

59 In the same vein, G.W. Grogan ('Christ and his People', p. 60) comments: 'Jesus is the new Moses–Joshua who leads the people of God to the promised land which now becomes fused in thought with that dominion over all things which God has ordained for man and which Psalm 8 celebrates. It is "the world to come".'

60 The sense of 'originator' or 'source' is most prominent in Micah 1: 13 (ἀρχηγὸς ἁμαρτίας); 1 Macc. 9: 61 (τῶν ἀρχηγῶν τῆς κακίας); 10: 47 (αὐτοῖς ἀρχηγὸς λόγων εἰρηνικῶν); and Acts 3: 15 (τὸν ἀρχηγὸν τῆς ζωῆς).

61 C.F.D. Moule (*An Idiom Book of New Testament Greek*[2] (Cambridge, 1959), p. 64) supports the view that it is inaccurate to

draw too hard a line between ὑπέρ and ἀντί: ' "in most cases one who acts on behalf of another takes his place" (Winter)'. Although patristic commentators tend to view ὑπέρ παντός as including the whole creation, most modern commentators read the masculine here ('for every man'), since Hebrews nowhere else betrays any interest in the cosmic aspect of Christ's work. Moffatt (p. 26) notes that 'the neuter is always expressed in "Hebrews" by the plural, with or without the article, and, as verse 16 shows, the entire interest is in human beings'.

62   J. Behm, *TNDT*, vol. I, p. 677. Moffatt (p. 26) points out, as many have done, how incorrect it is to suggest that 'to taste death' means only to take a 'rapid sip' of death: it means experiencing death *in all its bitterness*.

63   So Moffatt (p. 32). See below pp. 91ff, 174ff.

64   So Käsemann, (p. 141) and Müller (p. 291).

65   Vanhoye, *Situation*, p. 335. Cf. Lev. 20: 8; 21: 8; 15: 23; 22: 9, 16, 32 and Ezek. 20: 12; 37: 28; 2 Macc. 1: 25. Compare Michel, p. 149.

66   *Ibid.* Cf. Exod. 28: 41; 29: 33; 30: 30; 40: 13; Lev. 8: 12; 1 Sam. 16: 5; Exod. 19: 14; Josh. 7: 13.

67   Moffatt, p. 32 (my emphasis). 'The full meaning of ἁγιάζειν is not developed till 9: 13f, where we see that to be "sanctified" is to be brought into the presence of God through the self-sacrifice of Christ.'

68   This is particularly obvious in 10: 10, 14 because of the explanatory citation in 10: 15–18. In 10: 29 ('the blood of the covenant by which he was sanctified'), the imagery of 9: 15–22 and 10: 14–18 is recalled, where the blood of Christ inaugurates the New Covenant. This will also be in focus in 13: 12. In 9: 13 the purely material and cultic sanctification that the Old Covenant provided is contrasted with the inner consecration to God effected by the New Covenant (verse 14).

69   Michel, p. 150. In note 1 he criticises those who obscure the differences between τελειοῦν, ἁγιάζειν and καθαρίζειν. On pp. 338f he describes ἁγιάζειν as, above all, a term for the cultic-priestly action of Christ for us, but then a special work of God that describes the whole Christian position.

70   Moffatt, p. 32 (but on p. 28 he takes ἐξ ἑνός in Acts 17: 26 to be a neuter). So also Westcott (p. 50), who acknowledges that they 'spring from the same source, though in different ways'. Michel's argument (p. 150) that ἐξ ἑνός is a recognisable title for God on the basis of Deut. 6: 5 is too far-fetched. The proposal of Michel and Spicq (vol. II, p. 41) that the author must be referring to the divine origin of Christ because of the title ὁ ἁγιάζων is not valid. Hebrews stresses that Christ fulfils this divine prerogative as a man, and the expression says nothing necessarily about his divinity (cf. Vanhoye, *Situation*, p. 332).

71   A. Snell, p. 65. So also Procksch (*TDNT*, vol. I, p. 112), Vanhoye (*Situation*, p. 332), who argues against the suggestions that either

God or Abraham might be meant, and Hughes (pp. 104ff). Buchanan (p. 32) relates it to Abraham but gives little argument to support this. Although verse 16, with its reference to the 'seed of Abraham', helps to define more specifically the context in which the incarnation takes place, it can hardly be the direct reference in verse 11, where no clue is given to encourage that reading of the expression.

72 P.E. Hughes (p. 105) argues that ἐξ ἑνός is best taken as a neuter rather than as a specific reference to Adam (so Vanhoye (*Situation*, pp. 332f) despite the fact that Psalm 8 in the context recalls the creation narratives). Hughes goes on to argue that 2: 16 'places the incarnation within the perspective of the covenant, of which the incarnate Son is the focal point' (p. 119).

73 Cf. the expression 'holy brethren, who share in a heavenly call' (3: 1). It is difficult to escape the particularist thrust of the writer's thinking from 2: 10 to 3: 6. Cf. note 46 above.

74 Michel, p. 150. Of course there are significant differences between the sonship of Christ and the sonship of believers (so Hughes, p. 104), but this does not stop our writer from emphasising the similarities.

75 Vanhoye, *Situation*, p. 340. 'If the first part of the psalm is fulfilled in the passion of Jesus, the second part, which announces the deliverance, should be understood as a prediction of the paschal triumph.' Cf. Michel (p. 154) and F.F. Bruce (pp. 45f). The picture of Christ in the eschatological assembly (ἐκκλησία) is taken up again in 12: 23f.

76 So F. Doormann, 'Deinen Namen will ich meinen Brüdern verkünden', *Bibel und Leben* 14 (1973), 245ff. Buchanan (p. 33) also implies that the earthly ministry of Jesus is included in this expression.

77 Vanhoye (*Situation*, pp. 344f), following L. Malevez ('Le Christ et la foi', *NRT* 98 (1966), 1009–43). Michel (p. 154) also argues that Christ in his exalted state must continue to trust in the Father to fulfil his promises, as he did in his incarnate state. However, there is no basis for this in Hebrews (Michel reads it into Psalm 110: 1).

78 S. Kistemaker, *The Psalm Citations in the Epistle to the Hebrews* (Amsterdam, 1961), p. 84.

79 F.F. Bruce, p. 48. Moffatt (p. 33) argues that the children are *God's children*, the fellow 'sons' of Christ, but Westcott (p. 52) suggests that 'Christ is the "father" no less than the "brother" of his people.' There is no NT parallel to this latter assertion, but Isa. 53: 10 and 9: 6 ('Everlasting Father') could be taken as OT precedents. It is also possible that τὰ παιδία in Isa. 8: 18 is to be understood as a reference to 'disciples' (cf. 8: 16), which would make the text particularly applicable to Christians in relation to Christ. So Vanhoye, *Situation*, p. 345. Cf. John 21: 5; 17: 6.

80 Vanhoye, *Situation*, p. 348 (cf. Matt. 26: 41 = Mk 14: 38; Sir. 14: 17). This Hebraic expression for 'human nature' in contrast

to God is commonly found in the order σάρξ καὶ αἷμα (cf. Matt.
16: 17; 1 Cor. 15: 50; Gal. 1: 16) but is in the reverse order in
Eph. 6: 12.

81 Westcott, p. 52. Vanhoye (*Situation*, p. 349) argues that the aorist
μετέσχεν limits the affirmation to a definite time (cf. 5: 7 'in the
days of his flesh').

82 AG, p. 627. It is used nowhere else in the Bible, though the
adjective παραπλήσιον is found at Phil. 2: 27. Grimm-Thayer also
points out that it is possibly to be taken as equivalent in sense to
κατὰ πάντα in verse 17 and hence is used 'of a similarity which
amounts to equality'.

83 So Michel (p. 159), who describes the terminology of both these
verses as reminiscent of the Adam speculation in Jewish
Apocalyptic and Phil. 2: 6–7 (cf. Rom. 8: 3). However, note the
distinction between verses 14 and 17 suggested in connection
with the exegesis of the latter. Although the writer makes the
qualification 'without sin' (4: 15), it is sinlessness of life rather
than a built-in predisposition against sin that he refers to there
(see Appendix A).

84 Westcott (p. 53) stresses that διὰ τοῦ θανάτου means '*by death*
and not *by his death*', though 'this application is necessarily included: death that is truly death (1 John 3: 14), which was the
utmost effect of Satan's power, became the instrument of his
defeat'.

85 Michel, p. 160. He maintains that the trilogy 'death, devil, fear of
death' corresponds with ancient Jewish thinking and has its own
authority compared with the Pauline trilogy 'law, sin and death'.
However, our writer goes on to assert that a further purpose of
Christ's incarnation was to deal with the problem of sin (verses
17–18). It is true that we find no explicit connection between
sin, death and the Devil here, but the wording of verse 17 seems
to be somewhat patterned on that of verse 14 and the resumptive
nature of verse 17 could be taken as an indication that these
things were very much related in the author's thinking. There is
no mention of the law as 'the power of sin' (1 Cor. 15: 56), but is
there not the hint that 'the sting of death is sin'?

86 Delling (*TDNT*, vol. I, p. 453) says καταργήσῃ means that Satan
is 'condemned to inactivity or ineffectiveness in relation to the
Christian'. RSV 'destroy' is probably not as good as NEB 'break
the power': the work of Christ undoes the work of Satan by
taking away his power over death, but he is not yet destroyed.

87 Vos, *The Teaching of Hebrews*, p. 117. In the following pages,
Vos seeks to show parallels between Hebrews and the Pauline
language of redemption. See also P. Knauer, 'Erbsünde als Todes
Verfallenheit. Eine Deutung von Röm. 5: 12 aus dem Vergleich
mit Hebr. 2: 14f', *Theologie und Glaube* 58 (1968), 153ff.

88 Moffatt, p. 36. He renders δήπου as 'it need hardly be said' or 'of
course'. It is 'an appeal to information shared by the reader'
(BDF para. 441) and is a *hapax* in the Greek Bible.

89 E.K. Simpson, *Words Worth Weighing in the Greek New Testament* (London, 1946), pp. 27ff. In Acts 18: 17, 21, 30 it means 'hostile intervention' and in Matt. 14: 31 and Hebrews 8: 9 it means rescue from danger. The latter is certainly closer to the general sense of Isa. 41: 8f (LXX). Moffatt is too strongly influenced by the supposed parallel with βοηθῆσαι (verse 18) and the desire to avoid the sense of 'appropriate', which is constantly given by the Greek fathers.

90 The Greek fathers and others subsequently (e.g., P.E. Hughes, pp. 115f) have maintained that the verse simply describes the fact of incarnation.

91 Michel, p. 163. Abraham is presented in Hebrews as promise-bearer and as the example of faith and obedience for Christians (6: 13ff; 7: 6; 11: 8ff).

92 Dey (pp. 185ff) expounds the theory that the high-priestly Christology of Hebrews was influenced by Philo's Logos speculation and the connection with the high priest of Judaism. Michel (pp. 165ff) argues, on the other hand, that the apocalyptic speculation of late Judaism — above all, The Testament of the Twelve Patriarchs — points to an eschatological priestly office which parallels Hebrews at a number of points. The problem in the last case is the degree to which the Jewish texts have been revised by Christian scribes. The problem in the first case is the degree to which Hebrews can actually be shown to reflect significant parallels to the thought of Philo. The debate as to whether late Judaism awaited two Messiahs, a priestly and a royal one, still continues. Favouring two Messiahs, see R. Brown, 'The Messianism of Qumran', *CBQ* 19 (1957), 53—82, and 'J. Starcky's Theory of Qumran Messianic Development', *CBQ* 28 (1966), 51—7. See also K.G. Kuhn, 'The Two Messiahs of Aaron and Israel' in *The Scrolls and the New Testament*, ed. K. Stendahl (New York, 1957), pp. 54—64. Favouring one Messiah, see A.J.B. Higgins, 'The Priestly Messiah', *NTS* 13 (1966—7), 211—39, and B. Vawter, 'Levitical Messianism and the NT' in *The Bible in Current Catholic Thought*, ed. J.L. McKenzie (New York, 1964), pp. 83—9. Despite the fact that we are presented with many possible sources of influence on Hebrews, there is much to be said for the argument of S. Nomoto ('Herkunft und Struktur der Hohenpriestervorstellung im Hebräerbrief', *NovT* 10 (1968), 10—25) that *earlier Christian tradition* and *the distinctive theological originality of our author* are more significant factors in this debate than many scholars have allowed.

93 So Higgins, 'The Priestly Messiah', (p. 236) and J.R. Schaefer ('The Relationship between Priestly and Servant Messianism in the Epistle to the Hebrews', *CBQ* 30 (1968), 382). Cf. note 141 below.

94 Schaefer, 'Priestly and Servant Messianism', p. 382. In the earlier part of this article he shows how, by coincidence or design, Hebrews holds much in common with the various 'literary relics of the priestly circles' hope for the ideal priest to come' (p. 369).

However, he then goes on to show 'how radically the author outstripped his precursors' — notably in joining together the figures of the messianic priest and royal Messiah in one person and in presenting the sacrifice of Jesus the high priest as the voluntary offering of his human life. He rightly criticises the view of O. Cullmann (*The Christology of the New Testament* (ET, 2nd edn, London, 1963), pp. 87–9) that Jesus was conscious of fulfilling a priestly role from his use of Psalm 110: 1.

95   So Higgins, 'The Priestly Messiah', p. 236, and his *Jesus and the Son of Man* (London, 1964), pp. 146f, 184. Higgins sees the Johannine form of the Son of Man Christology as being the decisive link between the Synoptic teaching and that of Hebrews. However, Schaefer (CBQ 30, pp. 372ff) rightly questions whether this theory adequately accounts for our writer's emphasis on the suffering of Jesus, as the basis of his qualification to act as heavenly high priest. Any theory as to the development of our writer's high-priestly Christology must allow for *a synthesis of several ideas.*

96   Moffatt, pp. 37f. He goes on to say that the term 'high priest' was evidently familiar to the readers, but I will question this assumption in connection with 4: 14.

97   Vos, 'The Priesthood of Christ in the Epistle to the Hebrews', *PTR* 5 (1907), 447.

98   Westcott, p. 56.

99   Jeremias (*Jerusalem in the Time of Jesus* (ET, London, 1969), pp. 180f) shows how the Talmud is full of complaints about merciless and faithless priests. Furthermore, we may note that *severity against sin*, rather than pity, is the emphasis of passages like Exod. 32: 27–9; Num. 25: 6–13; Deut. 33: 8–11; Sir. 45: 23f, with respect to the priests.

100   Moffatt, p. 37. He propounds the view that Christ is merciful to those he came to save and faithful to the one who sent him, rejecting the suggestion that πιστός in 2: 17 can also mean 'reliable' and refer to the fact that we can trust Christ with complete confidence.

101   Vanhoye, *Situation*, pp. 375ff, and in more detail 'Jesus "fidelis ei qui fecit eum" (Heb. 3: 2)', *Verbum Domini* 45 (1967), 291ff. Moses is accredited as 'worthy of faith' and one who 'merits confidence' in Num. 12: 7 (LXX), which is cited in 3: 5. Thus the 'faithfulness' of Christ in 3: 2 and 2: 17 must be similarly interpreted.

102   So Westcott, p. 57. J. Swetnam ('Form and Content in Hebrews 1–6', *Biblica* 53 (1972), 378) argues that the purpose of the entire section from 3: 1 to 4: 14 is for the readers to 'contemplate the faithfulness of Jesus in order to imitate it'.

103   F. Büchsel, *TDNT*, vol. III, p. 316. P.E. Hughes (p. 121 note 123) argues that τὰς ἁμαρτίας is an accusative of respect and that the verb should be understood intransitively, giving the sense 'to make propitiation with reference to the sins of the people'.

However, this is not the most natural reading of the Greek here.

104   S. Lyonnet and L. Sabourin, *Sin, Redemption and Sacrifice* (Rome, 1970), p. 124.

105   *Ibid.* p. 122. So also Büchsel (*TDNT*, vol. III) concludes: 'the cultic action denoted by the words was designed to make God gracious again to the sinner ... Materially the effect on God could not be separated from the effect on man and his sin.'

106   Schrenk, *TDNT*, vol. III, p. 280.

107   Westcott, p. 58. Vos ('The Priesthood of Christ', p. 582) argues that '$i\lambda\acute{a}\sigma\kappa\epsilon\sigma\theta\alpha\iota$ does not here denote the single act of atonement on the cross, but the subsequent activity whereby the Saviour continually applies the propitiatory power of his sacrifice. Taken in this wider sense it could easily be replaced by the general term $\beta o\eta\theta\tilde{\eta}\sigma\alpha\iota$ "to succour".' Clearly, the atoning death of Christ is the basis of the 'mercy' he shows to his people (4: 16). However, I will argue that the 'help' he offers includes more than showing mercy to sinners.

108   Vanhoye, *Situation*, pp. 380f. However, he defines expiation as 'l'exercice d'un pouvoir en faveur du peuple' and intercession as 'une démarche tournée vers Dieu'. See also his 'De aspectu oblationis Christi in Ep. ad Heb.', *Verbum Domini* 37 (1959), 32–8. Lyonnet and Sabourin (*Sin*, pp. 141–6) have demonstrated that ($\grave{\epsilon}\xi$) $i\lambda\acute{a}\sigma\kappa\epsilon\sigma\theta\alpha\iota$ with God as object in the LXX can be understood in terms of intercession (Zech. 7: 2; 8: 22; Mal. 1: 9), but that is clearly not the construction here in Hebrews 2: 17. Moffatt (p. 39) also seems to identify the expiation of 2: 17 with the intercession of 7: 25.

109   J.H. Davies, *The Heavenly Work of Christ in Hebrews*, Studia Evangelica, vol. IV (*Texte und Untersuchungen* 102 (Berlin, 1968), ed. F.L. Cross, pp. 386f.

110   This seems a more logical way of reading the sequence 2: 17–18 than Moffatt's proposal that Christ 'suffered by his temptations' (p. 39). Moffatt goes on to say that the temptations especially in view were 'temptations to avoid the suffering that led to the cross', and yet strangely asserts that the temptations of Jesus were 'not simply due to what he suffered. He was strongly tempted by experiences which were not painful at all – e.g., by the remonstrances of Simon Peter at Caesarea Philippi.' I would argue that the latter is certainly an example of Jesus' being 'tempted to avoid the suffering that led to the cross'. Even the temptations recorded in Matt. 4 and Lk. 4 can be understood as providing alternatives to the way of suffering for Jesus.

111   Vos, 'The Priesthood of Christ', p. 582.

112   E. Riggenbach, *Der Brief an die Hebräer* (Leipzig, 1913), pp. 62f.

113   Kögel, 'Der Begriff $\tau\epsilon\lambda\epsilon\iota o\tilde{\upsilon}\nu$', p. 61.

114   See pp. 22f above on Herodotus III.86, Sophocles, *Electra* 1508–10 and the usage of the LXX with regard to the installation of the priests, which may be related (pp. 26ff). Compare Lk. 13: 32.

115 W. Manson, pp. 101, 110.
116 Moffatt, pp. 31f. The writer is 'thinking of God's purpose to realize a complete experience of forgiveness and fellowship (σωτηρία)'.
117 pp. 65f.
118 Du Plessis, p. 218.
119 Vos, 'The Priesthood of Christ', p. 589.
120 Riggenbach, *Der Brief an die Hebräer*, p. 47 note 20. Compare Kögel, p. 56 note 1 and pp. 67–8.
121 *Ibid.* p. 136.
122 Käsemann, *Das wandernde Gottesvolk*, p. 86. Cf. R. Bultmann, *Theology of the New Testament* (ET London, 1952), vol. I, pp. 176f. Although Käsemann acknowledges (pp. 89f) that Christ's perfecting involved suffering – 'because only thus did he become ἁγιάζων of his own and only thus did they as ἁγιαζόμενοι obtain a share in his perfection' – he gives little stress to this and describes the obedience of Jesus as simply an attribute of his earthly existence: not moral testing but 'recognition of the plan of salvation and a sign of humiliation, which puts him on the same footing with the earthly church' (p. 86).
123 A. Cody, *Heavenly Sanctuary and Liturgy in the Epistle to the Hebrews: the Achievement of Salvation in the Epistle's Perspective* (St Meinrad, Indiana, 1960), p. 89 (see the whole section pp. 77–89). Cody sees the Hellenistic concept of ἀνὴρ τέλειος at work in Hebrews, with Christ, the Son of God, as 'the "ideally" perfect' and the other sons as 'the perfect by participation' (p. 100 note 1). However, this does not find support in the relevant passages as I understand them.
124 W. Michaelis, *TDNT*, vol. V, p. 934. He agrees with Riggenbach (*Der Brief an die Hebräer*, p. 63 note 62) that 'the suffering cannot be confined to the moment of death', but not with Riggenbach's suggestion that it includes 'all the painful accompaniments leading up to it'. The plural παθήματα in 2: 10 refers only to 'the total process of the crucifixion' (cf. διὰ τοῦ θανάτου), according to Michaelis.
125 The verb πάσχειν is used in 2: 18; 5: 8; 9: 26 and it is characteristic of Acts (1: 3; 3: 18; 17: 3) and 1 Pet. (2: 21, 23; 3: 18 in some MSS, and 4: 1) to use the verb with reference to the death of Jesus. The verb does not occur in this connection in Paul, though he speaks of the παθήματα τοῦ Χριστοῦ (e.g., 2 Cor. 1: 5, 7; Phil. 3: 10). In 1 Pet. the verb and noun (5: 1) seem to be used not only as synonyms for death but with particular focus on the suffering associated with Christ's death. Believers are instructed how to cope with suffering themselves by the exemplary behaviour of Christ under suffering (see particularly 2: 18–25). I am suggesting a similar usage in Hebrews.
126 Westcott, p. 443. Note the challenge to bear τὸν ὀνειδισμὸν αὐτοῦ. This is a call to adopt their former bold stance and be willing to suffer as a consequence of their identification with Christ (10:

32–4; 12: 2–4). Michaelis' insistence that the expression 'outside the gate' (13: 12) indicates that the suffering can only denote the death of Jesus (cf. 'through his own blood'), 'not the preceding events in the city (the trial, mocking etc.)', is clearly valid but cannot be made the key for interpreting all the other references to the suffering of Jesus in Hebrews (*TDNT*, vol. V, p. 917).

127 Michaelis (p. 917) says the εἰσακουσθείς of 5: 7 'takes us already to the end of the Gethsemane incident' and that the next verse describes the suffering of death. But the pressing of such a chronological sequence here is precarious, to say the least. 5: 8 is an assessment of the significance of the events described in 5: 7, rather than a further stage in the 'narrative' of events.

128 Cf. Riggenbach, *Der Brief an die Hebräer*, p. 63 note 62.

129 See below on ἐντυγχάνειν (7: 25), pp. 114ff.

130 Silva, 'Perfection and Eschatology', pp. 62ff. However, his decision to look for an interpretation that 'minimizes, or even eliminates, the suggestion of moral progression in Jesus' character' is arbitrary and does not allow him to do justice to the full scope of our writer's presentation.

131 *Ibid.* p. 64. He relates this to Rom. 1: 4 and says 'the contrast is not between the two natures of Christ, but between two successive stages in his human–messianic existence'.

132 In this respect I agree with Cody (*Heavenly Sanctuary*, p. 108): 'Christ is the heir of the universe by reason of his divine nature, and all things are subject to him because he is God, and yet, there is the role played by his humanity and by his historical acts of salvation in *the actual realization of his dominion over the cosmic universe*, an idea which shows affinity to Col. 1: 16–20' (my emphasis).

133 Michel, p. 224. When he goes on to suggest that τελειωθείς (5: 9) may refer especially to Christ's exaltation, he is influenced too much by a syntactical argument (the possible parallelism of εἰσακουσθείς, ἀπὸ τῆς εὐλαβείας (5: 7), τελειωθείς (5: 9) and προσαγορευθείς (5: 10)), and not sufficiently by the wider picture of what qualifies Christ to be a 'merciful and faithful high priest'.

134 J. Calvin, *Commentaries on the Epistle of Paul to the Hebrews* (trans. J. Owen, Edinburgh, 1853), pp. 63f. He translates τελειωθείς (5: 9) by *sanctificatus* but τετελειωμένον (7: 28) by *perfectum*.

135 See above, pp. 6f (Häring), pp. 9–11 (Dibelius) and compare O. Moe, 'Der Gedanke des allgemeinen Priestertums im Hebr.', *TZ* 5 (1949), 165. Michel accepts that the verb has a cultic sense but questions whether the linguistic usage of Hebrews can be generally taken in this way (p. 146). Delling (*TDNT*, vol. VIII, pp. 82f) argues for this general cultic interpretation in Hebrews on the basis of LXX usage. Compare T. Torrance, 'Consecration and Ordination', *SJT* 11 (1958), 228ff. Many writers simply assume that the verb has a cultic meaning in Hebrews (e.g. Cullmann, *Christology*, p. 92).

136 Du Plessis, pp. 212f.
137 See above, pp. 27–30.
138 Du Plessis, p. 215.
139 See below pp. 149–53.
140 For the use of ἁγιάζειν in Hebrews essentially in connection with the establishment of New Covenant relations between God and man see note 68 above.
141 Spicq (vol. I, pp. 121–3) argues that John is the only other NT writing to present Christ as 'Pontife suprême, exerçant un ministère proprement sacerdotal'. In the volume in honour of M. Goguel (*Aux sources de la tradition chrétienne*, 1950, pp. 258–69) he argues that Hebrews actually took over the concept of Jesus as high priest from the Johannine writing. However, the emphasis in John on 'an epiphany of God in Christ, the living temple and centre of the cult' does not require us to understand his ministry as a sacerdotal one by any means. The reference to the 'seamless robe' (19: 23, compare Apoc. 1: 13) will be a very oblique reference to Christ as high priest, if indeed such symbolism is really intended. Only the prayer of John 17 can be said to offer possible indications of a priestly Christology in John. Yet even here, the prayer of verse 17 is for *the Father to 'consecrate' the disciples 'in truth'* (though Jesus' self-consecration to the will of the Father is the essential pre-requisite for this, verse 19). Theirs is a consecration for *mission to the world* (verse 18), even as Christ was consecrated by the Father for mission (10: 36). Spicq's argument in his commentary (vol. I, p. 123 note 3 and vol. II, pp. 214ff) that John and Hebrews have the same concept of perfection is simplistic. See above pp. 35–7. See further O. Moe, 'Das Priestertum Christi im Neuen Testament ausserhalb des Hebräerbriefes', *TLZ* 72 (1947) col. 335ff, E. Clarkson, 'The Antecedents of the High-Priest Theme in Hebrews', *ATR* 29 (1947), 92ff, and P. Giles, 'Jesus the High Priest in the Epistle to the Hebrews and the Fourth Gospel' (unpublished M.A. thesis for the University of Manchester, 1973).
142 Barrett (*The Gospel According to St. John*, p. 426) notes that 'the language is equally appropriate to the preparation of a priest and the preparation of a sacrificè; it is therefore doubly appropriate to Christ' (the passion is in view in 17: 19).
143 *Ibid.* p. 320. Contrast Brown (*The Gospel According to John*, vol. I, p. 411) who argues that a priestly consecration is in view. But is there enough evidence for a priestly Christology in John to warrant such a reading of 10: 36? See note 141 above.

4 The perfecting of Christ: his earthly struggle

1 Vanhoye, *Structure*, pp. 115–82.
2 So also T.C.G. Thornton (*JTS* n.s. 15 (1964), 137–41) observes in a review of Vanhoye's book. Note, for example that 3: 1, 6 involve parenesis and that there is exposition in 4: 3–10, 12–13.

3 J. Swetnam ('Form and Content in Hebrews 1–6', *Biblica* 53 (1972), 383) argues against Vanhoye that 'just as the word ὁμολογία in 3: 1 began the exhortation of 3: 1 – 4: 13 by making the link with the exposition of Christ's divinity in 1: 5 – 2: 4, so the word ὁμολογία in 4: 14 begins the exhortation of 4: 14 – 6: 20, by making a link with the exposition of Christ's humanity in 2: 5–18'. On the other hand, Spicq (vol. II, p. 86) makes 4: 12–16 'a practical appeal to submissiveness and confidence which concludes the theme of Christ the faithful priest' and heads the section 'Objet et fondement de la fidélité chrétienne: La Parole de Dieu et le Christ-Prêtre'.

4 Spicq (vol. II, p. 91). He notes the verbal links with 2: 17f: ἔλεος – ἐλεήμων; καθ᾽ ὁμοιότητα – ὁμοιωθῆναι; βοήθειαν – βοηθῆσαι.

5 *TDNT*, vol. V, pp. 215f. When he goes on to identify the confession with the thanksgiving, 'which has a firm place in the Lord's Supper in the form of a hymnic confession of Christ (Heb. 1: 3; 13: 15)', he is surely on shaky ground. Cf. R. Williamson, 'The Eucharist and the Epistle to the Hebrews', *NTS* 21 (1974–5), 300–12.

6 G. Bornkamm, *Studien zu Antike und Christentum*, vol. II (München, 1959), pp. 188–203. Buchanan (*To the Hebrews*, pp. 80f) rightly comments that 'Jesus was certainly important to the confession, but the limit and entire content of the creed are not known.' D.W.B. Robinson ('The Literary Structure of Hebrews 1: 1–4', *Australian Journal of Biblical Archaeology* 2 (1972), 178–86) argues for a chiastic pattern underlying the whole of 1: 1–4, in which case it is unlikely that verse 3 should be cut off and treated as a putative hymn-fragment.

7 V.H. Neufeld, *The Earliest Christian Confessions* (Leiden, 1963), pp. 34–41, 141. In seeking to show how the words 'apostle' and 'high priest' (3: 1) can be linked with the traditional content of the confession, Swetnam (*Biblica* 53, pp. 370–3) argues that 1: 5 – 2: 4 is concerned to present Christ as the one especially sent by God, and ἀπόστολος in the confession of 3: 1 refers to 'Christ's divinity as *the* one sent', whereas 2: 5–18 portrays Christ as brother of men and high priest.

8 Neufeld, *Confessions*, pp. 134ff. He acknowledges that certainty as to the exact content of the confession seems to be unattainable. On his theory, the title Son of God is given in 4: 14 'as the identification of ἀρχιερεύς (cf. 7: 3, 28)', but ἀρχιερεύς 'does not constitute the basic *homologia*' (p. 135).

9 *Ibid.* p. 137. Although the context of 10: 23 may suggest some liturgical expression of the Christian hope, this is hardly so at 4: 14. It will be argued in connection with the former that a non-liturgical confession of hope is the most suitable interpretation there as here.

10 NEB translates 10: 23 'let us be firm and unswerving in the confession of our hope' and gives a similarly dynamic and non-specific rendering of 4: 15 – 'let us hold fast to the religion we

profess' (so also in 3: 1, but with a marginal alternative). In the
light of traditions such as Lk. 12: 8, Matt. 10: 32 and the hymn
of 2 Tim. 2: 11–13, it is perfectly reasonable to suppose that the
writer was simply challenging them to continue their confession
of Christ in the general sense of maintaining their open allegiance
to him.

11 Westcott, p. 106. Neufeld (p. 137) is too cautious when he says
such open acknowledgement of faith before a hostile audience
'cannot be decided upon the basis of the letter but it need not be
excluded'. The challenge of 10: 35 most obviously points to the
need for a boldness in the face of unbelief and hostility. Holding
fast the Christian confession can be an act of 'confession' itself,
even though words may never be uttered. Cf. T. W. Lewis, ' "And
if he shrinks back" (Heb. 10: 38*b*)', *NTS* 22 (1975–6), 88–94.

12 Moffatt, p. 58.

13 Michel, pp. 204f. Hebrews gives no indication of how many
'spheres' Christ had to pass through to reach the holy place' (not
even in 9: 11). Cody (*Heavenly Sanctuary*, pp. 77–116) gives a
helpful systematisation of the material on heaven in Hebrews.

14 Westcott, p. 108.

15 *Ibid.* Michaelis (*TDNT*, vol. V, p. 936) relates the verb 'to
sympathise' (4: 15) to the description of Jesus as 'merciful' (2:
17) and says it denotes 'disposition rather than act, i.e., fellow-
feeling with the ἀσθένειαι'. Yet the same verb in 10: 34 is said to
refer to 'help given by both word and deed' (cf. 10: 33). Clearly,
the fellow-feeling of Christ also issues in 'help' (2: 18) and 'grace
to help in time of need' (4: 16).

16 Vos, 'The Priesthood of Christ in the Epistle to the Hebrews',
PTR 5 (1907), p. 583. Compare Westcott (p. 108) and Spicq (vol.
II, p. 92). The latter says 'it encompasses all the deficiencies and
limits of a created being ... in the intellectual order (Rom. 6: 19),
the religious (Rom. 8: 26) and the moral (1 Cor. 8: 7, 12). This
last nuance is that of 7: 28, setting the ἀσθένεια of the Jewish
priests in opposition to the τελειοῦν of Christ.' Both Spicq and
Michel (p. 207 note 3) note how ἀσθένεια (for *mikšôl*) in the
LXX becomes a virtual equivalent for σκάνδαλον.

17 Stählin, *TDNT*, vol. I, p. 492.

18 Westcott, p. 200. Like 7: 28, 5: 2 has in view the weakness of the
Jewish high priests.

19 Vos, 'The Priesthood of Christ', pp. 583f (my emphasis).

20 Spicq (vol. II, p. 94) makes the apposite comment: 'the perfect
πεπειρασμένον underlines the permanent benefit of this experience'.

21 R. A. Stewart, 'The Sinless High Priest', *NTS* 14 (1967–8), 135.

22 *Ibid.* p. 136. 'The one seeming exception so far has been the
Testament of Levi ch. xviii. However, ἐκλείψει ἡ ἁμαρτία only
implies the sinlessness of ἱερέα καινόν and the question remains as
to whether this was a Jewish work or a Christian one.'

23 *Ibid.* p. 135. So also Moffatt (p. 59): 'the idea of the Logos as

unstained by contact with the material universe is very different
from this conception of Jesus as actually tempted and scatheless
... Jesus is sinless, not in virtue of a divine prerogative, but as the
result of a real human experience which proved successful in the
field of temptation'. Contrast Dey (*The Intermediary World*, pp.
192f) who erroneously argues that sinlessness in Hebrews, as in
Philo, is 'equivalent to being "separated from sinners"', "higher
than the heavens" ... and being sinful is equivalent to having
"weakness"'. This ignores the emphasis of 4: 15 and 5: 7—9.

24 Michel, p. 211.
25 *Ibid.* p. 212 (e.g., Pss. Sol. 17: 21ff speaks of him as καθαρὸς
    ἀπὸ ἁμαρτίας, as a sequel to his possession of the Spirit, but does
    not go into the question of how his sinlessness comes into being
    or how far he is a contributor to it).
26 *Ibid.* p. 211. On p. 213 he notes how the Gospels 'know only of
    the overcoming of temptation and of the fact that neither law nor
    sin nor Satan could condemn Christ'.
27 So RSV ('tempted as we are'), AV, RV. Cf. 7: 15 and Buchanan
    p. 81.
28 F.F. Bruce p. 85 and Michel p. 208 (note 3 'one actually expects
    καθ᾽ ὁμοιότητα ἡμῶν').
29 Michel, p. 208.
30 *Ibid.* p. 211.
31 See p. 65.
32 R. Williamson, 'Hebrews 4: 15 and the Sinlessness of Jesus', *ExpT*
    86 (1974–5), 4f.
33 In some contexts in the LXX, προσέρχεσθαι is used to describe
    the action of all the Israelites, coming before the Lord in solemn
    assembly (e.g., Exod. 16: 9, 34, 32; Num. 10: 3—4). However,
    whereas the congregation may draw near to the tent of meeting
    to 'stand before the Lord' (Lev. 9: 5), only the priests may draw
    near to the altar to make offerings (e.g., Lev. 9: 7f; 21: 16f, 21,
    23; 22: 3; compare Num. 16: 40; 18: 3f, 22; Ezek. 44: 16). Al-
    though some scholars seek to limit the verb in Hebrews 10: 1 to
    the priests, it is argued below in connection with that verse (pp.
    145f) that the broader meaning suits the context best (so also
    Westcott, p. 307).
34 When προσέρχεσθαι is used to express the idea of foreigners
    coming to join the congregation of Israel as proselytes (e.g.,
    Exod. 12: 48f; Lev. 19: 33; Num. 9: 14), the notion of entering
    into a relationship with the God of Israel is thereby implied. In
    Sir. 1: 28, 30; 2: 1, the more general sense of a relationship with
    God by serving him is prominent (cf. the idea of drawing near to
    Wisdom with all your soul in Sir. 4: 15; 6: 26). Philo shows a
    development of this concept in his assertion that 'only for souls
    who regard it as their goal fully to be conformed to God who
    begat them is it lawful to draw nigh to him' (*Op. Mund.* 144,
    compare *Deus Imm.* VIII.161). The 'levite mind' is perfectly
    cleansed and purified, 'renounces all the things pertaining to

creation' and is acquainted with God 'to whom it has drawn nigh, by whom also it has been taken to himself' (*Plant.* 64, cf. *ibid.* 97, *Conf. Ling.* 55, *Fug.* 41, *Mut. Nom.* 13). In Hebrews 11: 6, the one who would 'draw near' to God is the one who seeks him in faith.

35 Windisch, p. 113. Barrett ('The Eschatology of the Epistle to the Hebrews', in *The Background of the New Testament and its Eschatology*, ed. W.D. Davies and D. Daube (Cambridge, 1956), p. 376), F.F. Bruce (p. 732) and Spicq (vol. II, p. 405) likewise. Compare the LXX usage (e.g., Exod. 12; 48f; Lev. 19: 33; Num. 9: 14) and Philo (*Spec. Leg.* I.51).

36 F.F. Bruce, p. 86 (cf. 9: 5 τὸ ἱλαστηρίον).

37 Michel, p. 209 (see especially note 1).

38 Cf. Jer. 7: 16; 49: 1f (ET 42: 1f), Psalm 33: 6 (ET 34: 5) and the sense of 'applying to a court or authority' in *P. Oxy.* VIII.1119.8 (προσήλθομεν τῇ κρατίστῃ βουλῇ). So Moffatt, p. 60 and H.W. Montefiore, *A Commentary on the Epistle to the Hebrews* (London, 1964), p. 92.

39 Michel, p. 346. Cf. W. Thüsing (' "Lasst uns hinzutreten ..." (Hebr. 10: 22). Zur Frage nach dem Sinn der Kulttheologie im Hebräerbrief', *BZ* 9 (1965), 1−17), who argues that the verb in that context refers to 'a eucharistic celebration' *and* 'the whole Christian life together with faith, prayer, worship and suffering' (p. 12). See my discussion on 10: 22 (p. 155 below).

40 H. Schlier, *TDNT*, vol. V, pp. 872ff.

41 *Ibid.* p. 875. So often the παρρησία of the righteous finds expression in prayer (e.g., Job 27: 9f; 22: 23−7).

42 W.C. van Unnik, 'The Christian's Freedom of Speech in the NT', *BJRL* 44 (1961−2), 472.

43 Schlier, *TDNT*, vol. V, p. 884.

44 van Unnik, 'The Christian's Freedom of Speech', p. 485. Schlier does not give sufficient stress to the latter element (*viz.* the manward direction of this παρρησία) whereas van Unnik rightly observes the writer's exhortation to 'profess their Christian hope amidst the surrounding dangers'.

45 Michel, p. 210.

46 Westcott, p. 110.

47 Delling (*TDNT*, vol. III, p. 462) suggests that the noun εὐκαιρία means 'the propitious time' in the LXX and that Hebrews 4: 16 means 'at the divinely appointed time': 'here the time of help is left to the judgement of God, but the human ὁμοιότης of the high priest (verse 15) ensures that the coming of this time does not stretch the patience of Christians too far'. Cf. Psalms 9: 9 (LXX 9: 22); 104(103): 27.

48 Michel, p. 210.

49 So, for instance, Westcott (p. 119) and Vanhoye (*Structure*, pp. 108−13). See note 79 below.

50 Spicq, vol. II, p. 105. *Contra* Vanhoye, 'Situation et Signification de Hébreux 5: 1−10', *NTS* 23 (1976−7), 446ff.

51 Dibelius, *Botschaft und Geschichte*, vol. II, pp. 169f, and J. Thurén, 'Gebet und Gehorsam des Erniedrigten', *NovT* 13 (1971), 136–46.

52 Moffatt, p. 62.

53 See particularly the discussion by Michel (pp. 216f) and F.F. Bruce (p. 89). Michel acknowledges that the Rabbis are inclined to describe all sacrifices as having atoning effect but that they elevate the sin-offerings, ascribing to them special weight.

54 Against Westcott (p. 120) who wants to attach it to θυσίας alone. The early omission of τε in p46, B, Dᶜ was probably motivated by a desire to make the connection with θυσίας more specific (cf. 7: 27; 10: 12).

55 See Michel (pp. 216f) for a discussion of the vexed question of the high priest's involvement in offerings other than those of the Day of Atonement.

56 Cody, pp. 93f. So also Montefiore, p. 97. Cf. Spicq, vol. II, pp. 118f.

57 E.K. Simpson ('The Vocabulary of the Epistle to the Hebrews I', *EQ* 18 (1946), 36f) speaks of a blend of 'forbearance' and 'condolence' in the use of this word elsewhere. LSJ suggest 'to be moderate, to bear reasonably with' and NEB translates 'to bear patiently'.

58 E.J. Yarnold, 'ΜΕΤΡΙΟΠΑΘΕΙΝ apud Heb. 5: 2', *Verbum Domini* 38 (1960), 149–55. He renders 5: 2 'qui iram suam contra ignorantes cohibere possit'. So, essentially, Moffatt (p. 62).

59 His criticism is probably not valid in the case of Michel who, in his latest edition at least, makes a distinction between μετριοπαθεῖν, which 'keeps its distance', and συμπαθῆσαι (p. 217). R. Williamson (*Philo and the Epistle to the Hebrews* (Leiden, 1970), pp. 25–30) shows how 'there is no indication in the way the Writer of Hebrews employs the word to suggest he was influenced either in his choice or his use of the word by Philo' (p. 30). Hebrews is closer to the use of Josephus (*Ant.* XII. 3.2). Williamson rightly suggests that one can detect, even in the latter, 'the increased significance of the more positive notion of clemency or compassion' (p. 26). Of course, to restrain one's feelings of anger is to act with clemency but the more negative aspect of this word seems to prevail in the examples cited by Yarnold. NEB and RSV do not adequately convey this.

60 Michaelis, *TDNT*, vol. V, p. 938.

61 Moffatt, p. 64.

62 See Appendix A and my comment on the suggestion that Christ 'offers' for himself in the prayers and supplications of 5: 7 and then for the people through his suffering in 5: 8–9 (p. 84).

63 So Moffatt (p. 62) and F.F. Bruce (p. 91). Compare Michel, pp. 217f.

64 Philo regards the daily meal offerings as the offering for the priest (Lev. 6: 20) and the lamb as the offering for the people (*Rer. Div. Her.* 36). However, most commentators think our writer restricts himself to the ritual of the Day of Atonement here.

65 Westcott, pp. 121f (my emphasis).
66 So Dibelius (*Botschaft und Geschichte*, vol. II, p. 170) and Thurén (*NovT* 13, pp. 138ff).
67 Moffatt, p. 64. A.B. Davidson (*The Epistle to the Hebrews* (Edinburgh, 1882), p. 113 note 1) rightly observes: 'what is said of Christ belongs not to his function as an high priest but to his preparation for becoming an high priest (verse 10)'. See my Appendix B. Riggenbach (*Der Brief an die Hebräer*, pp. 129f) argues that the writer would have used προσφέρειν with the dative and not with πρός, had he wished to give the sense that Christ's prayers were a sacrificial offering to God (see his note 41 for examples).
68 Westcott, p. 122. 'Even Aaron himself, though specially marked out before (Exod. 16: 33) did not assume the office without a definite call' (p. 123). Cf. Exod. 28: 1; Num. 16–18; Psalm 105: 26.
69 Moffatt, p. 64. Compare Westcott (p. 124 'the position of sonship includes every special honour, kingly or priestly') and Hay (*Glory at the Right Hand*, p. 144f) who stresses the parallel between 5: 5–10 and 1: 1–13.
70 Vanhoye, *Structure*, p. 112. He says that καθὼς καί will have the sense 'selon que' rather than 'de même que'. Cf. Davidson, *The Epistle to the Hebrews*, p. 111.
71 Westcott (p. 21) comments that γεγέννηκα 'marks the communication of a new and abiding life represented in the case of an earthly king by the royal dignity and in the case of Christ by the divine sovereignty, established by the Resurrection of the Incarnate Son in which His Ascension is included'. F.F. Bruce (p. 13) describes the σήμερον as 'the day when he was vested with his royal dignity as the Son of God' after his suffering and resurrection (cf. Rom. 1: 4).
72 Psalm 2: 8f is used with reference to the exaltation of Christ and his heavenly rule in Apoc. 2: 27; 12: 5; 19: 15, and Psalm 2: 1f is said to have its fulfilment in the rejection of Jesus as the Lord's Messiah at his crucifixion and subsequently in the rejection of the gospel of the ascended Christ in Acts 4: 25ff.
73 Spicq, vol. II, p. 111.
74 *Ibid.* p. 110. See my arguments on pp. 81f above.
75 Michel, p. 110.
76 Käsemann (p. 73) is rightly criticised by Michel (p. 148) on this issue. It is not adequate to speak of a 'proleptic use of the title "Son"' in 1: 2 or 5: 7f (Käsemann, p. 59) when 5: 8 seems to be making so much of the fact that the one who was (ὤν) Son had to learn through suffering as he did. Cf. Cody, p. 90 note 23.
77 G. Schrenk, *TDNT*, vol. III, p. 276.
78 According to AG (p. 811), κατὰ τὴν τάξιν means more than 'order' or 'rank' in the understanding of Hebrews. It refers also to 'the entirely different nature of Melchizedek's priesthood as compared with that of Aaron, 7: 11*b*'. Jesus is a high priest '*according to*

the nature of = *just like Melchizedek'*. Note 7: 15 (κατὰ τὴν ὁμοιότητα Μελχισεδεκ). Of course, 'in the strict sense of the term there was no τάξις or succession of Melchizedek priests' (Moffatt, p. 64). When our writer quotes Psalm 110: 4 in full, he naturally adopts the ἱερεύς found there (5: 6; 7: 17, 21 and 7: 15, 11). However, 'the exposition always has the ἀρχιερεύς in view' (G. Schrenk, *TDNT*, vol. III, p. 277 note 54) because of our writer's focus on the imagery of the Day of Atonement, and that title comes to be adopted even in connection with citations of Psalm 110: 4 (as in 5: 5, 10; 6: 20).

79 The pattern of the argument in 5: 1–10 is:
    (A) *Human High Priesthood* (5: 1–4)
        verse 1   General description of function
        verses 2f A Necessary Quality
        verse 4   The Necessary Calling
    (B) *The High Priesthood of the Son of God* (5: 5–10)
        verses 5f The Necessary Calling
        verses 7f The Acquisition of the Necessary Quality
        verses 9f General Description of Function

80 Vos, 'The Priesthood of Christ', p. 585.

81 Westcott, p. 128. Cf. M. Rissi, 'Die Menschlichkeit Jesu nach Hebr. 5: 7 und 8', *TZ* 11 (1955), 39.

82 P.T. O'Brien, 'Prayer in Luke–Acts', *Tyndale Bulletin* 24 (1973), 111–21. Lk. 3: 21 seems to have involved an act of commitment to the role of Servant-Messiah and 5: 16; 6: 12ff; 9: 18, 28 are in contexts where Jesus may have been tempted to swerve from that role to which he had committed himself.

83 So Riggenbach, p. 130, Spicq, vol. II, p. 113 and R.E. Omark, 'The Saving of the Saviour', *Interpretation* 12 (1958), 41ff.

84 R.P. Martin (*Mark: Evangelist and Theologian* (Exeter, 1972), p. 120) points out how 'Jesus dies as a man torn with anguish and immersed under a tide of separation from God.' Nevertheless, even the words 'My God, my God' (15: 34) profess 'a belief in God who is hidden in darkness': Jesus still retained his faith and 'made his appeal to God, though with a question and an anguished cry'. There is also evidence that Jews interpreted the opening words of Psalm 22 in the light of what follows as a *prayer for help* in time of need (G.F. Dalman, *Jesus–Jeshua* (ET, London, 1929), p. 206). For all that, the cry of Mk 15: 34 (= Matt. 27: 46) does not come across in the context as being a cry for rescue from death so much as an expression of anguish and alienation.

85 So Moffatt, p. 65. He draws attention to the Rabbinic stress on the value of tears to God. Cullmann (*Christology*, p. 96) suggests that these additions were made by the writer but then suggests that another tradition, independent from our Gospels, was used (p. 97). Dey (pp. 224f) argues that the language of 5: 7 has its origin in the tradition of Hellenistic–Jewish prayer represented by 3 Macc. 1: 16; 5: 7, 25 and Philo, *Quaest. in Gen.* IV. 233, *Deus Imm.* 115.

86   So Riggenbach, p. 131, Spicq, vol. II, p. 113, Cullmann, p. 97 and
     Dibelius, *Botschaft und Geschichte*, vol. II, pp. 171f. Dibelius
     argues that the OT conviction that a time of distress awaits the
     Messiah (e.g., Psalms 41: 6, 12; 42: 5; 21: 25; 68: 4 LXX) is the
     root of the Gethsemane scene in Mark and Hebrews 5: 7. The
     latter is only influenced by the former in a secondary sense: 'the
     presentation of Hebrews thus does not rest upon a taking-over of
     the Gethsemane scene; it presents only a parallel to it'.
87   Michel, p. 224.
88   Cf. note 86 above. Psalm 21 (LXX) is most often suggested as a
     possible source of influence (especially verse 3, verse 25 and the
     whole sequence in verses 23–5). God answers the prayer of the
     just one who fears him and saves him. It is noteworthy that Justin
     Martyr (*Dialogue* 99) interprets Psalm 21: 3 (LXX) as a prediction
     of the agony of Gethsemane and the latter part of the psalm with
     reference to the resurrection (106).
89   A. Strobel, 'Die Psalmengrundlage der Gethsemane-Parallele Hebr.
     5: 7f', *ZNW* 45 (1954), 266.
90   E. Brandenburger, 'Text und Vorlagen von Hebr. 5: 7–10', *NovT*
     11 (1969), 212ff. Brandenburger's basic thesis is that all previous
     investigations have failed to take satisfactory account of the
     break between verse 7 and verses 8–10 in terms of language,
     presentation and theme (p. 195). He proposes that the writer is
     introducing *two passages* from liturgical texts, known to the
     readers. The 'hymn' in verses 8–10 follows the pattern of 1: 3
     and Phil. 2: 6ff and Col. 1: 15ff, with the basic scheme 'eternal
     pre-existence, humiliation, exaltation' (pp. 200ff). Despite the
     influence of Psalm 116 (LXX 114), Brandenburger argues for 'the
     original thematic independence' of Hebrews 5: 7. It was formu-
     lated by the Hellenistic-Jewish Christian congregations, declaring
     God's mighty deed in rescuing Jesus from death. The motive of
     obedient submission is not reflected in this piece of tradition. Mk
     14 should not be used as a basis for interpreting Hebrews 5: 7
     because the former is concerned with Jesus' obedience and the
     latter with *God's justice*. This is an ingenious and well-argued
     proposal. However, as Thurén suggests ('Gebet und Gehorsam',
     p. 136), the apparent break between verse 7 and verses 8–10 is
     only the result of a failure to appreciate the flow of the author's
     argument. It is difficult to imagine that one so careful and precise
     in his argument and presentation as the author of Hebrews
     appears to be either deliberately or inadvertently blending
     together two traditions as imperfectly as Brandenburger proposes.
     Thurén's alternative is not completely satisfactory because of his
     argument that verse 7 represents Jesus' offering for himself (as a
     parallel to verse 3), but he rightly emphasises the connection
     between prayer and Christ's learning obedience (pp. 140ff). See
     note 67 above.
91   Vos, 'The Priesthood of Christ', p. 585.
92   B.F. Westcott, *The Gospel According to St. John* (London, 1908),

vol. II, p. 125. It is hard to believe that the Johannine words mean anything more than those of Mk 14: 35 ('that the hour might pass from him').

93   In the examples given by Westcott in his commentary on Hebrews (p. 128), it is by no means certain that ἐκ θανάτου in James 5: 20 means rescue from 'the peril *in* which the sufferer is immersed': it is more likely that death here represents the future judgement for disobedient 'souls'. This would be parallel to Rom. 5: 9 (ἀπὸ τῆς ὀργῆς). Acts 2: 40 uses ἀπό in a sense paralleling Jude 5 — rescue out of a situation in which one is immersed — and 2 Pet. 2: 21 (ἐκ) can equally mean 'away from' after ὑποστρέψαι.

94   J. Jeremias, *Abba* (Göttingen, 1964), pp. 319—23 (reprint of article 'Hebr. 5: 7—10', *ZNW* 44 (1952—3), 107—11). See similarly K.S. Wuest, *Hebrews in the Greek NT* (Grand Rapids, 1947), p. 99 and G.H. Lang, *The Epistle to the Hebrews* (London, 1951), pp. 91f.

95   Brandenburger, 'Text und Vorlagen', p. 216. However, I have already disputed his further point that Hebrews 5: 7 is closer to the cry of dereliction in Mk 15: 34 than to the Gethsemane scene in Mk 14: 33ff.

96   R.E. Brown (*The Gospel According to John* (London, 1971), vol. I, pp. 470f) argues that there are 'elements scattered through John that parallel the Synoptic agony scene' (12: 23, 27f, 29; 14: 30f; 18: 11). He does not conclude that John presents us with a dismembered form of the Synoptic agony scene but rather maintains that 'the Johannine picture where such prayers and sayings are scattered may actually be closer to the original situation than the more organized Synoptic scene'. However, I would argue that 12: 27f is much closer to the Synoptic account than Brown allows, even though it is not in the garden setting. The later references (14: 30f; 18: 11) do not give any hint of Jesus' praying as he did in 12: 27f, thus invalidating Brown's suggestion of scattered prayers in this vein.

97   C.K. Barrett (*The Gospel According to St. John* (London, 1967), p. 354) comments: 'in this prayer Jesus merely repeats the principle that has guided his life 7: 18, 8: 50. God is glorified in the complete obedience of his servant and the servant who does not his own will but the will of him that sent him desires only the glory of God.'

98   Moffatt (p. 66) and Spicq (vol. II, p. 115) have a similar explanation with respect to the two stages of Jesus' prayer but Spicq presses the parallel with Gethsemane more closely than Moffatt.

99   Cf. Moffatt, p. 66. The Old Latin had *exauditus a metu* and Beza rendered it *liberatus ex metu*. John Calvin (*Paul to the Hebrews*, pp. 120f) argues in favour of this interpretation. Cf. the list of those who have taken this position more recently in E. Grässer, 'Der Hebräerbrief 1938—63', *Theologische Rundschau* 30 (1964), 220.

100 Cullmann, p. 96. So also R. Bultmann, *TDNT*, vol. II, p. 753 (but

he prefers Harnack's solution), Montefiore, p. 99 and P. Andriessen, 'Angoisse de la mort dans l'Épître aux Hébreux', *NRT* 96 (1974), 282–92.

101 Brandenburger, 'Text und Vorlagen', p. 217.

102 Montefiore, p. 99.

103 Andriessen, 'Angoisse de la mort', p. 290.

104 *Ibid.* p. 292.

105 Andriessen discounts the fact that the adjective εὐλαβής occurs in Lk. 2: 25; Acts 2: 5; 8: 2; 22: 12 with the sense of 'devout' or 'God-fearing'.

106 Andriessen's suggestion that περὶ τῶν μηδέπω βλεπομένων (11: 7) depends on εὐλαβηθείς rather than on χρηματισθείς, does not decide the issue one way or the other. What is most likely in the context is that the opening πίστει gives εὐλαβηθείς much more of the sense of reverential fear or circumspection (cf. Moses in 11: 27 who did *not* fear because of his faith). Cf. Simpson ('Vocabulary', p. 19) for background to this verb and its substantive.

107 Jeremias, *Abba*, p. 321. He suggests similar parentheses at 7: 19*a*; 7: 20*b*–21 and 7: 12. Michel (p. 224) discusses the relationship between the three aorist participles εἰσακουσθείς, τελειωθείς, προσαγορευθείς.

108 See, for example, the suggestion of Blass-Debrunner (para. 211) that ἀπὸ τῆς εὐλαβείας should be taken with the following clause: 'because of his godly fear, Son though he was (and) because of the things which he suffered, he learned obedience'. However, Bultmann (*TDNT*, vol. II, p. 753 note 3) rightly criticises this as 'very artificial' and as not giving full weight to καίπερ ὢν υἱός. See also the comments of Jeremias (pp. 320f) on this syntactical issue.

109 A. Harnack, 'Zwei alte dogmatische Korrekturen im Hebräerbrief', *Studien zur Geschichte des NT und der alten Kirche* (Berlin–Leipzig, 1931), pp. 245ff, followed by R. Bultmann, *TDNT*, vol. II, p. 753, H. Windisch *et al.* There is a certain intrinsic probability to this suggestion – early corruption of the text can be explained on the ground that Christ's not being heard was theologically offensive – but there is no textual evidence to support it and one should not consider it until 'all other seriously discussable possibilities are exhausted' (Brandenburger, p. 193).

110 See note 90 for details.

111 Michel (p. 222) also draws a comparison between the two verses when he describes εὐλάβεια as 'the trust which is ready to obey': it characterises perhaps more 'the inner side' and obedience 'the outward-turned aspect of faith'. Although I have argued that Gethsemane is given as the example *par excellence* of Christ learning obedience through suffering, I would not limit the aorists of verse 8 to that event. As Du Plessis (p. 221) notes, these aorists will be 'complexive', 'subsuming all the humiliating experiences throughout his entire life under a single protracted statement'.

112 Bultmann, *TDNT*, vol. II, p. 753.

113 Thus, T.H. Robinson (*The Epistle to the Hebrews* (London, 1933), p. 64) even suggests that the report of an angel coming to strengthen Jesus in Lk. 22: 43 is a confirmation of this view (however, according to Lk. 22: 44 the struggle became more intense after this). He also adds that 'it did not follow that because the Father *heard* the request of his *Son* that he would therefore grant it'. The point in Hebrews would then be to stress that although the request was refused, 'the bond of friendship between Father and Son remained unimpaired' (p. 65). A.B. Bruce (*The Epistle to the Hebrews* (Edinburgh, 1899), p. 186) argues strongly for the interpretation that Christ was given courage to face death, although he is uncertain how to render εὐλάβεια.

114 Davidson, *The Epistle to the Hebrews*, p. 112. A.S. Peake (*The Epistle to the Hebrews* (Edinburgh, 1914), p. 135) attempts to combine both views.

115 Omark, 'The Saving of the Saviour', p. 47. He does not explicitly state that Jesus prayed to escape the sort of death he describes, though he implies it. Jesus may well have seen this 'potential forfeiture' and it may well be true that his 'salvation' consisted in part in rescue from it. However, Spicq's interpretation (my note 118) is a more accurate description of the plain sense of the texts concerned.

116 *Ibid.* p. 48.

117 *Ibid.* p. 51.

118 Spicq, vol. II, p. 115. The answer given to the prayer of Jesus in John 12: 28 implies the Father's intention to glorify his name in the death and exaltation of Jesus. Moffatt (p. 66) also relates the two stages of Jesus' prayer in Mk 14: 36 to the 'bitter tears and cries' and 'godly fear' of Hebrews 5: 7 respectively, but does not go as far as Spicq in suggesting that εἰσακουσθείς relates specifically to the second petition of Jesus only.

119 Riggenbach, p. 134. Jesus in Gethsemane, 'in the certainty of God's power and love, could beg to be kept from death, but in reverent awe for God, submit himself and in complete union with God's will achieve the answer to his prayers' (p. 136).

120 Jeremias, *Abba*, p. 321.

121 Moffatt, p. 66. So also F.F. Bruce (p. 103) and Westcott (p. 130) who says: 'the nature of Christ's sonship at first sight seems to exclude the thought that he should learn obedience through suffering'. The full significance of this clause is best represented by J.B. Phillips' 'Son though he was' and TEV 'though he was God's Son' (rather than AV, RV, RSV 'although he was a Son' or NEB 'son though he was').

122 Westcott, p. 130. Vos ('The Priesthood of Christ', p. 585) goes too far when he says 'it is natural for a son to obey' and misses the point of 12: 3–17 when he says 'it is not natural for a son to have to learn obedience in this way' (i.e., through suffering).

123 Any suggestion of a proleptic use of the title 'Son', either here or in 1: 2 (so Käsemann, p. 59), destroys the real force of the expression 'Son though he was'.

124 J. Coste, 'Notion Grecque et Notion Biblique de la "Souffrance Éducatrice" (à propos d'Hébreux 5: 8)', *Recherches de Science Religieuse* 43 (1955), 496. So also Moffatt (pp. 66f) concludes: the idea was invariably applied to 'the thoughtless or stupid, and to open and deliberate offenders' – to those who could only be taught by suffering. Coste says a cultivated Greek of the first century, ignorant of the Biblical perspective, might interpret Hebrews 5: 8 thus: 'Christ, who previously failed to recognize the necessity of obedience, has thus learned to submit to the wishes of the deity and his example has instructed his brothers.' This is an idea 'not without grandeur', but falling short of the Biblical perspective.

125 *Ibid.* p. 498. Job's friends develop the theme of educative suffering (5: 17; 33: 19; 36: 15) but he is not consoled and can only respond with a cry, an appeal to God (19: 23ff; 31: 35ff).

126 *Ibid.* p. 505. The emphasis on suffering as leading to acknowledgement of God and a crying to him is found in Ezek. 6: 7; 13: 14 etc.; Psalms 107, 78, 34; Neh. 9: 5-37; Jer. 31: 18ff; 1 Kgs 8: 23.

127 For a summary of Coste's views on Philo's use of this expression see note 134 below. In reviewing the application of Prov. 3: 11f to the readers in 12: 5-11, I will discuss the extent to which such teaching could have been applied to Christ (see pp. 175f).

128 C. Westermann, *Isaiah 40–66* (ET, London, 1969), pp. 227, 230.

129 *Ibid.* p. 268. He continues: 'the ἐφ' ἅπαξ of the Epistle to the Hebrews and its logical conclusions are already implicit here'.

130 αἴτιος does not occur elsewhere in the NT, but note LXX 1 Kgs 22: 22 ('I am the *cause* [of the death] of the persons in your father's house'), 2 Macc. 13: 4 ('that this man was the *cause/ source* of all the evil'), Bel and the Dragon 42 etc. Philo uses the expression αἴτιος σωτηρίας of the brazen serpent (*Agric.* 96) and of Noah in relation to his sons (*Virt.* 202). Cf. *Vit. Cont.* 86; *Spec. Leg.* I.252 (God). The salvation Christ achieves for others is not mere rescue from temporal destruction (Hebrews 11: 7) but, 'in accordance with the unique significance of its founder (7: 25), possesses absolute value and everlasting existence (Isaiah 45: 17)' (Riggenbach, p. 137).

131 Cf. W. Zimmerli and J. Jeremias, *The Servant of God* (ET, London, 1957), pp. 93, 96, and A. Richardson, *An Introduction to the Theology of the New Testament* (London, 1958), pp. 220ff.

132 P.E. Hughes, p. 187. Christ's obedience was learned in the sense that 'it was achieved as a personal reality, *through what he suffered*' (p. 186).

133 So K.H. Rengstorf (*TDNT* vol. IV, p. 411), who dismisses such interpretations as falling into 'the error of idealism' and as overlooking the fact that 'for biblical Greek μανθανεῖν takes place in the handling of Scripture as the revealed will of God'. However,

it is far-fetched to suggest that the verb carries this meaning into our context and that Jesus learned *from Scripture* 'that even to the smallest details (ἀφ' ὧν) his passion was grounded in the saving will of God and could not be separated from his calling'. This statement, though theologically true, cannot be argued simply from the use of ἔμαθεν here.

134 Coste shows that Philo uses the ἔμαθον – ἔπαθον word-play in two different ways. In *Vit. Mos.* I.102; II.55, 280, the educative value of chastisement is stressed, with the *negative* emphasis common to ordinary Greek usage, but with something also of the Biblical emphasis on coming to know God as he really is through such experiences (cf. *Spec. Leg.* IV.29). However, in *Rer. Div. Her.* 73; *Som.* II.107 and *Fug.* 138, Philo uses the combination to describe 'the experiences of the soul in its journey to God' (p. 519). Here, there is an emphasis on 'experimental knowledge', as when πάσχειν is used with εἰδέναι (e.g., *Leg. All.* III.156 and *Migr. Abr.* 34). Thus, ἔπαθεν is used more with the sense of 'experiencing' than suffering and ἔμαθεν takes on a much more positive meaning. Coste disagrees with Spicq (vol I, pp. 46f) that this is 'a formula and a fundamental principle of education' for Philo and that it has directly influenced our writer. The only real parallel between Hebrews 5: 8 and Philo is the use of ἔπαθεν in the sense of 'experience', rather than educative suffering, and the consequent adaptation in meaning of ἔμαθεν. *Contra* Dey, pp. 224f.

135 Vos, 'The Priesthood of Christ', p. 585. See also note 132 above.

136 F.F. Bruce, p. 103.

137 C. Spicq, vol. II, p. 117.

138 J. Calvin, *Paul to the Hebrews*, p. 123.

139 On 4: 15, Calvin says (p. 108): 'he not only proved himself to be a real man, but had also been taught by his own experience to help the miserable: not because the Son of God had need of such training but because *we could not otherwise comprehend the care he feels for our salvation*' (my emphasis). To say that the Son of God had no need of such training really plays down the significance of 5: 8.

140 *Ibid*. p. 124.

141 In 12: 1f, Jesus is presented as the last and greatest witness to that faith which persists against all odds and obtains its reward, thus bringing the exposition of Hebrews 11 to its climax. The theme of Jesus as *exemplar* is continued in 12: 3-4*a*, but here the emphasis is on his unjust treatment from 'sinners' – presumably a reference to mankind in rebellion against God and thus hostile to God's representative. In this respect, Jesus stands with the prophets of the OT as one persecuted because of his stand for God (cf. my discussion of Isa. 50: 4-9 with regard to Hebrews 5: 8). The link between 12: 3 and 12: 4 is important: believers are involved in the same struggle 'against sin'. All the hostility and opposition they experience because they are Christians must

be viewed in this light. It is because of their stand for Christ (13: 12–14; 10: 32–9). For a detailed treatment of this passage see my concluding chapter.

142 Calvin, p. 125.
143 *Ibid*. p. 124. Despite the emphasis on the uniqueness of Christ's experience here, Calvin makes it clear in commenting on 2: 10 that this depends on the ordinary way that God adopts in dealing with his own people:
> 'for his will is to exercise them with various trials, so that they may spend their whole life under the cross. It was hence necessary that Christ, as the first-begotten, should by the cross be inaugurated into his supremacy, since that is the common lot and condition of all. This is the conforming of the head with the members of which Paul speaks in Romans 8: 29.'

144 Du Plessis, p. 215. Although he allows that τελειοῦν may carry with it the sense of 'consecration' to priesthood from its use in the LXX, Du Plessis rightly concludes that the sense of vocational qualification in Hebrews cannot be restricted to the concept of priesthood. He notes that any such official understanding of the verb is likely to obscure the sense of personal consummation that is suggested by the usage of Hebrews.
145 See note 130 above. In 5: 9 αἴτιος σωτηρίας αἰωνίου is not the direct object of the verb 'to perfect', as is the expression 'the leader who delivers them' in 2: 10. However, as the complement of ἐγένετο it naturally refers to the subject of that verb who is described by the participle τελειωθείς as having been perfected.
146 Dibelius, *Botschaft und Geschichte*, vol. II, p. 170. He outlines his objections to the 'ethical–religious' development concept on p. 165.
147 Käsemann, p. 141. He views Christ's function as 'source of eternal salvation' as a *heavenly* role and ἀρχηγός as the role of the heavenly Man in his humiliation, in which 'he began to lead many sons to glory' (pp. 79–82; 89). See my comments on p. 56 above.
148 *Ibid*. p. 142.
149 *Ibid*. Cf. K. Bornhäuser, 'Die Versuchungen Jesu nach dem Hebräerbriefe', *Theologische Studien für M. Kähler* (Leipzig, 1905), pp. 74ff.
150 *Ibid*. p. 143.
151 Kögel, 'Der Begriff τελειοῦν', p. 65.
152 That the perfecting of Christ included the process of learning obedience through what he suffered is further suggested by the words 'to all who obey him' (5: 9). As noted above, the point is that Christians should by Christ's example 'be taught and prepared by various sorrows and at length by death itself, to render obedience to God' (Calvin, p. 124). Christ became the unique source of eternal salvation by that obedience which led him to death and heavenly exaltation. He also became an example and challenge to believers by his obedience. See also note 153.

153 Riggenbach, p. 136. Since 2: 10 pictures the perfecting of Christ 'through sufferings', it is most natural to read the sequence of thought in 5: 7–9 in a similar fashion. The τελειωθείς will be *resumptive* in 5: 9 and include within its scope the process of learning obedience through suffering described in 5: 7f. Christ's perfecting is not simply the *result* of his suffering, but *includes* suffering as a necessary part of the process. To restrict 5: 8 to the accomplishment of his redemptive sacrifice, the necessary prelude to his glorification, is to obscure our writer's emphasis on personal preparation of Christ for his high-priestly ministry (2: 17f; 4: 15f).

154 Cullmann, p. 97. He compares Phil. 2: 8 (ὑπήκοος μέχρι θανάτου), where μέχρι 'indicates a climax and thus also a certain development within Jesus' humiliation'.

155 *Ibid.* p. 95.

156 *Ibid.* p. 94.

157 *Ibid.* p. 93.

158 *Ibid.* p. 97.

159 P.E. Hughes, pp. 187f.

160 Cullmann, p. 92.

161 Westcott, p. 67.

162 *Ibid.* pp. 66f.

163 J. Denney, *The Death of Christ* (London, 1964), p. 121. 'The atonement, and the priestly or reconciling ministry of Christ, are the end to which the incarnation is relative as the means.' It is 'the atonement which explains the incarnation' (pp. 131f).

164 Westcott, pp. 49f.

165 See pp. 33f above.

166 Vanhoye, *Situation*, p. 321. See further on his position below pp. 122–4.

167 *Ibid.* pp. 322f. Cf. Cullmann, p. 97.

168 Vanhoye, *Situation*, pp. 323.

169 Spicq, vol. II, p. 222.

170 Michel, p. 224.

5 The perfecting of Christ: his exaltation

1 Spicq, vol. I, p. 179.

2 Michel, p. 255 ('Hier finden wir "vollkommene Lehre" für "Vollkommene"').

3 Vanhoye, *Structure*, pp. 141ff.

4 So Spicq, vol. II, pp. 179ff; Michel, p. 259 and F.F. Bruce, pp. 133ff. Although these commentators give slightly different names to the sections, their subdivisions of the text correspond exactly.

5 Vanhoye, *Structure*, pp. 125ff. The link between τελείωσις and τετελειωμένον is simply verbal at this point, since 7: 11–19 is discussing the failure of the Law and the levitical priesthood to perfect believers and 7: 28 the perfecting of Christ. However, Vanhoye's further subdivision of 7: 11–28 makes better sense by separating 7: 11–19 from 7: 20–8.

6   Hay, *Glory at the Right Hand*, p. 142. This is the conclusion to a
    helpful survey of the evidence (from pp. 134ff). Hebrews is the
    first Christian writing before Justin's *Dialogue* (33: 2; 63: 3; 83:
    2; 118: 1) to mention Melchizedek.
7   *Ibid.* p. 142. Cf. G. Wuttke, *Melchisedech der Priesterkönig von
    Salam*, BZNW 5 (Giessen, 1927), pp. 6ff; Käsemann, pp. 134ff;
    and Michel's survey (pp. 259–63).
8   Hay, *Glory at the Right Hand*, p. 143. This caution is essential in
    view of the number and diversity of traditions that could have been
    known to the writer. Thus, to isolate Philo or 11Q Melchizedek
    or Rabbinic exegesis seems unwarranted in such a context. 'The
    marvel about the argument concerning Melchizedek in Hebrews
    5–7 is not that the author has made so much out of so little, but
    that he has made so little out of so much' (pp. 152f).
9   Cf. G.B. Caird, 'The Exegetical Method of the Epistle to the
    Hebrews', *Canadian Journal of Theology* 5 (1959), 48 and F.
    Schröger, *Der Verfasser des Hebräerbriefes als Schriftausleger*,
    Biblische Untersuchungen 4 (Regensburg, 1968), pp. 156–9.
    The latter sees a parallel in Rabbinic concern to interpret one
    Scriptural text in the light of a second.
10 J. Schneider (*TDNT*, vol. V, p. 198) and AG (*s.v.* ἀφομοιόω)
    prefer the first rendering but Moffatt (p. 93) rightly points to the
    second possibility both here and in The Letter of Jeremiah 70. So
    also Westcott (p. 175).
11 Michel, p. 263. Spicq (vol. II, p. 184), following Javet, likewise
    suggests that the Biblical portrait of Melchizedek is a *mirror* in
    which we can contemplate the Son of God. Dey (pp. 187ff) so
    pursues the interpretation of this chapter in the light of Philonic
    parallels that he has the writer envisaging Melchizedek as a
    heavenly intermediary who is actually immortal as Jesus is. Such
    literalism is unwarranted in the interpretation of this passage.
12 Westcott, p. 175.
13 *Ibid.* p. 174. Cf. Jer. 33: 15; Isa. 9: 6.
14 Michel, p. 262. This, rather than the mythical, is the interpret-
    ation favoured by most modern commentators. Contrast Spicq,
    vol. II, p. 184.
15 See Spicq (vol. II, p. 208 note 4, Excursus V) for a comparison
    with Philo's use of the argument from silence and F.F. Bruce
    (p. 136 note 18) for the importance of this argument for Rabbinic
    exegesis.
16 B.A. Demarest, *A History of Interpretation of Hebrews 7: 1–10
    from the Reformation to the Present*, BZGBE 19 (Tübingen,
    1976), p. 136.
17 *Ibid.* p. 135. 'The silence of the record invests Melchizedek with
    an intransmissible and hence continuous priesthood which
    symbolically portrays the unbounded perpetuity of the priest-
    hood of Christ' (p. 136).
18 Westcott, p. 177. 'The Levitical priests tithed their brethren:
    Melchizedek, a priest of another race, tithed Abraham their

common father. His priesthood was absolute and not a priority in the same family.' For Philo's interpretation of Gen. 14: 17ff see Dey, pp. 199–203.

19 Westcott, p. 179.

20 See Michel (p. 267) on the special significance of μαρτυρεῖσθαι in Hebrews (seven times). Scripture emphasises with all its authority for our writer that 'God has given [Melchizedek] a share in his life.' The special greatness of Melchizedek lies in this typological representation (cf. *TDNT*, vol. IV, p. 497).

21 F.F. Bruce, p. 142. Cf. Gen. 25: 23; Mal. 1: 2f; Rom. 9: 11ff; 5: 12.

22 A *hapax* in the Greek Bible, but see Williamson (*Philo and Hebrews*, pp. 103–6) for numerous extra-Biblical examples. Buchanan (p. 122) paraphrases: 'one might even (extend the figure to) say (that) ...'

23 Hay, *Glory at the Right Hand*, p. 146.

24 Moffatt, p. 96. So also Westcott (p. 183), Spicq (vol. II, p. 189) and NEB ('it is on this basis that the people were given the Law'). Compare the use of ἐπί with the genitive in this way in Lk. 4: 29; 2 Cor. 13: 1. The suggestion of Dey (p. 194, especially note 6) that the ἐπί is equivalent to a περί with the genitive, meaning 'the people have received legislation concerning the Levitic priesthood (i.e., concerning their genealogical descent)', would certainly give a uniform sense to the argument of 7: 11–18. However, verse 19 ('the law perfected nothing') suggests that νόμος in the more general sense was in view in the passage as a whole, with the ἐντολή of verses 16, 18 giving the more specific sense at that stage of the argument.

25 Michel, p. 270.

26 W. Gutbrod, *TDNT*, vol. IV, p. 1072. He concludes that 'the law is weak for Paul because man does *not* do it, whereas it is weak for Hebrews because *man* does it. The two propositions start from different points but fundamentally then contain the same verdict' (p. 1079).

27 Windisch, p. 66. There is validity, however, in the argument of W. Manson (p. 115) that 'in St. Paul the abrogation of the Law as a source of rightness with God implicitly carries the fall of the cultic with it. In Hebrews the supersession of the cultus explicitly involves the repeal of the Law.'

28 Michel, p. 284. W. Manson (p. 115) also notes 'the positive relation in which the Jewish system of religion stands to Jesus Christ' in much that our writer says.

29 Michel, p. 285.

30 Michel (p. 271) notes that the descent of Jesus from Judah here probably hints at the early Christian confession of Jesus as Son of David. Cf. Jeremias, *Jerusalem in the Time of Jesus* (ET, London, 1969), p. 291 (note) and F.F. Bruce, p. 146. Contrast the unnecessary caution of Buchanan (pp. 123f) in denying any connection between Jesus and the Son of David in Hebrews.

31 So Hay, *Glory at the Right Hand*, p. 149.

32 Westcott, p. 185.

33 *Ibid.* p. 186.

34 W. Gutbrod, *TDNT,* vol. IV, p. 1078. Cf. Michel (p. 272) and Westcott (p. 186). NEB ('a system of earth-bound rules') rather obscures the important contrast between 'Law' and 'power'.

35 Michel, p. 272. The distinction between σάρκινος and σαρκικός, as made by Westcott (p. 186), is discussed by Michel (p. 272 note 1).

36 E. Schweizer, *TDNT,* vol. VII, p. 144. Note the description of the Law in 9: 10 as δικαιώματα σαρκός (NEB: 'outward ordinances'). The RSV paraphrase of 7: 16 ('not according to a legal requirement concerning bodily descent') is justifiable in the light of the context (verses 13f).

37 See the discussion by Michel (p. 272).

38 Montefiore, pp. 125f. Cf. Spicq (vol. II, p. 193), who also argues that Christ was 'in possession of his priesthood since his birth (γέγονεν)' on the basis of the divine and human in his nature. Buchanan (p. 125) oversimplifies the relationship between Christ and Melchizedek and reads too much into the verb ἀνατέταλκεν (7: 14) when he interprets the writer to mean 'that he was *not* born (7: 13)'. Christ was 'neither conceived nor born, he arose (ἀνατέταλκεν): he "came into existence"'.

39 See especially Appendix B.

40 B.A. Demarest, 'Priest After the Order of Melchizedek. A History of Interpretation of Hebrews 7 from the Era of the Reformation to the Present' (Ph.D. thesis, University of Manchester, 1973), pp. 337f. As to whether Christ's death was part of his priestly service, he says: 'it is probable that the writer envisaged no time interval between Christ's self-sacrifice and his entrance into the heavenly sanctuary. Having brought the perfect sin offering ἐφάπαξ, *the victim became almost simultaneously the high priest*. (p. 345, my emphasis).

41 So Käsemann (pp. 58f, 140–51), F.F. Bruce (p. 148) and Michel (pp. 272f).

42 F. Büchsel, *TDNT*, vol. IV, p. 339.

43 Westcott, p. 187. 'Although the form of its manifestation was changed and in the earthly sense he died, yet his life endured unchanged even through earthly dissolution.' This is not the NT way of thinking about death and resurrection at all: resurrection is a totally new beginning after the experience of death.

44 *Ibid.* p. 188.

45 AG *s.v.* ἀθετέω 1.*a.* Michel (p. 273) quite reasonably speaks of ἀθέτησις here as 'a periphrasis for divine activity' and implies that the abrogation took place with the promulgation of Psalm 110: 4. See also Moffatt (p. 97) and F.F. Bruce (p. 148).

46 Westcott, p. 189.

47 Moffatt, p. 98. Thus also Michel (p. 273) speaks of the better hope as 'a guaranteed, certain one, which leads to the goal'. The

hope is better because the promises are better (8: 6ff; cf. 7: 27; 10: 34).

48   Westcott, p. 189. O. Moe ('Der Gedanke des allgemeinen Priester-tums', *TZ* 5 (1949), 162f) makes similar use of this argument from linguistic usage.

49   There is certainly a hierarchy of drawing near to God in such references as Exod. 19: 21f, where only the priests who consecrate themselves for this purpose may draw near to God on Mt Sinai, and Exod. 24: 2, where Moses alone is to draw near to God at the top of the mountain, leaving the elders (including Aaron!) to wor-ship 'afar off' (verse 1). The verb is used as a technical term for the actions of the priests in Lev. 10: 3; 21: 21, 23: Ezek. 40: 46; 42: 13; 43: 19; 44: 13; 45: 4. However, ἐγγίζειν is used of Abraham drawing near to God in prayer in Gen. 18: 23 (note Philo's use of this reference to support his own idea of drawing near to God through wisdom and partaking of life immortal in *Leg. All.* III.9; *Deus Imm.* 161; *Migr. Abr.* 132). In Eccles. 4: 17 (ET 5: 1) to 'draw near to listen' and to 'draw near to sacrifice' are two different ways of approaching God in his 'house', and in Hosea 12: 7 (ET 12: 6); Zeph. 3: 2; Haggai 2: 15; Isa. 29: 13; 58: 2, the drawing near to God refers to *all* the people (either in cultic worship or in the more spiritualised sense of prayer). Indeed, the people of God are characterised in Psalm 148: 14; Judith 8: 27 as τοὺς ἐγγίζοντας αὐτῷ. Note also the way ἐγγύς is used to express the relation between God and the righteous in Psalms (LXX) 33: 19; 118: 151; 144: 18 etc.

50   H. Preisker, *TDNT,* vol. II, p. 331. Westcott himself acknowledges (p. 307) that the whole congregation is included in the title τοὺς προσερχομένους in 10: 1, 'which cannot be limited to the priests or to special offerers'. Although it is true to a certain extent that the ritual of the Old Covenant 'was calculated rather to keep men at a distance from God than to bring them near' (F.F. Bruce, p. 149), it is significant that our writer could describe the wor-shippers as 'those who draw near to God' *in such a context* (10: 1–4). In 11: 6 he makes it clear that anyone who could encounter God in a living relationship of faith may be described as τὸν προσερχόμενον τῷ θεῷ. Men of faith in the OT enjoyed this drawing near in a non-cultic context, though cultically certain bounds were placed on them.

51   Michel, p. 274. O. Hofius ('Die Unabänderlichkeit des göttlichen Heilsratschlusses. Erwägungen zur Herkunft eines neutestament-lichen Theologumen', *ZNW* 64 (1973), 135ff) argues that the theme in 6: 17f has its roots ultimately in the OT but is not derived from a single passage there. Neither Philo nor Qumran offers an exact parallel, though Rabbinic exegesis of Num. 23: 19 is similar (compare Rom. 11: 29; 9: 6; 3: 3–4).

52   T.W. Manson, *Studies in the Gospels and Epistles* (Manchester, 1962), p. 249. Cf. Gal. 3: 15ff.

53   The inheritance into which the New Covenant brings the people

of God is eternal (9: 15), just as the redemption it provides is
eternal (9: 12), and therefore it can be called an 'eternal covenant'
(13: 20). It is this 'better hope' that makes the covenant better.

54 Michel, p. 275 (my emphasis). Moses is called 'mediator' of the
Old Covenant (Gal. 3: 19) but not 'surety'. The latter term, which
only occurs at Hebrews 7: 22 in the NT, is used in Sir. 29: 15f
and 2 Macc. 10: 28 in the sense in which it is found frequently in
Greek legal documents. Sir. 29: 14–17 speaks of a good man
becoming a surety for his neighbour and, in effect, giving his life
for the other person (verse 15), so acting as his rescuer (verse 17).

55 Westcott (p. 191) unnecessarily limits the concept when he asserts
that Christ is not 'a surety for man to God, but a surety of a
covenant of God with man'. The whole presentation of Christ's
ascension and entrance into the heavenly sanctuary as forerunner
on his people's behalf seems to imply that, as his people's
representative, he satisfies the terms of God's covenant from the
manward side. By virtue of his position as the seated priest-king
in the heavenly sanctuary he also guarantees the covenant from
God to man (12: 23f). Cf. F.F. Bruce, p. 151 note 70.

56 Buchanan consistently translates εἰς τὸν αἰῶνα as 'for the age'
and takes εἰς τὸ παντελές (7: 25) as a parallel ('for the entire
(age)'). Apart from the awkwardness of the latter, the rendering
of the former is unwarranted. There is no limitation placed on the
exercise of Christ's priesthood in Hebrews. On the contrary, as
Spicq (vol. II, p. 197) argues, the use of μένειν in the LXX to
signify the 'everlastingness' of God in contrast to man allows us
to perceive in 7: 24 'a clear declaration of the eternity of Christ
and his priesthood, and indirectly of his divinity'.

57 Παραμένειν is a common euphemism in the papyri for 'to remain
in office or serve' (Moffatt, p. 99) and appears to have a stronger
sense than μένειν (Michel, p. 276). Cf. Josephus, *Ant.* IX.273;
XI.309; Phil. 1: 25 and Jas. 1: 25.

58 W. Lorimer ('Hebrews 7: 23f', *NTS* 13 (1967), 386f) suggests
that the original reading in verse 24 was ἀμετάβατον ('not passing
to another'), a corruption due to παρα(μένειν) in verse 23. However, there is no textual evidence for such a change and despite
the dispute over the meaning of ἀπαράβατον we are not justified
in seeking to solve the dilemma by supposing a corruption where
no real evidence exists. Moffatt (p. 99) is representative of those
who would render this word 'in the uncommon sense of non-
transferable ... as an equivalent for μὴ παραβαίνουσαν εἰς ἄλλον'.
Although this may suit the context well, contrasting Jesus with
the levitical priests who must hand on their priesthood to others,
it is better to understand the word in the common sense of
'permanent, unchangeable' (AG *s.v.* ἀπαράβατος), and understand
the sense 'passing to no successor' only as a subsidiary notion. Cf.
Michel, p. 276; Westcott, p. 192 and Simpson, 'Vocabulary', pp.
187f.

59 Michel, p. 276. Cf. 2: 17; 3: 1; 8: 3; 9: 18.

60 Westcott, p. 193. He takes the words 'to make intercession for them' to indicate that 'the final end of Christ's life in heaven as it is here represented is that he may fulfil the object of the incarnation, the perfecting of humanity'.

61 AG (*s.v. παντελής*) note examples for usage in both ways but point to the evidence of a number of ancient versions to support the temporal sense 'forever, for all time'. Lk. 13: 11 may similarly be interpreted in both ways. See note 56.

62 Michel, p. 276 note 2 (commenting on Riggenbach's emphasis on the *completeness* of salvation, rather than on its *eternity*).

63 Moffatt, p. 100. It is noteworthy that Moffatt and RSV do not translate the first *καί*, which would be redundant according to their interpretation.

64 In an appendix to his thesis (see my note 40), B.A. Demarest shows how Roman Catholic interpretation of this concept has tended to be more literal, and Reformed theology has comprehended it in a strictly figurative and metaphorical sense. Thus, Calvin on Rom. 8: 34 says Christ 'appears continually before the Father in his death and resurrection which takes the place of eternal intercession', though he acknowledges (*Institutes* III. 20 20) that Christ mediates the petitions of believers on earth. On Hebrews 7: 25 Calvin says 'Christ prays for us not with prayers expressed in words, not in weepings, nor even with the measure of distress displayed in the Garden of Gethsemane. The intercession of Christ is his unchanging desire for the salvation of his elect.' Demarest shows how Puritans like John Owen suggested more than 'a desire for the salvation of his elect' from this verse. Older Lutherans, too, conceived of Christ's petitionary activity as more real and vocal than the strictly metaphorical understanding of Calvin and others. The Lutherans tended to include the world as well as the elect in the scope of Christ's heavenly intercession (analogous with his earthly prayers for his enemies). Arminian theologians pressed for the idea of Christ's intercession as the continuation in the heavenly world of his expiatory sacrifice once offered upon earth. The latter view finds echoes in contemporary Anglo-Catholic theology. Regardless of how literally we wish to interpret the intercession, it is important to remember that, in the perspective of our writer, 'heaven is not a place of sacrifice and our Lord is no longer a sacrificing priest. He has "offered one sacrifice for sin for ever" (10: 12). But his presence in the holiest is a perpetual and effective presentation before God of the sacrifice once offered' (H.B. Swete, *The Ascended Christ* (London, 1910), p. 43).

65 Hay, p. 130. Cf. Mark 8: 38 par.; Matt. 10: 32 par. In Matthew 7: 21ff and 25: 31ff, 'Jesus acts as both star witness and judge.' See also 2 Tim. 2: 12; Apoc. 3: 5. Hay argues that 'this heavenly action seems limited in time to the last judgement', though he excepts 1 John 2: 1; Lk. 22: 32 and John 17.

66 C.F.D. Moule, 'From Defendant to Judge – and Deliverer',

Studiorum Novi Testamenti Societas Bulletin 3 (Oxford, 1952), 40–53 and Cullmann, *Christology*, p. 183 and Hay, pp. 75f, 132f.

67 Hay (pp. 133f) has good reasons for including 1 Pet. 3: 21f in this category.

68 *Ibid.* p. 150. Hay also argues that it conflicts with the image of *passivity* in the picture of Jesus' heavenly session in 10: 12f and 12: 2. However, this latter feature would simply imply that Christ's intercession involved no ritual actions or prostrations before the Father. See my note 64.

69 Hay himself suggests that 'perhaps the author connects it with the prayers they offer' (p. 132), but that the intercession can hardly be for minor or occasional sins only, since 'the author declares (7: 25) that it is a matter of salvation (σῴζειν)' (p. 150). Setting 4: 14–16 within the context of the previous section (3: 1 – 4: 15), I would argue that the invitation of 4: 16 must concern any sin or sense of failure that would prevent believers from reaching their heavenly destination and so enjoying salvation 'for all time'. Cullmann (p. 102) also connects the imagery of intercession in 7: 25 with 4: 14–16.

70 So A. Nairne, *The Epistle of Priesthood* (1913), p. 201. However, see the arguments of Cody (pp. 168–202) against such literalism and my note 75.

71 Cullmann, pp. 101f.

72 Westcott, p. 231. He draws attention to the significance of Exod. 28: 29, as many commentators do in this regard: 'in the Levitical ritual the truth was foreshadowed in the direction that "Aaron shall bear the names of the children of Israel in the breastplate of judgement upon his heart when he goes in unto the holy place" ' (p. 194).

73 Cody, p. 195 (see his chapter 4 on the subject of Christ's heavenly 'liturgy'). The following reference is from p. 199.

74 Montefiore, p. 129. Cf. Westcott (p. 194) for this view amongst the Fathers.

75 Cody, p. 199. W. Stott ('The Conception of "Offering" in the Epistle to the Hebrews', *NTS* 9 (1962–3), 67) stresses that the fundamental meaning of ἐντυγχάνειν is 'to approach on behalf of' rather than 'to plead' (cf. also *TDNT*, vol. VIII, pp. 242f) and that in Christ's ' "approach" we too as "his brethren" have the right παρρησία (4: 16) of approach and speech, a right not allowed in the Tabernacle ritual'. He goes on to observe that the only passage in Scripture where prayer is spoken of with the posture of sitting is 2 Sam. 7: 18, where David as king is seated before God, 'claiming that the covenant, which has been promised, shall be fulfilled'. Thus, Hebrews 7: 25 may be understood not in terms of 'pleading the sacrifice' but in terms of Christ, having accomplished already the cleansing and mediated the New Covenant, 'now seated in royal state and claiming the fulfilment of the covenant promises for his seed'.

76 Windisch (p. 67) proposed that 7: 26–8 was a small hymn and

liturgical conclusion to the Melchizedek section. Michel (p. 278), however, argues that only verse 26 is such a hymn and that the author draws exegetical conclusions from the whole argument of chapter 7 in verses 27−8. However, even the suggestion that verse 26 is a hymn-fragment seems hard to accept in view of the words 'for it was fitting that we should have such a high priest', clearly presupposing the argument of the preceding verses (and verse 27 in its turn depending so much on verse 26).

77 Westcott (p. 195) rightly argues that believers are in focus with the word ἡμῖν because 'the dominant thought is of the struggles of the Christian life, which are ever calling for divine succour'.

78 So Westcott (p. 195) and Michel (pp. 278f), who argues that this is not a rationalising nor anthropocentric approach but an understanding that proceeds from the cross (cf. 2: 10 ἔπρεπεν γὰρ αὐτῷ).

79 F. Hauck, *TDNT*, vol. V, pp. 490f. In the LXX, ὅσιος most often represented ḥāsîd for the godly man (Psalm 16: 10), the people of God (Psalm 149: 1, 5) or God himself (Psalm 145: 17). 'In mind and conduct [Christ] perfectly fulfils the divine requirements' (*ibid.* p. 492).

80 Spicq, vol. II, p. 200. Cf. Moffatt, p. 101.

81 Philo (*Spec. Leg.* I.113; *Fug.* 108ff) uses ἀμίαντος to describe 'the undefiled character of the Logos as the truth denoted allegorically by the law forbidding the high priest to touch a corpse or mourn for the dead (Lev. 21: 10f)' (F.F. Bruce, p. 156 note 86). However, Christians have as their high priest 'one who does not remain in the realm of ideas but is the incarnate Logos, one who preserved his purity while treading the common ways of this world and sharing our human lot' (*ibid.* pp. 156f).

82 Montefiore, pp. 129f (e.g., ritual purity (Lev. 21: 11) and bodily integrity (Lev. 21: 17) are highlighted). J.A.T. Robinson (*The Human Face of God* (London, 1973), p. 89) argues that assertions such as Hebrews 7: 26 are in the first instance *theological*, rather than historical judgements: 'for, in order to "do away with sins" he had, according to the sacrificial theory of the day, himself to be spotless, whether as priest or as victim'. However, he later shows how believable is the testimony of Jesus' having 'no trace of the consciousness of sin or guilt' (p. 97).

83 AG *s.v.* χωρίζω 2.c. The following καί would then be understood in the sense of 'also', rather than in the sense of 'even'.

84 F.F. Bruce, p. 157 note 88. Michel (p. 280) notes that the priests of Israel were 'set apart' by men, but our high priest by God himself (cf. Test. Levi 4: 2). However, χωρίζειν is not a technical term for ordination or consecration and cannot be pressed too far in this direction.

85 Michel, p. 281. The statement of Moffatt (p. 101) that Christ is 'no levitical priest in daily contact with (sinners), and therefore obliged to sacrifice repeatedly' obscures the fact that Christ *was* in daily contact with sinners and still did not need to sacrifice for

his own sins because he remained 'without sin'. See also 9: 14 (ἄμωμον) for the cultic—moral perfection of Christ as sacrifice and high priest.

86 The reference to a double sacrifice by the high priests of Judaism on a *daily* basis (7: 27) is a source of much debate. The double sacrifice — 'first for his own sins and then for those of the people' — was certainly the central feature of the great Day of Atonement ritual and our writer knows this to have been a *yearly* event (9: 7, 25; 10: 1, 3). To interpret καθ' ἡμέραν as 'on every day on which he had to offer' (Strack—Billerbeck, vol. III, p. 698) would certainly solve the problem but it is not the most natural reading of that expression. In the Rabbinic tradition, the daily food offering for the high priest (Lev. 6: 19—23) seems to be connected with the *tamid* sacrifice for the people, offered morning and evening (Michel, p. 282). Our author seems to have viewed the double sacrifice of the Day of Atonement as so decisive and important that he has interpreted the daily offerings in connection with it.

87 Buchanan, p. 130.

88 Westcott, p. 199. That is, the analogy with the Aaronic offerings breaks down when one remembers the preceding statements about the sinlessness of Christ (4: 15; 5: 7f; 7: 26).

89 F.F. Bruce, p. 160. This statement is more accurate than Westcott's (p. 199): 'the offering upon the cross was a high-priestly act, though Christ did not become "high priest after the order of Melchizedek", that is, royal high priest till the Ascension'. The latter introduces a distinction into our writer's thinking about the high priesthood that he himself does not make. Christ does not fulfil 'the type of Aaron' (p. 229) by literally carrying out a double sacrifice as on the Day of Atonement but by the offering of an entirely novel sacrifice, with reference to the heavenly sanctuary, in his capacity as high priest after the order of Melchizedek. See Appendix B.

90 In assessing the significance of μετριοπαθεῖν in 5: 2 it was suggested that συμπαθῆσαι in 4: 15 actually implies a more positive ability to help. Thus, despite the fact that Christ was not 'beset with weakness', as human high priests were, his experience as a man in temptation and suffering enabled him to gain perfect understanding of and sympathy with the problem of human weakness. Cf. p. 83 above.

91 Westcott, p. 200, cf. p. 77 above.

92 Michel, p. 284 (*Versuchungen preisgegeben*).

93 Riggenbach, pp. 214f.

94 An incarnational theology similar to John 1: 14 is implied in Hebrews 2: 9, 14, 17 (though not by the use of ἐπιλαμβάνεται in 2: 16, as some have argued) and 10: 5. See also my discussion on the writer's use of Psalm 2 in 1: 5 and 5: 5 (pp. 84ff above).

95 Hofius, *Der Christushymnus*, p. 79 (contra Windisch, pp. 12f). On pp. 93ff he seeks to explain this in terms of OT assertions about God being *king already* (Exod. 15: 18; Psalms 10: 16;

146: 10) and yet *becoming king 'on that day'* (Zech. 14: 9; Obad. 21; Num. 14: 21/Psalm 72: 19).

96 Kögel, p. 64.

97 M. Silva ('Perfection and Eschatology in Hebrews', *Westminster Theological Journal 39* (1976), 63ff) rightly relates the perfecting of Christ in Hebrews to the idea of the Son inheriting the name (1: 4ff) by the fulfilment of his messianic work. However, he inappropriately places the emphasis on 'some type of change *in his human nature*' and relates this to 1 Cor. 15: 45. I have argued that this is not our writer's focus, though he does imply 'two successive stages in (Christ's) human-messianic existence'. See above pp. 70f.

98 Käsemann, p. 86.

99 *Ibid*. p. 85.

100 *Ibid*. p. 86.

101 *Ibid*. p. 143. The virtual identification of *Opfertod* and *Himmelfahrt* is discussed on p. 148.

102 Cody, p. 102.

103 *Ibid*. p. 173. He rightly argues that the resurrection and ascension have to do with what is essentially the same thing when considered from this metaphysical standpoint. Our writer focusses on the ascension because of its suitability in connection with the imagery of the Day of Atonement ritual (p. 174).

104 *Ibid*. p. 176.

105 Assuming that 9: 11f refers to the ascension, which many commentators question. This is discussed below on pp. 143f.

106 *Ibid*. pp. 101f.

107 *Ibid*. p. 103.

108 See above pp. 81f. and Appendix B. Cody (pp. 102f) modifies this traditional Catholic perspective, however, as follows: 'only after his suffering and his perfection, when his priestly human nature has reached the celestial plane of divine power and glory, is he formally proclaimed "high priest after the order of Melchizedek" (5: 8ff), an "eternal" priest, although radically he was priest from the instant of the incarnation'.

109 *Ibid*. p. 97.

110 Davidson, p. 151.

111 Vanhoye, *Structure*, pp. 42ff.

112 *Ibid*. p. 135 note 1.

113 Vanhoye, 'La Structure Centrale de l'Épître aux Hébreux (Héb. 8: 1 – 9: 28)', *Recherches de Science Religieuse* 47 (1959), 44ff.

114 *Ibid*. p. 56.

115 *Ibid*. p. 56 note 10. Vanhoye makes the usual parallel with LXX usage and argues with respect to our writer's application that the connection is 'very close'.

116 Vanhoye, *Situation*, p. 323. Spicq (vol. II, p. 118) notes how this is the perspective of Phil. 2: 9 but goes on to argue that our writer is focussing on Christ's 'qualité de prêtre-sauveur'. L.

Sabourin (*Priesthood: a Comparative Study* (Leiden, 1973) pp. 191f) also argues that the perfecting of Christ is 'the sacrificial transformation of (his) body'. His humanity was 'in the likeness of sinful flesh (Rom. 8: 3)' and 'had to be transformed, to appear before God'. His own sacrifice (9: 23) is said to achieve this transformation for him. However, the introduction of Pauline texts, rather than texts from Hebrews itself, indicates that the line of thought is by no means obvious in the latter. It is really only by way of his own peculiar interpretation of 9: 23f that Sabourin arrives at the conclusion that 'Christ himself underwent a sacrificial purification (τελείωσις) to enter the sanctuary' (p. 204).

117 In his book *Structure* (p. 243), Vanhoye connects the concept with the sacrificial theme of Hebrews: 'the accomplishment to which Christ is subjected is none other than his sacrifice'. The aorist τελειωθείς in 5: 9 'envisages the sanctifying action itself' (p. 245). However, he does not relate this to his remarks on 8: 1– 9: 28. In his book *Situation*, Vanhoye fails to relate his remarks to either the preceding article or his book *Structure* on this subject in a satisfactory way.

6 The perfecting of believers

1 Kögel, *Der Begriff* τελειοῦν, p. 56. He ties this in with the use of Psalm 8 in 2: 5ff. The basis of our writer's use of τελειοῦν lies in his view of God's purpose in salvation, which is the restoration of the image and glory of man. However, it is doubtful that our writer expresses such a full-blown image of God theology and views the perfecting of mankind essentially in terms of glorification.

2 So, Riggenbach *Der Brief an die Hebräer*, (p. 383 note 87) and Delling (*TDNT*, vol. VIII, p. 83 note 29). See my note 202 below.

3 Delling, *TDNT*, vol. VIII, pp. 85f. He takes 2 Chr. 29: 35 to refer to the 'execution' of the peace offerings (τῆς τελειώσεως τοῦ σωτηρίου).

4 The combination θυσίαν ἐγκαινισμοῦ καὶ τῆς τελειώσεως τοῦ ἱεροῦ has suggested to some interpreters a cultic use of τελείωσις, parallel to the sense of ἐγκαινισμός ('dedication', 'consecration'). However, Delling's rendering is more likely (so RSV 'sacrifice for the dedication and completion of the temple'). Compare my discussion on a similar use of the terminology in Patristic literature (p. 45 above).

5 Delling has 'the time of becoming sexually mature' for ἀγάπης τελειώσεώς σου. The parallelism with ἐλεούς νεότητός σου is said to suggest this sense of maturity. Cf. the usage of Aristotle (*Gen. An.* IV.8, p. 776b.1) and Philo (*Leg. All.* I.10 etc.).

6 In Exod. 29: 22, 26, 27, 31, 34; Lev. 7: 37 (LXX 7: 27); 8: 22 (21), 29 (28), we have a reference to the sacrifice associated with the installation of priests and in Lev. 8: 26(25), 31, a reference to

the 'basket of ordination offerings' (ἐν τῷ κανῷ τῆς τελειώσεως). Lev. 8: 33 speaks of ἡμέρα τελειώσεως ὑμῶν and links this clearly with the common use of the verb in this respect. Note Philo's use of this terminology in *Rer. Div. Her.* 251; *Leg. All.* III.130; *Migr. Abr.* 67; *Vit. Mos.* II.149.

7   Delling p. 85. See similarly Du Plessis (p. 229), who deduces from the use of τελείωσις in Hebrews 7: 11, which 'refers us to Levitic ordination', that the perfection envisaged was 'the totality of being in a divine relationship'. M. Dibelius (*Botschaft und Geschichte*, vol. II, p. 168) speaks of *die vollendende Weihe*, which is the qualification for heavenly priestly and sacrificial service (compare Michel, p. 269, especially note 2). Moe ('Der Gedanke des allgemeinen Priestertums', pp. 167f) makes the common assumption that τελειοῦν in Hebrews is to be related to the cultic use of the LXX but significantly says this is not so in 7: 11, 19; 11: 40; 12: 23! Here, however, the thought of priestly approach to God is said to be evident in the context.

8   Against the cultic interpretation of τελειοῦν/τελείωσις in Hebrews see especially Riggenbach, 'τελείωσις', pp. 191f.

9   Cf. the 'actualisation' or 'execution' of a resolve (Philo, *Spec. Leg.* II.9) or of the words of the prophets (*Vit. Mos.* II.288).

10   Michel, p. 269, note 2. He is clearly influenced by the argument of Dibelius here. Compare Buchanan, p. 122.

11   See note 24 to my previous chapter.

12   Kögel, p. 60. He is criticised by Du Plessis (p. 228) for his 'preconceived criterion of a formal concept of perfection applied here as a general principle'. Du Plessis says the cultic sense of τελείωσις/τελειοῦν limits the writer's use of οὐδέν to 'the default of the sacrificial system and the law'. However, this is obvious from the context and not from the alleged cultic sense of the verb, and is recognised by Kögel when he speaks of the regulations that have 'a purpose and task within the divine field of salvation'.

13   Riggenbach, *Der Brief an die Hebräer*, p. 201.

14   Moffatt, p. 98. His reference to 'an adequate forgiveness of sins' cannot be supported from the context but enters into the picture at 9: 9 (cf. 9: 14) and 10: 14 (cf. 10: 15–18).

15   W. Manson, p. 115.

16   Du Plessis, p. 230.

17   See my discussion of ἐγγίζειν on p. 112 and of προσέρχεσθαι on pp. 78f. *Contra* Dey (p. 94) it cannot simply be asserted that 'perfection and access to God are alternative forms of expression, exactly as in Philo'. Those who drew near to God under the Old Covenant were *not* perfected (10: 1). Those who draw near on the basis of Christ's sacrifice *are* perfected (10: 14, cf. 7: 25; 9: 14).

18   As Kögel proposes (pp. 55f). The verb δοξάζειν is not used in Hebrews but the idea of glorification is present in 2: 10 (εἰς δόξαν). See note 1 above.

19   Westcott, p. 189. All his supporting arguments are from Paul,
      not Hebrews.
20   Windisch (p. 66) rightly describes the Law in our writer's thinking
      as 'the sum of sacrificial regulations for the ancient cultic com-
      munity'. See pp. 108f above.
21   Westcott, p. 66.
22   κεφάλαιον can mean 'summary, sum' or 'chief point' (cf. Westcott,
      p. 214).
23   τοιοῦτος ... ἀρχιερεύς in 7: 26 also looks in both directions, as I
      suggest is the case with 8: 1. Moffatt (p. 104) renders the latter:
      'such, I have said, was the ἀρχιερεύς for us and such is the
      ἀρχιερεύς we have – One who is enthroned ἐν τοῖς οὐρανοῖς
      next to God himself'. So also Michel, p. 287. However, Westcott
      (pp. 214f) sees the τοιοῦτον in 8: 1 as totally *prospective* (so
      also Spicq, vol. II, p. 234).
24   Vanhoye, *Structure*, pp. 138ff. Cf. the use of Psalm 110: 1 in
      10: 12–13.
25   Hay, *Glory at the Right Hand: Psalm 110 in Early Christianity*
      (New York, 1973), p. 151.
26   Moffatt, p. 104. So also Westcott, p. 216; Michel, pp. 287f;
      F.F. Bruce, p. 161 note 3. P.E. Hughes (p. 281 note 54) gives
      a brief history of exegesis.
27   P. Andriessen ('Das grössere und vollkommenere Zeit (Hebr.
      9: 11)', *BZ* 15 (1971), pp. 87f) argues for a distinction in 8: 1f
      as well as in 9: 11f. So also Vanhoye, 'Par la tente plus grande et
      plus parfaite ... (Héb. 9: 11)', *Biblica* 46 (1965), p. 4 and L.
      Sabourin, 'Liturge du Sanctuaire et de la Tente véritable', *NTS*
      18 (1971), pp. 87ff. However, each of these writers comes to
      different conclusions as to the theological significance of the
      distinction.
28   P.E. Hughes, p. 289. However, I differ with his argument that no
      distinction is implied in 9: 11f (p. 141). If F.J. Schierse is
      correct (*Verheissung und Heilsvollendung* (Munich, 1955), pp.
      30ff, 40ff), the 'first tent' in 9: 8ff is a symbol of earth and the
      'second tent' a symbol of heaven. This allows him to take the
      τῶν ἀγιῶν of 8: 2 as a reference to the heavenly sanctuary as
      the true 'inner shrine'.
29   Michel (p. 288) argues that the heavenly–earthly contrast in
      Hebrews is 'certainly Hellenistic, but is not philosophically
      meant'. Our writer is controlled by an exegesis of the OT in
      terms of 'original–copy' thinking (note the key word τύπος in
      8: 5 from Exod. 25: 40). R. Bultmann (*TDNT*, vol. I, p. 250)
      shows how ἀληθινός is often used in the same sense as ἀληθής
      in the NT. The latter does not occur in Hebrews, but the former
      is found in 8: 2; 9: 24 and 10: 22. In the first two instances
      the meaning is 'that which truly is' or 'that which is eternal'.
      Cf. H. Bietenhard, *Die himmlische Welt im Urchristentum und
      Spätjudentum* (Tübingen, 1951), pp. 125–30 and 136 note 2.

30 Michaelis, *TDNT*, vol. VIII, p. 376 (and Bultmann in note 29 above). In 9: 1 the Mosaic tabernacle is described as ἅγιον κοσμικόν ('an earthly sanctuary'), and the antonym is clearly ἐπουράνιος (cf. G. Schrenk, *TDNT*, vol. III, p. 278 on κοσμικός).

31 Moffatt, p. 105. H. Schlier (*TDNT*, vol. II, p. 33) also suggests a hendiadys.

32 *Ibid.* p. 106. Cody (pp. 20f) suggests that Wis. 9: 8 affords the best background for understanding the notion of the heavenly sanctuary in Hebrews, where Solomon's temple is said to have been 'a copy of the holy tent' which God prepared 'from the beginning'. However, in Wis. 9: 8 'the earthly sanctuary's being a copy of the heavenly model is something good because it is signed with the heavenly, while for Hebrews the earthly sanctuary's being merely a copy is something unfortunate because it is marked with the sign of the changing and the transitory and must sooner or later pass away'. Thus, Wisdom stays in the Platonic line of thought. Compare Philo, *Leg. All.* III.33; *Vit. Mos.* II.74 (where Philo treats Exod. 25: 40 in a cosmological– philosophical way that is hardly similar to our writer's use in 8: 5).

33 Williamson, *Philo and Hebrews*, p. 557. Compare Michel, p. 289 and Buchanan, p. 134.

34 S. Nomoto, 'Herkunft und Struktur der Hohenpriestervorstellung im Hebräerbrief', *NovT* 10 (1968), pp. 17ff. He argues that the contrast between the earthly and heavenly sanctuaries is not Alexandrian metaphysics, but the author's way of presenting the typological relation between the Old and New Covenants. The terms σκιά, ὑπόδειγμα, παραβολή, ἀντίτυπος, must be understood thus (p. 19).

35 *Ibid.* F. F. Bruce (p. 111) compares 10: 1 (σκιάν ... τῶν μελλόντων ἀγαθῶν) and Col. 2: 17 (σκιὰ τῶν μελλόντων).

36 The LXX τύπος renders MT taḇnit̠ (building or construction), which indicates something more objective than verbal instructions. So F.F. Bruce, p. 165 note 27. Cf. Exod. 25: 9; 26: 30; 27: 8.

37 Moffatt (p. 107) rightly suggests that the passive νενομοθέτηται implies that 'God is ὁ νομοθετῶν (as in LXX Psalm 83: 7).'

38 Vanhoye, *Structure*, pp. 143f. Similarly Westcott, p. 221. However, Moffatt (p. 108) stresses rather less convincingly the positive function of the citation at this point.

39 I have discussed this in some detail in 'The Prophecy of the New Covenant in the Argument of Hebrews', *RTR* 38 (1979), 74–81. Moffatt (p. 112) rightly observes that the stress on worship and priesthood in 9: 1ff is actually outside the purview of Jer. 31: 31ff. 'The writer takes a special view of διαθήκη which involves a celestial counterpart to the ritual provisions of the old order.' However, the link between the themes is particularly provided in 10: 15–18, where the *forgiveness* that is basic to the New Covenant is shown to be the achievement of Christ as high priest.

40 Vanhoye, *Structure*, p. 145. He notes how δικαιώματα is used

only in 9: 1, 10 and how κατασκευάζειν in 9: 2, 6 'marks the
limits of the description of the temple (9: 2–5)'. Note how he
establishes that 8: 3–5 and 9: 1–10 are complementary (p. 146).

41 H. Sasse, *TDNT*, vol. III, p. 897 ('the earthly sanctuary'). This
terminology does not reflect the view that the Tabernacle was a
symbol of the world (Josephus, *War* IV.324; Philo, *Spec. Leg.*
I.66; *Vit. Mos.* II.77ff). Our writer views the OT sanctuary as
taking its pattern from the *heavenly* original, not from the
creation (Michel, p. 298).

42 Riggenbach, p. 238. Michaelis (*TDNT*, vol. VII, p. 376), discusses
the unusual use of πρώτη in 9: 2 in a *spatial sense* ('the front
tent'). O. Hofius ('Das "erste" und das "zweite" Zelt. Ein Beitrag
zur Auslegung von Hebr. 9: 1–10', *ZNW* 61 (1970), pp. 274ff),
points to the interesting linguistic parallels in Josephus (*War* V),
where the whole temple area is called τὸ ἱερόν (184, 186), but the
inner sanctuary for the Jews alone is called τὸ δεύτερον ἱερόν
(193f), and the area for the Gentiles ἀπὸ τοῦ πρώτου (*sc.* ἱεροῦ
195). A similar spatial use of πρῶτος and δεύτερος is found in
War V.208f, with respect to οἶκος.

43 Westcott, p. 252.

44 The reference here is not simply to the Holy Spirit's inspiration
of the text of the OT (P.E. Hughes, p. 321). The writer is claiming
special insight from the Spirit into the meaning and purpose of
the law's provisions, which comes in the light of the fulfilment in
Christ and was not previously available to Jewish readers of the
OT (Michel, p. 306).

45 Ἐχούσης στάσιν means more than 'being in existence' (so Moffatt,
p. 118). Westcott (p. 254), suggests that this means 'while the first
tabernacle still has an appropriate place answering to the divine
order'. F.F. Bruce (p. 192 note 48), similarly speaks in terms of
the 'sanctuary status' of the first tent in the divine economy.

46 So Buchanan, pp. 144f; Riggenbach, p. 249; Moffatt, p. 118 and
Hofius, 'Das "erste" und das "zweite"', p. 276 (especially his
note 28). Hofius goes on to conclude that the first tent is 'a
parable or symbol of the old age'.

47 F.F. Bruce, pp. 194f; P.E. Hughes, pp. 322f. Schierse (*Verheissung*,
pp. 30ff), takes the first tent as symbolic of 'the earthly world'
and the second tent of the 'heavenly sanctuary'. However, since
our writer's basic contrast is between the two covenants and the
'ages' which they represent, it is best to express the symbolism of
the verse as suggested above.

48 Spicq, vol. II, p. 254. See on 8: 2 above (pp. 130f), where τῶν
ἀγίων seems to be equivalent to τῶς σκηνῆς τῆς ἀληθινῆς.

49 The ἥτις of verse 9 may refer to the whole situation described in
verses 6–8, in which case, the ἥτις is 'attracted to the gender and
number of παραβολή' (F.F. Bruce, p. 195 note 60). However, if
the ἥτις relates specifically to the πρώτη σκηνή of verse 8
(Moffatt, p. 118), the meaning is simply that the first tent
symbolises the whole Tabernacle/temple system as a barrier to
true fellowship with God.

50 Michel, p. 307. Käsemann (p. 30 note 6), relates the establish-
    ment of this new order of salvation to the enthronement of the
    Redeemer. Both Michel and Westcott (pp. 254f), relate the
    'present age' and the 'age of reformation' to the doctrine of the
    two ages and stress the overlap that Christians experience.

51 W. Manson, pp. 132f. If the readers were 'a Jewish–Christian
    group who, for one reason or another, were opposing the ritual
    freedom of the larger Church', it can be seen how apposite our
    writer's warning would have been. Adherence to the 'first sanc-
    tuary' prevents a realisation of the benefits of Christ's work and
    true access to God.

52 The καθ' ἥν of verse 9 will relate back to the πρώτης σκηνῆς of
    verse 8.

53 Michel, p. 308; H. Strathmann, *TDNT*, vol. IV, pp. 63f; G. Delling,
    TDNT, vol. VIII, p. 83 note 22 and Du Plessis, p. 231. Michel is
    particularly inconsistent with respect to 10: 2, since he acknowl-
    edges that the τοὺς προσερχομένους of 10: 1 refers to the 'wider
    circle of the members of the congregation, for whom the sacrifice
    is meant' (pp. 331f).

54 H. Strathmann, *TDNT*, vol. IV, p. 63.

55 The modified application of λατρεύειν in 9: 14 and 12: 28 shows
    that the writer was not consistent in his use of the verb. The
    contrast in 9: 13f indicates that the New Covenant has achieved
    that cleansing of the conscience that *all* the worshippers lacked
    under the former system and that all sought through its rituals
    (10: 1f).

56 C. Maurer, *TDNT*, vol. VII, pp. 900ff and C. A. Pierce, *Conscience
    in the New Testament* (London, 1955), pp. 13ff.

57 Maurer, *TDNT*, vol. VII, p. 904. Even after the 1st century BC,
    when the nouns are established in this sense, the continuing non-
    moral application of συνείδησις in particular reminds us that the
    moral sense arose only secondarily in the history of the term.

58 Pierce, *Conscience in the NT*, p. 60. See his pp. 54–9 for LXX
    usage.

59 Maurer, *TDNT*, vol. VII, pp. 908ff.

60 *Ibid.* p. 917. See the whole section pp. 914–17 and M. E. Thrall,
    'The Pauline Use of ΣΥΝΕΙΔΗΣΙΣ', *NTS* 14 (1967–8), 118–25.

61 Συνείδησις occurs seven times in 1 Cor. 8–10 but not at all in the
    parallel argument of Rom. 14, suggesting that the concept of
    conscience was particularly used in dealing with the Corinthians
    because it was already a term used by them, perhaps in their
    communications with Paul.

62 E. Jacob, *TDNT*, vol. IX, pp. 626f. Cf. F. Baumgärtel, *TDNT*,
    vol. III, pp. 606f.

63 Westcott, p. 324. Cf. Spicq, vol. II, p. 317 and Isa. 38: 3 (*lēb
    šālēm*); Test. Dan 5: 3.

64 G. von Rad, *Old Testament Theology* (ET London, 1965), vol.
    II, pp. 213ff notes that 'this is Jeremiah's way of speaking of a
    future outpouring of God's Spirit, for what he thinks of is nothing

other than the spiritual knowledge and observance of the will of God'. See further my article 'The Prophecy of the New Covenant in the Argument of Hebrews', *RTR* 38 (1979), 74–81.

65 Although we may take συνείδησις in the cognitive sense of 'consciousness of sins' in 10: 2, it should be translated 'conscience' elsewhere in Hebrews (*contra* Du Plessis, p. 231). So Michel, p. 332 note 4.

66 Michel, p. 308. Maurer, p. 902, argues that in extra-Biblical usage 'neither in a philosophical nor a moral sense has conscience a great deal to do with the deity'. However, OT teaching about man's responsibility to God and the need for a clean heart in relation to God prepares the way for NT usage of συνείδησις (pp. 908f).

67 Against Pierce (p. 102f), the καλή συνείδησις of 13: 18 is not simply the joy experienced from *no pain* of conscience. There are certain things known to be pleasing to God (e.g., 13: 15f), and even the desire to act accordingly ('desiring to act honourably in all things', 13: 18), can give one the joyful sense of being responsive to God's will. The sense of ultimate accountability to God (e.g., 9: 27; 12: 28f; 13: 17), is a safeguard against self-righteousness and self-deception (as in 1 Cor. 4: 4f). The request for prayer in 13: 18 is similar to Paul's in 2 Cor. 1: 11f. The good conscience is 'a particular form of protection against evil slander' (Michel, p. 332 note 4).

68 Cf. AG *s.v.* κατά II.6. Schierse (*Verheissung*, p. 152) rightly points out that καθαρίζειν has a basically negative sense ('removal of the filth of sin'), but that this enables positive consecration to God (9: 14; 10: 19ff). However, his attempt to read τελειοῦν in 9: 9 eschatologically is inappropriate: the purified conscience is said to be perfected because it 'really reflects again an eschatologically-oriented frame of mind, the free access to God' (p. 156). Such exegesis pays scant regard to the syntax of the verse and the function of τελειοῦν within it.

69 Michel, p. 308. However, I dispute his simplistic identification of τελειοῦν in 9: 9 and καθαρίζειν in 9: 14 (p. 333 note 4). The true parallel to the idea of man being perfected κατὰ συνείδησιν (verse 9), is to be found in the full statement of verse 14: the conscience must be cleansed in order that one might serve God effectively. The concept of perfection refers to the whole process by which a person is thus consecrated to God.

70 Vanhoye (*Structure*, pp. 147ff), shows how 'blood' is only employed once in the previous section (9: 7) but many times in 9: 11–28 (9: 12 (twice), 13, 14, 18, 20, 21, 22, 25). The concept of Christ's self-offerings is found in 9: 14, 25, 28 and necessarily involves the shedding of his blood. In contrast with Spicq's suggestion (vol. II, p. 247), of a 'rigorous parallelism' between 9: 11–14 and 9: 1–10, Vanhoye argues for an antithetical parallelism.

71 Γενομένων (B, D*, 1739, it^[d,e], syr^[p,h,pal], Origen, Cyril–Jerus.,

Chrys[gr,lat], p. 46 γεναμένων), appears to have 'a superior attestation on the score of age and diversity of text type' to μελλόντων (Aleph, A, D[c], I[vid], K, P, many minuscules, it, vg, syr, cop, arm, eth, and many fathers), and the latter is best explained as appearing under the influence of 10: 1. So B.M. Metzger *et al.*, p. 668 and Zahn; Westcott; F.F. Bruce; Buchanan. Compare J.M. Boyer, *Biblica* 32 (1951), 232–6. Michel (p. 310), and Moffatt (p. 120), argue to the contrary. However, compare Michel, p. 331.

72 J. Denney, *The Death of Christ* (London, 1951), p. 131.

73 RSV '*taking* not the blood' is unwarranted. In Westcott's words, the διά is to be understood 'as marking the means but not defining the mode (μετά)' (pp. 260f). Cf. Moffatt, p. 121 note 1 and F.F. Bruce, pp. 200f.

74 Westcott, p. 261.

75 Michel, pp. 312f.

76 There are no grounds for a distinction between λύτρωσις (9: 15) and ἀπολύτρωσις (9: 12), in the NT. The latter is used in 11: 35 in the more literal sense of liberation and in 9: 15 in the modified sense of cancellation or remission. F. Büchsel (*TDNT*, vol. IV, pp. 352ff), and Buchanan, p. 148, give OT background.

77 Spicq, vol. II, pp. 256ff.

78 Michel (p. 313 note 1), presents evidence linking the two rituals in later Jewish tradition, but our writer may have made the connection spontaneously. The ritual of the red heifer illustrates most aptly the external nature of the sanctification provided by the old cult. Contrast P.E. Hughes (pp. 362–4), on the purpose of the reference here.

79 E. Schweizer (*TDNT*, vol. VII, p. 142), suggests that this phrase in 9: 10 means 'statutes of the earthly sphere'. The δικαιώματα of 9: 1 are 'related to the sanctuary in the κόσμος in contrast to that not made with hands 9: 11, 24 ... Purity of conscience is found only in the priest of the temple not made with hands, which does not belong to this creation.'

80 Although Hebrews asserts that 'under the law almost everything is purified with blood' and 'without the shedding of blood there is no forgiveness of sins' (9: 22), it would seem from 9: 15 that the writer viewed forgiveness under the Old Covenant as coming from the death of Christ. Thus, the animal sacrifices operated in a parabolic or sacramental fashion, pointing to the reality that was to come with the death of Christ. However, the unsatisfactory nature of this method of approaching God is well illustrated in 10: 1–4.

81 Michel, p. 314 (my emphasis). Westcott's interpretation of blood as the symbol of 'a life made available for others' (p. 263 and pp. 295ff), is particularly inappropriate in this context. See L. Morris, 'The Biblical Use of the Term "Blood"', *JTS* 3 (n.s. 1952), 216ff, and J. Behm, *TDNT*, vol. I, pp. 172ff.

82 Ἄμωμος becomes a technical term in the LXX for the cultic (physical) perfection required in animal sacrifices (e.g., Exod. 29:

2 for *tāmîm*, Lev. 1: 3; 4: 3). It is also used to render *tāmîm* in the sense of 'religious and moral blamelessness' (LXX Psalms 14: 2; 36: 18; Prov. 11: 5; 20: 7). In 1 Pet. 1: 19 and Hebrews 9: 14 both senses are implied, though there is no suggestion of physical perfection *per se*: Christ is the perfect sacrifice because he is morally blameless (4: 15; 7: 26). Cf. F. Hauck, *TDNT*, vol. IV, pp. 830f.

83 Moffatt, p. 124 (my emphasis). Cf. Riggenbach, pp. 264ff. For a history of exegesis see J.J. McGrath, *'Through the Eternal Spirit'. An Historical Study of the Exegesis of Hebrews 9: 13–14* (Rome, 1961).

84 Cody, pp. 103ff. Cf. Westcott, pp. 236f and Spicq, vol. II, pp. 258f.

85 So Michel, p. 314. Early copyists saw this possibility and rendered the text διὰ πνεύματος ἁγίου (Aleph^c, D*, P etc. with lat, cop). However, this is clearly a secondary reading. The anarthrous πνεύματος ἁγίου is found in 2: 4 and 6: 4, and in 10: 29 the Holy Spirit is characterised as τὸ πνεῦμα τῆς χάριτος.

86 F.F. Bruce, pp. 205f (and p. 223 notes 169–72). In Isa. 42: 1 the Servant is empowered for his ministry by the divine Spirit. P.E. Hughes (pp. 385f) says there is 'nothing inappropriate' in this sort of explanation, but prefers the line proposed by Moffatt.

87 NEB reads ἡμῶν but RSV ὑμῶν here. Metzger *et al.* (p. 668), argue that the external evidence for the two readings is rather evenly balanced, but prefer the former because 'the author uses the direct address only in the hortatory sections of his Epistle'. However, since the writer turns here from general exposition to particular application of the work of Christ to the experience of believers, the latter seems just as likely.

88 Moffatt, p. 74. Cf. Eph. 2: 1 ('dead in trespasses and sins'), and the Jewish teaching on the 'way of life' and the 'way of death' (Test. Jud. 20: 1–5; Test. Ash. 1: 3 – 6: 6; 1QS 3: 18 – 4: 26; Didache 1: 1 – 5: 2; Barnabas 18: 1 – 20: 2).

89 *Ibid.* Cf. Michel, p. 308. No allusion to the defilement resulting from contact with a dead body (from which sprinkling with the heifer's ashes effected purification 9: 13), can be supposed at 6: 1f, and it is extremely doubtful at 9: 15 (so P.E. Hughes, p. 361).

90 Westcott (p. 146), says: 'all the works corresponding with the Levitical system, not in their original institution but in their actual relation to the Gospel as established in the Christian society' have been made 'dead works' by the work of Christ. This statement is generally true to our writer's message, but unlikely to have been the meaning here. These 'works' are not such as would give a person a guilty conscience. The levitical system did not provide for the cleansing of the conscience (9: 9f), and really accentuated the problem with the reminder of sin (10: 1–3). But nowhere does the writer imply that the system itself was the *cause* of guilty consciences. A similar criticism could be levelled at the interpretation of R.V.G. Tasker (*The Gospel in the Epistle to the*

Hebrews[2] (London, 1956), p. 21), who speaks of 'repentance from dead works' as 'an abandonment of the attempt to obtain righteousness by seeking to obey the precepts of a lifeless moral code'.

91 Du Plessis, p. 231.

92 H. Strathmann, *TDNT*, vol. IV, p. 64.

93 Pierce, *Conscience in the NT*, pp. 101f. G. Harder (*TDNT*, vol. VI, p. 557 note 72), observes: 'a bad conscience is one which is thus injurious to sincerity in prayer and the spirit of truth' (*Barnabas* XIX.12; *Didache* IV.14; Hermas, *Mandate* III.4).

94 See below pp. 154–6 and pp. 78–81 above.

95 H. Strathmann, *TDNT*, vol. IV, p. 64. He makes the helpful observation that the exhortation to offer to God 'acceptable worship' serves as a transition to the admonitory section in chapter 13. Cf. the use of $\lambda\alpha\tau\rho\epsilon\acute{u}\epsilon\iota\nu$ in Lk. 1: 74; Acts 24: 14; 27: 23; 2 Tim. 1: 3; Rom. 1: 9; Phil. 3: 3.

96 In 13: 15 the 'sacrifice of praise' that Christians are to offer to God through Jesus is further defined in language borrowed from Hosea 14: 2 LXX – it is 'the tribute of lips which acknowledge his name' (NEB). This could clearly have reference to the celebration of God's character in personal or corporate acts of praise. The words could even have special relevance to 'worship of a eucharistic kind' (Snell, p. 161). However, our writer's meaning cannot be restricted to Christian cultic activity. The use of $\acute{o}\mu o\lambda o\gamma \epsilon\~i\nu$ here undoubtedly includes the concept of confessing Christ before the world, either in words or deeds (cf. Matt. 10: 32 par; John 9: 22; 12: 42; Rom. 10: 9f; 1 Tim. 1: 16; Titus 1: 16).

97 My translation, following Vanhoye, 'Par la tente plus grande et plus parfaite ... (Héb. 9: 11)', *Biblica* 46 (1965), 2. Compare L. Sabourin 'Liturge du Sanctuaire et de la Tente véritable (Héb. 8: 2)', *NTS* 18 (1971–2), 86.

98 See NEB translation. Montefiore (p. 153), argues for an identification of the 'tent' and the 'sanctuary' here, as does P.E. Hughes (pp. 289f, originally in *Bibliotheca Sacra* (1973), vol. CXXX, no. 520, pp. 305–14). Hughes rightly argues for a hendiadys in 8: 2 but proposes that the sanctuary into which Christ has entered in 9: 12 is 'the same as that tent which is described as "true" and "greater and more perfect" '. However, even the linguistic correspondence with 9: 24 is insufficient to override the fact that the 'greater and more perfect tent' and 'his own blood' are the *means* ($\delta\iota\acute{\alpha}$ + genitive), by which Christ enters the sanctuary. The interpreter's desire for consistency should not take precedence over his concern for grammatical and syntactical accuracy in the immediate context.

99 The $\sigma\kappa\eta\nu\acute{\eta}$ of 9: 11 is thus compared with the nearest use of $\sigma\kappa\eta\nu\acute{\eta}$ in verse 8 with the words 'greater and more perfect, not made with hands, that is, not of this creation'. The 'first tent' of the earthly Tabernacle has a heavenly or eschatological parallel as the way or means of entry into the sanctuary of God.

100 See P.E. Hughes (pp. 283ff), for a helpful survey and critique of these views. Cody (pp. 164f), gives modified support to the Patristic line of exegesis: the σκηνή of 9: 11 is 'not exactly to be equated with the body of Christ or the humanity of Christ, but it is a figure primarily of the humanity of Christ as an instrument in the work of salvation (διά instrumental), and secondarily of the entire span of Christ's saving passage through the earthly plane (διά local), and on into heaven'. Schierse (*Verheissung*, p. 57), similarly speaks of the whole span of Christ's life from his entrance into the world (10: 5), to his exaltation (10: 12), as an 'ascending way' into the heavenly sanctuary.

101 Vanhoye, 'Par la tente plus grande', p. 12.

102 *Ibid.* pp. 21f. J. Swetnam (*Biblica* 47 (1966), 91–106), develops this to include the idea of the 'eucharistic body' of Christ!

103 Vanhoye, 'Par la tente plus grande', p. 26. On the relationship between the 'tent' and 'the sanctuary' he says: Christ 'does not leave the tent to arrive in the presence of God, the greater tent being the mode under which his human nature is introduced properly into the divine sanctuary'.

104 See above pp. 131f.

105 Cody, pp. 172ff. Resurrection and ascension are 'a continuous movement from the nadir of the tomb to the zenith of the celestial world'. If Hebrews emphasises the second rather than the first, it is because 'in the Epistle's typological exposition Our Lord's crossing over into the new, spiritual, divine world of ultimate reality fits very well into the type-complex of the Day of Atonement's sin-expiating ritual, while the Resurrection from the dead does not'. Cf. Windisch, p. 79.

106 See below on 10: 19f (pp. 153f).

107 Sabourin, 'Liturge du Sanctuaire', p. 88. He develops his interpretation of 9: 11f in *Priesthood: a Comparative Study* (Leiden, 1973), pp. 198ff. There he offers further criticisms of Vanhoye's position. However, to say that 'in the new liturgy the passage (to the Holy of Holies), takes place in the sacrifice itself' (p. 202), is to obscure the significance of the ascension in our writer's use of the imagery of the Day of Atonement ritual. See Michel (p. 309), and note 105 above. We must not make an artificial division between the death and exaltation of Christ in terms of his redemptive achievement, though the Gospel records speak of a temporal separation between these events.

108 Westcott, p. 260. Cf. Cornelius à Lapide, cited by P.E. Hughes (p. 286).

109 P.E. Hughes, p. 287. He also rightly notes how the metaphor of the 'tent for the body' becomes the basis for another metaphor, the 'body for the church', in this sort of interpretation. This gives the exegesis 'a distinctly mystical quality'. It proposes a cryptic use of language that is totally out of character for our writer.

110 Moffatt, p. 120. Cf. Spicq, vol. II, p. 256; Héring, p. 84; Michel, pp. 310ff.

111 The theory is dismissed along these lines by P.E. Hughes (p. 289), and Vanhoye, 'Par la tente plus grande', pp. 7ff.

112 Michel, pp. 311f. On p. 205 he describes the expression in 4: 14 as 'a summary term for ascension, which comes from Apocalyptic and Gnosis', indicating 'the different layers of supernatural spheres which are situated between God and man, the holy place and earth'. Cody (pp. 77ff), distinguishes 'cosmological', 'axiological' and 'eschatological' uses of the terminology in Hebrews, but does not recognise Michel's two levels in the axiological usage.

113 So Andriessen ('Das grössere und vollkommenere Zelt (Hebr. 9: 11)', *BZ* 15 (1971), 84f), who shows a counterpart in Rabbinic thinking. Michel (p. 312), argues that Apocalyptic and Gnostic writers speak also of 'transcendental but spatially delimited areas beyond the cosmos'. For the OT background see L.I.J. Stadelmann, *The Hebrew Concept of the World*, Analecta Biblica 39 (Rome, 1970), pp. 49–52.

114 So Vanhoye, 'Par la tente plus grande', p. 10 note 1.

115 Michel, p. 309. Cf. Käsemann, pp. 146–56 and John 3: 14; 12: 23; 13: 31f.

116 Andriessen proposes that Christ's passage through this 'heaven of the angels' (pp. 84f) shows that he is exalted above the angels as unique mediator between God and man (pp. 89f), that he thus becomes 'the greatest officiant of the whole tent' (p. 90) and has made a *Kultraum* for his 'brothers' (p. 91). Our writer is not using the ascension theme here to assert Christ's triumph over evil spirits (1 Pet. 3: 22 cf. verses 18ff), but simply continuing the emphasis of 1: 4–13 on Christ's superiority to the angels. Yet, it must be admitted that such an allusion is only possible here, given a common understanding of the heavenlies on the part of writer and readers.

117 Kögel (p. 55) relates the use of the term here to our writer's general and ongoing comparison between the covenants and their spheres of influence.

118 Michel, p. 311.

119 Vanhoye (*Structure*, p. 170) clearly shows the concentric symmetry of 10: 1–18. While his arguments in favour of linking verse 4 with the following verses, rather than with verses 1–3, have some merit, it seems more natural, with most commentators and versions, to see verse 4 as a conclusion to verses 1–3.

120 The substitution of καί for οὐκ αὐτήν in p. 46 cannot be original, because 'the constitution of the sentence implies a contrast between εἰκών and σκιά ' (Metzger *et al.*, p. 669). Cf. F.F. Bruce, p. 255 note 1. *Contra* F. Sen, *Cultura Biblica* 23 (1967), 165–8, following R. Cantalamessa, *Aegyptus* 45 (1965), 194–215. NEB seems to be less effective than RSV in bringing out the contrast between σκιάν and οὐκ αὐτὴν τὴν εἰκόνα.

121 W. Manson, p. 184. Cf. F.F. Bruce, p. 226; S. Schulz, *TDNT*, vol. VII, p. 398; and Michel, p. 330. *Contra* Moffatt, p. 135; Spicq, vol. I, p. 75, vol. II, pp. 301f.

122 H. Kleinknecht, *TDNT*, vol. II, pp. 388f. G. Kittel (*TDNT*, vol. II, p. 395) says 'all the emphasis is on the equality of the εἰκών with the original' in the usage of 2 Cor. 4: 4; Col. 1: 15 (εἰκών τοῦ θεοῦ). Indeed, 'in the NT the original is always present in the image. What is depicted here is given visible manifestation.' Thus, in Hebrews 10: 1, 'the Law deals only with the σκιά and not with the essence of things'.

123 Against Westcott (p. 307), who takes τῶν πραγμάτων as expressing τὰ μέλλοντα ἀγαθά 'so far as they were embodied' and Moffatt (p. 135), who says the two expressions in 10: 1*a* are equivalent, but inappropriately takes them to mean 'the boons and blessings still to be realized in their fulness for Christians, being thought of from the standpoint of the new διαθήκη, not of the Law' (so also Montefiore, p. 164).

124 Michel, p. 331. Cf. Schierse, pp. 44f.

125 Although the plural δύνανται is strongly attested (Aleph, A, C, D^b, P, 33, 81 etc.), 'it appears to have been introduced by copyists who were influenced by προσφέρουσιν ' (Metzger *et al.*, p. 669). The plural reading would make our author guilty of 'a hanging nominative at the beginning of the sentence, whereas he is usually careful to observe grammatical accuracy'. (F.F. Bruce, p. 225 note 2).

126 Against H. Strathmann (*TDNT*, vol. IV, pp. 63f), who argues that λατρεύειν must be a technical term for priestly ministry here, on the basis of 8: 5 and 13: 10. See my argument on p. 134 above.

127 Michel, pp. 331f; Delitzsch, p. 450; Riggenbach, p. 297 and Westcott, p. 307. *Contra* Delling (*TDNT*, vol. VIII, p. 83), who says the OT cultus 'could not "qualify" the priest "for cultic ministry" (10: 1)', taking both προσέρχεσθαι and τελειῶσαι as technical terms, relating to priestly ministry.

128 A number of commentators argue that the κατ' ἐνιαυτόν and εἰς τὸ διηνεκές are 'placed (irregularly) at the head of the clause to which they belong in order to bring out the conceptions of "yearly repetition" and "perpetuity" of effect, which respectively characterise the old and new covenants' (Westcott, p. 305. Compare Montefiore, p. 164; Michel, p. 331 and most German commentators). So NEB 'it can never bring the worshippers to perfection for all time'. The use of εἰς τὸ διηνεκές in 10: 12, 14, stressing the permanency of result is evidence in favour of this view (cf. 7: 3). However, the position of εἰς τὸ διηνεκές immediately after προσφέρουσιν suggests that it is more likely to be related to this verb. In which case, the expression takes on the meaning 'continually', and with κατ' ἐνιαυτόν ('yearly') gives *double emphasis* to the futility of the yearly ritual of the Day of Atonement: the law 'can never, by the same sacrifices which are continually offered year after year, make perfect those who draw near' (RSV). Although our writer speaks in general terms in 5: 1 and 9: 9 (which is the closest parallel to 10: 1), the expression ἐν αὐταῖς ἀνάμνησις ἁμαρτιῶν κατ'ἐνιαυτόν (10: 3)

most naturally suggests the annual Day of Atonement, not the yearly round of sacrifices. So Michel, p. 331 and Riggenbach, p. 295. *Contra* Westcott, p. 307 and Spicq vol. II, p. 302.

129 Pierce, *Conscience in the NT*, pp. 101f. C. Maurer (*TDNT*, vol. VII, p. 918) takes συνείδησις in the cognitive sense here ('knowledge of sins'). H.K. LaRondelle (*Perfection and Perfectionism* (Kampen, 1971), pp. 240ff) warns against the danger of understanding this as 'mere intellectual or moral reflection'. Our writer has in mind the Hebrew sense of a burdened, smiting heart or haunting guilt consciousness, 'which became most pronounced on the Day of Atonement' (p. 241).

130 J. Behm, *TDNT*, vol. I, pp. 348f. Moffatt (p. 137) suggests that 'public notice had to be taken of such sins ("commemoratio" Vg.)', and notes a possible echo of Num. 5: 15, quoted by Philo to illustrate his statement that the sacrifices of the wicked simply serve to recall their misdeeds. However, the resemblance is 'more apparent than real' (P.E. Hughes, p. 392, esp. note 53) and our writer's estimate of the effectiveness of Jewish sacrifices 'is wholly opposed to the Jewish view in spite of Num. 5: 15 and Philo' (Behm).

131 Cf. 10: 11 (περιελεῖν ἁμαρτίας). Cf. Spicq, vol. II, p. 304. R.A. Stewart (*Rabbinical Theology* (Edinburgh, 1961), pp. 120ff) points out that many pious Jews in the closing years of the Second Temple, while paying lip-service to the sacrificial cult, realised that this was not the means by which sin could be removed (cf. Jubilees 34: 19). Cf. Michel, p. 334 note 2 for a good summary of Philo's views on this issue. Nevertheless, Hebrews 10: 4 goes beyond anything that a contemporary Jew would have said (even those in the Qumran community – F.F. Bruce, p. 196 note 63). It is an understanding that comes to our writer as a consequence of his teaching on the sacrifice of Christ.

132 Despite the fact that Aleph, B, A etc. have σῶμα, the Rahlfs edition of the LXX surprisingly reads ὠτία (with G, following MT). Rather than arguing that the reading σῶμα is a corruption of an original ὠτία (Moffatt, p. 138), it is better to see here a free interpretation of the Hebrew: 'the "body" is the instrument for fulfilling the divine command, just as the "ear" is the instrument for receiving it' (Westcott, p. 310). Thus, we may suppose that the Greek translators regarded the wording of the Hebrew as an example of *pars pro toto* and rendered the text 'in terms which express *totum pro parte*' (F.F. Bruce, p. 232). Cf. P.E. Hughes p. 396 (esp. note 58).

133 F.F. Bruce, p. 234. Compare Montefiore, p. 166. Westcott (p. 311) will not confine these words to the moment of the incarnation, 'though they found their complete fulfilment then', but applies them 'to each manifestation of Christ in the realm of human life'. However, our writer offers no evidence for such successive manifestations – it is not his way of thinking. Snell (p. 123) takes the first part of the citation as an utterance of the

pre-incarnate Christ through the Psalmist: only after God had
made plain that the former system could not implement his will
(τότε) could Christ deliberately accept 'his vocation to become
incarnate in the body prepared for him'. However, this interpretation tends to exaggerate the significance of the contrast in the
citation and ignores the fact that it is all placed into the mouth
of Christ 'coming into the world'.

134 So Westcott, p. 311; Spicq, vol. II, p. 304; Hughes, p. 397 (esp.
note 60).

135 W. Manson, pp. 144f.

136 See Spicq (vol. II, p. 306) for a list of the various interpretations
that have been given to this expression (cf. Hughes, p. 397 note
61). It seems best to take βιβλίου as a genitive of definition −
'the book in scroll-form' or 'the scroll of writing' − and the
κεφαλίς (meaning the knob at the top of the stick around which
the scroll was rolled) as a metonymy for the scroll itself (so
F.F. Bruce, p. 234 note 44).

137 Westcott, p. 315. Although most commentators and EVV take
the ἐν as *instrumental* here, Westcott understands it to imply
that Christians are 'included in the Father's will, which Christ
fulfilled'. This may be implied in 2: 9ff, but goes beyond the
plain meaning of 10: 10.

138 Spicq, vol. II, p. 306 and Hughes, p. 399. *Contra* Westcott,
p. 314; Michel, p. 339 and G. Stählin, *TDNT*, vol. I, p. 384.

139 In 7: 27, the contrast is between Christ's self-offering (ἐφάπαξ)
and the continual sacrifices of Jewish high priests. In 9: 12,
Christ's ἐφάπαξ entrance into the heavenly sanctuary is διὰ δὲ
τοῦ ἰδίου αἵματος (compare the use of ἅπαξ in 9: 25ff, where
suffering, sacrifice, death and offering are parallel concepts). If
ἐφάπαξ in 10: 10 is taken as referring both to the death of
Christ and to its effects, Stählin is to be followed (*TDNT*, vol. I,
p. 384).

140 Denney, *The Death of Christ*, pp. 131f.

141 However, the κατ' ἐνιαυτόν of 10: 1 is more likely to refer to
the annual Day of Atonement ritual than to the yearly cycle of
daily sacrifices mentioned here. See note 128 above.

142 So Westcott (p. 316) and F.F. Bruce (p. 237 note 57) relate
εἰς τὸ διηνεκές to προσενέγκας, which seems more natural
than relating it to ἐκάθισεν and reading it as the beginning of
the next clause, as do Moffatt (p. 140) and Michel (p. 340).

143 Michel, p. 340. He compares the 'rest' of God at the completion
of his creative activity (4: 4). Hay (*Glory at the Right Hand*,
pp. 87f) has argued that attention in 10: 12 is 'centred not on
where Jesus sits but simply on the fact that he sits'. The
expression τὸ λοιπὸν ἐκδεχόμενος (10: 13) suggests to Hay that
our writer, like Paul in I Cor. 15: 25, finds in Psalm 110: 1 'a text
for the period between Jesus' resurrection and his final return.
Yet he describes Christ not as actively subduing his foes but as
sitting motionless.' Hay concludes that it is a serious mistake to

claim that early Christian references to Psalm 110: 1 regularly express convictions about Christ reigning as royal lord in the present era (p. 91, pp. 125f). However, Hay's interpretation is too narrowly literalistic. The fact that Jesus sits in the presence of God, in the royal seat, is an important basis for assuring the readers that they have access to God (4: 14–16; 7: 25; 10: 19ff). No Aaronic priest ever sat down in the presence of God in the earthly sanctuary, but Christ has done so in the heavenly sanctuary, and that at God's right hand. Even though it is as a seated priest-king, and not as a suppliant, that Christ appears in Hebrews, we are not left with the image of someone sitting motionless. The activity of Christ in 'upholding all things by his powerful word' (1: 3) finds its parallel in salvific terms in 7: 25, where the image is that of Christ acting to bring men into a proper relationship with God. Psalm 110 itself speaks of the Lord sending forth from Zion the king's 'mighty sceptre' with the challenge to 'rule in the midst of your foes' (verse 2). God's subjection of the king's enemies is *coextensive* with the king's exercise of his sovereign rights. Christ's rule is exercised in the present age through the Gospel, by virtue of his sacrifice, as many of his 'enemies' are thus brought into subjection. The final victory occurs with the judgement of those who fail to respond to his gracious offer in the present (9: 27f; 10: 26–31; 13: 4).

144 Hay, *Glory at the Right Hand*, p. 152. 'The author comes closer here than anywhere else in his epistle to exhibiting death and heavenly session as a single theological event.'

145 Westcott, p. 317. Du Plessis (p. 232) argues that τετελείωκεν εἰς τὸ διηνεκές indicates that the work of Christ is 'qualitatively and quantitatively wholly efficacious'.

146 Westcott's attempt to distinguish θυσία (10: 12; 9: 26) and προσφορά (10: 10, 14, 18) — making the latter a reference to 'his perfect life crowned by a willing death' (p. 317) — is artificial. Although προσφορά is used in Psalm 39: 7 LXX for *minḥâh* (the meal-offering for sanctifying consecration, compare Daniel 3: 38), a special application is implied in the usage of 10: 18. Here, the reference is to a προσφορά which has the effect of a περὶ ἁμαρτίας (*ḥaṭṭā't*) or sin-offering. Our writer views all the sacrifices of the OT as finding their fulfilment in the death of Christ as our sin-offering, and both θυσία and προσφορά refer to that death alone. Cf. 9: 25–8 where the concepts of offering, sacrifice, suffering, death and blood are interchangeable.

147 Moffatt (p. 141) observes that 'the oracle, even in the LXX version, contemplates no sacrifice whatever as a condition of pardon, but our author assumes that such an absolute forgiveness was conditioned by some sacrifice'. Even if no sacrifice is implied, it would seem from the wording of the oracle in both MT and LXX that Jer. 31: 34 (the last promise) is presented as being the basis of the preceding promises (MT *kî*, LXX ὅτι).

148 Westcott, p. 347.

149 Michel, p. 341. This is certainly a more logical way of relating these two verbs than Käsemann's solution (p. 87), discussed below. Spicq (vol. II, p. 310) similarly views the present participle as an indication of 'an incessant and progressive application of the merits of the offering of Christ in the soul of the faithful'. He then goes on to relate this to the doctrine of the sacrifice of the Mass (p. 312).

150 Kögel, p. 58.

151 Davidson, p. 66. So W. Manson (p. 146) renders 'he has perfected the sanctified for ever' and RSV 'those who are sanctified' (NEB 'he has perfected for all time those who are thus consecrated').

152 Riggenbach, p. 307.

153 Spicq, vol. II, p. 282. On the development of the terminology of holiness and sanctification in the OT see O. Procksch, *TDNT*, vol. I, pp. 89ff. See also pp. 59, 72f above.

154 Westcott, p. 317.

155 *Ibid.* p. 50. However, in 12: 10, God *gives* man a share in his holiness through παιδεία. This could refer both to a participation in his presence in the heavenly city, which is only reached through persevering faith, or to present growth in godliness. Both of these ideas seem to be combined in 12: 14, where ἁγιασμός is something man must pursue in order to 'see the Lord'. Moffatt (p. 204) equates ἁγιότης here with 'the divine life'.

156 *Ibid.* p. 347. The work is said to be complete on the divine side (ἡγιασμένοι τετελείωκεν), but 'gradually appropriated on man's side'. On p. 348 he speaks of 'the progressive hallowing by which the divine likeness is slowly formed'.

157 Riggenbach, p. 402. Cf. F.F. Bruce, p. 359.

158 Michel, p. 451 note 3. He insists that sanctification is God's work on us, and only calls for our 'Yes' to this work.

159 *Ibid.* p. 451. He identifies the pursuit of peace in the community with 'being ready for forgiveness' and relates the demand for ἁγιασμός to this: 'if he is consecrated through the cross, he is appointed to make sacrifices for others'.

160 Procksch, *TDNT*, vol. I, p. 113.

161 Dibelius, *Botschaft und Geschichte*, vol. II, p. 168 ('die vollendete Weihe').

162 Riggenbach, *Der Brief an die Hebräer*, p. 308. Cf. Rom. 8: 30 ('those whom he justified he also glorified').

163 Barrett, in *Background of the NT*, p. 365.

164 Käsemann, p. 88. He notes how everything 'consecrated' in Hellenism tends towards a 'share in the heavenly sphere of perfection'. However, on p. 89 he says believers are only ἁγιαζόμενοι provisionally too.

165 *Ibid.* p. 89. Man's perfecting is only immediate by virtue of his connection with Christ as ὁ ἁγιάζων ('the heavenly man'), according to Käsemann.

166 Note the treatment of 9: 15 on p. 158 below.

167 Westcott, p. 320. Compare Spicq, vol. II, p. 315 (commented on below).

168 H. Schlier, *TDNT*, vol. V, p. 884 ('In content, παρρησία is freedom of access to God, authority to enter the sanctuary, openness for the new and living way which Jesus has opened for us'). Compare Windisch (p. 93). Riggenbach (pp. 312f), and Michel (p. 344), who concludes that the 'objective element includes the subjective and not the subjective the objective'. This is a proper corrective to Spicq (vol. II, p. 315) who actually says that 'the subjective significance of παρρησία can enrich itself with an objective nuance (cf. 3: 6) manifestly imposed here by the context'.

169 W.C. van Unnik 'The Christian's Freedom of Speech in the NT', *BJRL* 44 (1961–2), 485. See my detailed analysis of the use of this concept in Hebrews above (pp. 79f).

170 Most commentators render εἴσοδος with an infinitive (e.g., Michel, p. 344). However, Westcott (p. 320) rightly points out that εἴσοδος means primarily the *way* ('the parallel with ὁδός (verse 20) seems to fix this as the dominant sense here') and only secondarily refers to the *use* of the way. He translates: 'boldness to use the entrance into the holy place'.

171 N.A. Dahl 'A New and Living Way: the Approach to God According to Hebrews 10: 19–25', *Interpretation* 5 (1951), 409.

172 J. Behm, *TDNT*, vol. III, p. 454 argues for the cultic meaning of ἐγκαινίζειν ('to consecrate') in 9: 18, referring to the inauguration of the Old Covenant with a blood ritual. However, on 10: 19f he says ἐγκαινίζειν ὁδόν could 'just as well mean "to make a way which was not there before" as "to use a way for the first time", "to open it", "to dedicate it". The way to God which Jesus has newly opened and trodden is the way on which Christians can now find access to God.'

173 Dahl ('A New and Living Way', pp. 403f) argues for the cultic reading here.

174 Although the veil is not qualified, as in 9: 3 (τὸ δεύτερον καταπέτασμα), the context implies that this is our writer's meaning, and not the 'veil' into some heavenly *outer* court (cf. F.F. Bruce, p. 246, esp. note 87).

175 So, for example, Westcott, Nairne, Spicq, Héring, Montefiore, NEB.

176 So, for example, Windisch, Riggenbach, Moffatt, T.H. Robinson, F.F. Bruce, Michel, RSV.

177 N.H. Young, 'τοῦτ᾿ ἔστιν τῆς σαρκὸς αὐτοῦ (Hebrews 10: 20): Apposition, Dependent, or Explicative?', *NTS* 20 (1973–4), 103. He points to the example of Romans 10: 8 in this regard and continues: 'it is, of course, impossible to connect σαρκός appositionally to ὁδόν for the former is a genitive and the latter an accusative. This also rules out any direct relationship with ἐγκαινίζω.' This last remark refers to an argument of Hofius ('Inkarnation und Opfertod Jesu nach Hebr. 10: 19f', *Der Ruf Jesu und die Antwort der Gemeinde* ed. E. Lohse (Göttingen, 1970), pp. 132–41) that τοῦτ᾿ ἔστιν introduces a phrase explicative

of the preceding sentence as a whole, and especially with reference to ἐγκαινίζειν.

178 Andriessen, 'Das grössere und vollkommenere Zelt', pp. 80f.

179 Young, *NTS* 20, p. 104. He agrees with Andriessen in respect to 13: 15 and 7: 5 but only takes this as sufficient evidence (with Westcott) for the fact that the word order is not decisive.

180 Moffatt, p. 143. Endorsed by Young (p. 104) and P.E. Hughes (p. 409). J. Jeremias ('Hebräer 10: 20 τοῦτ᾽ ἔστιν τῆς σαρκὸς αὐτοῦ', *ZNW* 62 (1972), 131) accepts the basic arguments of Hofius (my note 177) but disagrees that τῆς σαρκὸς αὐτοῦ applies to the acceptance of the flesh in the incarnation: it points to the *devotion of Christ's flesh in the crucifixion.*

181 So Young, 'Apposition; Dependent or Explicative', p. 103. He comments: 'to one who knew Greek as the writer of this epistle did, the ambiguity of διά would be close to mind as he added the appositional phrase'.

182 Ἰερεύς μέγας is a rendering of *hakōhēn haggādôl* in Lev. 21: 10, Num. 35: 25, 28, and no special difference is to be discerned in our writer's usage here, as distinct from ἀρχιερεύς or ἀρχιερεύς μέγας (Michel, p. 346, esp. note 1; F.F. Bruce, p. 249, esp. note 97).

183 Schierse (p. 171), in discussing the various interpretations of οἶκος τοῦ θεοῦ, rightly points out that the imagery suggests a combination of ideas − 'heaven', 'heavenly sanctuary', 'church on earth' (viz. the congregation addressed). Compare Westcott (p. 323), who relates the 'church on earth' to the concept of the heavenly assembly thus: 'the church on earth, so far as it has a true existence, lives by its embodiment of the heavenly idea'.

184 Michel, p. 346. Cf. 1 Pet. 2: 4ff.

185 Michel, p. 346 note 3. W. Thüsing (' "Lasst uns hinzutreten ..." (Hebr. 10: 22). Zur Frage nach dem Sinn der Kulttheologie im Hebräerbrief', *BZ* 9 (1965), 1−17) argues that προσερχώμεθα in the context (10: 19−25) refers to a 'eucharistic celebration' but also, in view of our writer's total perspective, 'the whole Christian life together with faith, prayer, worship and suffering' (p. 12). It would be more accurate to say that Christian hope and love are the outworking of that personal and corporate drawing near to God through Christ which is the essence of being a Christian.

186 Michel, p. 460 note 2.

187 *Contra* O. Glombitza ('Erwägungen zum Kunstvollen Ansatz der Paraenese im Brief an die Hebräer 10: 19−25', *NovT* 9 (1967), 138ff), these two participial clauses belong together and relate to the preceding προσερχώμεθα.

188 So Snell (p. 129), who points to 12: 24 and 1 Pet. 1: 2 in this connection. Dahl ('A New and Living Way', p. 406) acknowledges that 'we must regard the sprinkling of the blood on the people at the inauguration of the covenant at Sinai as the type of the sprinkling of the people of the New Covenant'. However, he then goes on to argue for the imagery of sacerdotal installation (cf.

Exod. 29: 4, 21; Lev. 8: 6, 30). This is the most common interpretation of the verse (e.g., Moffatt, p. 144; Michel, p. 346) and is
taken by Moe ('Der Gedanke des allgemeinen Priestertums', pp.
162f) as decisive for the view that the priesthood of all believers
is being expounded here. However, the idea of Christians being
inaugurated into the New Covenant by the blood of Christ
pervades the chapter, and the specific imagery of the verse is
anticipated in 9: 18ff. Furthermore, it is doubtful that the priesthood of all believers is being expounded in this passage with as
much explicit detail as Moe and others propose.

189   James D.G. Dunn (*Baptism in the Holy Spirit* (London, 1970),
pp. 211ff) sees a 'complementary parallelism' here in 10: 22,
viewing Christian conversion—initiation in its inward and outward aspects (so also Windisch, p. 93 and F.F. Bruce, pp. 250f).
Christian baptism is 'both one with the Jewish lustrations in its
merely external operation, and different in that it belongs to the
fulfilment and the reality of which these other lustrations were
only shadows'. It is 'accompanied by the reality which it
symbolizes, as they were not and could not be'. This view seems
to be more satisfactory than the view that takes the two clauses
as a form of rhetorical parallelism (so Michel, pp. 346f; Spicq,
vol. II, p. 317).

190   Westcott, p. 324. Compare Spicq, vol. II, p. 317.

191   See note 64 above and the discussion on pp. 135f.

192   V.H. Neufeld, *The Earliest Christian Confessions* (Leiden, 1963),
p. 137. See my discussion on pp. 75f above.

193   Michel (p. 347) rightly points out that the genitive τῆς ἐλπίδος
indicates the *object* of the confession (Col. 1: 15; 1 Tim. 1: 1),
not the act of hoping itself. The whole Christian life can be comprehended in the concept of ἐλπίς (3: 6; 6: 11, 18; 7: 19; 10: 23;
11: 1). The ὁμολογία need not be made up solely of 'eschatological items' (*contra* Westcott, p. 326), since the whole Christian
life is 'christologically and eschatologically stamped for Hebrews'.

194   Μαρτυρεῖσθαι occurs seven times in Hebrews (7: 8, 17; 10: 15;
11: 2, 4, 5, 39) where the reference is always to the witness of
the Scriptural record. Cf. Michel, p. 267; Montefiore, p. 212 and
Ignatius, *Phil.* 11, *Eph.* 12; Justin, *Dial.* 29.

195   Michel, p. 421.

196   Moffatt, p. 190. Note how Barrett (in *Background of the NT*, pp.
378f) deals with the difficulty of relating 6: 15ff to chapter 11.

197   Hebrews sees a need for a similarly patient faith on the part of
Christians, so that they might do the will of God and 'obtain the
promise' (10: 36 κομίσησθε τὴν ἐπαγγελίαν, cf. 6: 12). Furthermore, although Christians have in one sense approached the
heavenly city, like the men of faith in chapter 11 they too must
seek 'the city which is to come' (13: 14). In what sense, then, are
Christians in any better position than their OT counterparts?
Barrett (in *Background of the NT*, pp. 382f) argues that for
Christians 'the unseen truth which God will one day enact is no

longer entirely unseen; it has been manifested in Jesus ... the "end" in which all believe and towards which all move, has been anticipated and proleptically disclosed'. I would add to this the perspective of 10: 14 that Christians have been 'perfected' already by the sacrifice of Christ. Barrett disregards this when he includes Christians in the μὴ ... τελειωθῶσιν of 11: 40.

198 Moffatt (p. 190) and F.F. Bruce (p. 343 note 298) both argue that the sense of προβλέπειν here is 'to provide'. Similarly, Michel (p. 421) notes the parallel sense of the Pauline προγινώσκειν (Rom. 8: 29) and the Johannine ἀγαπᾶν (John 17: 23) and concludes that God's foreknowledge implies 'a divine resolution of will beforehand' (cf. Psalm 33: 13 LXX; Barn. 6: 14; 9: 7; 3: 6).

199 So Westcott, p. 384. He continues: 'for we have actually seen in part that towards which they strained ... The fathers with a true faith looked for a fulfilment of the promises which was not granted to them. To us the fulfilment has been granted.' This is true to our writer's general perspective (see note 197 above) but does not take proper account of the epexegetical ἵνα clause in 11: 40, which shows how the κρεῖττόν τι should be taken.

200 Riggenbach, p. 382. Although κρείττων is regularly used almost as a technical term in Hebrews to describe the new dispensation and its benefits (8: 6; 7: 22; 11: 35*b*), that is not its specific function here. *Contra* Montefiore, p. 212.

201 Moffatt, p. 191. The elders were denied 'the historical experiencing of the Messianic τελείωσις of Jesus Christ until we could share in it' (Du Plessis, pp. 244f).

202 Riggenbach, p. 383 note 87 (compare Barn. 6: 19; 4 Ezra 4: 35ff; Apoc. Bar. 30: 2). Michel (p. 421 note 4) says the perfecting here is manifestly an eschatological event: 'each individual Christian must acquire it, but he receives the gift in association with the whole church'. Perfection is thus personal, eschatological consummation, experienced in the fellowship of the elect. Delling (*TDNT*, vol. VIII, p. 83) argues that τελειοῦν is used as a synonym for ἀγιάζειν in previous passages but in 11: 40; 12: 23 to describe the attaining of the goal of heavenly rest (see esp. his note 29). There is no escaping the fact that τελειοῦν describes an eschatological event in Hebrews, but I have argued from its close association with the fulfilment of Jer. 31: 31–4 that the terminology is used by our writer to stress the realised aspect of man's salvation, from the view-point of the Christian era. A radical change of meaning need not be sought for the application of τελειοῦν in 11: 40.

203 So Kögel, 'Der Begriff τελειοῦν', pp. 55f.

204 Riggenbach, p. 308. Cf. Käsemann, pp. 84ff.

205 F.F. Bruce (p. 208 note 111) rightly notes that this could only have direct relevance to readers of Israelite birth or adoption. Cf. P.E. Hughes, pp. 366ff. This verse does not prove that all the readers were of Israelite birth or adoption, but it would indicate that a fair proportion of them were such. All are addressed in 3: 1 as those who 'share in a heavenly call'.

206 Moffatt p. 127.
207 *Ibid.* p. 191. Cf. Westcott (p. 384): 'in part that end has been reached by the old saints, in some degree, in virtue of Christ's exaltation (12: 23), but in part it waits for the final triumph of the Saviour, when all that we sum up in confessing the truth of the resurrection of the body is fulfilled'. However, see pp. 163–6 below. F.F. Bruce (p. 344) says: 'they and we together now enjoy unrestricted access to God through Christ as fellow citizens of the heavenly Jerusalem'.
208 Spicq, vol. II, p. 368. However, his assertion that 'disciples of Jesus Christ, contrary to their ancestors in the faith, obtain immediately after their death their final achievement, the definitive consummation of their life, that is access to the heavenly sanctuary', does not follow if the resurrection of the body is to be the consummate state of all God's people. Why are OT believers only 'in limbo' and not in the heavenly city with Christians? In actual fact, when he describes the 'spirits of just men made perfect' (12: 23) as including the just of Old and New Covenants, waiting for their resurrection bodies (p. 408), he makes nonsense of the former distinction between the present state of OT and NT dead. See note 251 below. Cf. Snell, p. 146.
209 Michel, pp. 421f. Whereas Michel suggests this interpretation with a series of rhetorical questions, Buchanan (p. 206) confidently asserts that it is our writer's perspective. Cf. Nairne, p. 404.
210 So Montefiore (pp. 212f): 'so long as a single member of the family is not present, the household of faith can never be made perfect'. Compare Westcott, p. 384. This ignores the fact that the subject of the verb is specifically οὗτοι πάντες, in contrast with 'us', and that the verb itself refers back to the accomplishment of salvation by the sacrifice of Christ (10: 14). The perfecting in view is a personal eschatological consummation of believers in a relationship with God, experienced in the fellowship of the 'household of faith'.
211 Compare 1 Pet. 1: 10ff, 20 (δι' ὑμᾶς), Matt. 13: 16f.
212 Westcott, p. 384. However, his further comments on the significance of 12: 23 should be assessed in the light of the exegesis of that verse presented below.
213 So Moffatt (pp. 213f) rightly connects the arguments of verses 18ff to the warning of verses 14–17, the γάρ in verse 18 suggesting such a link. So also Vanhoye, *Structure*, pp. 205ff. Spicq (vol. II, p. 403) inappropriately regards the case of Esau as a parenthesis to the argument, and links verses 18ff with the challenge of verses 11–14.
214 Westcott, p. 412.
215 Michel, pp. 461f. Cf. Exod. 19: 12, 16–21; Deut. 4: 11f; 5: 22f; 9: 19. Thus, the point is made that the Law was 'to guard the holiness of God and to demonstrate to men the distance between men and God' (p. 462).
216 W.J. Dumbrell, 'The Spirits of Just Men Made Perfect', *EQ* 48

(1976), 158 (my emphasis). This is more suitable to the details of the passage, as his exegesis shows, than Käsemann's explanation in terms of an *epiphany* on Mt Zion, corresponding to the revelation on Mt Sinai (Käsemann, pp. 27ff).

217 Barrett, in *Background of the NT*, p. 376. See my discussion of 4: 16; 10: 22. Cf. Spicq (vol. II, p. 405), who refers to Christians here as 'proselytes of heaven', and F.F. Bruce (p. 372), who compares Philo, *Spec. Leg.* I.51.

218 Käsemann, p. 31. Cf. Michel (p. 461), who says προσέρχεσθαι in 12: 22 describes 'participation in the worship of the congregation: in confession, in prayer, in baptism and eucharist, one draws near to God. This "drawing near" remains a cultic event.' However, there is no justification for such a restriction of meaning. Cf. Michel's own stress on p. 460 note 2.

219 Michel, p. 460 note 2. See pp. 154ff above.

220 Käsemann (pp. 30f), who rightly stresses that προσεληλύθατε may not simply be interpreted as if the end of the race had already been reached. Yet, the privileges of citizenship in 'the city which is to come' (13: 14) are already enjoyed by faith: 'the people of God are still a pilgrim people, treading the "highways to Zion", but by virtue of his sure promise they have already arrived there in spirit' (F.F. Bruce, pp. 374f).

221 G. Fohrer, *TDNT*, vol. VII, pp. 300ff.

222 *Ibid.* pp. 312ff.

223 E. Lohse, *TDNT*, vol. VII, p. 337 (esp. note 287) and compare pp. 325ff. Like Hebrews, Paul makes it clear in Gal. 4: 26ff, by the use of this metaphor that 'eschatological salvation is not awaited in the indefinite future, but has already come. We who believe in Christ are children of our mother, the Jerusalem which is above.'

224 See Spicq, vol. II, pp. 406f, and cf. his 'La Panégyrie de Héb. 12: 22', *Studia Theologica* 6 (1953), 30–8. His own preference is to see πανηγύρει as being in apposition to μυριάσιν ἀγγέλων (so also Luther, Calvin, Peake, Riggenbach, Seesemann in *TDNT*, vol. V, p. 722 *et al.*). This enables him to conclude that verses 22*b*f provide a triple designation of the angels (cf. Montefiore, p. 231). However, this interpretation is criticised below.

225 So Westcott, Vaughan, Farrar, Moffatt, Robinson, F.F. Bruce *et al.* Westcott notes that this rendering has ancient authority uniformly in its favour and observes that 'the rhythm of the sentence appears to require that μυριάσιν ἀγγέλων should go together though πανηγύρει sounds harsh by itself' (p. 416). If πανηγύρει is related to the preceding words, the author may be seen to be following a consistent pattern – the introduction of each group or individual in the heavenly city with a καί. If πανηγύρει is in apposition to μυριάσιν ἀγγέλων or related to the following clause, this pattern is interrupted (see P.E. Hughes, pp. 552ff).

226 F.F. Bruce, p. 370 note 131.

227 So also AV, RV, ASV, RSVmg. So Hofmann, von Soden, Windisch, Michel and Dumbrell, 'Just Men Made Perfect', pp. 151ff.

228 Dumbrell, 'Just Men Made Perfect', p. 156. Cf. Michel p. 464.

229 So Westcott, p. 416. Whether we attach πανηγύρει to the angels or to 'the assembly of the firstborn', it is remarkable that the character of this whole concourse is not one of fear before the 'God of all as judge'. Here we find angels and men 'no longer separated, as at Sinai, by signs of great terror, but united in one vast assembly' (p. 415). Cf. Michel (pp. 463f) and Hughes (pp. 552ff).

230 Spicq (vol. II, pp. 407f) argues that they are the 'firstborn of all creation' (Hermas, *Vis.* III.4.1) who constitute the 'primordial celestial society (ἐκκλησία, cf. 2: 12; Psalm 82: 1), the great elders of Christians in the church triumphant' (cf. Psalm 88: 6 LXX and my note 224). So Käsemann, p. 28; Montefiore, p. 231. *Contra* P.E. Hughes, pp. 554f.

231 F.F. Bruce, pp. 376f. Note 1: 6 where Jesus is πρωτότοκος and 2: 12f where believers are his 'brothers' and 'children' (cf. Apoc. 1: 5; Col. 1: 15; Rom. 8: 29). Cf. Westcott, p. 417; Moffatt, p. 217; Michel, p. 461 and Michaelis, *TDNT*, vol. VI, p. 881.

232 So Calvin (p. 334): 'the description *firstborn* is not given here to the children of God indiscriminately, as Scripture sometimes does, but he gives this distinction to honour particularly the patriarchs and other prominent men of the old church'. Cf. Nairne, *Priesthood*, pp. 19, 415.

233 Spicq, vol. II, p. 407; Michel, pp. 464f; Käsemann, p. 28 note 3.

234 Michel, p. 464. However, his attempt to restrict this to the earthly church of Jesus whose 'names are written in heaven' is hard to square with the overall picture in 12: 22ff of God as judge, in the midst of a *heavenly assembly*. 'Written in heaven' does not prove that we are dealing with the earthly community of the people of God (cf. Moffatt, p. 217 and Dumbrell, 'Just Men Made Perfect', p. 157, note 17). NEB rightly translates 'first-born *citizens of heaven*'.

235 F.F. Bruce, pp. 376f; P.E. Hughes, pp. 548f; and Dumbrell, p. 157. Spicq (vol. II, p. 408) objects: 'how would Christians have "approached" Christians?' The answer is simply that, by becoming members of this supernal ἐκκλησία through faith, the recipients of Hebrews have approached God in the company of a vast multitude of believers in all ages.

236 Westcott, p. 417. Although he goes on to say 'Christian believers in Christ, alike living and dead, are united in the body of Christ', it appears from what follows that he thinks of the first-born as Christians only — the expression does not comprehend faithful Israelites for him. Michel (p. 465 note 1) inappropriately classifies Westcott along with himself, Delitzsch and Riggenbach as arguing only for the *earthly* Church here.

237 So Westcott, p. 158, Moffatt, p. 218 (RSV 'to a judge who is God of all'). The word order seems to favour this rendering, rather than NEB 'God the judge of all'.

238 Moffatt (p. 218), who rightly argues that the punitive sense of 9: 27 and 10: 30 makes it impossible to understand κριτής as 'defender' or 'vindicator' (so also Hofmann, Delitzsch, Riggenbach *et al.*); cf. F.F. Bruce, p. 377.

239 Dumbrell (pp. 158f) notes how the 'festive mood of the immediate context must express the conviction that the verdict to be pronounced upon those assembled can be nothing else than complete divine favour and acceptance, a verdict which has already been anticipated in the experienced gift of Christian forgiveness'.

240 Charles, *Apocrypha and Pseudepigrapha*, vol. II, p. 274. He concludes that 103: 3f seems only to refer to 'a resurrection of the spirit', and similarly Jubilees 23: 30f (*ibid.* p. 49). However, E. Sjöberg (*TDNT*, vol. VI, p. 379) views the latter more in terms of the immortality of the spirit: 'the ref. here, then is not to the resurrection of the body of the righteous, but only to the joy of their spirit, which still lives on'. See his further discussion of the development of Apocalyptic ideas in Rabbinic literature (*ibid.* pp. 376ff) and Jeremias, *TDNT*, vol. I, pp. 146–9 (ᾅδης).

241 Westcott, p. 418. They are said to be ' "spirits" not yet "clothed upon" (2 Cor. 5: 4)', for which he compares 1 Pet. 3: 19; Wis. 3: 1 and Apoc. 6: 9ff. However, only the latter forms a possible parallel, since 1 Pet. 3: 19 is more likely to be a reference to angels (see my note 249) and Wis. 3: 1 (cf. 4: 7; 5: 15ff) speaks of immortality rather than an intermediate state before resurrection.

242 Dumbrell, 'Just Men Made Perfect', p. 159. However, the reference in Hebrews 12: 23 cannot be restricted to Christian martyrs, as in the Apocalypse, since our writer says nothing of them elsewhere and there would presumably have been too few of them at that period to warrant the significance attached to them in 12: 23.

243 Montefiore, p. 232. Cf. Paul's σῶμα πνευματικόν (1 Cor. 15: 44).

244 We may compare the vision of 1 Enoch 39: 4ff, where we find the 'dwelling places of the righteous' with the righteous angels under the protection of the 'Lord of the Spirits'. Charles (*Apocrypha and Pseudepigrapha*, vol. II, p. 210) describes this as 'a vision of the future Messianic kingdom', in which 'the unities of time and place are curiously neglected' (compare 1 Enoch 41: 1f). It is not clear whether a resurrection of the body or of the spirit is implied here (see note 240 above). E. Schweizer (*TDNT*, vol. VI, pp. 445f) argues that the dualism of a carnal and spiritual world lies behind 12: 23. This is shown by the designation of God in 12: 9 as πατὴρ τῶν πνευμάτων, meaning that he is 'not just the Father of the corruptible flesh but also of the innermost I which will one day have to answer before him'.

245 Michel, pp. 466ff. In some sense, the judgement of God is said to have been passed on them already.

246 *Ibid.* p. 467. He acknowledges that the 'soteriological' understanding of τελειοῦσθαι is possible here, but difficult to relate to the preceding expression ('assembly of the firstborn who are enrolled in heaven'), This difficulty is overcome by interpreting

the latter, as I have, as a picture of the whole communion of saints, the eschatological church in its final and complete state. On p. 468 he argues that both the ideas he has presented must be held together.

247   F.F. Bruce, p. 378 and F. Loofs, *Encyclopaedia of Religion and Ethics*, vol. IV, p. 662 (ed. J. Hastings, Edinburgh, 1911). Delling (*TDNT*, vol. VIII, p. 83) refers this to the elders who did not reach the perfection that is only given in the saving work of Christ (μὴ χωρὶς ἡμῶν, 11: 40) and concludes: 'But they have now received a share in the consummation, 12: 23.' In note 29 he suggests that τετελειωμένων may be used in the sense of Wis. 4: 13 (i.e., 'at the goal of heavenly rest'). However, he takes τελειοῦν as having 'materially the same sense' as ἁγιάζειν in all places apart from 11: 40; 12: 23.

248   Riggenbach, pp. 416ff. He does not think the writer considers whether the 'righteous in question have departed this life already so or as a result of the perfecting of Christ's work'.

249   W.J. Dalton (*Christ's Proclamation to the Spirits* (Rome, 1965), pp. 135ff) argues that 1 Pet. 3: 19f refers to Christ's proclamation of his victory over all the forces of evil to the angelic 'spirits', who brought about the flood by their sinful association with men (Gen. 6). Christ's 'proclamation' coincided with his ascension to the right hand of God (1 Pet. 3: 22 cf. Eph. 4: 9f; 1: 20f; Phil. 2: 9; 1 Tim. 3: 16). On this view, 1 Pet. 3: 18 – 4: 6 says nothing about Christ offering salvation to OT dead or bringing about any change in their situation. Similarly, the description of Christ's descent to 'the lower parts of the earth' in Eph. 4: 9f may only be a description of the incarnation (so J. Gnilka, *Der Epheserbrief* (Freiburg, 1977), pp. 208f). However, if it refers to his penetration to Hades, his leading 'captivity captive' does not refer to the liberation of the dead but rather to his subduing of all the forces of evil in his resurrection and exaltation (cf. Eph. 1: 20f; 2: 1–7. So F. Büchsel, *TDNT*, vol. III, p. 641f). *Contra* Loofs, *Encyclopaedia of Religion and Ethics*, vol. IV, p. 662.

250   Westcott, pp. 418f. He compares the picture of the 'harrowing of hell' in the Gospel of Nicodemus (21ff), which does not really parallel Westcott's own representation of the work of Christ at all.

251   Spicq (vol. II, pp. 408f) argues that the 'righteous of Old and New Testament' are in view here, but takes τελειοῦν as a virtual equivalent to δοξάζειν. His argument on 11: 40 – that Christians obtain 'final achievement, the definitive consummation of their life' upon death, whereas OT believers must wait 'in limbo' until the resurrection – does not tally with his exegesis of 12: 23 (p. 368). If all the faithful are in the heavenly city in 12: 23, nothing can be essentially lacking in their relationship with God. If the resurrection is necessary in the case of OT believers so that they can enter the enjoyment of the heavenly city, why is this not necessary also in the case of Christians?

252 P.E. Hughes, p. 516. He later argues that the OT saints, 'imperfect though their situation formerly was, now share with us the perfection which has been procured by the incarnate Son's all-sufficient sacrifice, the effect of which reaches back to include them no less than it reaches forward to include us who belong to the post-advent era'. He seems to imply that the enjoyment of the messianic τελείωσις occurred for them at the end of their earthly pilgrimage, when they 'experienced for themselves that Jesus is not only the pioneer but also the perfecter of their faith (12: 2)' (p. 550).

253 Käsemann, p. 87. Cf. Spicq (vol. II, p. 409), who takes the perfect here as a sign of the stable and definitive character of their condition', clothed with δόξα.

254 The αἵματι ῥαντισμοῦ is best connected with the blood-sprinkling rite by which the Old Covenant was inaugurated (pp. 19f), as the covenant reference in 12: 24 shows (cf. 10: 22, where the effect of the New Covenant on believers is described in terms of ῥεραντισμένοι τὰς καρδίας).

255 To identify the 'speaking' with the warning of verse 25 (so Käsemann, p. 29) is too simplistic. The whole eschatological scene in 12: 22−4 speaks to men of acceptance. The warning that follows relates to those who turn their backs on this gracious offer.

256 So NEB. *Contra* Westcott (p. 419, 'better than Abel'), this is 'a compendious construction for "in comparison with Abel's" ' (F.F. Bruce, p. 370 note 136). Westcott's argument that the blood symbolises the 'life' of Christ seems highly inappropriate in view of Gen. 4: 10, where it was the *death* of Abel that called for vengeance. So too, in 12: 24, it is the death of Christ that speaks − but of God's grace, rather than vengeance − and not 'the abiding virtue of Christ's offered life'.

257 Dey, p. 124.

7 Perfection and the purpose of Hebrews

1 The rendering of καταρτίσαι ὑμᾶς ἐν παντὶ ἀγαθῷ (13: 21) as 'make you perfect in all goodness' (NEB) is more elegant than RSV ('equip you with everything good') but obscures the fact that a different verb is used here, with an application significantly different from that of τελειοῦν, by our writer. Although there may be a formal similarity in the way these verbs are used (AG *s.v.* καταρτίζω), τελειοῦν is never employed in Hebrews as καταρτίσαι is here to refer to the 'completion' or 'fitting out' of believers in a moral sense. The perfecting of man in a New Covenant relationship with God is something already achieved by the sacrifice of Christ (10: 14), though it clearly has moral implications (9: 14 'to serve the living God'). The prayer that God will provide everything necessary for doing his will (13: 21) is significantly based on a recollection of all that the death and resurrection of Christ achieves for believers.

2 So Spicq (vol. II, p. 382), who notes that the attitude of the
   Christian disciple is indicated by the four participles ἔχοντες,
   ἀποθέμενοι, ἀφορῶντες, μὴ ἐκλυόμενοι.

3 Westcott, p. 393.

4 Vanhoye (*Structure*, p. 196) notes four mentions of the theme of
   endurance (verses 1, 2, 3, 7) for one of faith (verse 2). I would
   add that the exhortation of verses 12—13 implies the same idea.

5 Michel, p. 426.

6 E. Stauffer, *TDNT*, vol. I, p. 135. See especially Herodotus, *Hist.*
   IX.60.1 (ἀγῶνος μεγίστου προκειμένου) for an example of how
   the terminology could be adapted to the idea of conflict in the
   broadest sense.

7 Contrary to J.D. Robb (*ExpT* 79 (1967—8), 254), H.N. Bream
   (*ExpT* 80 (1968—9), 150f) argues that 'run the race' is the best
   translation in the context and is consistent with the recognised
   pre-eminence of the foot-race in the Greek games.

8 Ἀγωνίζομαι (4 Macc. 17: 13), ἀγών (11: 20; 13: 15; 15: 29; 16:
   16; 17: 11), and other details noted by Moffatt (p. 195) and F.F.
   Bruce (pp. 348ff). Stauffer (p. 136) remarks that the athletic
   imagery of 4 Macc. is the 'more relevant as the torturing and
   execution of martyrs often took place in the same arena and
   before the same spectators as the γυμνικοὶ ἀγῶνες'.

9 Moffatt, p. 193. It refers to 'the weight of superfluous things, like
   clothes, which would hinder and handicap the runner' (p. 194), but
   equally may apply to 'excess bodily weight' (F.F. Bruce, p. 349).

10 H. Seesemann, *TDNT*, vol. V, p. 41. He shows how ὄγκος, which
   occurs only here in the Biblical documents, first means 'mass',
   'weight', 'compass' in classical Greek. To read the figurative sense
   of 'pride', often found in Philo, 'does not take the metaphor
   sufficiently into account' (*ibid.* note 3).

11 Westcott, p. 395.

12 RSV here captures the sense argued by Westcott (p. 396), Moffatt
   (pp. 194f), and Simpson (*Words*, pp. 26f, 'the sin *so prone to
   hamper* or *trammel*'). Zuntz (*Text*, p. 28) argues that the variant
   εὐπερίσπαστον (NEB mg. 'the sin which all too readily distracts
   us') in p. 46 and 1739 is original because it 'suits the context of
   Hebrews supremely, or even uniquely, well'. However, it is hard
   to see why scribes would change this for the more obscure
   εὐπερίστατον. Cf. Metzger *et al.*, p. 675.

13 Michel, pp. 428f; Westcott, p. 395 and F.F. Bruce, p. 349. P.E.
   Hughes (p. 520) follows Delitzsch in arguing that this expression
   is a 'clarification of what is meant by the weight or encumbrance
   of every kind which must be laid aside', but this obscures the
   clear distinction in the text.

14 Käsemann, p. 25. In 3: 7ff ἁμαρτία is said to be characterised as
   ἀπείθεια, identical with ἀπιστία (especially in verses 17—19).

15 *Ibid.* p. 26. In particular cases he says the question must be asked
   whether this apostasy happens unconsciously (5: 2 ἀγνοεῖν) or
   consciously (10: 26 ἐκουσίως). Yet how can unconscious sin be

characterised as apostasy when we consider our writer's description of the latter in 6: 4–6 and 10: 26–31?

16 Westcott, p. 393. H. Strathmann (*TDNT*, vol. IV, p. 491) agrees, but sees a certain ambivalence in the terminology here in the light of μαρτυρεῖσθαι in chapter 11.

17 Moffatt, p. 193. He acknowledges the validity of Westcott's argument up to a point — περικείμενον particularly suggests the idea that they are witnesses of our struggle — but says this is not developed.

18 Riggenbach (p. 385) endorsed by Michel (p. 427 note 3), who argues vigorously against the approach of Westcott and Strathmann (note 16).

19 Moffatt, p. 196. Like many commentators he notes the parallel with 4 Macc. 17: 10 (compare Epictetus II.19).

20 Hofius, in *Der Christushymnus*, p. 15 (Compare Hebrews 6: 6; 11: 26; 13: 13). P. E. Hughes (p. 525) says: 'it is important to recognise that the shame of the cross, where Christ bore the sins of the world, is something infinitely more intense than the pain of the cross'.

21 *Ibid*. p. 65 (emphasis removed). Cf. his p. 75.

22 Montefiore, p. 215. Cf. Hughes, p. 523 note 117 for a brief survey of the history of interpretation and criticism of this approach. P. Andriessen and A. Lenglet ('Quelques passages difficiles de l' Épître aux Hébreux (5: 7, 11; 10: 20; 12: 2)', *Biblica* 51 (1970), 215ff) seek to relate this to the glory which was Christ's all along, and was especially manifested at the Transfiguration. This was exchanged for the λύπη and παιδεία of Calvary, in order to identify with his brothers and share their lot. Cf. Spicq, vol. II, p. 387.

23 This is confirmed by the subsequent interpretation of their suffering as the παιδεία of God, after which comes joy (verse 11).

24 Cf. BDF para. 208 and Moffatt (pp. 196f) who answers the charge that this in some way diminishes the value of Christ's self-sacrifice. Michel (pp. 434f) relates the joy to 'the exaltation appointed for Christ, following his suffering' and says this is consistent with OT and Johannine association of χαρά with eschatological salvation for believers (cf. Isa. 55: 12; 66: 10; Bar. 4: 22).

25 Like the verb (cf. John 19: 12; Rom. 10: 21), the noun ἀντιλογίαν 'covers more than verbal opposition as in Numbers 20: 13 and Jude 11' (Moffatt, p. 198). It can imply all forms of hostility and opposition. Michel suggests that the τοιαύτην implies an allusion to the immediate situation of the readers (p. 436).

26 Westcott (p. 400) and the majority of commentators. This seems most likely in view of parallels such as 2 Macc. 13: 14 (ἀγωνίσασθε μέχρι θανάτον). *Contra* J. Behm, *TDNT*, vol. I, p. 172 and compare Michel p. 437.

27 Michel, p. 437. He argues in connection with verse 3 that

ἁμαρτωλοί are 'the men who are hostile to the representative of faith in the concrete situation and cause his suffering' (p. 436). Westcott (p. 400) similarly views the struggle in verse 4 as essentially with 'open enemies' but speaks of a personification of sin 'in order to emphasise its essential character (even believers are "sinners") and to include its various forms'. Contrast Spicq, vol. II, p. 390.

28 Moffatt, p. 199. The writer does not even imply by οὔπω that martyrdom is 'the inevitable result of tenacity'. The wording of verse 3 anticipates the μηδὲ ἐκλύου of verse 5 and the challenge of verses 12–13. Together with 10: 35ff, this suggests that the writer had good cause to fear some weakening of resolve and failure of faith on the part of some of his readers. Cf. note 48 below.

29 Hay, *Glory at the Right Hand*, p. 89. He notes that this is the only place in Hebrews where Psalm 110: 1 is not set in a doctrinal passage but has a *hortatory* significance (pp. 88f).

30 *Ibid.* p. 95. Compare the emphasis on looking to the reward in 11: 16, 26 and 13: 13–14.

31 This sense is argued for by E.K. Simpson ('The Vocabulary of the Epistle to the Hebrews I', *EQ* 18 (1946), 36) and Delling (*TDNT*, vol. I, p. 488). Windisch (p. 109) suggests a deliberate ambiguity.

32 P.G. Müller, ΧΡΙΣΤΟΣ ΑΡΧΗΓΟΣ: *Der religionsgeschichtliche und theologische Hintergrund einer neutestamentlichen Christus-prädikation* (Frankfurt, 1973) pp. 308f.

33 Westcott, p. 397. Cf. Riggenbach (pp. 389f) and P.E. Hughes (pp. 522f) for different variations on this theme.

34 Moffatt, p. 196. Cf. F.F. Bruce p. 351 ('Jesus ... is presented as the one who has blazed the trail of faith and as the one who himself ran the race of faith to its triumphant finish').

35 *De Prin.* III.1.19 (232.1).

36 *De Simeone et Anna* 5 (Migne, *PG* 18, 360B) ὁ τῶν τελεουμένων τελειωτὴς καὶ δεσπότης.

37 *Orationes* XL. 44 (Migne, *PG* 36, 421C). Delling (*TDNT*, vol. VIII, p. 86 note 4) rightly attacks the view of Dibelius (*Botschaft und Geschichte*, p. 171) that τελειωτής in Hebrews 12: 2 can mean 'mystagogue'. The significance of πίστις elsewhere in Hebrews must be kept in view: it is not to be equated with σωτηρία or with 'the Christian faith'.

38 *TDNT*, vol. VIII, p. 86. Moffatt (p. 196) suggests that our writer coined the term.

39 Riggenbach, p. 390. Compare Müller, ΧΡΙΣΤΟΣ, p. 310 ('He strode ahead of all believers in faith and led faith to its definitive end').

40 Du Plessis, pp. 222f.

41 *Ibid.* p. 224.

42 *Ibid.* p. 226. Cf. pp. 224f. He relates τελειωτής to 11: 39f, arguing that the perfecting of the saints is wholly dependent on Christ's achievement as 'perfecter of faith'.

43 Delling, *TDNT*, vol. VIII, p. 86. Müller (ΧΡΙΣΤΟΣ, p. 309)
   makes the interesting suggestion that Jesus endured the cross
   with the sort of faith mentioned in 11: 19 — that God was able
   to raise men even from the dead — and perfected *that sort of
   faith* in his resurrection.
44 Michel, pp. 431, 434.
45 G. Bornkamm ('Sohnschaft und Leiden', *Judentum, Urchristentum, Kirche*, ed. W. Eltester (Berlin, 1960), p. 195) inappropriately suggests that the theodicy problem that lies behind Prov.
   3: 11f 'in our context generally plays no further role'. This is
   because our writer's Christology opens up 'a new horizon of
   godly παιδεία' (5: 8; 12: 1ff) and gives the sonship of believers
   a new meaning (p. 198). The latter statement explains in part
   how our writer deals with the theodicy problem, but it is inadequate to suggest that there is no theodicy problem for our
   writer to face. Furthermore, our writer makes more of the
   perspective of Prov. 3: 11f on this issue than Bornkamm allows.
   Compare Michel pp. 439f.
46 διαλέγεται in Hebrews 12: 5 treats the utterance of the written
   word of Scripture as 'the voice of God conversing with men'
   (Westcott, p. 401). Similarly Michel, p. 438. With most commentators, it seems best to read verse 5 as an *interrogative* (*contra*
   NEB).
47 Westcott, p. 401.
48 T.W. Lewis ('And if he shrinks back (Hebrews 10: 38*b*)', *NTS* 22
   (1975–6), 92) concludes that we are dealing here with a situation
   in which 'a community, after embracing the word ἐν υἱῷ and
   manifesting boldness in its initial confrontation with public
   hostility towards itself, has grown weary (cf. 12: 12) in its
   intercourse with the world and is now drawing back from such
   contact'. This defection is a *process*, rather than a single event,
   and is partly based on a misguided interpretation of Isa. 26: 20
   (p. 94).
49 Bornkamm, in *Judentum*, pp. 196ff.
50 Westcott, p. 402.
51 Reading an imperative here, as Michel suggests (pp. 440f), seems
   rather awkward, though the indicative implies a challenge. Cf.
   Westcott, p. 402 and Moffatt, p. 201.
52 It is more appropriate to the context to read this expression as a
   designation for God as 'the author of man's spiritual being'
   (Moffatt, p. 203; F.F. Bruce, p. 360), than as 'the Father of all
   spiritual beings' (Westcott, p. 403). See the full discussion in
   Hughes, p. 530.
53 'To *be subject* to the Father who is the source of all life is
   indeed to *live*. To turn away from him is to turn away from
   life. To make the discipline of hardship and affliction an
   excuse for dropping out of the Christian race is to cast doubts
   on one's filial relationship to the heavenly Father and on the
   seriousness of one's desire to "share his holiness". The sphere

of redemption is indeed the sphere of holiness' (Hughes, p. 531).

54 O. Procksch, *TDNT*, vol. I, p. 114. Moffatt, p. 204 ('Here it denotes the divine life'). The ἀγιασμός of 12: 14 'derives from the verb ἁγιάζειν as a *nomen actionis'* (Procksch, p. 113) and expresses that practical holiness of life which believers must pursue (διώκετε). The stress in 12: 10 is not on human endeavour but on the fact that God *gives* a share in his holiness (static quality), by divine παιδεία.

55 Michel, p. 446. Cf. Psalm 85: 11; Isa. 32: 17; Jas. 3: 18 and Hebrews 7: 3; Spicq, vol. II, p. 396 and Hughes p. 533.

56 F.F. Bruce, p. 361. Compare Psalm 131: 2. NEB ('peaceful harvest of an honest life') is a very weak rendering. Michel (p. 445) seems to give the best understanding of εἰρηνικόν when he describes it as a substitute for a genitive ('the fruit which consists of peace, i.e., which is enjoyed in peace'). It is also, of course, 'the fruit which consists of righteousness'. Cf. Moffatt (p. 205) and P.E. Hughes (p. 533) for the suggestion that εἰρηνικόν speaks of the rest after the period of pain of discipline.

57 So also Wikgren, 'Patterns of Perfection', p. 164.

58 *Ibid*. p. 163.

59 Vanhoye (*Structure*, p. 115) argues that 'literary criteria do not favour this division'. An inclusion is formed between 5: 11 and 6: 12 by the use of νωθροί ,suggesting the divisions 5: 11 – 6: 12 (Parenesis: 'The Disposition of the Hearers') and 6: 13–20 (Exposition: 'The Value of God's Oath'). However, I judge this to be a good example of the situation where *content* must take precedence in determining structure.

60 Westcott, p. 133.

61 W. Manson (p. 61), opposing the view of E.F. Scott (*The Epistle to the Hebrews: Its Doctrine and Significance* (Edinburgh, 1922) pp. 30f, 42–5, 194f), that the readers were some kind of intellectual *élite*, to whom the writer desires to communicate some higher Christian *gnosis*. Michel (p. 232) warmly commends the arguments of Manson here. Compare Käsemann, pp. 122–4.

62 Some of the material in this section is taken from my article 'The Situation of the "Hebrews" (5: 11 – 6: 12)', *RTR* 35 (1976), 14–21.

63 J. Bonsirven, *Saint Paul: Épître Aux Hébreux* (Paris, 1943), p. 288. 'The Apostle estimates that the majority of his readers belong to the category of the perfect or that he can treat them as such' (p. 289).

64 Spicq, vol. II, p. 156.

65 'La Communauté des "Hébreux": était-elle tombée dans le Relâchement?', *Nouvelle Revue Théologique* 96 (1974), 1054ff (translation on p. 1059).

66 Wherever ἐπεί is used with the sense of 'otherwise', rather than 'since', the context clearly indicates that an unreal or contrary-to-fact situation is implied. This is so in 9: 26 and 10: 2 where we

have what Moule calls 'logically a conditional sentence' with an 'implied protasis' (*Idiom Book*, p. 151). Compare BDF para 360 (2). The fact that we are dealing with an 'unreal period' in the latter references is further shown by the use of an adversative in the next clause or sentence (9: 26 νυνὶ δέ; 10: 3 ἀλλ'). An entirely different syntactical pattern may be seen in other contexts where ἐπεί is used (2: 14; 4: 6; 5: 2, 6: 13; 9: 17; 11: 11): the relevant clause in each of these verses represents a further *positive* statement in what might be called an 'ascending argument', and 5: 11 belongs syntactically to this usage. It is noticeable too that Andriessen must ignore the force of γεγόνατε in order to make sense of the clause with the meaning 'otherwise'. Clearly we are dealing with a state of affairs that is a present condition, with the perfect tense perhaps suggesting some definite point in the past when this began. Cf. Hughes, p. 189.

67 Cf. 2: 1 (τοῖς ἀκουσθεῖσιν), the citation of Psalm 95: 7 at 3: 7*b*– 8*a*, 15 and 4: 7*b* to stress that in each fresh hearing of the words of God there is the possibility of offence, and 4: 1f where the writer fears lest the unresponsiveness of the Israelites on their way to Canaan to 'the message which they heard' (ὁ λόγος τῆς ἀκοῆς) be manifested amongst his readers.

68 Spicq (vol. II, p. 143) characterises it as 'the inertia or culpable negligence of the Hebrews to instruct themselves in Christian doctrine'. This limits the interpretation too much to the intellectual dimension. W. Manson (pp. 61f) rightly asks: 'Are they going forward from the first principles of their confession, or are they going back upon these principles?' The readers were 'immature Christians needing more of the gospel, rather than immature theologians whom the author wished to initiate into a higher *gnosis*'.

69 Thus Michel says νωθροὶ γεγόνατε ταῖς ἀκοαῖς refers to the 'spiritual receptivity' of the hearers, which has not increased and become more acute (5: 14), but has diminished. This retardation is not natural (διὰ τὸν χρόνον, verse 12) and is contrary to the development of faith. ' "Stumpf" wird man gegenüber dem Wort, gegenüber dem Heil, gegenüber dem Hoffnungsgut' (pp. 234f).

70 H. Preisker, *TDNT*, vol. IV, p. 1126. 'This is connected with the fact that the recipients of the epistle do not have the vitality of assured and persevering faith ... When Christian faith shows exhaustion both in breathing in (hearing and receiving) and in breathing out (believing confidence in the future) the author of Hebrews calls his readers νωθροί.'

71 Westcott, p. 158.

72 So Scott, *Hebrews*, pp. 30ff (a document 'written by a teacher for teachers'), and K. Bornhäuser, *Empfänger und Verfasser des Briefes an die Hebräer* (Gütersloh, 1932), pp. 16ff (the converted priests of Acts 6: 7), and Spicq (vol. I, pp. 266ff), who argues similarly that 'only priests have sufficient understanding and taste

for this theology of priesthood for one to be able to write to them an epistle exclusively dedicated to this theme'. In 'L'Épître aux Hébreux, Apollos, Jean-Baptiste, les Hellénistes et Qumrân' (*Revue de Qumrân* 1 (1958–9), 365ff), Spicq argues that the author addresses himself to 'Esseno-Christians, to Jewish priests among whom a certain number of ex-Qumranians could be found' (p. 390).

73 Michel, p. 235.

74 Montefiore, p. 102. In surprising contrast to his argument above (note 72), Spicq (vol. II, p. 143) says 'every Christian who has reached maturity is under obligation to profess and propagate his faith'!

75 If Lewis ('And if he shrinks back', pp. 92ff) is right, they were actually justifying this 'withdrawal' and 'concealment' on the basis of a false interpretation of Isa. 26: 20 (see note 48 above). Γεγόνατε χρείαν ἔχοντες γάλακτος (verse 12) seems to imply a regression in terms of spiritual apprehension (cf. Westcott, p. 135).

76 Van Unnik, 'The Christian's Freedom of Speech', p. 485.

77 A. Nairne, *The Epistle of Priesthood* (Edinburgh, 1913), pp. 333. See also T.H. Robinson, *The Epistle to the Hebrews* (London, 1948), p. 67.

78 H. Schlier, *TDNT*, vol. I, p. 646. Michel (p. 236) contrasts the use of the milk – solid food imagery in Philo and the Mysteries. Williamson (*Philo*, p. 280) argues that the similarities between Hebrews 5: 11ff and Philo's usage are often 'purely formal and not even verbal'.

79 Delling, *TDNT*, vol. VII, p. 687. Michel (p. 235 especially note 4) says the genitive τῆς ἀρχῆς is 'reminiscent of a descriptive adjective' (p. 236). F.F. Bruce (p. 109 note 83) describes τῆς ἀρχῆς here and in 6: 1 as a 'genitive of definition' and says 'one cannot well press a distinction between the στοιχεῖα and the ἀρχή'.

80 G. Kittel, *TDNT*, vol. IV, p. 138. Cf. Psalms 18: 14; 106: 11 LXX. Kittel restricts the reference in 5: 12 to 'the Christ revelation' which God spoke in the Son (1: 2). Similarly, Michel (p. 236) restricts it to 'the beginning of the preaching about Christ'.

81 Westcott, p. 135. This position is developed by Adams ('Hebrews', pp. 165f), who argues that τίνα should be read (accusative neuter plural of the interrogative pronoun) and that στοιχεῖα means 'elemental' or 'fundamental'. The readers need to be taught again 'what are the first principles' or 'fundamental principles of Scripture'. They must learn (or re-learn) 'a new way of looking at Scripture'. Spicq (vol. II, p. 143): 'To tackle the theology of Christ as priest according to the order of Melchizedek it is necessary to be initiated to the reading of the Bible and to the first principles of exegesis, notably to typology.' However, contrast Spicq, vol. II, p. 146.

82 Westcott, p. 144. He argues that ἡ ἀρχὴ and τοῦ Χριστοῦ go

together, and that ὁ τῆς ἀρχῆς λόγος does not form a compound noun. Contrast Michel (p. 238) who speaks of two genitive connections being merged into a unity (ὁ τῆς ἀρχῆς λόγος·ὁ λόγος τοῦ Χριστοῦ) to give 'das Anfangswort'.

83 Moffatt (p. 69) and Montefiore (p. 104) render the expression in 6: 1*a* 'elementary Christian doctrine', W. Manson (p. 60) 'the elementary principles of Christian teaching', P.E. Hughes (p. 195) 'the word (or instruction) of the beginning of Christ', NEB 'the rudiments of Christianity'.

84 Moffatt, p. 69, Michel, p. 236. The expression in 5: 12*a* is thus similar in meaning to that of 6: 1, but more general in its reference to 'divine oracles'. G. Hughes (*Hebrews and Hermeneutics* (Cambridge, 1979), p. 50) argues that the oracles contained in the OT Scriptures will be included in this expression and that the apathy of the readers threatens to make the task of OT interpretation difficult for the writer. The same disease of apathy is represented in 6: 1 in terms of an unwillingness to penetrate further than the beginnings of the Christian message. While the two expressions are distinguishable, 'they nevertheless represent symptomatically the same disease'.

85 J.C. Adams, 'Exegesis of Hebrews 6: 1f', *NTS* 13 (1966–7), 379f.

86 *Ibid.* p. 383.

87 Michel (p. 233) observes the lack of Christology in this 'proselyte catechism' but argues that 'the Messiahship of Jesus is certainly the presupposition of this enumeration'. P.E. Hughes (p. 195 note 33), in a specific reply to Adams, notes that the τοῦ Χριστοῦ of 6: 1, whether an objective or subjective genitive, makes these *specifically Christian doctrines* and observes: 'it is quite contrary to the attitude of the writers of the NT to regard the teaching of Christ, or any part of it, as no better than common Jewish beliefs and therefore dispensable. The very thought would have been shocking to the apostolic mind.'

88 Adams, 'Exegesis', p. 384.

89 Michel, p. 238 note 4.

90 F.F. Bruce, pp. 117f. G. Hughes (*Hebrews and Hermeneutics*, pp. 26–31, 55f) presents a modified form of the 'relapse theory': the readers are Jewish Christians in danger of relapse to Judaism but writer and readers are still talking *between themselves* and 'not (yet) across the boundaries of faith to Jewish opponents or would-be seducers' (p. 56).

91 Although it may be true that δυσερμήνευτος λέγειν (verse 11) suggests some difficulty in the subject matter itself (so Andriessen, 'La communauté des "Hébreux" ', p. 1058), the description of the readers in 5: 11ff shows that the readers were unprepared in themselves for deeper teaching.

92 G. Schrenk, *TDNT*, vol. II, p. 198. Compare Michel, pp. 236f and Riggenbach, pp. 144f.

93 Moffatt, p. 71. Compare Montefiore, p. 101 ('without experience

of discourse between right and wrong', i.e., 'without experience of moral truth') and NEB ('does not know what is right').

94   H.P. Owen, 'The "Stages of Ascent" in Hebrews 5: 11 – 6: 3', *NTS* 3 (1956–7), 244ff. He relates this to the terminology of 5: 14, where γεγυμνασμένα is said to 'demand the assumption that "the mature" are mature *before* they receive the solid food' and the training that they need in order to assimilate that solid food involves a discernment of right and wrong in a moral sense. In Marcus Aurelius XI λόγος δικαιοσύνης appears as an explicit parallel to ὀρθὸς λόγος ('principle of justice').

95   Williamson, *Philo*, pp. 290f.

96   Τὰ αἰσθητήρια means 'a plurality of capacities for moral decision which through ἕξις have already developed into specific qualities' (Delling, *TDNT*, vol. I, p. 188).

97   Michel, p. 237. Westcott is probably too specific in a non-moral direction when he describes the διάκρισις of 5: 14, 'in relation to the proper food of the soul', as 'the discrimination of that which constitutes its due strengthening' (p. 138). Cf. P. E. Hughes, p. 193.

98   Williamson, p. 289. Cf. his whole section from p. 280, comparing Philo's use of such terminology with that of Hebrews.

99   Westcott, p. 136. Cf. Spicq (vol. II, p. 144), who adds that the moral sense of λόγου δικαιοσύνης cannot be excluded in such a pedagogical context.

100   There is a danger of confusing our writer's perspective with Paul's teaching on justification by faith. Hebrews uses Hab. 2: 3–4 LXX at 10: 38 in a different way from Paul (Rom. 1: 17; Gal. 3: 11), to stress that ὁ δίκαιος is the man who continues to have faith in God through all the trying situations of life. The godly are similarly designated as 'the righteous' in 12: 23, where τετελειωμένων describes the effect of Christ's sacrifice on their relationship with God (and includes within its scope what Paul means by justification). Only 11: 7 suggests specifically the Pauline idea of God as the source of righteousness for believers. In 1: 9 righteousness is something the Son of God loves (Cf. 7: 2 'king of righteousness').

101   AG, *s.v.* ἄπειρος. Cf. Plato, *Rep.* IX.584*E*, Philo, *Agric.* 160.

102   Against Owen ('The "Stages of Ascent" ', pp. 244ff), this ability to distinguish good and evil need not be seen as a stage prior to the reception of solid food. If the terminology is consistently adapted in the way I have suggested, such discernment results from being fed 'solid food' and learning to appreciate its value. Alternatively, the 'training' could be related to the experience of divine παιδεία (γυμνάζειν in 5: 14 and 12: 11), which only benefits those who react to it with the *faith* that solid food is designed to encourage.

103   F.F. Bruce, p. 111. W. Thüsing (' "Milch" und "feste Speise" (1 Kor. 3: 1f und Hebr. 5: 11 – 6: 3). Elementarkatechese und theologische Vertiefung in neutestamentlicher Sicht', *Trierer Theologische Zeitschrift* 76 (1967), 275) defines 'solid food' as

'the teaching which derives from "perfection" ... and which leads to it'.

104 Pp. 207f. He argues that 'maturity' is not to be 'levelled to the plane of vague spiritual efficiency', but viewed in terms of '*maturity of apperception* in pedagogical or tutorial respect'.

105 G. Bertram, *TDNT*, vol. IV, p. 920. Compare my notes 61 and 68 above.

106 P.E. Hughes, p. 212. His discussion of the whole issue is very helpful (pp. 212–22). On p. 218 he suggests that some had been caught up in the group experience without really grasping 'even the first principles of the faith'.

107 Thus, 3: 12; 3: 13; 4: 1; 4: 11; 10: 25 and 12: 15 (with the warning that 'one bitter, noxious weed' in their midst can 'poison the whole'). The last reference shows why the state of a few should be the concern of all.

108 Andriessen, 'La communauté des "Hébreux" ', p. 1060 and Moffatt, p. 83. Καὶ ἐχόμενα σωτηρίας will be epexegetical of τὰ κρείσσονα, meaning 'which makes for salvation' or 'which accompanies salvation'.

109 10: 24; 12: 14*a*; 13: 1–3, 6 suggest that love needs development in their midst as much as faith and hope. Lewis ('And if he shrinks back', p. 92 note 1) suggests that the love of 6: 9–12 is 'intra-faith intercourse' still being manifested in the community, whereas 10: 32–6 refers to their attitude to outsiders, which the author calls his hearers to resume.

110 Westcott, p. 158.

111 Moffatt, p. 84.

112 Du Plessis, p. 129. Michel (pp. 249f) rightly argues that the writer does not wish to emphasise a distinction between the concepts of faith, hope and love here. 6: 11 is like 3: 14 and zeal should be shown for the complete development of hope to the end.

113 Cf. note 103 above. 'It is assumed that the position of inferiority occupied by the readers of the Epistle is not to be acquiesced in' (Westcott, p. 144).

114 The ἀφιέναι–φέρεσθαι contrast, which is evidenced in Euripides (*Andromache* 392f), is a rhetorical device here, not to be pressed too literally (Michel, p. 237). 'Leaving' the 'elementary doctrines of Christ' does not mean despising them or abandoning them 'any more than a pupil who has learned the ABC's can then dispense with the alphabet. The letters of the alphabet are indispensable in the formulation and communication of the most advanced learning; for progress to maturity is always cumulative' (P.E. Hughes, pp. 194f).

115 This is essentially the thesis of Thüsing ' "Milch" und "feste Speise" ', pp. 233–46, 261–80. He identifies the elementary teaching of 6: 1f with the ὁμολογία of 3: 1; 4: 14; 10: 23 and says: 'the "new interpretation" of the *homologia* through the high-priestly teaching contains nothing basically new as to

content but develops the sense which the *homologia* had from the beginning'. The author makes *explicit* the *'implicit christological structure of the "foundation"'*. Compare Owen, 'The "Stages of Ascent"', pp. 252f.

116 Moffatt, p. 72. (Cf. 6: 3 'and this we will do').

117 Westcott, p. 145. Montefiore (p. 104) suggests they are to be 'borne along on the floodtide of the author's argument' but the passive may equally suggest 'the agency of God' (so P.E. Hughes, p. 194 note 31).

118 *Ibid.* However, on p. 65 he speaks of 'the ripe perfectness (τελειότης) of Christian knowledge' as set against the 'first elementary teaching of the Gospel' in 6: 1.

119 Moffatt, p. 72.

120 Du Plessis, p. 209. Compare Montefiore, p. 104 ('the perfection of Christian doctrine'), Delling, *TDNT*, vol. VIII, p. 79 ('the highest stage' of Christian teaching), following Käsemann (pp. 117–224), who coins the phrase λόγος τέλεος, Spicq, vol. II, p. 146 ('perfection of doctrine').

121 Du Plessis, p. 209. Delling (*TDNT*, vol. VIII, p. 79 note 12) argues that 'lexically τελειότης in Hebrews 6: 1 is not used in the same way as τέλειος in 5: 14' but is to be related to the ἀρχή of 5: 12; 6: 1.

122 So Aristotle, *Metaph.* III.6.207ᵃ21; 261ᵃ36; Wisdom 6: 15 φρονήσεως τελειότης ('perfection of understanding'); 12: 17 δυνάμεως τελειότης ('perfection of power'). However, note the sense of moral integrity associated with the concept of acting ἐν ἀληθείᾳ καὶ τελειότητι (Jdg. 9: 15, 19). Cf. Prov. 11: 3(A). Note also that τελειότης is used as a variant in Jer. 2: 2 (Aleph) for τελείωσις. In Col. 3: 14 (τὴν ἀγάπην ὅ ἐστιν σύνδεσμος τῆς τελειότητος), the totality implied by τελειότης appears to be the *unity* of the Church as the body of Christ. Du Plessis renders: 'love which is the binding force of perfect unity' (p. 202).

123 *Rer. Div. Her.* 156 cf. *ibid.* 121 ('No one reaches perfection in any of his pursuits but undoubtedly all perfection and finality belong to the One alone'), *Mut. Nom.* II, *Spec. Leg.* II.177.

124 *Abr.* 54, Compare *Vit. Mos.* II.58 (διὰ τελειότητα τῆς ἐν αὐτῷ φύσεως *Sacr.* 120 and *Rer. Div. Her.* 310 ('the perfection of virtue').

125 *Agric.* 157 compare *ibid.* 165, 168. Perfection is the goal of 'those making progress'. The expression 'perfection of the soul' is found in *ibid.* 146 and *Spec. Leg.* I.80.

126 *Mut. Nom.* 12, cf. *ibid.* 24, 123 (Caleb); *Plant.* 135 (Leah, having given birth to Judah, who is 'confession of praise to God', reached the 'utmost bound of perfection'); *Fug.* 115 (in the character of the high priest we see perfection in something like its highest form).

127 *Ebr.* 82 cf. *Migr. Abr.* 73. There is an inner and an outer aspect to human perfection (*Ebr.* 85, *Spec. Leg.* IV.69) but true τελειότητες belong ultimately to God alone (*Rer. Div. Her.* 121 in note 123 above).

128 *NTS* 3, p. 250. Hebrews 'never uses such key-words as θεωρία, ἐπιστήμη, γνῶσις or even the most striking omission of all σοφία'. The author is hardly a pioneer of Christian gnosticism (p. 251): the truth he expounds cannot be termed secret or esoteric.

129 *Ibid.* p. 251.

130 *Ibid.* p. 249. However, on p. 252 he seems to relate this to the 'heavenly perfection which it is the destiny of Christians to achieve after the example of Jesus their ἀρχηγός and τελειωτής'.

131 Du Plessis, p. 208 (emphasis removed).

132 AV ('Let us go on unto perfection') is misleading because it implies either a simple progress in moral terms or a direct reference to our writer's teaching on perfection elsewhere. The latter cannot be the case, since perfection is already achieved for believers by the work of Christ and enjoyed in the present (10: 14).

133 Käsemann (p. 122) compares Barnabas 5: 4 (ὁδοῦ δικαιοσύνης γνῶσις) with 1: 5 (τελεία γνῶσις) and says 'the τελειότης of teaching preserves the perfection of the people of God gained in baptism and awakens them to new life in temptation and attack'. But this hardly justifies the equation of τελειότης with λόγος τέλειος in Hebrews 6: 1.

134 Wikgren, 'Patterns of Perfection', p. 166.

Appendix A

1 'Hebrews 4: 15 and the Sinlessness of Jesus', *ExpT* 86 (1974), 4—8.

2 Buchanan, pp. 130f.

3 Westcott, p. 108.

4 Moffatt, p. 59. The writer is 'too eager, to enter into psychological analysis' of Jesus' condition at this point.

5 Michel, p. 213 (cf. the extended note on pp. 211—13). Neither the Gospels nor Isa. 53: 9, which could be taken as the OT precedent for NT assertions about the sinlessness of the Messiah, speak about the sinlessness of his *nature.* The Gospels know only about the overcoming of temptation and about the fact that neither Law, nor sin, nor Satan could condemn Christ.

6 Buchanan, p. 130 (endorsed by Williamson, p. 6). While the cross may be regarded as the perfecting of his life of obedience, this by no means implies that there was a time when he was disobedient and sinful. His obedience had to be proved with the severest testing, but this does not permit us to conclude that he was ever imperfect in a moral sense. As I have shown, the perfecting of Jesus refers essentially to his vocational qualification or the fulfilment of his messianic role. This includes the concept of moral development, but not from the starting point of sinlessness. The fact that the ascension is to be included in the concept of his perfecting, forbids a simple equation with his learning obedience. Furthermore, Hebrews nowhere suggests that Jesus had to

'overcome his own personal estrangement from God' (Williamson, p. 5).

7 D. Bonhoeffer, *Christology* (ET London, 1971), p. 112. Jesus 'entered man's sinful existence past recognition'. Cf. Williamson, p. 7.

8 Westcott, p. 264.

9 See Michel (p. 211) for a helpful comparison of our writer's picture of the testing of Christ and that of the Gospels. J.A.T. Robinson (*The Human Face of God* (London, 1973), p. 96), argues: 'we simply have not the evidence to say even that (Jesus) was always loving. All that we can say is that these were the marks for which he was remembered – by his followers.'

10 Robinson, *The Human Face*, p. 94, 'What Augustine called the greater freedom not to sin *presupposes* rather than *precludes* the lesser freedom to sin.'

11 p. 7. He continues: 'if the life of Jesus is to have any relevance, relevance as a life which offers to others the prospect of sin's defeat, because it embodies such a defeat within itself, that defeat of sin must have been, it seems to me, within a life wholly like that of other men'. This suggests redemption from sin by following Christ's example, which is hardly our writer's position.

Appendix B

1 Bruce Demarest, *A History of Interpretation of Hebrews 7: 1–10 from the Reformation to the Present* (Tübingen, 1976), p. 22.

2 *Ibid.* p. 22 note 2, quoting Socinus.

3 See above pp. 110f. Spicq (vol. II, p. 193) is typical of those who argue that this verse refers to Christ's becoming high priest through his *incarnation.*

4 Davidson, *Hebrews,* p. 150.

5 G. Vos, 'The Priesthood of Christ in the Epistle to the Hebrews', *PTR* 5 (1907), 599. In a helpful discussion of this issue, he compares Paul's view of the exalted Lord, who 'sums up and carries in himself all the saving power which flows from his work in the flesh, from his death on the cross' (p. 601).

6 Westcott, p. 199. Cf. A.B. Bruce (*The Humiliation of Christ* (Edinburgh, 1895), p. 309), for a similar view.

7 *Ibid.* pp. 229f.

8 J.H. Davies, 'The Heavenly Work of Christ in Hebrews', *Studia Evangelica,* vol. IV, pp. 386f.

9 Davidson, p. 149 (criticising A.B. Bruce, *Humiliation*).

10 *Ibid.* p. 150.

11 Cody, *Heavenly Sanctuary,* p. 97. He argues that Christ is only formally proclaimed 'high priest after the order of Melchizedek' after his 'suffering and his perfection, when his priestly human nature has reached the celestial plane of divine power and glory'. This is so 'although radically he was priest from the instant of incarnation' (pp. 102f).

12 *Ibid.* p. 96. The idea of Christ's priesthood is closely related to that of his being 'mediator of a new covenant' in 8: 6 (cf. 7: 22; 9: 15; 12: 24). The mediation of Christ in Hebrews is not inter-preted in terms of the union of two natures. Jesus is not described as the mediator between God and man, but rather as the mediator of the New Covenant, and as such its guarantor. He achieves this mediatorial role by the shedding of his own blood, for the establishment or inauguration of that covenant.

13 G. Schrenk, *TDNT*, vol. III, p. 276.

14 See Vos, 'The Priesthood of Christ', p. 599.

15 Schrenk, p. 279.

16 *Ibid.* p. 276. This view is endorsed by Käsemann (p. 148), who argues that the proclamation of Jesus' priesthood at the time of his enthronement (e.g., 5: 10), 'only represents the juridical acknowledgement of Jesus as the high priest and the public confirmation by the angels' (p. 150). Käsemann argues that the idea of Jesus' 'becoming' high priest with his sacrificial death is found in *Acta Petri et Pauli* 30, *Passio Andreae* 6, Ignatius, *Phil.* 9: 1.

17 Davidson, p. 151.

18 Cody, *Heavenly Sanctuary*, pp. 97 and 102f.

BIBLIOGRAPHY

Adams, J.C., 'The Epistle to the Hebrews with Special Reference to the Problems of Apostasy in the Church to which it was addressed' (unpublished M.A. thesis, University of Leeds, 1964).

'Exegesis of Hebrews 6: 1f', *NTS* 13 (1966–7), 378–85.

Andriessen, P. and Lenglet, A., 'Quelques passages difficiles de l'Épître aux Hébreux (5: 7, 11; 10: 20; 12: 2)', *Biblica* 51 (1970), 207–20.

Andriessen, P., 'Das grössere und vollkommenere Zelt (Hebr. 9: 11)', *BZ* 15 (1971), 76–92.

'La communauté des "Hébreux": était-elle tombée dans le relâchement?', *NRT* 96 (1974), 1054–66.

'Angoisse de la mort dans l'Épître aux Hébreux', *NRT* 96 (1974), 282–92.

Arnim, H. von, *Stoicorum veterum fragmenta* (4 vols, Lipsiae, 1903–24).

Arnold, W.R., *Ephod and Ark*, HTS, vol. III (Cambridge, Mass., 1917).

Ballarini, T., 'ARCHEGOS (Acts 3: 15; 5: 31; Hebrews 2: 10; 12: 2): autore o condottiero?', *Sacra Doctrina* 16 (1971), 535–51.

Bampfylde, G., 'John 19: 28. A Case for a different translation', *NovT* 11 (1969), 247–60.

Barr, J., *The Semantics of Biblical Language* (Oxford, 1961).

Barrett, C.K., 'The Eschatology of the Epistle to the Hebrews' in *The Background of the NT and its Eschatology* (C.H. Dodd *FS*), ed. W.D. Davies and D. Daube (Cambridge, 1956), pp. 363–93.

The Gospel According to St. John (London, 1967).

Baumgärtel, F. and Behm, J., καρδία, *TDNT*, vol. III, pp. 605–15.

Beare, F.W., *A Commentary on the Epistle to the Philippians*, BNTC (London, 1959).

Behm, J., αἷμα, αἱματεκχυσία, *TDNT*, vol. I, pp. 172–7.

Ἀνάμνησις, *ibid.* pp. 348–9.

Γεύομαι, *ibid.* pp. 675–7.

Ἐγκαινίζω, *TDNT*, vol. III, pp. 453–4.

Bertram, G., νήπιος, *TDNT*, vol. IV, pp. 912–23.

Bietenhard, H., *Die himmlische Welt im Urchristentum und Spätjudentum*, WUNT 2 (Tübingen, 1951).

Black, M., *The Scrolls and Christian Origins* (London, 1961).

An Aramaic Approach to the Gospels and Acts, 3rd edn (Oxford, 1967).

Blass, F. and Debrunner, A., *A Greek Grammar of the New Testament and Other Early Christian Literature*, translated and edited by R.W. Funk (Chicago–London, 1961).

Bligh, J., Review of A. Vanhoye: *La structure littéraire de l'Épître aux Hébreux* (Paris–Bruges, 1963), in *Heythrop Journal* 5 (1964), 170–7.
    Chiastic Analysis of the Epistle to the Hebrews (Oxford, 1966).
Bonhoeffer, D., *Christology* (ET, Fontana Library, London, 1971).
Bonsirven, J., *Saint Paul: Épître aux Hébreux*, Verbum Salutis (Paris, 1943).
Bornhäuser, K., 'Die Versuchungen Jesu nach dem Hebräerbriefe' in *Theologische Studien für M. Kähler* (Leipzig, 1905), pp. 69ff.
    Empfänger und Verfasser des Briefes an die Hebräer (Gütersloh, 1932).
Bornkamm, G., 'Das Bekenntnis im Hebräerbrief' in *Studien zu Antike und Christentum* 2 (Munich, 1959), 188–203.
    'Sohnschaft und Leiden' in *Judentum, Urchristentum, Kirche* (J. Jeremias *FS*), ed. W. Eltester (Berlin, 1960), BZNW 26, pp. 188–98.
Boyer, J.M., 'Las variantes *Mellontōn y genomenōn* en Hebr. 9: 11', *Biblica* 32 (1951), 232–6.
Brandenburger, E., 'Text und Vorlagen von Hebr. 5: 7–10. Ein Beitrag zur Christologie des Hebräerbriefes', *NovT* 11 (1969), 190–224.
Bream, H.N., 'More on Hebrews 12: 1', *ExpT* 80 (1968–9), 150–1.
Brooke, A.E., *The Johannine Epistles*, ICC (Edinburgh, 1912).
Brown, R.E., 'The Messianism of Qumran', *CBQ* 19 (1957), 53–82.
    The Gospel According to John, Anchor Bible, vols. XXIX, XXIXA (London–Dublin–Melbourne, 1971).
Bruce, A.B., *The Humiliation of Christ* (Edinburgh, 1895).
    The Epistle to the Hebrews: The First Apology for Christianity (Edinburgh, 1899).
Bruce, F.F., ' "To the Hebrews" or "To the Essenes"?' *NTS* 9 (1962–3), 217–32.
    Commentary on the Epistle to the Hebrews (London–Edinburgh, 1964).
    The Epistles of John (London, 1970).
Buchanan, G.W., *To the Hebrews*, Anchor Bible, vol. XXXVI (New York, 1972).
Büchsel, F., ἰλάσκομαι, *TDNT*, vol. III, pp. 314–8.
    Κατώτερος, *ibid.* pp. 640–2.
    Ἀκατάλυτος, *TDNT*, vol. IV, pp. 338–9.
    Λύτρωσις, ἀπολύτρωσις, *ibid.* pp. 351–6.
Bultmann, R., *Theology of the New Testament*, vol. I (ET, London, 1952); vol. II (ET, London, 1955).
    The Gospel of John (ET, London, 1971).
    The Johannine Epistles (ET, Philadelphia, 1973).
    Ἀληθής, ἀληθινός, *TDNT*, vol. I, pp. 247–50.
    Εὐλαβής, εὐλαβεῖσθαι, εὐλάβεια, *TDNT*, vol. II, pp. 751–4.
Burton, E.D., *Syntax of the Moods and Tenses in New Testament Greek* (Edinburgh, 1894).
Butterworth, G.W., *Clement of Alexandria* (London, 1939).
Caird, G.B., 'The Exegetical Method of the Epistle to the Hebrews', *Canadian Journal of Theology* 5 (1959), 44–51.
Calvin, J., *Commentaries on the Epistle of Paul to the Hebrews*, translated by J. Owen (Edinburgh, 1853).

Campenhausen, H. von, *The Fathers of the Greek Church* (ET, London, 1963).
Carlston, O.C., 'The Vocabulary of Perfection in Philo and Hebrews', in *Unity and Diversity in New Testament Theology*, ed. R.A. Guelich (Grand Rapids, Michigan, 1978).
Charles, R.H., *Apocrypha and Pseudepigrapha of the Old Testament in English* (2 vols., Oxford, 1913).
Clarkson, E., 'The Antecedents of the High-Priest Theme in Hebrews', *ATR* 29 (1947), 92ff.
Cody, A., *Heavenly Sanctuary and Liturgy in the Epistle to the Hebrews. The Achievement of Salvation in the Epistle's Perspective* (St. Meinrad, Indiana, 1960).
Colson, F.H., Whitaker, G.H., and Earp, J.W., *Philo*, Loeb Classical Library (10 vols., London–Cambridge, Mass., 1929–62).
Coste, J., 'Notion grecque et notion biblique de la "souffrance éducatrice". À propos d'Hébreux 5: 8', *Recherches de science religieuse* 43 (1955), 481–523.
Creed, J.M., *The Gospel According to St. Luke* (London, 1950).
Cullmann, O., *The Christology of the New Testament*, 2nd edn (ET, London, 1963).
Dahl, N.A., 'A New and Living Way – The Approach to God According to Hebrews 10: 19–25', *Interpretation* 5 (1951), 401–12.
Dalman, G.F., *Jesus–Jeshua* (ET, London, 1929).
Dalton, W.J., *Christ's Proclamation to the Spirits. A Study of I Peter 3: 18 – 4: 6*, Analecta Biblica 23 (Rome, 1965).
Davidson, A.B., *The Epistle to the Hebrews*, Handbooks for Bible Classes (Edinburgh, 1882).
Davies, J.H., 'The Heavenly Work of Christ in Hebrews', *Studia Evangelica*, vol. IV, ed. F.L. Cross; *Texte und Untersuchungen* 102 (Berlin, 1968), pp. 384–9.
Deasley, A.R.G., 'The Idea of Perfection in the Qumran Texts' (unpublished Ph.D. thesis, University of Manchester, 1972).
Delitzsch, F., *Commentary on the Epistle to the Hebrews* (ET 2 vols, Edinburgh, 1872).
Delling, G., αἰσθάνομαι, etc. *TDNT*, vol. I, pp. 187–8.
    Ἀργός, ἀργέω, καταργέω, *ibid.* pp. 452–4.
    Ἀρχηγός, ἄρχων, *ibid.* pp. 487–9.
    Ἄκαιρος, etc. *TDNT*, vol. III, p. 462.
    Πλήρης, πληρόω, etc. *TDNT*, vol. VI, pp. 283–311.
    Στοιχέω, etc. *TDNT*, vol. VII, pp. 666–87.
    Τέλος, τελέω, τελειόω, etc. *TDNT*, vol. VIII, pp. 49–87.
Demarest, B., 'Priest After the Order of Melchizedek. A History of Interpretation of Hebrews 7 from the Era of the Reformation to the Present' (unpublished Ph.D. thesis, University of Manchester, 1973).
    A History of Interpretation of Hebrews 7: 1–10 from the Reformation to the Present, Beiträge zur Geschichte der biblischen Exegese 19 (Tübingen, 1976).
Denney, J., *The Death of Christ* (London, 1951).
DeVaux, R., *Ancient Israel, its Life and Institutions* (ET, London, 1961).

Dey, L.K.K., *The Intermediary World and Patterns of Perfection in Philo and Hebrews*, S.B.L. Dissertation Series 25, edited by H.C. Kee and D.A. Knight (Missoula, Montana, 1975).

Dibelius, M., 'Der himmlische Kultus nach dem Hebräerbrief' in his *Botschaft und Geschichte*, vol. II (1956), pp. 160–76 (reprinted from *Theologische Blätter* 21 (1942), pp. 1–11).

Dodd, C.H., *The Interpretation of the Fourth Gospel* (Cambridge, 1963).

Doormann, F., 'Deinen Namen will ich meinen Brüdern verkünden', *Bibel und Leben* 14 (1973), 245–52.

Dumbrell, W.J., 'The Spirits of Just Men Made Perfect', *EQ* 48 (1976), 154–9.

Dunn, J.D.G., *Baptism in the Holy Spirit* (London, 1970).

Du Plessis, P.J., ΤΕΛΕΙΟΣ: *The Idea of Perfection in the New Testament* (Kampen, 1959).

Easton, B.S., *The Gospel According to St. Luke* (Edinburgh, 1926).

Elliott, J.K., 'When Jesus was Apart from God: an examination of Hebrews 2: 9', *ExpT* 83 (1971–2), 339–41.

Ellis, E.E., *The Gospel of Luke*, New Century Bible (London, 1966).

Farrar, F.W., *The Epistle of Paul the Apostle to the Hebrews* (Cambridge, 1891).

Festugière, A.J., *La révélation d'Hermès Trismégiste, Études Bibliques* (4 vols, Paris, 1950–4).

Foerster, W., *Gnosis: a collection of Gnostic Texts* (ET, Oxford, 1972).

Fohrer, G. and Lohse, E., Σιών, Ἰερουσαλήμ etc. *TDNT*, vol. VII, pp. 292–338.

Giles, P., 'Jesus the High Priest in the Epistle to the Hebrews and the Fourth Gospel' (unpublished M.A. thesis, University of Manchester, 1973).

'The Son of Man in the Epistle to the Hebrews', *ExpT* 86 (1974–5), 328–32.

Glombitza, D., 'Erwägungen zum kunstvollen Ansatz der Paraenese im Brief an die Hebräer 10: 19–25', *NovT* 9 (1967), 132–50.

Gnilka, J., *Der Epheserbrief*, TKNT, vol. X, 2, 2nd edn (Freiburg–Basel–Vienna, 1977).

Goodenough, E.R., *By Light, Light* (New Haven, 1935).

An Introduction to Philo Judaeus, 2nd edn (Oxford, 1962).

Goodrick, A.T.S., *The Book of Wisdom* (London, 1913).

Grässer, E., 'Der Hebräerbrief 1938–1963', *Theologische Rundschau* 30 (2–3, 1964), 138–236.

Gray, G. Buchanan, *Sacrifice in the Old Testament* (Oxford, 1925).

Gregg, J.A.F., *The Wisdom of Solomon* (Cambridge, 1922).

Grimm, G.L.W., *Das Buch der Weisheit* (Leipzig, 1860).

Grogan, G.W., 'Christ and his People: An Exegetical and Theological Study of Hebrews 2: 5–18', *Vox Evangelica* 6 (1969), 54–71.

Gutbrod, W., νόμος, *TDNT*, vol. IV, pp. 1036–85.

Hadas, M., *The Third and Fourth Books of Maccabees*, Dropsie College Edition: Jewish Apocryphal Literature (New York, 1953).

Häring, Th., 'Über einige Grundgedanken des Hebräerbriefs', *Monatsschrift für Pastoraltheologie* 17 (1920–1), 260–76.

'Noch ein Wort zum Begriff τελειοῦν im Hebräerbrief', *NKZ* 34 (1923), 386–9.

Harder, G., Article πονηρός, πονηρία, *TDNT*, vol. VI, pp. 546–66.

Harnack, A. von, 'Zwei alte dogmatische Korrekturen im Hebräerbrief' in his *Studien zur Geschichte des NT und der alten Kirche* (Berlin–Leipzig, 1931), pp. 245ff.

Hauck, F., μῶμος, ἄμωμος, ἀμώμητος, *TDNT*, vol. IV, pp. 829–31.

Ὅσιος, ὁσίως, etc. *TDNT*, vol. V, pp. 489–93.

Hay, D.M., *Glory at the Right Hand: Psalm 110 in Early Christianity*, S.B.L. Monograph 18 (Nashville–New York, 1973).

Hengel, M., *Der Sohn Gottes* (Tübingen, 1975).

Héring, J., *L'Épître aux Hébreux* (Paris–Neuchâtel, 1954).

Higgins, A.J.B., *Jesus and the Son of Man* (London, 1964).

'The Priestly Messiah', *NTS* 13 (1966–7), 211–39.

Hoekema, A.A., 'The Perfection of Christ in Hebrews', *Calvin Theological Journal* 9 (1974), 31–7.

Hofius, O., 'Das "erste" und das "zweite" Zelt. Ein Beitrag zur Auslegung von Hebr. 9: 1–10', *ZNW* 61 (1970), 271–7.

'Inkarnation und Opfertod Jesu nach Hebr. 10: 19f' in *Der Ruf Jesu und die Antwort der Gemeinde* (J. Jeremias *FS*) ed. E. Lohse (Göttingen, 1970), pp. 132–41.

'Die Unabänderlichkeit des göttlichen Heilsratschlusses. Erwägungen zur Herkunft eines neutestamentlichen Theologumenon', *ZNW* 64 (1973), 135–45.

Der Christushymnus Philipper 2: 6–11, WUNT 17 (Tübingen, 1976).

Hort, F.J.A. and Mayor, J.B., *Clement of Alexandria: Stromateis Book VII* (London, 1902).

Hughes, G., *Hebrews and Hermeneutics* (Cambridge, 1979).

Hughes, P.E., *Paul's Second Epistle to the Corinthians* (London–Edinburgh, 1962).

A Commentary on the Epistle to the Hebrews (Grand Rapids, Michigan, 1977).

Hyatt, J.P., *Exodus*, New Century Bible (London, 1971).

Jacob, E., *et al.* ψυχή etc. *TDNT*, vol. IX, pp. 608–31.

Jeremias, J. and Zimmerli, W., *The Servant of God* (ET, London, 1957).

Jeremias, J., ᾅδης, *TDNT*, vol. I, pp. 146–9.

'Hebräer 5: 7–10' in *Abba* (Göttingen, 1964) pp. 319–23, reprinted from *ZNW* 44 (1952–3), 107–11.

Jerusalem in the Time of Jesus (ET, London, 1969).

'Hebräer 10: 20 τοῦτ' ἔστιν τῆς σαρκὸς αὐτοῦ', *ZNW* 62 (1971), 131.

Jewett, R., 'Conflicting Movements in the Early Church as Reflected in Philippians', *NovT* 12 (1970), 362–90.

Käsemann, E., *Das wandernde Gottesvolk. Eine Untersuchung zum Hebräerbrief* (4th ed, Göttingen, 1961).

Kistemaker, S., *The Psalm Citations in the Epistle to the Hebrews* (Amsterdam, 1961).

Kittel, G. and Rad, G. von, δοκέω, δόξα etc. *TDNT*, vol. II, pp. 232–55.

Kittel, G. and Rad, G. von and Kleinknecht, H., εἰκών, *ibid.* pp. 381–97.

Kittel, G., λόγιον, *TDNT*, vol. IV, pp. 137–41.

Kleinknecht, H. *et al.* εἰκών, *TDNT*, vol. II, pp. 381–97.

Klijn, A.F.J., 'Paul's Opponents in Philippians 3', *NovT* 7 (1964), 278–84.

Knauer, P., 'Erbsünde als Todes Verfallenheit. Eine Deutung von Röm. 5: 12 aus dem Vergleich mit Hebr. 2: 14f', *Theologie und Glaube* 58 (1968), 153–8.

Koester, H., 'Outside the Camp: Hebrews 13: 9–14', *HTR* 55 (1962), 299–315.

'The Purpose of ... a Pauline Fragment', *NTS* 8 (1961–2), 317–32.

Kögel, J., 'Der Begriff τελειοῦν im Hebräerbrief im Zusammenhang mit dem neutestamentlichen Sprachgebrauch' in *Theologische Studien für M. Kähler* (Leipzig, 1905), pp. 37–68.

Kuhn, K.G., 'The Two Messiahs of Aaron and Israel' in *The Scrolls and the New Testament* ed. K. Stendahl (New York, 1957), pp. 54–64.

Lake, K., *The Apostolic Fathers*, Loeb Classical Library (2 vols., London, 1912–13).

Lampe, G.W.H., *A Patristic Greek Lexicon* (Oxford, 1961).

Lang, G.H., *The Epistle to the Hebrews* (London, 1951).

LaRondelle, H.K., *Perfection and Perfectionism. A Dogmatic–Ethical Study of Biblical Perfection and Phenomenal Perfection* (Kampen, 1971).

Lewis, T.W., ' "... And if he shrinks back" (Hebrews 10: 38*b*)', *NTS* 22 (1975–6), 88–94.

Liddell, H.G., and Scott, R., *A Greek–English Lexicon*, revised by H.S. Jones (Oxford, 1940).

Lightfoot, J.B., *St. Paul's Epistle to the Philippians*, 2nd edn (London–Cambridge, 1869).

Lindars, B., *New Testament Apologetic* (London, 1961).

Linss, W.C., 'Logical Terminology in the Epistle to the Hebrews', *Concordia Theological Monthly* 37 (1966), 365–9.

Lohse, E. and Fohrer, G., Article Σιών, Ἰερουσαλήμ etc. *TDNT*, vol. VII, pp. 292–338.

Loofs, F., Article 'Descent to Hades (Christ's)' in *Encyclopedia of Religion and Ethics*, vol. IV, ed. J. Hastings (Edinburgh, 1911), pp. 654–63.

Lorimer, W., 'Hebrews 7: 23f', *NTS* 13 (1966–7), 386–7.

Lyonnet, S. and Sabourin, L., *Sin, Redemption and Sacrifice. A Biblical and Patristic Study*, Analecta Biblica 48 (Rome, 1970).

Malevez, L., 'Le Christ et la Foi', *NRT* 98 (1966), 1009–43.

Manson, T.W., *Ministry and Priesthood: Christ's and Ours* (London, 1958). *Studies in the Gospels and Epistles* (Manchester, 1962).

Manson, W., *The Epistle to the Hebrews. An Historical and Theological Reconsideration*, The Baird Lecture, 1949 (London, 1951).

Martin, R.P., *Mark: Evangelist and Theologian* (Exeter, 1972). *Philippians*, New Century Bible (London, 1976).

Maurer, C., Article σύνοιδα, συνείδησις, *TDNT*, vol. VII, pp. 899–919.

Mayer, G., *Index Philoneus* (Berlin, 1974).

McGrath, J.J., 'Through the Eternal Spirit'. *An Historical Study of the Exegesis of Hebrews 9: 13–14* (Rome, 1961).

Metzger, B.M., Aland, K., Black, M., Martini, C.M., and Wikgren, A., *A Textual Commentary on the Greek New Testament*, A companion volume to the United Bible Societies' Greek NT, 3rd ed (London–New York, 1971).

Michel, O., 'Die Lehre von der christlichen Vollkommenheit nach der Anschauung des Hebräerbriefes', *Theologische Studien und Kritiken* 106 (1934–5), 333–55.

Der Brief an die Hebräer, 13th edn, MK (Göttingen, 1975).

Οἰκουμένη, *TDNT*, vol. V, pp. 157–9.

Ὁμολογέω, etc. *ibid.* pp. 199–220.

Michaelis, W., πάσχω etc. *TDNT*, vol. V, pp. 904–39.

Πρῶτος etc. *TDNT*, vol. VI, pp. 865–82.

Σκηνή etc. *TDNT*, vol. VII, pp. 368–94.

Migne, J.-P., *Patrologia, Series Graeca* (Paris, 1844ff).

Moe, O., 'Das Priestertum Christi im Neuen Testament ausserhalb des Hebräerbriefes', *TLZ* 72 (1947), cols. 335ff.

'Der Gedanke des allgemeinen Priestertums im Hebräerbrief', *TZ* 5 (1949), 161–9.

Moffatt, J., *A Critical and Exegetical Commentary on the Epistle to the Hebrews*, ICC (Edinburgh, 1924).

Montefiore, H.W., *A Commentary on the Epistle to the Hebrews*, BNTC (London, 1964).

Morris, L., 'The Biblical Use of the Term "Blood"', *JTS* n.s. 3 (1952), 216ff.

Moule, C.F.D., 'From Defendant to Judge – and Deliverer', *Studiorum Novi Testamenti Societas* Bull. 3 (Oxford, 1952), pp. 40–53.

An Idiom Book of New Testament Greek, 2nd edn (Cambridge, 1959).

'Fulfilment Words in the NT: Use and Abuse', *NTS* 14 (1967–8), 293–320.

Moulton, J.H., *A Grammar of New Testament Greek*, *Prolegomena* (Edinburgh, 1908).

Müller, P.G., ΧΡΙΣΤΟΣ ΑΡΧΗΓΟΣ. *Der religionsgeschichtliche und theologische Hintergrund einer neutestamentlichen Christusprädikation* (Frankfurt, 1973).

Nairne, A., *The Epistle of Priesthood* (Edinburgh, 1913).

Neufeld, V.H., *The Earliest Christian Confessions*, NT Tools and Studies, vol. V (Leiden, 1963).

Nomoto, S., 'Herkunft und Struktur der Hohenpriestervorstellung im Hebräerbrief', *NovT* 10 (1968), 10–25.

Noth, M., *Exodus* (ET, London, 1962).

O'Brien, P.T., 'Prayer in Luke-Acts', *Tyndale Bulletin* 24 (1973), 111–21.

Omark, R.E., 'The Saving of the Saviour. Exegesis and Christology in Hebrews 5: 7–10', *Interpretation* 12 (1958), 39–51.

O'Neill, J.C., 'Hebrews 2: 9', *JTS* n.s. 17 (1966), 79–82.

Owen, H.P., 'The "Stages of Ascent" in Hebrews 5: 11 – 6: 3', *NTS* 3 (1956–7), 243–53.

Peake, A.S., *The Epistle to the Hebrews* (Edinburgh, 1914).

Peterson, D.G., 'The Situation of the "Hebrews" (5: 11 – 6: 12)' *RTR* 35 (1976), 14–21.

'The Prophecy of the New Covenant in the Argument of Hebrews', *RTR* 38 (1979), 74–81.

Pfitzner, V.C., *Paul and the Agon Motif. Traditional athletic imagery in the Pauline Literature*, Supplement to *NovT* 16 (Leiden, 1967).

Pierce, C.A., *Conscience in the New Testament*, Studies in Biblical Theology 15 (London, 1955).

Plummer, A., *A Critical and Exegetical Commentary on the Second Epistle of St. Paul to the Corinthians*, ICC (Edinburgh, 1915).

Powell, J.E., *Herodotus* (2 vols, Oxford, 1949).

Preisker, H., ἐγγύς, ἐγγίζω, προσεγγίζω, *TDNT*, vol. II, pp. 330–2. Νωθρός, *TDNT*, vol. IV, p. 1126.

Procksch, O. and Kuhn, K.G., Article ἅγιος, ἁγιάζω etc. *TDNT*, vol. I, pp. 88–115.

Prümm, K., 'Das neutestamentliche Sprach- und Begriffsproblem der Vollkommenheit', *Biblica* 44 (1963), 76–92, reviewing P.J. Du Plessis, ΤΕΛΕΙΟΣ.

Rad, G. von, *Old Testament Theology* (2 vols, ET, London, 1975).

Reider, J., *The Book of Wisdom* (New York, 1957).

Reiling, J. and Swellengrebel, J.L., *A Translator's Handbook of the Gospel of Luke*, Helps for Translators, vol. X (Leiden, 1971).

Rengstorf, K.H., μανθάνω etc. *TDNT*, vol. IV, pp. 390–461.

Richardson, A., *An Introduction to the Theology of the New Testament* (London, 1958).

Richardson, C.C., *Early Christian Fathers*, Library of Christian Classics, vol. I (London, 1953).

Rigaux, B., 'Révélation des mystères et perfection à Qumrân et dans le Nouveau Testament', *NTS* 4 (1957–8), 237–62.

Riggenbach, E., *Der Brief an die Hebräer*, ZK (Leipzig, 1913). 'Der Begriff der τελείωσις im Hebräerbrief. Ein Beitrag zur Frage nach der Einwirkung der Mysterienreligion auf Sprache und Gedankenwelt des Neuen Testaments', *NKZ* 34 (1923), 184–95.

Rissi, M., 'Die Menschlichkeit Jesu nach Hebr. 5: 7 und 8', *TZ* 11 (1955), 28–45.

Robb, J.D., 'Hebrews 12: 1', *ExpT* 79 (1967–8), 254.

Robinson, D.W.B., 'The Literary Structure of Hebrews: 1–4', *Australian Journal of Biblical Archaeology* 2 (1972), 178–86.

Robinson, J.A.T., *The Human Face of God* (London, 1973).

Robinson, T.H., *The Epistle to the Hebrews* (London, 1933).

Sabourin, L., ' "Liturge du sanctuaire et de la tente véritable" (Héb. 8: 2)', *NTS* 18 (1971–2), 87–90. *Priesthood: a Comparative Study*, Studies in the History of Religions 25 (Leiden, 1973).

Sanday, W. and Headlam, A.C., *A Critical and Exegetical Commentary on the Epistle to the Romans*, ICC, 5th ed (Edinburgh, 1902).

Sasse, H., κοσμέω, κόσμος etc. *TDNT*, vol. III, pp. 867–98.

Schaefer, J.R., 'The Relationship between Priestly and Servant Messianism in the Epistle to the Hebrews', *CBQ* 30 (1968), 359–85.

Schierse, F.J., *Verheissung und Heilsvollendung. Zur theologischen Grundfrage des Hebräerbriefes* (Munich, 1955).

Schlatter, A., *Der Glaube im Neuen Testament*, 5th edn (Stuttgart, 1963).

Schlier, H., γάλα, *TDNT*, vol. I, pp. 645–7.

Δείκνυμι etc. *TDNT*, vol. II, pp. 25–33.

Παρρησία etc. *TDNT*, vol. V, pp. 871–86.

Schmithals, W., 'The False Teachers of the Epistle to the Philippians' in his *Paul and the Gnostics* (ET, Nashville, 1972), pp. 65–122.

Schnackenburg, R., *Die Johannesbriefe*, TKNT, vol. XIII, 3, 3rd edn (Freiburg–Basel–Vienna, 1979).

Schneider, J., ὅμοιος etc. *TDNT*, vol. V, pp. 186–99.

Παραβαίνω etc. *ibid.* pp. 736–44.

Schrenk, G. and Quell, G., δίκη, δίκαιος etc. *TDNT*, vol. II, pp. 174–225.

Schrenk, G., ἱερός etc. *TDNT*, vol. III, pp. 221–83.

Schröger, F., *Der Verfasser des Hebräerbriefes als Schriftausleger*, Biblische Untersuchungen 4 (Regensburg, 1968).

Schulz, S., σκία etc. *TDNT*, vol. VII, pp. 394–400.

Schweizer, E. *et al.*, πνεῦμα etc. *TDNT*, vol. VI, pp. 332–455.

Σάρξ etc. *TDNT*, vol. VII, pp. 98–151.

Scott, E.F., *The Epistle to the Hebrews: its Doctrine and Significance* (Edinburgh, 1922).

Scroggs, R., *The Last Adam* (Oxford, 1966).

Seesemann, H., ὄγκος, *TDNT*, vol. VI, p. 41.

Πανήγυρις, *ibid.* p. 722.

Sen, F., 'Se recupera la verdadera lectura de un texto muy citado, cuyo sentido cambia substancialmente (Heb. 10: 1)', *Cultura Bíblica* 23 (1967), 165–8.

Silva, M., 'Perfection and Eschatology in Hebrews', *Westminster Theological Journal* 39 (1976), 60–71.

Simpson, E.K., 'The Vocabulary of the Epistle to the Hebrews', *EQ* 18 (1946), 35ff.

Words Worth Weighing in the Greek New Testament (London, 1946).

Sjöberg, E., *et al.* πνεῦμα etc. *TDNT*, vol. VI, pp. 332–455.

Smith, J., *A Priest for Ever: a Study of Typology and Eschatology in Hebrews* (London–Sydney, 1969).

Snell, A., *New and Living Way. An Explanation of the Epistle to the Hebrews* (London, 1959).

Soden, H. von, *Der Brief an die Hebräer*, Hand-Kommentar zum NT, vol. III, 2, ed. H.J. Holtzmann, 3rd edn (Freiburg, 1899).

Spicq, C., 'L'origine Johannique de la conception du Christ-Prêtre dans l'Épître aux Hébreux' in *Aux sources de la tradition chrétienne*, (M. Goguel *FS*) (Paris, 1950), pp. 258–69).

L'Épître aux Hébreux, Études Bibliques (2 vols, Paris, 1952).

'La panégyrie de Héb. 12: 22', *Studia Theologica* 6 (1953), 30–8.

'L'Épître aux Hébreux, Apollos, Jean-Baptiste, les Hellénistes et Qumrân', *Revue de Qumrân* 1 (1958–9), 365–90.

Stadelmann, L.I.J., *The Hebrew Concept of the World*, Analecta Biblica 39 (Rome, 1970).

Stählin, G., ἅπαξ, ἐφάπαξ, *TDNT*, vol. I, pp. 381–4.

Ἀσθενής etc. *ibid.* pp. 490–3.

Stauffer, E., ἀγών etc. *ibid.* pp. 135–40.

Stewart, R.A., *Rabbinical Theology* (Edinburgh, 1961).

'The Sinless High Priest', *NTS* 14 (1967–8), 126–35.

Stott, W., 'The Conception of "Offering" in the Epistle to the Hebrews', *NTS* 9 (1962–3), 62–7.

Strack, H.L. and Billerbeck, P., *Kommentar zum Neuen Testament aus Talmud and Midrasch*, vol. III (Munich, 1925), pp. 672–750.

Strathmann, H., λατρεύω, λατρεία, *TDNT*, vol. IV, pp. 58–65. Μάρτυς, μαρτυρέω etc. *ibid.* pp. 474–514.

Strobel, A., 'Die Psalmengrundlage der Gethsemane-Parallele Hebr. 5: 7f', *ZNW* 45 (1954), 252–66.

Swete, H.B., *The Ascended Christ* (London, 1910).

Swetnam, J., '"The Greater and More Perfect Tent". A Contribution to the Discussion of Hebrews 9: 11', *Biblica* 47 (1966), 91–106.
'On the Literary Genre of the "Epistle" to the Hebrews', *NovT* 11 (1969), 261–9.
'Form and Content in Hebrews 1–6', *Biblica* 53 (1972), 368–85.
'Form and Content in Hebrews 7–13', *Biblica* 55 (1974), 333–48.

Tasker, R.V.G., *The Gospel in the Epistle to the Hebrews*, Tyndale Monograph, 2nd edn (London, 1956).

Taylor, V., *Jesus and his Sacrifice. A Study of the Passion Sayings in the Gospels* (London, 1959).

Thornton, T.C.G., Review of A. Vanhoye: *La structure littéraire de l'Épître aux Hébreux* (Paris, 1963), *JTS* n.s. 15 (1964), 137–41.

Thrall, M.E., 'The Pauline Use of ΣΥΝΕΙΔΗΣΙΣ', *NTS* 14 (1967–8), 118–25.

Thüsing, W., '"Lasst uns hinzutreten ..." (Hebr. 10: 22). Zur Frage nach dem Sinn der Kulttheologie im Hebräerbrief', *BZ* 9 (1965), 1–17.
'"Milch" und "feste Speise" (I Kor. 3: 1f und Hebr. 5: 11 – 6: 3). Elementarkatechese und theologische Vertiefung in neutestamentlicher Sicht', *Trierer Theologische Zeitschrift* 76, 4 (1967), 233–46, and 5 (1967), 261–80.

Thurén, J., 'Gebet und Gehorsam des Erniedrigten', *NovT* 13 (1971), 136–46.

Torrance, T., 'Consecration and Ordination', *SJT* 11 (1958), 228ff.

Unnik, W.C. van, 'The Christian's Freedom of Speech in the New Testament', *BJRL* 44 (1961–2), 466–88.

Vanhoye, A., 'La structure centrale de l'Épître aux Hébreux (Héb. 8/1 – 9/28)', *Recherches de science religieuse* 47 (1959), 44–60.
'De "aspectu" oblationis Christi secundum Epistulam ad Hebraeos', *Verbum Domini* 37 (1959), 32–8.
La structure littéraire de l'Épître aux Hébreux, 2nd edn, Studia Neotestamentica 1 (Paris–Bruges, 1963; revised and augmented 1976).
'"Par la tente plus grande et plus parfaite ..." (Héb. 9: 11)', *Biblica* 46 (1965), 1–28.
'Jesus "fidelis ei qui fecit eum" (Heb. 3: 2)', *Verbum Domini* 45 (1967), 291–305.
Situation du Christ. Hébreux I et II, Lectio Divina 58 (Paris, 1969).
'Discussions sur la structure de l'Épître aux Hébreux', *Biblica* 55 (1974), 349–80.
'Situation et signification de Hébreux 5: 1–10', *NTS* 23 (1976–7), 445–56.

Vaughan, C.J., *The Epistle to the Hebrews* (London, 1890).

Vawter, B., 'Levitical Messianism and the NT' in *The Bible in Current Catholic Thought*, ed. J.L. McKenzie (New York, 1964), pp. 83–9.

Völker, W., *Fortschritt und Vollendung bei Philo von Alexandrien*, Texte und Untersuchungen zur Geschichte der altchristlichen Literatur 49, 1 (Leipzig, 1938).

Vos, G., 'The Priesthood of Christ in the Epistle to the Hebrews', *PTR* 5 (1907), 423–47, 579–604.

'Hebrews, the Epistle of the Diathēkē', *PTR* 13 (1915), 587–632, and 14 (1916), 1–61.

The Teaching of the Epistle to the Hebrews (Grand Rapids, Michigan, 1956).

Weiser, A., *The Psalms* (ET, London, 1962).

Weiss, B., *Der Brief an die Hebräer*, 6th edn MK (Göttingen, 1897).

Westcott, B.F., *The Epistles of John* (London, 1883).

The Gospel According to St. John (2 vols, London, 1908).

The Epistle to the Hebrews, 3rd edn (London, 1914).

Westermann, C., *Isaiah 40–66* (ET, London, 1969).

Wikgren, A., 'Patterns of Perfection in the Epistle to the Hebrews', *NTS* 6 (1959–60), 159–67.

Williamson, R., *Philo and the Epistle to the Hebrews*, Arbeiten zur Literatur und Geschichte des hellenistischen Judentums 4 (Leiden, 1970).

'Hebrews 4: 15 and the Sinlessness of Jesus', *ExpT* 86 (1974–5), 4–8.

'The Eucharist and the Epistle to the Hebrews', *NTS* 21 (1974–5), 300–12.

Wilson, R.McL., *Gnosis and the New Testament* (Oxford, 1968).

Wilson, W., *The Writings of Clement of Alexandria* (2 vols, Edinburgh, 1871–2).

Windisch, H., *Der Hebräerbrief* (Tübingen, 1931).

Wuest, K.S., *Hebrews in the Greek New Testament for the English Reader* (Grand Rapids, Michigan, 1947).

Wuttke, G., *Melchisedech der Priesterkönig von Salam*, BZNW (Giessen, 1927).

Yadin, Y., 'The Dead Sea Scrolls and the Epistle to the Hebrews', *Scripta Hierosolymitana*, vol. IV (1958), pp. 36–55.

Yarnold, E.J., 'ΜΕΤΡΙΟΠΑΘΕΙΝ apud Heb. 5: 2', *Verbum Domini* 38 (1960), 149–55.

Young, N.H., 'τοῦτ᾽ ἔστιν τῆς σαρκὸς αὐτοῦ (Hebrews 10: 20): Apposition; Dependent or Explicative?', *NTS* 20 (1973–4), 100–4.

Zimmerli, W. and Jeremias, J., *The Servant of God* (ET, London, 1957).

Zuntz, G., *The Text of the Epistles*, British Academy Schweich Lectures, 1946 (London, 1953).

INDEX OF PASSAGES QUOTED

Amos
  5: 21 (LXX)   163

Micah
  1: 13   218n60

Intertestamental and Other Jewish Writings

1 Enoch
  9: 3   163
  9: 10   163
  22: 3ff   163
  39: 4ff   277n244
  91: 10   163
  92: 3   163
  102: 4f   163
  103: 3f   163, 277n240
  103: 7f   163

Josephus
  Ant. XII.3.2   232n59
  Ant. XV.4   204n69

Judith
  10: 8   25, 201n26
  10: 9   127, 203n55

Jubilees
  23: 30f   277n240

1 Maccabees
  9: 61   218n60
  10: 47   218n60

2 Maccabees
  2: 9   45, 127, 203n55
  10: 28   247n54
  13: 4   239n130

4 Maccabees
  4: 10   80
  7: 13–15   202n36
  7: 15   25, 45, 201n29
  13: 22ff   199n42

Philo
  Abr. 52–3   205n76
  Abr. 54   184
  Abr. 62   204n69
  Agric. 42   31
  Agric. 96   239n130
  Agric. 157   184
  Cher. 35   30
  Conf. Ling. 95   32

Habakkuk
  2: 3f (LXX)   164, 288n100

Ebr. 82   31, 185
Fug. 138   240n134
Fug. 168   31
Gig. 54–5   32, 205n79
Jos. 26   199n42
Leg. All. I.10   30
Leg. All. II.61   30
Leg. All. III.44   31
Leg. All. III.45   30f, 202n36
Leg. All. III.74   31
Leg. All. III.129–35   199n42
Leg. All. III.244–5   31
Mut. Nom. 12   184f
Op. Mund. 89   30
Op. Mund. 144   230n34
Plant. 64   230n34
Praem. 49–53   31
Quaest. in Gen. I.86   202n36
Rer. Div. Her. 36   232n64
Rer. Div. Her. 73   240n134
Rer. Div. Her. 121   290n123
Rer. Div. Her. 156   184
Sacr. 5–8   31
Som. II.107   240n134
Som. II.231–5   204n71
Spec. Leg. I.79   203n46
Spec. Leg. II.9   254n9
Spec. Leg. IV.209   30
Virt. 202   239n130
Vit. Cont. 25   205n79
Vit. Mos. I.102   240n134
Vit. Mos. I.283   30
Vit. Mos. II.55,280   240n134
Vit. Mos. II.149–50,153   204n58
Vit. Mos. II.150   202n40
Vit. Mos. II.275   204n69
Vit. Mos. II.288   254n9

Psalms of Solomon
  17: 21ff   230n25

Qumran Documents
  11Q Melch.   243n8
  IQS 3: 13 – 4: 26   13

Other Ancient and Early Christian Writings

DATE DUE